THE ORIENTAL INSTITUTE OF THE UNIVERSITY OF CHICAGO

STUDIES IN ANCIENT ORIENTAL CIVILIZATION · NO. 39

George R. Hughes

STUDIES
IN HONOR OF
GEORGE R. HUGHES

JANUARY 12, 1977

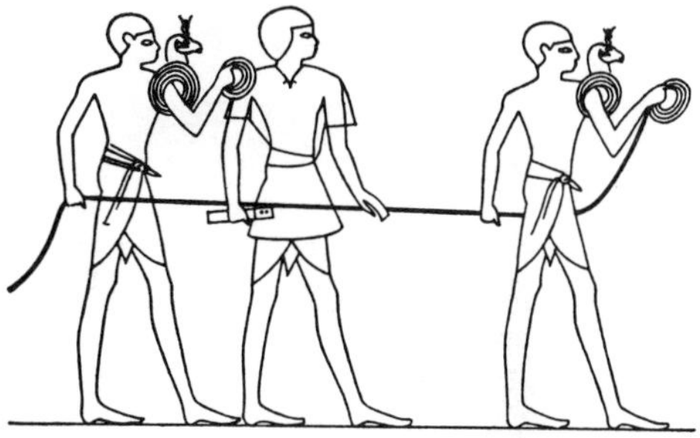

THE ORIENTAL INSTITUTE OF THE UNIVERSITY OF CHICAGO

STUDIES IN ANCIENT ORIENTAL CIVILIZATION · NO. 39

THE ORIENTAL INSTITUTE · CHICAGO · ILLINOIS

Library of Congress Catalog Card Number: 76-47851

The Oriental Institute, Chicago

TABLE OF CONTENTS

LIST OF ILLUSTRATIONS

LIST OF ABBREVIATIONS

AJSL	American Journal of Semitic Languages and Literatures. Chicago, 1884–1941.
"AK"	Robert Haardt. "Versuch einer altkoptischen Grammatik." Ph.D. diss., University of Vienna, 1948.
ANET	J. B. Pritchard, ed. Ancient Near Eastern Texts Relating to the Old Testament. Princeton, 1955.
ASAE	Annales du Service des Antiquités de l'Egypte. Cairo, 1900–.
BASOR	Bulletin of the American Schools of Oriental Research. New Haven, 1919–.
BD	Book of the Dead.
BIFAO	Bulletin de l'Institut français d'archéologie orientale. Cairo, 1901–.
BiOr	Bibliotheca Orientalis. Leiden, 1943–.
BJRL	Bulletin of the John Rylands Library. Manchester, 1903–.
BM	British Museum.
BMMA	Bulletin of the Metropolitan Museum of Art. New York, 1906–.
BSAC	Bulletin de la Société d'archéologie copte. Cairo, 1935–.
"CCG"	"Catalogue général des antiquités égyptiennes du Musée du Caire."
CdE	Chronique d'Egypte. Brussels, 1926–.
CRAIBL	Comptes rendus à l'Académie des Inscriptions et Belles-Lettres. Paris, 1857–.
CT	Coffin Texts.
"DFIFAO"	"Documents de fouilles publiés par les membres de l'Institut français d'archéologie orientale du Caire."
ECT	A. de Buck. The Egyptian Coffin Texts I–VII ("OIP" XXXIV, XLIX, LXIV, LXVII, LXXIII, LXXXI, LXXXVII). Chicago, 1935–61.

"FIFAO"	"Fouilles de l'Institut français d'archéologie orientale du Caire."
JANES	Journal of the Ancient Near Eastern Society of Columbia University. New York, 1968–.
JARCE	Journal of the American Research Center in Egypt. Boston, 1962–.
JCS	Journal of Cuneiform Studies. New Haven, Conn. and Cambridge, Mass., 1947–.
JdE	Journale d'Entrée.
JEA	Journal of Egyptian Archaeology. London, 1914–.
JESHO	Journal of the Economic and Social History of the Orient. Leiden, 1958–.
JNES	Journal of Near Eastern Studies. Chicago, 1942–.
MDAIK	Mitteilungen des Deutschen Archäologischen Instituts, Abteilung Kairo. Berlin and Wiesbaden, 1930–.
MFA	Museum of Fine Arts, Boston.
"MIFAO"	"Mémoires publiés par les membres de l'Institut français d'archéologie orientale du Caire." Cairo, 1902–.
MIO	Mitteilungen des Instituts für Orientforschung. Berlin, 1953–.
MMA	Metropolitan Museum of Art, New York.
"MMAF"	"Mémoires publiés par les membres de la Mission archéologique française au Caire." Cairo, 1884–.
MOR	Mouth-Opening Ritual.
OI	Oriental Institute, University of Chicago.
"OIC"	"Oriental Institute Communications." Chicago, 1922–.
"OIP"	"Oriental Institute Publications." Chicago, 1924–.
OLZ	Orientalistische Literaturzeitung. Berlin and Leipzig, 1898–.
OMRO	Oudheidkundige Mededelingen uit het Rijksmuseum van Oudheden te Leiden. Leiden, 1920–.
Or	Orientalia, Nova Series. Rome, 1932–.
PSBA	Proceedings of the Society of Biblical Archaeology. London, 1879–1918.
PT	Pyramid Texts, utterance numbers.
Pyr	Pyramid Texts, section numbers of Kurt Sethe, Die altägyptischen Pyramidentexte. 2 vols.; 2d ed., Hildesheim, 1960.

Ram	Wolfgang Helck, Die Ritualdarstellungen des Ramesseums I. ("Ägyptologische Abhandlungen," Vol. 25) Wiesbaden, 1972.
RdE	Revue d'Egyptologie. Paris and Cairo, 1933–.
RT	Recueil de travaux relatifs à la philologie et à l'archéologie égyptiennes et assyriennes. Paris, 1870–1923.
SAK	Studien zur altägyptischen Kultur. Hamburg, 1974–.
"SAOC"	"Studies in Ancient Oriental Civilization." Chicago, 1931–.
"UGAÄ"	"Untersuchungen zur Geschichte und Altertumskunde Ägyptens." Leipzig and Berlin, 1896–.
"Urk"	"Urkunden des ägyptischen Altertums." Leipzig and Berlin, 1903–.
Wb	Adolf Erman and Hermann Grapow, Wörterbuch der ägyptischen Sprache. 7 vols., plus 5 vols. Belegstellen; Leipzig and Berlin, 1926–63.
ZÄS	Zeitschrift für ägyptische Sprache und Altertumskunde. Leipzig and Berlin, 1863–.
ZDMG	Zeitschrift der Deutschen Morgenländischen Gesellschaft. Leipzig and Wiesbaden, 1847–.

PREFACE

"Good sir, may you endure and have victuals with you every day, you being cheerful, flourishing daily, and praised a million times. May joy and delight cleave fast to you, and your limbs proclaim health: you shall feel younger every day, and no harm shall draw nigh you. A year will come when one will recall your virtue and find not the like of you, your eye being bright every day and your stride firm. May you multiply happy years, your months in prosperity, your days in life and dominion, your hours in health, your gods pleased with you. They are content with your utterances, and a goodly West has been sent forth to you. You are not old (yet), you are not ill. May you complete 110 years upon earth, your limbs being vigorous, even as what is done for one who is praised like you when his god favours him. [. . .] For the benefit of an excellent, trustworthy righteous one, greatly praised of his god Thoth" (P. Anastasi III, 4/4–11, translated by Ricardo A. Caminos, *Late-Egyptian Miscellanies*, pp. 85–86).

On the occasion of his seventieth birthday, George R. Hughes's students and colleagues take great pleasure in offering this modest tribute to a man who is a renowned scholar and generous friend. The editors would like to take this opportunity to thank all the contributors who have given of themselves and their time in order to express their esteem for his many and varied contributions. They would also like to thank Mr. W. Raymond Johnson, who provided all the calligraphy included in the articles. Special thanks go to the members of the Editorial Office of the Oriental Institute, especially Ms. Olga Titelbaum, for the skill and promptness they have shown in dealing with a difficult manuscript under a time deadline.

Janet H. Johnson
Edward F. Wente

GEORGE R. HUGHES

George R. Hughes was born a farm boy near Wymore, Nebraska, January 12, 1907, the elder child of Evan and Pyne Hughes. His was a Welsh community; until he went to school, he spoke only Welsh, and he has remained proud of his Welsh heritage all his life. He began his schooling in the proverbial one-room schoolhouse, one year later than most, since his parents wanted him to wait until his younger sister would also be old enough to go, so they could walk back and forth together. When the time came to transfer to high school, the nearest high school would not accept his credentials, and he had to take an entrance exam. Although he passed easily, he was almost denied admission because the school system lost his exam paper. Just before he was to take a repeat exam, the original was found, and he was on his way. He went on from high school to the University of Nebraska, where he felt lost in the crowd. But despite the new environment he excelled in his studies and graduated Phi Beta Kappa in 1929.

The next fall the small-town boy ventured out of Nebraska, moving to Chicago to attend McCormick Theological Seminary. He studied introductory Egyptian under O. R. Sellers and, in the summer of 1931, took a course with William F. Edgerton at the Oriental Institute. Edgerton recognized his ability and urged him to devote himself to the study of ancient Egyptian. During his last year in the seminary, when he was class president, he not only won the class prize for best preacher, but he also was awarded the Nettie F. McCormick Fellowship in Old Testament to continue his formal education. In the fall of 1932 he formally registered in the Divinity School of the University of Chicago, by which time he had become an ordained minister and had taken as wife Maurine G. Hall, who has remained his constant companion and helpmate for over forty years. Once at the University of Chicago, he studied both Hebrew and ancient Egyptian in the Department of Oriental Languages and Civilizations.

Within a couple of years of his arrival at the University of Chicago he transferred from the Divinity School to the Department, and, when it came time to choose a dissertation topic, he decided that there was more range in Egyptology and so began a dissertation on Demotic land leases under William F. Edgerton. He was already a research assistant in the Oriental Institute, working for Edgerton on Spiegelberg's materials for a Demotic dictionary at the then lavish salary of $2000 per year. For about eight years he shared a tiny, low-ceilinged, hot, stuffy office on the third floor with other young research assistants, known collectively and informally as "Breasted's Brain Trust." To this day the venetian blind that he helped purchase to keep out the hot afternoon sun hangs in his former office, providing shade for new generations of orientalists, busy at their work. But not all his time was spent in purely academic pursuits—he was also a noted member of the Oriental Institute softball team.

During World War II he went to Washington along with several of his colleagues from the Oriental Institute, including his former teacher Edgerton, and spent the years from 1942 to 1946 in Intelligence, applying his abilities in deciphering ancient Demotic to modern cryptography. Following the war, in 1946, he went to Chicago House, Luxor, as an epigrapher working first in the Temple of Khonsu and at the Bubastite Portal in Karnak. When Professor Richard A. Parker resigned his position as field director of the Epigraphic Survey, George Hughes became field director on New Year's Day, 1949, a post he was to hold through difficult years until the spring of 1964. Even the bombing of Luxor during the 1956 war could not force him to abandon his responsibilities at Chicago House.

He is by nature a thorough and painstaking person, and perhaps these traits are best exhibited in the reams of collation sheets he prepared over the years that he served as epigrapher and field director of the Epigraphic Survey. Backing the accuracy of many drawings of the expedition's past publications, as well as of some yet to appear, are the exacting, often minute corrections and additions made on the collations sheets in Hughes's neat hand. To work as a fellow epigrapher with him in temple and in tomb was a real educational experience; one learned how to interpret traces on a badly damaged wall by visualizing what the scene or text looked like originally. In this way he was a great teacher in the field as well as in the classroom.

While he was demanding as a field director, he was far from being a "Cruel Father" (the title of one of his articles). As head of Chicago House he was a kind and generous father to those who lived and worked with him. In Luxor he is still remembered not only for his devotion to the task of recording ancient monuments but also for the magnanimity and graciousness that he displayed through his interest in the personal welfare of those with whom he came in contact. His charity and his ability to sympathize with personal problems have made him a rare and very special person, both at home and abroad.

He eschews lavishness and bravado; the simple things of life give him great enjoyment. In Luxor he would sometimes accompany an ailing staff member into town on a visit to the pharmacy on Station Street. While waiting for the prescription to be filled, he seemed to derive great contentment from merely chatting and watching the people come and go. A big event during the Luxor days might be going down to the railroad station to meet someone. Once Stephen Glanville and the then young Harry Smith were visiting Chicago House.

Smith, who had gone off for the day on a side trip, was returning on the night train, so Glanville and Hughes went to the station to meet him. Sitting on a bench on the platform, the two scholars talked about Demotic and related subjects. Smith's train arrived and discharged him into the customary bedlam of shouting, running, and pushing. He saw no one there to meet him and walked to Chicago House. When he arrived there and learned that Glanville and Hughes were at the station, he walked back and found the two professors still talking with deep absorption, happily cocooned away from the distractions around them.

Postcard dated October 1955: "Dear Carl: This proves we are here. . . . Tim . . . Healy collect[s] us at the station. I hadn't been fishing, but it wouldn't have been a bad specimen at that. . . ."

Although epigraphers and artists generally wear pith helmets or hats while working in the sun, one of the staff of Chicago House during Hughes's directorship was so concerned about the dangerous effects of solar radiation that he always wore a hat whenever he stepped out-of-doors, even if only briefly. Among the Egyptologists he was called "the Hat." One day, while Hughes was perched high on a ladder at the temple of Medinet Habu (Hughes often spoke of epigraphers' getting "notched feet" like some toy circus figures he used to play with as a boy), intent on his collating, he rather absent-mindedly asked Selim, the ladder-man who stood below him, *Fên el-Burnêṭa?* in Arabic, "Where is 'the Hat'?" The gentle Selim innocently replied, *Ya mudîr, fôq râsek*, "Oh director, on top of your head."

Hughes developed an ulcer, which fortunately was cured by surgery in Chicago; it required a diet of bland foods, for which he acquired a taste. Understandably, he has not had much liking for fancy cookery. On numerous occasions in the Chicago House dining room he would inveigh against the innocuous artichoke and avocado. Not even the therapeutic qualities of the artichoke, especially for those who had suffered liver ailments, could convince him that it was fit for consumption. For him that vegetable was simply too much of a nuisance to eat.

In 1961/62 he took on the added duties of acting field director of the Oriental Institute Excavations in the Sudan. On January 1, 1964, he stepped down as field director of the Epigraphic Survey and returned to Chicago, thinking he would be able to devote his time and energy to teaching and research. But his colleagues had other plans for him. Without a single dissenting vote, he was soon selected as the seventh director of the Oriental Institute, a position he held for four years, from 1968 to 1972. He served the Institute so faithfully and so successfully that the central administration of the University continued to support the Institute when other parts of the University were suffering financial retrenchment. No ranting, no posturing, just a quiet sincerity, which was persuasive. He is extremely modest. Shortly before the end of his tenure as director he and his wife were dinner guests of some wealthy members of the Institute. The subject of finance must have come up during the evening at some time because these members made a very generous donation to the Institute and stated that this was being done because of their admiration for George Hughes. But he, in his quiet, unassertive way, could never fully believe that it was really because of him that this money had been given.

In 1972, having handed over the directorship to his successor, he was again able to devote all his energy to teaching and research. In 1975 he formally retired from active teaching, but he has remained a source of aid and encouragement to colleagues, students, and his many friends. It was only after his retirement from the University of Chicago that he was able, for the first time, to make use of his other gift, noted by his peers at McCormick Theological Seminary so many years earlier, that of preaching. He stepped in as acting pastor of the church he had been attending for years.

His temperament is reflected in the ancient Egyptian aphorisms he once chose to quote in a convocation address to a University of Chicago graduating class:

"Do not be arrogant because of your knowledge."

"Take counsel with the ignorant as well as with the learned."

"If you are one to whom petition is made, be kind when you listen to the petitioner. . . . A petitioner likes attention to his words better than the accomplishment of that for which he came."

These reflect closely the principles by which he has led his own life. He remains so skilled in his main love, Demotic, that his fellow Demoticists the world over look to him for help with new and puzzling documents, and he remains a warm, generous human being, the "quiet man" who has found "the sweet well for a man thirsting in the desert" (*ANET*, p. 379).

THE FUNERARY TEXTS OF KING WAHKARE AKHTOY ON A MIDDLE KINGDOM COFFIN

James P. Allen

The funerary texts of King Wahkare Akhtoy appear among the texts inscribed on the outer coffin of a pair belonging to a certain *jmj-rꜣ pr Nfrj*. The coffins were discovered at el-Barsha, in one of six shaft tombs in front of the Middle Kingdom tomb of *Ḏḥwtj-ḥtp* II, and are now in the Cairo Museum (catalogue numbers 28087–88).[1] From philological criteria they can be dated to the early Twelfth Dynasty.[2] A terminus a quo is provided by the use of the tongue (𓄓) in writings of the title *jmj-rꜣ*, a practice that begins early in the reign of Sesostris I.[3] Peculiarities in the *ḥtp-ḏj-nzw* formulae suggest as a lower limit the reign of Amenemmes II.[4]

Both coffins are inscribed on their inner surface with hieratic texts set in vertical columns, the greater part of which are spells from the Coffin Texts. The inner coffin (B17C) contains CT 45–51 on the back and front and CT 154–60, 146, 165–68, 453–54 on the top; on the bottom, which has not been published, is a copy of the Book of Two Ways (CT 1029–1130) similar to that of B3C (C 28085).[5] Nine short spells of original content occupy the head and foot.[6]

[1] Georges Daressy, "Fouilles de Deir el Bircheh (novembre–décembre 1897)," *ASAE* 1 (1900) 40–42.

[2] See Wolfgang Schenkel, *Frühmittelägyptische Studien* ("Bonner Orientalistische Studien," n.s. Vol. 13 [Bonn, 1962]) p. 120. Textual and orthographic criteria are the phrases *nb jmꜣḫ* and *dj.f prt-ḫrw* and the determinatives of *wt* and *tꜣ-ḏsr*, in the *ḥtp-ḏj-nzw* formulae.

[3] *Ibid.*, p. 36.

[4] C. J. C. Bennett, "Growth of the *ḥtp-di͗-nsw* Formula in the Middle Kingdom," *JEA* 27 (1941) 77–82. Two criteria are the sequence *nb Ḏdw*, *ḫntj-jmntj.w*, *nṯr* ꜥꜣ, *nb ꜣbḏw* of the epithets of Osiris and the term *jmꜣḫy* without preceding *n kꜣ nj*, both of which are common in the period from Sesostris I to Amenemmes II but rare afterwards.

[5] "Textes . . . très incorrects et négligés": Pierre Lacau, *Sarcophages antérieurs au nouvel empire* II ("CCG" [1906]) 9.

[6] CT temp. 164, 378, 79, 166+276, 228, 107, 57, 154, 359; see Thomas George Allen, *Occurrences of Pyramid Texts with Cross Indexes of These and Other Egyptian Mortuary Texts* ("SAOC," No. 27 [1950]) p. 122, n. 4. Part of Pyr 1854 occurs in CT temp. 166+276.

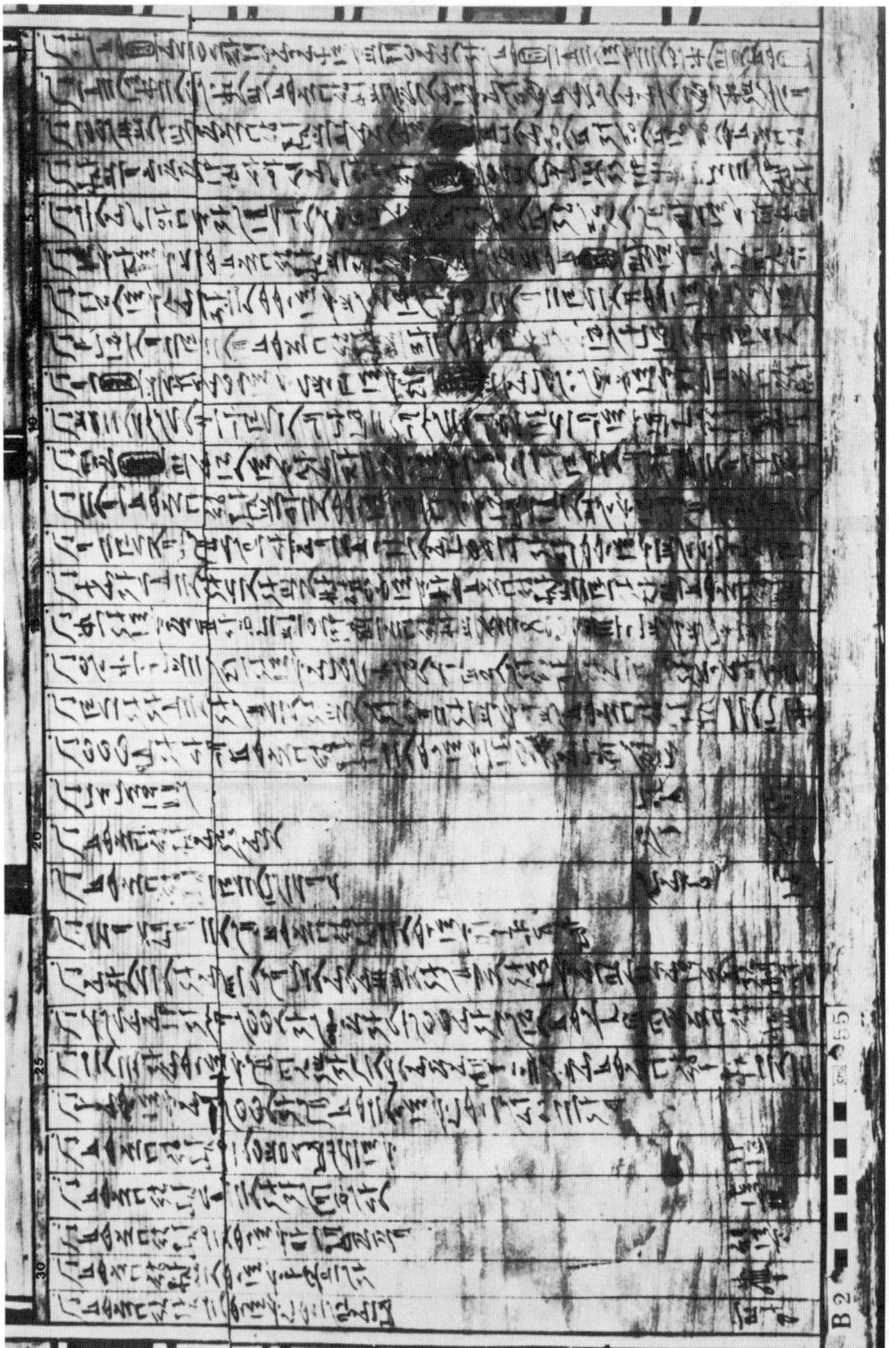

FIG. 1.—B16C, lines 1–31 (head)

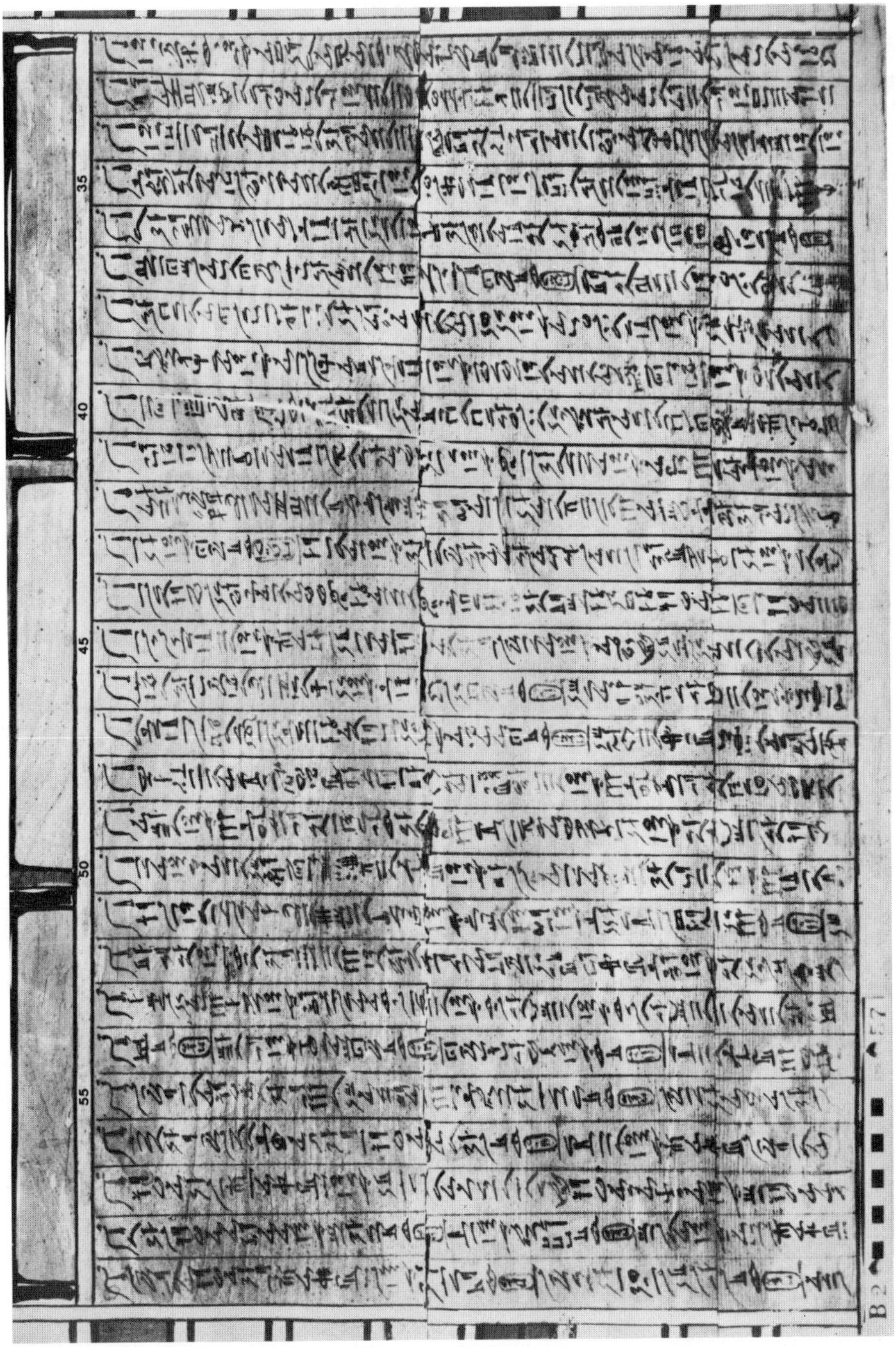

FIG. 2.—B16C, lines 32–59 (foot)

The outer coffin (B16C) is inscribed on the back, front, and part of the bottom with a series of Coffin Texts: CT 45–53 (CT 45–50 copied in wrong order from a retrograde original[7]) and CT 32–40. The rest of the bottom contains a copy of the Book of Two Ways, in Lesko's "version A," with a text like that of B12C (C 28089).[8] The top is uninscribed.

It is the texts on the head and foot of B16C that have elicited the greatest scholarly interest, for they show the cartouches of an otherwise unattested king *Wꜣḥ-kꜣ-Rʿw Jẖty*, presumably one of the Akhtoy family of the Ninth to Tenth dynasties (Figs. 1–2).[9] The significance of these cartouches was first discussed by Pierre Lacau in 1902, and a partial analysis of the content of the texts was included in his publication of the coffin in 1906.[10] The texts were among those subsequently copied by the Oriental Institute's Coffin Texts Project, but they were omitted from the final corpus of Coffin Texts. They are published here through the kind permission of Professor John A. Brinkman, director of the Oriental Institute.

An initial reading of the texts on the head and foot of B16C indicates that they were copied onto the coffin in reverse order from a retrograde original with vertical columns; that is, the copyist began at the end of his original and copied toward the front, presumably misled by the fact that the signs in the original faced in the same direction as that in which the columns were to be read. The same phenomenon is to be noted among the Coffin Texts on the back of B16C; earlier examples occur among the texts in the pyramids of *Wdbt-n.j* (Oudj. 233–41) and *Jbj* (Aba 523–34, 579–86).[11] Reconstructing the original columns involves essentially reading the copy backwards. This is complicated by the fact that the integrity of the original columns was not always respected by the copyist. When he had finished copying the text of one column of the original, the scribe would continue with the top of the next column of the original, usually

[7] *ECT* I 222.

[8] Leonard H. Lesko, *The Ancient Egyptian Book of Two Ways* ("University of California Publications, Near Eastern Studies," Vol. 17 [Berkeley, 1972]) p. 134. The texts are not included in *ECT* VII; the notes of the Oriental Institute's Coffin Texts Project describe them as "all too corrupt to be worth copying."

[9] The most recent discussions are those of J. von Beckerath, "Die Dynastie der Herakleopoliten (9./10. Dynastie)," *ZÄS* 93 (1966) 16; Hans Goedicke, "Probleme der Herakleopolitenzeit," *MDAIK* 24 (1969) 141–42; Jesus Lopez, "L'Auteur de l'enseignement pour Mérikarê," *RdE* 25 (1973) 187–90.

[10] Pierre Lacau, "Le roi ," *RT* 24 (1902) 90–92; *idem, Sarcophages* II 12–13.

[11] References to sources of Pyramid Texts employ the abbreviations of Allen, *Occurrences*, pp. 12–41, with the exception of "Nt" for "Neit"; a full bibliography may be found there. The abbreviation "Pyr" refers to the section numbers of Kurt Sethe, *Die altägyptischen Pyramidentexte* I–II (2d ed.; Hildesheim, 1960) Pyr 1–2217; Utterance numbers are preceded by the abbreviation "PT" (PT 1–714).

without moving to the top of the next column on the coffin and giving no graphic indication of the juncture. In some cases the juncture may be recognized from the break in the sense of the text; in others, its location may be confirmed through parallels in other copies.

Figures 3–6 contain a hieroglyphic transcription of the text, arranged in columns corresponding to those of B16C's original. The line numbers of the coffin are given in the body of the text (lines 1–59); the top of each column bears an asterisked numeral indicating the order in which the original was to be read (cols. *1–*73). The order in which the scribe of B16C copied his original is the reverse of that indicated by the asterisked numerals. Contrary to the usual practice, the scribe also began his copy on the foot of the coffin; the same procedure is evident on the ends of the inner coffin, B17C, but with the texts copied in proper order.[12]

The texts of cols. *1–*73 are primarily copies of Utterances from the Pyramid Texts. In a number of instances they represent the earliest—in some cases, the only—complete copy of texts that are incompletely preserved in the pyramids themselves. An index of these texts follows, together with an epigraphic commentary on the copy; I have included a translation of the less familiar Utterances only.

Col. *1. A spell paralleled in Nt 300: "Take the Eye of Horus, half of which he saw in Seth's hand."

Cols. *2–*6. PT 58–62. B16C agrees with all earlier copies in using between PT 59 and PT 61 a spell different from N's unparalleled and only partially preserved PT 60 (N 289). The spell is attested in Nt 305 and Aba 9. Sethe's PT 62 is actually two spells that share a common title (omitted in B16C); this accounts for the *ḏd-mdww* in the middle of col. *6.

NOTES

jbꜣ⟨t⟩.n.f (col. *2). The head of the bird looks like *ꜣḫ*, but the feet are different; compare the form in lines 41, 44, 50.

For the title of PT 58 read *ḏbꜣ*, "a kilt with tail" (*Wb* V 560, 8). The "enemy" determinative for  occurs again in line 15; the Coffin Texts use the normal form (Georg Möller, *Hieratische Paläographie* I [Leipzig, 1909] 462, Prisse): *ECT* I 163*c*, 164*h*, 170*d*/*h*, 174*m*. The corruption possibly derives from the hieratic form of an original , but in that case the omission of the *ḏbꜣ*-sign is abnormal (for the spelling without the final radical, see Pyr 1373*b*, 2108*a*).

In the titles of PT 59–61 (cols. *3–*5), *Ḥrw* is a plene writing for the falcon on a standard (Pyr 42*b*–*c* N); compare the spelling of *njswt* in *ECT* I 197*f*.

[12] Recognized already by Lacau, *RT* 24 (1902) 91. The lines of B16C were numbered by the Coffin Texts Project in accordance with the usual order head–foot–back–front–top–bottom; thus, col. *42 contains the text of the first line of the head (line 1), col. *43 the last line of the foot (line 59).

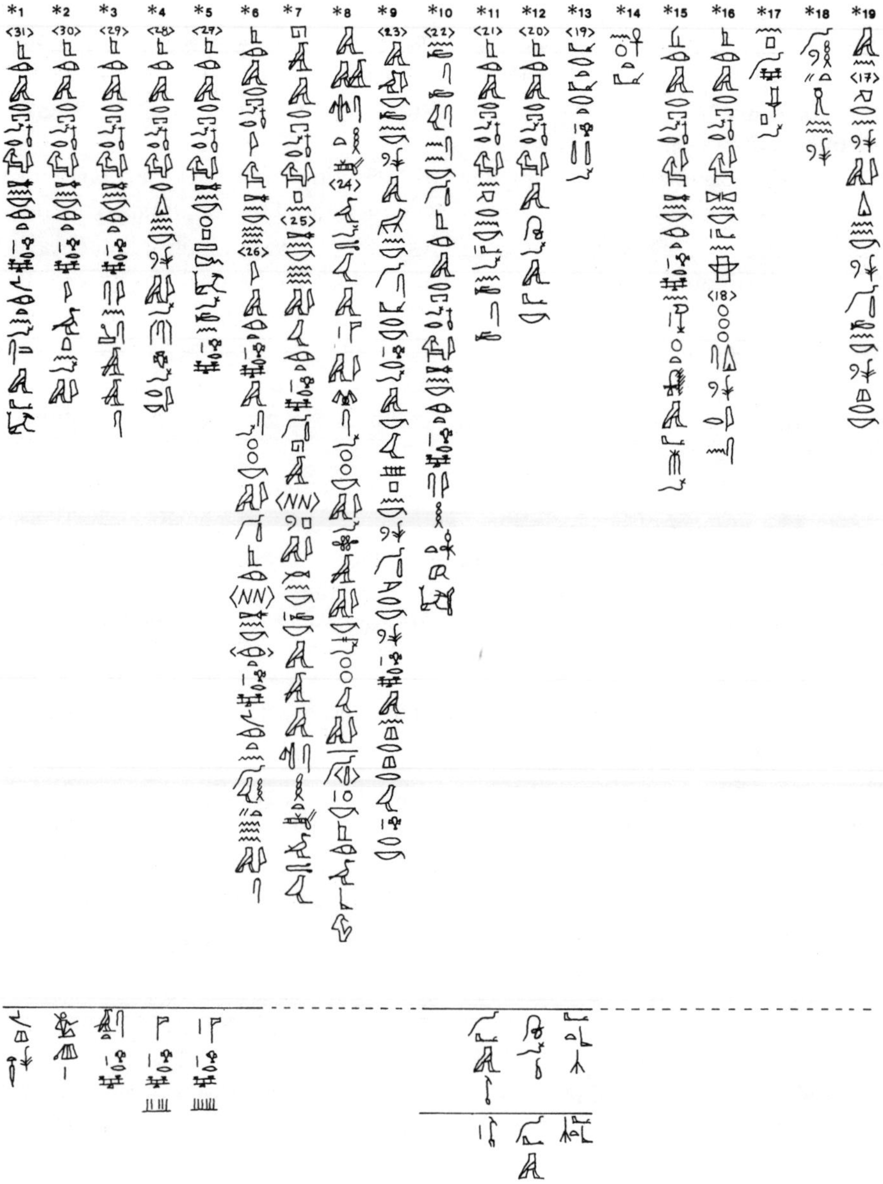

FIG. 3.—Transcription of cols. *1–*19 (B16C, 16–31)

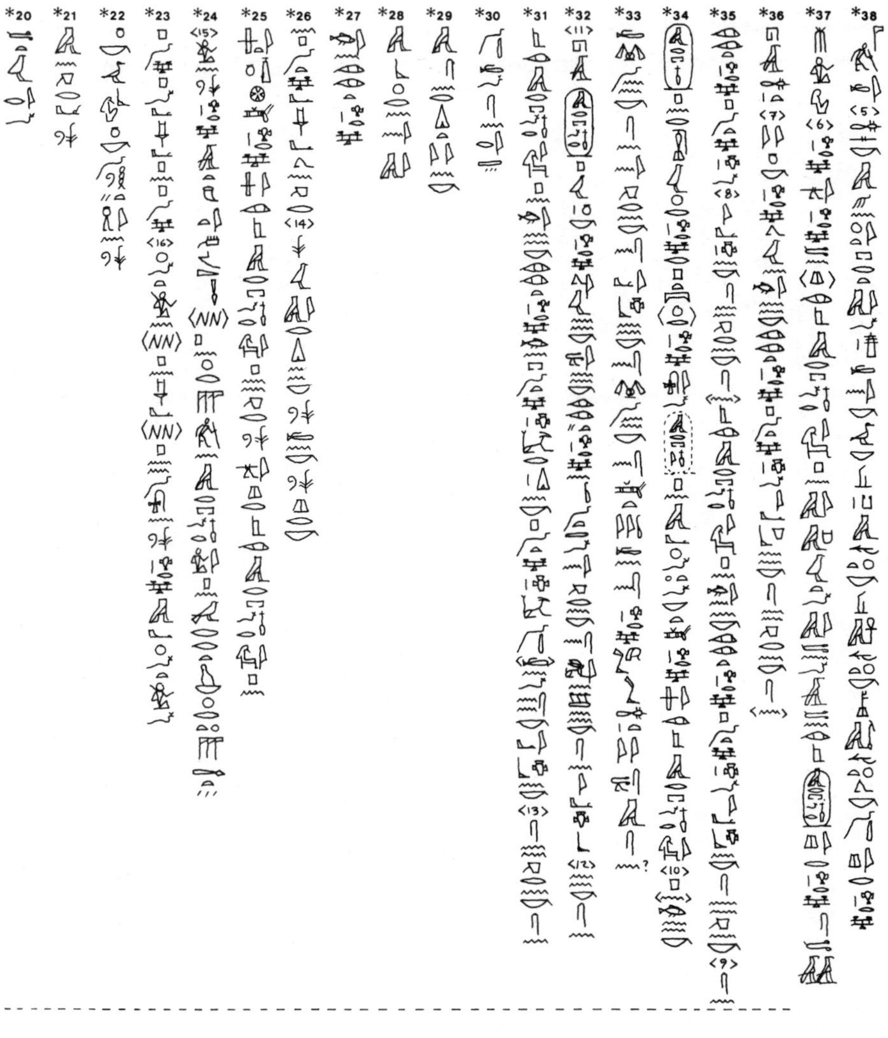

FIG. 4.—Transcription of cols. *20–*38 (B16C, 4–16)

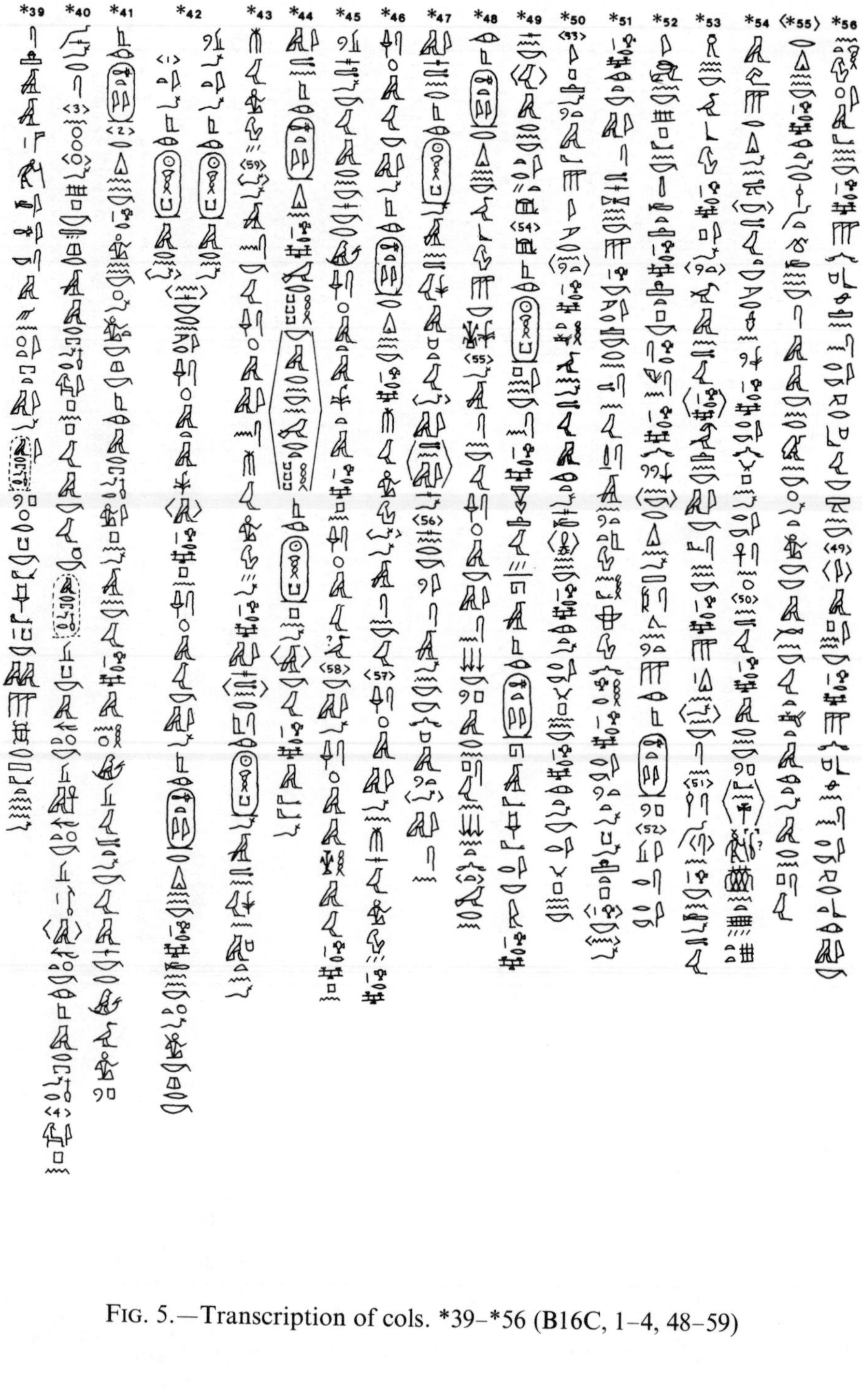

FIG. 5.—Transcription of cols. *39–*56 (**B16C**, 1–4, 48–59)

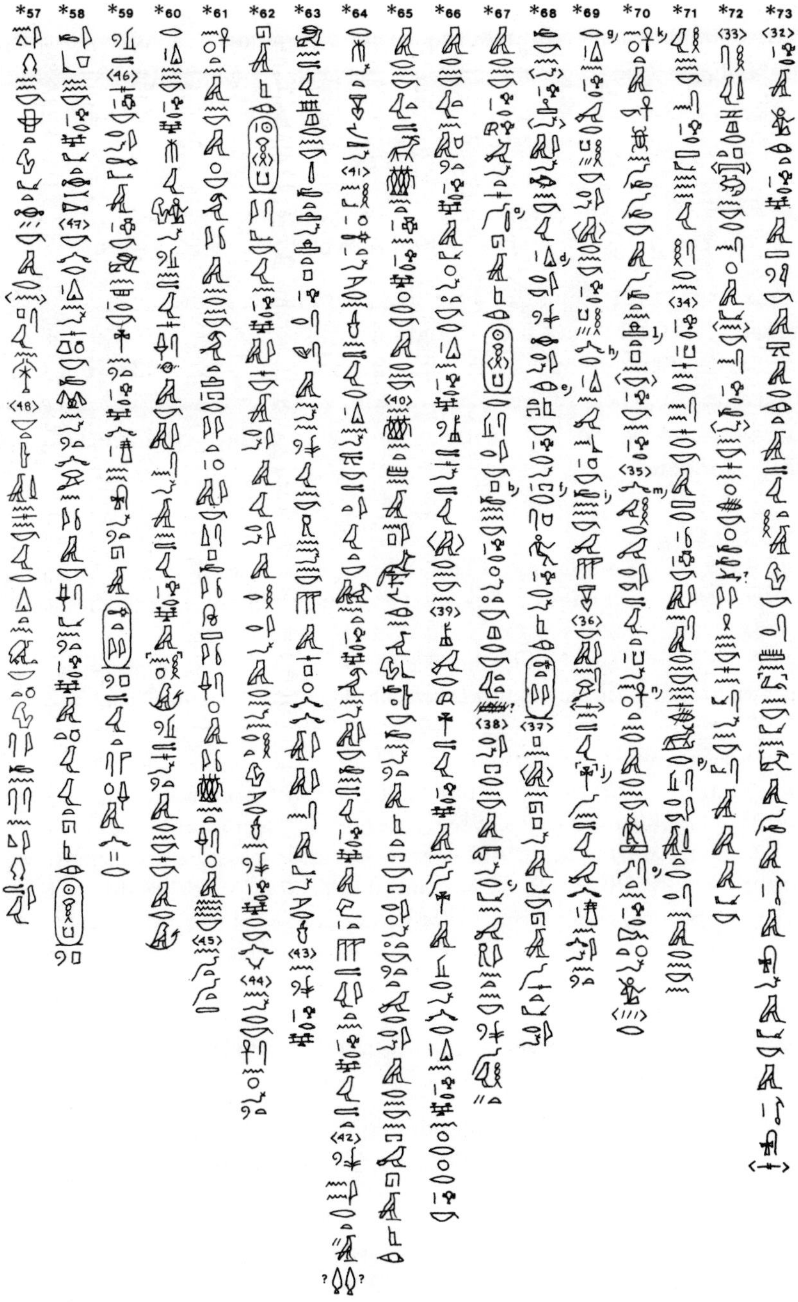

FIG. 6.—Transcription of cols. *57–*73 (B16C, 32–48)

Cols. *7–*8. PT 68, also two spells with a common title, as the *ḏd-mdww* in col. *7 shows. The placement of PT 68 between PT 62 and PT 63 is paralleled in Aba.

NOTES

ḏrt.k (col. *7). Perhaps corrupt for *ꜥ.k* of other copies.
m, "don't" (col. *8). The sign following is corrupt for the negative arms.

Cols. *8–*10. PT 63–65, 67. Five spells for different kinds of sceptres (PT 66 omitted), but treated as a unit, as the titles in Nt 309–12 (PT 64–67) illustrate. The text reads continuously: "Recitation: I am Osiris. Geb, take your son; put him within you. Clear off his face—behold, you have blinded him. Recitation: You, however, should love Horus. Don't let your face be downcast(?); they will . . . for you."

NOTES

jnk Wsjr (col. *8). Spoken by the deceased; but the parallels in Aba 13, Sq3C 97 (*ECT* VII 60*p*), and the Saite copies of Hekamsaf (*n.* 5) and Pediniese (122) have *jnk Jst*.
jm zꜣ.k (col. *9). N 293 apparently adds *Ḥrw*; cf. Hekamsaf *n.* 5–6.
ḏsr.k, "clear off." For this meaning, see Pyr 515*a*, 2013*a*. Geb, as god of the earth, is requested to clear away the soil that covers the king's face, "blinding" him.
šzp.n.k. For *šp.n.k* of Nt 309, Sq3C 97–98 (*ECT* VII 60*t*); perhaps already showing the loss of medial *z*, as in Coptic ϣⲱⲡ.
mr.k sw(*t*) *Ḥrw*. The *ḏd-mdww* preceding this spell (PT 65) indicates that the deceased rather than Geb is now being addressed; oddly, Nt 309 inserts it between the two clauses of PT 64. I take *sw*(*t*) to be the enclitic particle, here emphasizing the contrast with the preceding lines; Nt 310 has *swt*, as apparently does N 296. It is also possible to understand *sw*(*t*) as the personal pronoun, but this requires an awkward nominal-sentence construction in N and Nt. Sq3C 98 (*ECT* VII 60*u*–61*a*) has a quail chick after *k*, perhaps in a re-interpretation of the sentence: *mr kw swt Ḥrw* or *mr.k wj swt Ḥrw*.
B16C omits PT 66 and the second clause of PT 67 (*dj n.k sw m ꜥ.k*). The latter would have appeared at the end of col. *9 and may have been overlooked by the copyist; the omission of PT 66 is probably a feature of the original manuscript.

Col. *10 end. PT 70. The title, omitted at the end of line 22, is 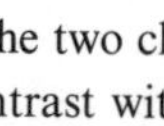, "a mace of fine gold" (N 303; Nt 317 is corrupt or miscopied).

Cols. *11–*31. A series of spells that follows PT 70 in both N and Nt and is therefore Sethe's provisional PT 71. The series comprises four major sections, described in the following.

Cols. *11–*16. PT 71A (N 304–306+3, Nt 318–23). Six spells for various kinds of staves, including two for the crook and the flail; hence, a continuation of PT 62–70: "Osiris Steward *Nfrj*, seize his hand, ⟨the hand of your enemy⟩; don't let him get away from you. Lean(?) on each of his two staves. Live,

⟨live⟩! Osiris Steward *Nfrj*, receive the Eye of Horus that dangled from the hand(s) of his children. Osiris Steward *Nfrj*, receive the hand of Nephthys; prevent her from giving it to them."

NOTES

After *ʿ.f* (col. *11) the scribe began to write col. *10 in the same line (line 21), but stopped after four signs and began in a new line (line 22). Nt 318 has *ʿnj ḫftj.k* in apposition after *ʿ.f*; compare the end of col. *73.

For the title of col. *12, read 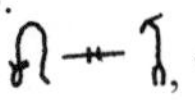, "*wꜣs*-sceptre"; 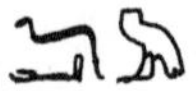 below is a plene writing for  (*wꜣs*).

ḏsr.tj (col. *13). The strong arm for ; compare the spelling in line 23.

mdw.wj.f. Nt 320 and Sq1Sq 102 (*ECT* VII 62*o*) have *ḏbʿ.wj.f*, "his two fingers"; but compare the phrase *ḏsr ḥr ḏʿm*, Pyr 339*c*, 1456*c*–58.

The strong arm below *ʿnḫ.tj* (col. *14) is from *ḏsr.tj* of col. *13, which the scribe started to write here, then began anew in line 19.

Cols. *17–*23. PT 71B (N 306+4–10, Nt 324–28). Five spells for bows and bow equipment, with a continuous text: "Laying low that (enemy) who stands (against Steward *Nfrj*). Thoth, bring him to me. Take, I have seized him; take, I have given him to you. Recitation: Put him beneath you; you are the one to whom he belongs; take, seize him. I am Geb; I am Thoth, who brings him. Lay low that one, and this one will stand up: lay low the enemy of ⟨Steward *Nfrj*⟩, and ⟨Steward *Nfrj*⟩ will stand up."

NOTES

The first clause of col. *19, *(j)m nḏr.n.j sw*, is omitted in Nt 325, but Sq1Sq 104 (*ECT* VII 62*u*–*v*) parallels the B16C copy. *Ḏd-mdww* apparently separates the speech of Thoth from that of another officiant.

For col. *21, Nt 326 has *ḏd-mdww Wsjr Njt nḏr n.k sw, j.zj ḫr Wsjr Njt*; the last clause is apparently paralleled in N, which shows the king's name at the end of line 306+8.

The parallel to col. *22 in Nt 327 omits *jnk* before *Ḏḥwtj* and adds *pḏ pf* after *jn sw*. Both may be the result of scribal errors: in the first instance, the miscopying of an original split column; in the second, dittography with Nt 328 (col. *23).

Cols. *23–*26. PT 71C (N 306+11–14). A longer spell with the instruction *dj ḥꜣ[.f]*, "Put around him," referring to the implements given in the preceding spells. In B16C, where the title is omitted, PT 71C follows PT 71B without pause. It serves as a summary of PT 71A–B and includes quotations from these two spells: "Horus has saved him from his enemy; Horus of Weaving-Town has adorned him. ⟨Steward *Nfrj*⟩ is justified before the gods; Steward *Nfrj* has taken possession of the crown before the Big Ennead in Heliopolis. Horus who is Osiris Steward *Nfrj*, seize him. Go to Osiris Steward *Nfrj*, lay low him who stands (against him); seize him. Take, I have given him to you. Put him beneath you; ⟨don't let him get away from you⟩."

NOTES

⌈*ḏbꜣ*⌉*.n* (col. *24). See the note to col. *2 title; for the clause, cf. Pyr 2094*a*.

ḫrw ⟨NN⟩ *pn*. Grouping in the manuscript.

⌈*jṯ*⌉*.n*. The aged man is corrupt for ; the hieroglyphic form is used, whereas the hieratic appears in line 4.

Ḥrw jmj Wsjr NN *pn* (col. *25). from original ? But the usual phrase has *Ḥrw* (Pyr 19*a*, 21*b*, 55*a–b*, 831). The same group occurs in this phrase in col. *34, q.v.

N 306+14 has [ ] at the end of PT 71C, probably for [*m w*]⌈ꜣ⌉*.f m* ꜥ*.k*, "don't let him get away from you," omitted here.

B16C shows that the fragment placed by Jéquier, *Le Monument funéraire de Pĕpi II* I ("Fouilles à Saqqarah" [Cairo, 1936]), at the top of N 306+4–13 actually belongs above lines 306+12–21; *jmt* in Jéquier's line 306+5 follows *psḏt* ꜥꜣ*t* at the top of line 306+13. The titles in the register above belong to lines 216+100–5; read [*ḫbz*]*t* over lines 306+16–17, the title of PT 652 (N 216+100–1 = Nt 297, 301, 304); the traces Jéquier saw over 306+10–11 may be the and stroke of *bzg*(?), the title of PT 653 (N 216+102–3 = Nt 298); for Jéquier's *m*[*str*]*t* over 306+12–13, read *m*[*ṯpn*]*t*, the title of the spell that follows PT 653 in Nt 299 (= N 216+[104–5]). The remaining two lines in N (216+106–7) are sufficient for Nt 300.

Cols. *27–*31. PT 71D (N 306+15–[23], Nt 283–91). A single spell of nine short clauses, each with separate title (for bows and bow equipment) but reading consecutively: "Bring the two Eyes of Horus from the place where they fell. Behold, they are given to you. Recitation: He ⟨has⟩ put them down. Osiris Steward *Nfrj*, I have brought you the two Eyes of Horus. I bring the two things that Seth exulted over; I give you the two things that Seth exulted over. Recitation: He has set them in place for you. Assimilate them; take hold of them."

NOTES

⟨*dj*⟩*.n.f sn n.k* (col. *31). The two preserved parallels, Sq3C 111 (*ECT* VII 61*x*) and Sq1Sq 107 (*ECT* VII 62*dd*), both have *dj.n.*(*j*) *sn n.k*. Despite the abnormal word order, the sense is clear. The third person in B16C is supported by the preceding *ḏd-mdww*, indicating a change in speaker, as in the similar clause in col. *30. The various speakers of PT 71D can be identified as: *a*. the deceased or an officiant (cols. *27–*28); *b*. the deceased's son Horus (col. *29); *c*. an officiant (col. *30); *d*. the deceased's son Horus (col. *31 beginning); *e*. an officiant (col. *31 end).

Cols. *32–*34. PT 106 (Pyr 69–70, as revised by Sethe, *Pyramidentexte* I 509); found in N 403–408 (title in Pyr 1644*c*), also in Sq3C 111–15 (*ECT* VII 61*z–dd*) and in the late copies of Pediniese (lines 137–41, 165–68, 340–44).

NOTES

hꜣ (jmj-rꜣ Nfrj)| *pw* (col. *32). The deceased's name varies with that of King Akhtoy in lines 2–11. The king's name (*Jḫty*) is original in line 1; also in lines 6–7 and 10, where it is written without cartouche and in a variant form. The deceased's name (*jmj-rꜣ pr Nfrj*) occurs over an erased cartouche in lines 3, 4, and 9 middle, and once within a cartouche from which the original name has been erased (line 11). In each case the later name is written small, in the space of the cartouche, indicating that the correction was not made immediately. In lines 6 and 9 top, the deceased's name is written (small) inside a cartouche but on apparently virgin surface. These probably represent corrections made after the ring had been drawn but before the royal name was written inside. In making the substitution of the later name immediately over the blank cartouche without first erasing it (compare line 6, where the head of the *m* projects above the top of the cartouche), the scribe followed his general practice of not cancelling errors (see the notes to cols. *11, *14, *62, *66). The deceased's name, written full size, is original in lines 2, 3, 3–4, 6, 8, and 9 bottom. But, the superfluous *pn* in line 3 suggests that these too replace an original royal name. From col. *42 on, only the royal names *Wꜣḥ-kꜣ-Rꜥw* and *Jḫty* appear, in alternation (alternation between praenomen and nomen is also to be noted in the pyramid of Aba). In cols. *32–*41, the original manuscript may have used only the nomen *Jḫty*: the preserved instances in lines 1, 6–7, and 10 are all of the nomen, and are spaced between occurrences of the later name such that the restoration of an original pattern of alternating royal names is impossible.

jṯ.n.j. Parallels have *jn.n.j*; may be corrupt for .

jꜥb.n.j n.k sn / *dmḏ.n.j n.k sn*, *j.nḏr n.k sn* (cols. *32–*33). A line not found in other copies, equivalent to Pyr 70*a* beginning plus a repetition of Pyr 69*c* beginning; Pyr 70*a* follows. In *dmḏ.n.j n.k*, is ligatured, like .

tm.ty (col. *33). is very large, like .

s⌈šm⌉.sn. for ; cf. line 11. The of *sn* is uncertain, possibly only the grain of the wood, but is required by context and parallels.

For Pyr 70*c–d*, other copies have *jr qbḥw ḫr Ḥrw jr pt ḫr nṯr ꜥꜣ, nḏ.sn* NN. B16C substitutes *Ḥrw* for *nṯr ꜥꜣ*; hence singular *j.nḏ.f* occurs in Pyr 70*d* (col. *34).

Cols. *34–*36. PT 107 (Pyr 71*a–b*, as revised by Sethe, *Pyramidentexte* I 509, plus Pyr 71*c* [ff.]). This spell consists of the lines *jn.n.j n.k jrt.j Ḥrw pḏt.j jb.f*, *jꜥb n.k sn, nḏr n.k sn* repeated three times with different introductions; the third one is like that of PT 106. A twofold repetition occurs in Sq3C 115–18 (*ECT* VII 62*a–g*) and Sq6C 82–84 (*ECT* VII 58*c–f*) but differs slightly from the B16C version. The N text is lost after Pyr 71*b* (three or four lines after N 409), but the version recorded in B16C fits well into five of N's columns including the beginning in line 408 (N 408–409 + 3). Utterances 106 and 107 may be a single spell: lines N 403 ff. have only one title beneath them (Pyr 1644*c*). But I have given them separate numbers on the strength of Nt 292 and Sq6C 82–84, where Pyr 71*a* is not preceded by Pyr 69–70.

NOTES

Ḥrw jmj Wsjr NN (col. *34). The preceding *tm* does not appear to belong to the end of PT 106, and copies of Pyr 71*a* have *Ḥrw* as the first word of the spell. B16C is paralleled by Sq3C 116–17 (*ECT* VII 62*c–d*), where  precedes *Ḥrw*. *Tm* would appear to be a verb, but its significance in these two copies is unclear.

The length of col. *36 suggests that the end was left blank in the original. Col. *37 begins a new series of spells.

Col. *37. PT 644 (N 552+14–16), with Pyr 1823*b* beginning omitted.

NOTES

jz⌈ꜣ⌉.ṯn. Probably from 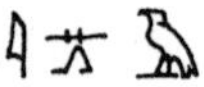 or 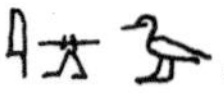, with the bird mistaken for the Horus-falcon and given plene spelling.

Cols. *37 end–*40. PT 643 end (N 552+8–13), in two versions. Pyr 1822 is also known from a version in Norman de Garis Davies, *The Tomb of Rekh-mi-Rēꜥ at Thebes* (2 vols.; New York, 1943) Pl. LXXXVII, reg. ii, but the entire spell is otherwise unparalleled. B16C indicates that Pyr 1819–20*a* belong to a different spell than Pyr 1820*b*–22. Sethe's Utterance 643 can therefore be separated into PT 643A and PT 643B. The former is Pyr 1819 (Sethe's 1820*a* renumbered 1819*c*); the latter contains Pyr 1820–22, which can be restored in N 522+8–13 as follows:

1820*a*) *[ḏd-mdww j.gr] wr*
b) *sšꜣꜣ [nṯr smsw, jdj ꜥꜣ skm] n jḫt*
1821*a*) *pr.tj jm.f [j Pjpj Nfr-kꜣ-Rꜥw pw ḥr kꜣ].k*
b) *ꜥḥꜥ kꜣ.k mm [nṯr.w, ḫpr šꜥt.f ḏs.f jr.sn*
c) *ḫw.f] tpj.k tꜣ*
1822*a*) *hꜣ Pjpj Nfr-kꜣ-Rꜥw [pw m-k wj jnk zꜣ.k*
b) *w]ṯz kꜣ m ḫt.k [wṯz ꜥnḫ m ḫt.k*
c) *wṯz] wꜣs m ḫt.k Wsjr Pjpj Nfr-kꜣ-Rꜥw.*

Translation: "The Great One grows still; the elder god sails away; he of much gray hair has been censed for the meal. Go forth as him, O Pepi Neferkare, to your ka. Let your ka take its place among the gods; let the terror proper to it come to be against them, that it may protect your survivor upon earth. Ho Pepi Neferkare, behold me—I am your son, who carries on ka in your wake, who carries on life in your wake, who carries on dominion in your wake, Osiris Pepi Neferkare."

NOTES

j.⌈g⌉r ⌈wr⌉ (cols. *37, *38).  for  also occurs in line 31 *mꜣgsw*; the normal hieratic form is used in the Coffin Texts (*ECT* I 200*b*, 202*d*, 219*f*, 225*a*). N 552+8 has *wr* before *sšꜣꜣ*, corresponding to *Ḥrw* in B16C; for the confusion between the two, see col. *69.

jdj ⌜ꜣ⌝ *skm n jḫt* (cols. *38, *39). The sequence of subjects in the three clauses of Pyr 1820 is paralleled in PT 558, a variant of PT 643B. The subject of the third clause (Pyr 1390*d*) is *qꜣj smk* (for *skm*), "he of long gray hair" (cf. *Wb* V 3, 8); in B16C is probably best understood as a corruption of , analogous to *qꜣj*. The verb of the third clause is shown by Pyr 1390*d* to be *jdj*, "sprinkle (with incense or water)" (*Wb* I 152, 5–6). The adverbial adjunct *n jḫt* corresponds to Pyr 1390*d m Jnw*, "in Heliopolis"; for the association of *jdj*, "cense," and *jḫt*, "meal," see Pyr 295*a*, 296*a*.

ḏd (col. *38). The first version of PT 643B omits most of Pyr 1821 and the opening words of Pyr 1822*a*. The deletion is marked by the *Rezitationsvermerk ḏd* (*Wb* V 629, 8–9), indicating that two lines are to be read without pause between them.

wṯz (cols. *38, *40). is usual in this manuscript for the ideograms of *wṯz* and *rs* (also corrupt for in line 18, for in line 39). The sign in *wṯz* occasionally has an extra tick (lines 5, 38–39), in which case I have transcribed .

ḏd-mdww (col. *38). The heading introduces a repetition of PT 643B, this time in the complete version. The substitution of the personal name for *zꜣ.k* in Pyr 1822*a* (col. *40) suggests that a different speaker is also involved.

j NN *pw* (col. *39). The deceased's name is written over an erased cartouche; the position of the reed leaf at the right is original.

⌜*h*⌝*ꜣ jmj-rꜣ Nfrj* {*pn*} *pw* (col. *40). The superfluous *pn* (ligatured) before *pw* suggests the thoughtless substitution of *jmj-rꜣ Nfrj pn* for an original royal name. In the particle *hꜣ*, is a misreading (and plene spelling) of original .

Col. *41 beginning. A short spell corresponding in theme to the spell that precedes PT 645–49 in Nt 358–59 and B4C 136 (*ECT* VI 374*h*–*j*). The lacuna in N 552+14, although generous for the beginning of PT 644, does not appear large enough to have held a parallel to this spell as well. Translation: "Osiris Akhtoy, I have given you Horus; I have set your enemy beneath you."

NOTES

⌜*dj*⌝.*n.j*. The dittography in line 1 indicates that the seated man is corrupt for . Some hieratic forms of the seated man look like hieratic with a vertical line through the center; damage in the original may explain the misinterpretation here.

Cols. *41–*42. PT 645.

NOTES

There is some confusion in the copy of col. *42 as a result of the hiatus between the foot and the head. The last few centimeters of line 59 (foot) contain the beginning of col. *42. The scribe then moved to the first line of the head (line 1) and repeated the beginning of col. *42 but omitted *wṯz.f*. The signs following *m rn*⟨*.f*⟩ in line 1 appear to be a corruption of ⟨*Z*⟩*kr*; is a rather bizarre misinterpretation of the determinative of *Zkr*: reflects the prow of the bark and its rope, part of the undercarriage (cf. Möller, *Hieratische Paläographie* I 378). In all, the omission and corruption of signs suggests that the original manuscript may have been damaged at this point.

Cols. *42–*44. PT 648, attested in the pyramids in N 552+24–28, Nt 363–65, and in a new fragment from the pyramid of Pepi I: *Or* n.s. 39 (1970) Pl. XXXVII, Fig. 36, reg. i 1. The copy of Nt, which follows that of Pepi I, differs slightly from the N text. The older version (P, Nt) has the line *ṯwt nṯr sḫm wꜥtj* between the vocative and text of Pyr 1828*a* and omits Pyr 1829*a–b*. B16C follows the later version (N); the copy in cols. *42–*44 omits Pyr 1829*c–d*, but the repetition in cols. *46–*47 has the complete spell.

NOTES

dj.n.j n.k ḫftj.k ẖr.k (col. *42 end). Apparently dittography of col. *41 beginning; *rḏj.n n.k Ḥrw* must be the verb phrase governing *ms.w⟨.f⟩* in col. *43. The mistake is probably in the original of B16C, since col. *42 was copied before col. *41.

j.mz ⟨ṯn⟩ ⌈*j*⌉*r Wsjr* (col. *43). B16C has *jr* for the *ẖr* of other copies (cf. col. *47); for  read .

ḥmj⌈*w*⌉*tj.fj*. 𓈖 is probably for the ligatured plural strokes, which are very flat in this manuscript (compare *ms.w* just above in line 59). The spelling is by analogy with the infixed *w* of the feminine plural.

Col. *44. PT 646, with the end omitted by homoioteleuton. The version of this spell in Nt 359–60 and S14C 191–92 (*ECT* VII 94*d–e*) has an additional line *ṯwt nṯr* ꜥꜣ at the end, omitted in B16C, S10C 271–72, and probably also in N.

Cols. *44–*46. PT 647. At the end of this spell, Nt adds the line *sḫm.k ḥw.k ḏt.k m* ꜥ *ḫftj.k*, also found in B4C 138 (*ECT* VI 375*c*) but omitted in N and B16C. Nt omits the beginning of PT 647 (Pyr 1826–27*a*) through homoioteleuton with Pyr 1824*e*, which precedes.

NOTES

*sḫmw z*ꜣ(?)*.k jm.f* (col. *45). The sign at the end of line 57 is not clear, possibly superfluous. S10C has *sḫm*(*w*)*.k*, as does the parallel phrase in Pyr 1827*b*. Sethe saw "the body of a bird" (*Pyramidentexte* III 103) at the end of the lacuna before [ ]*m.k* in N 552+23, and restored [*ḥt*]*m.k*. B16C may be interpreted as *sḫmw z*ꜣ*.k jm.f*, but the *m* before the suffix makes this impossible for N.

Cols. *46–*47. PT 648 (see cols. *42–*44).

NOTES

jm⟨.ṯn j.m⟩z.f (col. *47). Omission through homoioteleuton.

In line 56, read *jw f*ꜣ*.sn k*(*w*), "they carry you" (Pyr 1829*d*); *jw* is not paralleled in other copies.

Cols. *48–*49. PT 649A. Sethe's Utterance 649 comprises three spells. The first (PT 649A) is Sethe's Pyr 1830*a–d* plus 1831*a*, attested in N 552+28–31, Nt 365–66, S10C 279–81, and in the new P fragment, reg. i 2–3 (see cols.

*42–*44, commentary), as well as here; P and Nt omit Pyr 1830*d*. The second spell (PT 649B), omitted in N, is similar to PT 454, with the additional lines *stp.sn zꜣ m pḥtj.k, hꜣ Wsjr* NN *ṯwt nṯr ꜥꜣ* between Pyr 847*b* and 847*c*. It follows PT 649A in Nt 366–68 and the new P fragment, reg. i 4–6, and is also attested in Aba [x–]515 and B4C 138 (*ECT* VI 375*d–f*). The third spell (PT 649C) consists of Sethe's Pyr 1831*b*–32*a*, attested in N 552+32–34, Nt 368–69, Aba 515–16, B4C 138–39, and the new P fragment, reg. i 6–[8]. Sethe's Pyr 1832*b* is not found in the parallels and probably belongs to PT 650.

Cols. *49–*61. PT 364.

NOTES

jp.f tw (col. *50). This spelling of the 2ms dependent pronoun (also *twt*, col. *51) probably does not reflect the influence of Middle Egyptian phonology. It occurs only in this grouping, as a variant of older *ṯw* (over); the sign transcribed as may in fact be a miniature (cf. *j.mr.n.sn ṯw*, line 52).

At the end of col. *50, *Ḥrw jrt.f jr.k wp.n n.k* is a dittograph of Pyr 609*c* end–610*a* beginning. The text reads from the first *wp.n n.k* in col. *50 to *Ḥrw jrt.k* in col. *51; the verb *mꜣ.k* has been omitted between *jrt.k* and *jm.s*, possibly through homoioteleuton. The omission of *mꜣ.k* may be the fault of the scribe of B16C, but the dittography in col. *50 was most likely present in the original manuscript; its deletion would leave an abnormally short column.

Wsjr (*Jḫty*)| *pw* (col. *52). The pattern of alternating nomen and praenomen is broken between cols. *49 and *52.

ꜥnḏtj (col. *54). The sign to the right of the standing figure looks like , perhaps for with a preceding omission of other phonograms.

Between cols. *54 and *56 the scribe has omitted an entire column of his original (Pyr 614*b–d* except end); it is restored here as col. ⟨*55⟩, in the style of the surrounding lines.

ḏr bw jrt.k jm, "in the place where your Eye is" (col. *56). Pyr 615*d* has *ḏr bw nb mḥ.n.k jm*, "in any place to which you have swum." The *t* after *b*(*w*) may belong with *jrt.k* or to the relative pronoun ⟨*n*⟩*tj*. Similar clauses in the Pyramid Texts all have *ntj* (Pyr 434*d*, 1044*c*, 1045*c*, 1222*c*, 1717*a*).

At the end of col. *57 read *j.s*(*j*)⌈*ꜥ.tj*⌉ *n.s jnq*⌈*.s*⌉ *ṯw*, Pyr 616*f*/*e* without the paronomastic adjuncts. An exact parallel to the B16C version of Pyr 616*d–f* (as corrected) exists in S10C 291, probably also in S14C 181–82 (lost).

n sn.nw.⌈*k*⌉ (col. *59). Pyr 619*a* has *n nṯr mrwtj.k*. The B16C version may have been paralleled in B9C 310: it is now lost, but the lacuna is small for the traditional phrase.

⌈*ḥnw*⌉ (col. *60). The signs look like : the head of and the beneath are corrupt for , the tail of for .

The B16C version of Pyr 621*c* (col. *61 end) is also found in S10C 296 and S14C 188–89 (the latter erroneously included in *ECT* VII 94*a*).

Cols. *62–*67. A single spell comprising most of the older PT 370 and PT

371. The first half of the spell (cols. *62–*64) consists of PT 370 minus its beginning and end (Pyr 645*c*–47*c*). The second half (cols. *64–*67) is composed of the lines of PT 371 in variant order, with the last line of PT 369 (Pyr 644*d*–*e*) as conclusion to the whole.

NOTES

The praenomen (*Wꜣḥ-kꜣ-Rꜥw*)| in line 43 (col. *62) is written larger than usual, and in a variant spelling; the *wꜣḥ*-sign is incomplete (compare the form in lines 37 and 48). The size of the cartouche suggests that the scribe wrote the name first, then drew the ring around it, contrary to his usual practice. The variant forms of the nomen in lines 6–7 and 10 may reflect the same procedure. There, however, the scribe has omitted the cartouche—in lines 6–7 through necessity, in line 10 through neglect. For the use of different spellings, cf. Aba 328 (Gustave Jéquier, *La Pyramide de Aba* "Fouilles à Saqqarah" [Cairo, 1935] p. 21).

j.mz kw jr.f. The scribe first wrote *kꜣ* for *kw* and continued with *jr.f m* before realizing his error. He then corrected the mistake by writing the correct sign (quail chick) and repeating *jr.f m*, but neglected to cancel the original error and dittography.

šz⌈*p*⌉*.n.k* (col. *63). The *šzp*-sign is made like ;  is a misinterpretation (and plene spelling) of .

n bjꜣ jm.sn. The spelling of *bjꜣ* is possibly an example of the use of the negative arms with the value *b*: see J. J. Clère, "L'ancienneté des négations à *b* initial du néo-égyptien," *MDAIK* 14 (1956) 29–33.

The end of col. *64 contains a puzzling fragment whose significance is not clear. The last two signs look somewhat like *ḫsf*-signs (Möller, *Hieratische Paläographie* I 473) and appear to be determinatives of a dual noun—perhaps *jꜣ*⌈*r*⌉*rt.j*, "two vines," determined by two trees (for the spelling, cf. *Urk* I 4, 14), or "two sceptres" of a shape similar to that of the tree (*Wb* I 32, 11). In any case, the signs fit neither here, in Pyr 650*b*, nor on top of col. *63, between Pyr 646*b* and 646*c*. Grammatically it is possible to understand *jꜣ*⌈*r*⌉*rt.j* as the subject of *wṯṯ sw*, but this makes little sense and has no support in the parallels. Assuming that the present placement is correct, the signs may be intrusive from a title beneath cols. *62–*67 in the original (for the titles of longer spells, cf. Pyr 457*c*); the signs preceding the "determinatives" may represent the copyist's plene spelling of two original ideograms.

Ḫntj-(*j*)*mntj.w* (col. *65). *Jnpw* is plene spelling of the determinative of *Ḫntj-jmntj.w*; cf. Pyr 592*b* (a parallel of this line).

pr-⌈*wr*⌉. *Wr* is written with the round-tailed sparrow (Möller, *Hieratische Paläographie* I 197) instead of the fork-tailed swallow; compare the spelling of *ḥwr*/*ḥrj* in line 35 (col. *70).

The beginning of col. *66 is identical to that of col. *65. The scribe began to copy col. *65 after col. *67, realized his error after having written six signs, but simply continued with the adjacent portion of col. *66 instead of erasing the mistake and substituting the correct signs. The space occupied by the erroneous signs in col. *66 belongs to (*Jḫty*)| *pn*, the continuation of col. *65 *hꜣ Wsjr*; the omitted name preserves the alternation of praenomen and nomen.

nḥm.n tw Ḥrw (col. *66). Pyr 649*b* has *nḥm.n.f ṯw*. Akhtoy's new edition of PT 371 has reversed Pyr 649*a* and 649*b* and added the vocative *hꜣ Wsjr* ⟨(*Jḫty*)| *pn*⟩.

Cols. *67–*73. A new spell, containing PT 372 (Pyr 651–53) interspersed with lines from a number of other spells and some original text. The parallels (indicated by the letters *a–p* in Fig. 6) are the following: *a*) Pyr 651*a*; *b*) Pyr 650*a*; *c*) Pyr 651*b–c*; *d*) Pyr 652*b*; *e*) Pyr 651*d*; *f*) Pyr 652*a–b*; *g*) Pyr 1825*a–b*; *h*) Pyr 1633*a*; *i*) a new line, bearing some resemblance to Pyr 1831*a*; *j*) Pyr 591*a* or 618*b*; *k*) Pyr 1633*c*; *l*) a new line (cf. Pyr 611*a*); *m*) Pyr 610*d*; *n*) a new line; *o*) Pyr 653*a–d*; *p*) new text (compare the beginning with Pyr 1798*a*; compare col. *72 end with Pyr 1632*c*; compare col. *73 end with cols. *11–*12). Translation: "Ho Osiris Wahkare, awaken! Horus has spread out your enemy beneath you. You are older than him; you came forth before him. Horus has made Thoth fetch him for you; / he has placed you on his back, that he might not thwart you. Set (your) haunch on him(?), take your seat on him. Go up and sit on him, Osiris Akhtoy; don't let him escape you. Board (him), for you are more sacred than him. / Horus has made your magic greater than his, in your name of Great of Magic; Horus will not let you be eclipsed. Horus has stationed the gods for you, that you might join them and they might row you. Horus has cared for you; he will not fail to care for you. / Live in your (new) life; come into being and endure forever, in Mendes. Look favorably upon Horus; Horus will not be far from you, for you are his ka. Live, in your name of Andjty. Horus has cut up the foreleg(s) of your enemies; / Horus has smitten them into pieces for you; Horus has driven their ka away from them. Burn, . . . your heart among them, in your name of *Nzr*. Awaken sounder than them, in your name of / 'He who awakens sound, whom the sky bears,' for the fear of you is on them. Horus has gathered them together for you; he sets them before you upside down(?). Take them in your arms, for he lifts them up to you. Take hold of / Horus; set the Eye of Horus in your empty space(?). Do not be hostile to the Eye of Horus, for you are Ha, its owner. Lean on the arm of Seth, as a *ḏʿm*-sceptre; don't let him get away from you, as a *wꜣs*-sceptre."

NOTES

rdj.n ⌜*Ḥrw*⌝ *jn.t n.k sw Ḏḥwtj* (col. *67). Pyr 651*b*, with *sw* for *ḫftj.k*, mentioned in the preceding line (Pyr 650*a*). *Ḥrw* is written with the round-tailed sparrow, which the scribe also uses for *wr* in line 40. The same spelling of *Ḥrw* occurs again in col. *69 (three times) and col. *70, in variance with the normal spelling. The confusion undoubtedly arises through the similarity of the *wr*-bird and the Horus-falcon in hieratic (compare the note after next); the scribe's use of the round-tailed sparrow represents a simplification of both signs.

jm.f ⌜*ẖꜣ*⌝ *kw* (col. *68).  is a misinterpretation (and plene spelling) of the *ẖꜣ*-fish. The normal form of *ḫꜣ* in this coffin is like that used in Sinuhe (Möller, *Hieratische Paläographie* I 257); it occurs in the Coffin Texts (*ECT* I 154*c*, 173*d*, 198*c*).

rn.k ⌈*wr*⌉ *ḥkꜣ.w* (col. *69). is a misreading (and plene spelling) of the *wr*-bird, which is similar to the Horus-falcon in hieratic. For the confusion, see also *ECT* I 223*d*, 224*c*, 229*c*.

n rḏj.n ⌈*Ḥrw*⌉ *bnw.k*. The verb in Pyr 1633*a* has been interpreted previously as a hapax *bḫn* (*Wb* I 470, 13), but the spelling here and in Nt 431 shows that the round sign in N 649 is actually the *nw*-jar; compare the similar line in *ECT* I 287*e–f*. The root is 3ae-*w bnw* (= *Wb* I 456, 13 *bn*); the *w* is written in Sq3C 203 (Pyr 1633*a*) and in *Urk* I 36, 13 (*sḏmtj.fj*).

⌈*nḏ*⌉*.n ṯw* ⌈*Ḥrw*⌉, *n ḏd.n j.*⌈*nḏ*⌉*.f tw*. The initial sign of *nḏ.n* has a form like that of the *zmꜣ*-sign but with an arm to the right (cf. line 35, bottom); in *j.nḏ.f* the negative arms is corrupt for the *nḏ*-sign.

ʿnḫ.tj . . . Ḏdwt (col. *70). This parallel suggests that the Pyramid Texts' *ḫpr* is the imperative "come into being" rather than an ideogram for "beetle"; *ʿnḫ.k* is also in Nt's two copies of Pyr 1633*c* (Nt 431, 674). In *Ḏdwt*, may stand for (cf. Pyr 1301*c*).

n ḥ⌈*w*⌉*r* ⌈*Ḥrw*⌉. The verb and its subject are both spelled with the round-tailed sparrow, which the scribe uses elsewhere for *wr* (line 40) and *Ḥrw*. The verb is perhaps a corruption of Pyr 610*d ḥrj*, "be far," through a confusion of the two signs.

ḥw.n n.k sn Ḥrw šʿ.wj (col. *71). Pyr 653*b* has *jn.n*. For *ḥwj* with the old perfective of result, cf. Pyr 587*b*.

⌈*r*⌉*s-wḏꜣ ḫrj pt* (col. *72). The use of for may be an indication that the scribe began to copy col. *71 after col. *73, but realized his mistake after writing only one sign. The signs after *wḏꜣ* may be corrupt for *šzp* (cf. line 42); but this interpretation makes little sense. As they stand, the first sign is the determinative of *rs-wḏꜣ* (corrupt?; for ?), while the next two are the nisbe *ḫrj*. The significance of the entire phrase, an epithet of Osiris, is indicated by Pyr 741*a sḏr Wr ḥr mwt.f Nwt*, "The Great One sleeps on his mother Nut."

dj⟨*.f*⟩ *n.k sn ḫr.k ḫdd.y*(?). The meaning of the word(s) following *ḫr.k* is not clear. The signs and the double reed leaf are fairly certain; the sign between looks like the harpoon. If the phonograms are not corrupt, the word is a hapax, possibly to be related to *sḫd*(*ḫd*), "be upside down," with corrupt for the determinative of the overturned boat; the double reed leaf can be the ending of a 3mpl old perfective (cf. Pyr 1617*b* N *jʿb.y*). Hence perhaps *ḫdd.y* or ⟨*s*⟩*ḫd*⟨*ḫ*⟩*d.y*, "they being upside down." A form of *ḫdj*, "go downstream" (also with corrupt determinative), does not appear to suit the context.

šn n.k sn, s(*j*)*ʿ.f n.k s*⌈*n*⌉. For the association of these two clauses, see Pyr 140*c*, 160*b*, 213*a*.

ꜣmm.k Ḥrw, ⌈*wdj*⌉ *jrt Ḥrw m šw.k* (cols. *72–*73). A parallel for the use of *ꜣmm* in a friendly sense is possibly Pyr 1739*b ꜣmm ṯw Šw*, where *ṯw* may refer to the king; compare also the use of *nḏrj* with non-inimical object (PT 106–7, Pyr 1786*b*). The signs following *Ḥrw* at the top of col. *73 would appear to represent a verb governing *jrt Ḥrw*. The "enemy"-sign is almost certainly corrupt. Its use in lines 15 and 30 suggests the verb *ḏbꜣ*, but it is difficult to accommodate any of the various meanings of this verb in the present context without assuming the omission of one or more signs. As an alternative, the corruption in line 2 suggests that the seated man is a mistake for *dj*; the preceding may be a miscopied quail chick (cf. line 43; possibly also ⌜*w*⌝*ḏꜣ.tj*, line 34), the first sign of the full root *wdj*, "set in place." The adjunct *m šw.k* can mean "when you ascend," but in connection with *wdj šw* is probably better taken as the root "be empty": here perhaps a nominal form "blank (space)"; cf. *šw*, "blank (sheet of papyrus)" (*Wb* IV 428). Interpreted in this manner, the clause *wdj jrt Ḥrw m šw.k* forms the second of two paired clauses; compare the pairing of *nḏrj* and *wdj* in Pyr 997*a–b*, 1405*b–c*.

m šm jr jrt ⌜*Ḥrw*⌝, *ṯwt Ḥꜣ* ⌜*nb*⌝*.s*. The bird after *jrt* may be a misreading of an original Horus-falcon. The request in the first clause continues the theme of the preceding sentence; compare the phrase *ḥtp ḥr.k n Ḥrw*, "look favorably upon Horus," cols. *51, *70.

rmn n.k ʿ nj Stẖ. The sign between *rmn* and *n.k* is slightly different from and may be a badly made , the determinative of *rmnj*. For *rmnj*, "lean on," with direct object, compare possibly Pyr 1528*a*/*c*, 1638*c*. Alternatively, perhaps understand intransitive "The arm of Seth acts as support for you."

The texts on the head and foot of B16C form a ritual unit that has its parallels in the pyramids of Pepi II and his queen Neith. Columns *1–*36 contain the text of a ritual for the presentation of various objects of personal attire. In the pyramid of Pepi II this ritual is displayed in the upper three registers of the north wall of the burial chamber, east end (Fig. 7). The first register is largely destroyed; the second contains the texts corresponding to cols. *2–*31 in B16C. In the third register the end of the ritual (PT 106–7, B16C *32–*36) is preceded by a series of spells, mostly unique, similar in purpose to PT 71C. From their titles, these "supplementary" spells appear to accompany the actual deposition of the objects around the sarcophagus: "Set at his left hand" (Pyr 65*a*), "Set in his left hand" (Pyr 67*a*, 68*e*), "[Set] beneath his head" (over N 392+11 ff.); a ritual censing is performed at the same time (Pyr 1644*a–b*).

Neith's copy of the ritual of objects occurs in a similar location in her pyramid but is somewhat disjointed and abbreviated from lack of space (Fig. 8). The upper part of the wall contains the text of the Offering Ritual (PT 23–57, 72–96, 108–71, 173–98, 223–25), which in the pyramid of Pepi II is inscribed in the middle section of the north wall (to the left of Fig. 7). The ritual of objects appears at the bottom of the wall, to the west of the door. The sequence of spells begins in reg. v, the left half of which corresponds to N's reg. i, the right to N's reg. ii; the texts equivalent to the end of N's reg. ii have been placed in the space left over at the end of reg. iv. Neith has copied only the spells for the presentation of the objects themselves, omitting the longer texts that accompany the formal deposition of the objects in the burial chamber (PT 71C and PT 97 ff.). The conclusion of the ritual (PT 106–7) is represented by the first line of PT 107 (Nt 292).

In both N and Nt the beginning of the ritual includes PT 651–53 followed by two spells lost at the end of N's reg. i but preserved in Nt 299–300 (see the last note to cols. *23–*26, above). The sequence Nt 300–PT 58 in B16C *1–*2 thus

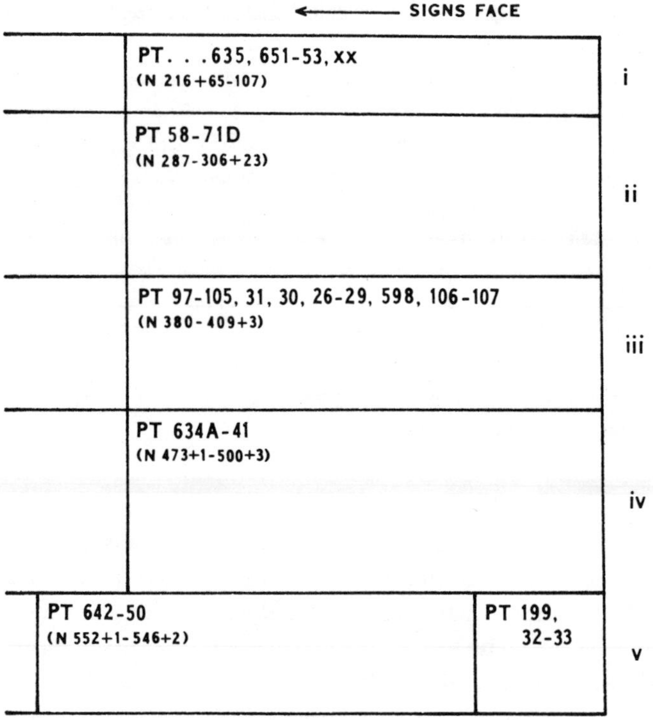

FIG. 7.—Burial chamber of Pepi II, north wall, east end

agrees with the sequence in the pyramids.[13] Moreover, as col. *1 (line 31) was the last to be inscribed, it can be assumed that the original of B16C continued to the left and contained at least the remainder of the texts in Nt 293–99 and possibly also those in N's reg. i (N 216+[65]–98).

Columns *37–*49 preserve the text of a ceremony involving a statue of the deceased, which is placed in a Sokar bark and carried by the Children of Horus.[14] The theme of the texts is similar to that which runs through the object ritual, describing the king's defeat of his enemies; here the emphasis is on the magic powers (*wrt-ḥkꜣ.w*) by means of which his triumph is accomplished. The corresponding texts in N occur below those of the object ritual (Fig. 7, reg. v); in Nt they are separated from the object ritual by the door (Fig. 8, reg. iii right). The

[13] Nt 301 contains a repetition of PT 652, as also Nt 304 (between PT 59 and PT 60).

[14] Scene 73 of the Mouth-Opening Ritual, whose text is composed of PT 644+648+645, specifies the "Children" as the four Sons of Horus (MOR 73 text e; Eberhard Otto, *Das ägyptische Mundöffnungsritual* ["Ägyptologische Abhandlungen," Vol. 3 (Wiesbaden, 1960)] I 201). The title of MOR 73 indicates that the ritual involves "carrying the statue to its shrine" (*ibid.*, p. 199). See the commentary, *ibid.*, II 164–66.

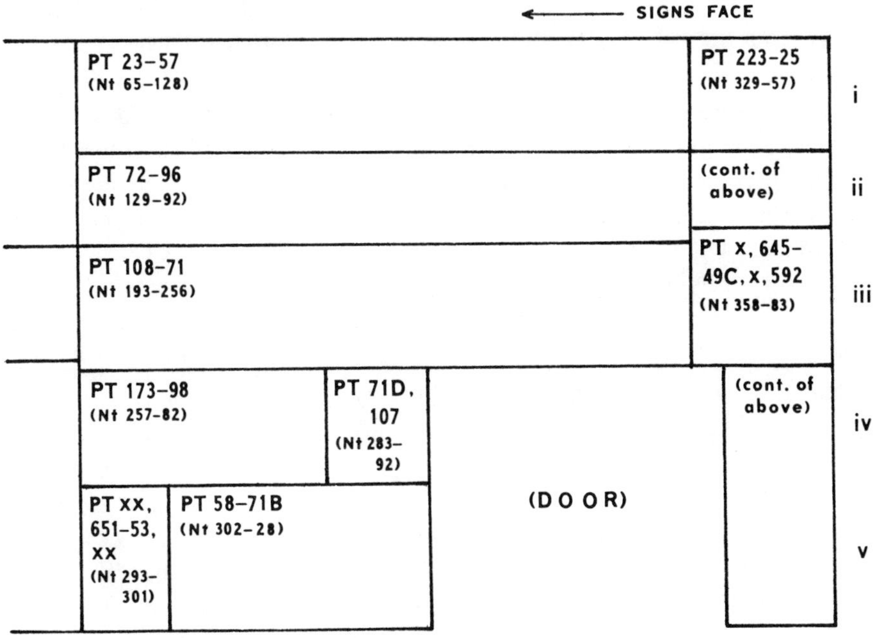

FIG. 8.—Burial chamber of Neith, north wall, east end

ceremony in N opens with a series of spells (reg. iv) in which the statue has its mouth and eyes opened (PT 634A), is clothed (PT 634C–36) and anointed (PT 637–39). Nt and B16C dispense with these preliminaries and begin immediately with the procession. The location of the statue rite at the end of the wall in both pyramids suggests that it is the final episode in the offering ceremonies of the north wall. This is supported by the legend accompanying PT 644 in TT 100: "Recession by the citizenry after making a good burial for Mayor Rekhmire."[15] The rite has some relationship to the later Mouth-Opening Ritual: N's opening spell (PT 634A) is preserved in MOR 27, and PT 644–45 + 648 make up the text of MOR 73.

The three long spells in cols. *49–*73 appear at first glance to belong to a separate section without specific ritual associations; but this initial impression is misleading. Physically at least, PT 364 belongs to the statue rite: although it is separated from PT 649A by a division line, it does not commence a new column. In S14C the spell precedes PT 646–48 (CT 884); in S10C it follows PT 645–49A before a new section of text (CT 1 ff.). The content of PT 364 makes it suitable as a summary of the statue rite: references are made to the opening of

[15] Davies, *The Tomb of Rekh-mi-Rēʿ*, Pl. LXXXIX, reg. ii. The end of reg. v in N contains spells for the formal "reversion" of the offerings of the entire wall (PT 199) and a final libation (PT 32–33).

the king's eye and mouth (Pyr 610*a*, 618*a*), to the "standing up" of the king by Horus (Pyr 617*c*), and to his being carried by the Children of Horus (Pyr 619*b*–20). In employing a long "hymn" as a coda to the statue rite, B16C follows the tradition of the pyramids, as represented in N's PT 650 and Nt's PT 592, both of which contain references to the rite and bear some resemblance to PT 364.

The spells in cols. *62–*73 begin at the top of a new column and are related to each other through their kernel of PT 370–72. They appear to have been edited out of these older spells for specific use in the original of B16C. The rewording of Pyr 649*b*, 651*b*, and 653*b* is clear evidence of a purposeful recomposition, as opposed to a senseless jumbling of the older lines. The first spell is more or less identical to PT 370–71. The second, although based on PT 372, has undergone more extensive editing; the use of  for *pḏj* and  for *rḏj* (col. *67) are signs that this took place at a relatively late date.[16] The re-editing of these spells may have been occasioned specifically by their use in the present context. They contain lines reminiscent of both the object ritual and the statue rite: compare col. *66 (Pyr 649*b*) with col. *23; col. *66 end (Pyr 644*d*) with col. *9 (Pyr 46*b*); col. *67 (Pyr 650*a*) with cols. *32–*36 (PT 106–7); col. *68 end (Pyr 652*b*) with col. *13; col. *69 with col. *44 (PT 646); and col. *73 end with cols. *11–*12. Such parallels suggest that cols. *62–*73 serve as summary and conclusion to the rites in cols. [x–]*1–*61 and are thus the final lines of the original of B16C (or at least of a discrete section of it).[17] This agrees with the conclusion reached earlier that the scribe began his copy at the end of his original.

The original beneficiary of these funerary rites was the king whose cartouches are preserved on the foot and in line 1 of the head. Lines 2–31 of the head must

[16] For $s > z$ see below. An interesting analogue to the use of Middle Egyptian orthography in col. *67 occurs in the 12th-Dynasty tomb of Sesostris-ankh (S). The texts in S consist of a nearly complete copy of the Pyramid Texts of Unis, with two additions. The first of these, PT 173–98, forms part of the Offering Ritual, attested first in the pyramid of Pepi II (PT 173 in Teti). Unis' texts and this addition regularly appear in S with the Old Kingdom orthography for the *sḏm.f* and *sḏm.n.f* of *rḏj* ( and ), with few exceptions ( in Pyr 53*a* and 139*c*,  in 145*b*–*c*). The second addition consists of a series of spells inscribed in space left over in the northeast corner of the tomb and on the walls of the corridor. Although all occur earlier, in the pyramids of Unis' successors (CT 516 first in N 1055+27–30 plus Gustave Jéquier, *Le Monument funéraire de Pépi* II I, Pl. XV, fragment 13), they are arranged in a sequence typical of Middle Kingdom sources: PT 593, 356+357, 364, 677, 365, 373, CT 516. The sequence is attested in B9C 291–329, B10C 256–81 and [395–422], Sq4C 157–233, and a partial example in Sq13C 14–41 (with PT 366 for PT 593); see Hartwig Altenmüller, *Die Texte zum Begräbnisritual in den Pyramiden des Alten Reichs* ("Ägyptologische Abhandlungen," Vol. 24 [Wiesbaden, 1972]) pp. 23–24. In this sequence S uniformly writes the *sḏm.f* and *sḏm.n.f* of *rḏj* with the typical Middle Kingdom spellings  and .

[17] The numerous corruptions in cols. *72–*73 suggest that the original manuscript may have been damaged at this end; a column or two may even have been lost.

originally have borne the same royal name(s), despite the occurrence of *Nfrj*'s name in the copy. The order of copy shows a transition from the royal names to that of *Nfrj*. The two sections of unaltered names are connected by a section in which the later name is frequently written over an erasure of the earlier. The retention of the royal names in lines 32–59+1 is consistent with the copyist's general inattention to the content of his original, as manifested above all in the fact that he has copied its columns backwards. Lines 2–11 reflect the point at which the scribe became aware of the necessity for substituting the name of the coffin's owner. The erased cartouches testify to his efforts to establish a pattern of substitution, which eventually succeed only in the last lines of the head. The two instances in which the later name is written over an empty cartouche suggest that the corrections in lines 2–11 represent errors apprehended fairly soon after their commission; the unemended cartouches of line 1 and the foot follow the scribe's general practice elsewhere of not erasing mistakes of which he has become aware.

The carelessness with which the scribe of B16C copied his original is evident throughout the copy. Signs are frequently omitted, only occasionally through homoioteleuton. In addition, there is evidence in the large number of errors involving the transposition of signs that the scribe suffered from dyslexia. The simple transposition of two signs is common, particularly among the longer texts of the foot: line 37 *rḫwt.f*, line 40 *mswt.f*, line 44 *nmnm.k*, line 49 *rḏj.n.f*, line 51 *dj.n.f*, line 52 *j.mr{kr}.n.sn ṯw*, line 55 *fꜣ.ṯn* and *ḥmjwtj.fj*, line 57 *wṯz*, and line 58 *Mḥw*; compound examples, involving three or more signs, occur in line 15 *Tꜣjtj*, line 32 *wꜣ⟨s⟩*, line 36 *dj.n⟨.f⟩ k(w)*, line 44 *m rn.k nj ꜣḫt*, line 45 *wṯz.sn ṯw*, line 49 *bw jrt.k jm*, and line 56 *fꜣ.sn*.[18]

Most errors in the text involve the misuse or substitution of single signs. In some instances it appears that the scribe has simply chosen the wrong hieratic sign or has distorted the proper hieratic form. Most notable in this respect is the *nḏ*-sign, which appears variously as  (lines 9, 16, 46),  and  (line 36); other abusive spellings substitute  for  in *npḏ*/*pḏj* (*passim*),  for  in *jʿb* (*passim*),  for  (line 18) and  (line 39), and hieroglyphic  for  (line 15). That these are the result of carelessness rather than ignorance seems clear from instances in which the correct sign is written.[19] The scribe's ability to read as well as to copy his original is displayed in a number of other alterations that he has made in the spelling of the text. The use of 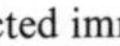 for , common

[18] Examples also in the Coffin Texts: *ECT* I 137*b*, 144*a*, 160*b*. An interesting example is *ECT* I 140*d rḫt.n.k*; the word was begun with a transposition but was corrected immediately, resulting in *ḫrḫt.n.k*.

[19] In our texts:  in lines 39, 46; in lines 7, 46;  *passim*;  in lines 41, 49. In Coffin Texts:  in *ECT* I 123*b* (*npḏ*);  in *ECT* I 172*a*, 196*b*, 236*c*, 240*g*.

throughout the coffin, is infrequent before the end of the Eleventh Dynasty and so probably represents an adaptation made by the Twelfth-Dynasty scribe rather than a feature of the Ninth- to Tenth-Dynasty original.[20] Another alteration is evident in the use of plene writing, the "spelling out" in phonograms of a (presumably) ideographic original.[21] The clearest instances are [glyph] for [glyph] (w3s) in line 20; [glyph] for the determinative alone, in line 40; and [glyph] for [glyph] (ḥ3) in line 36. That [glyph] represents an original [glyph] is probable on the basis of its substitution for [glyph] in lines 27–29 and *ECT* I 197f; the same group is used for [glyph] or [glyph] in line 6 and for [glyph] (wr) in lines 5, 6, and 35. These and similar revisions of the original account in part for the unequal length of the reconstructed columns.

In many cases the scribe's misspellings can be attributed to his misinterpretation of signs in the original manuscript. A number of such errors point to an original hieratic character. Most striking among these is the confusion of *wr* and *Ḥrw* (lines 5, 6, and 35–40), whose hieratic shapes are virtually identical in many hands. The scribe's common malformation of □ as [glyph] (and plene [glyph] in line 42) probably also derives from a misreading of the hieratic. Other likely corruptions of a hieratic original are:

[glyph] for [glyph], lines 15, 30(?); for [glyph], lines 2, 32

[glyph] for [glyph], lines 35, 46

[glyph] for [glyph], line 33

[glyph] for [glyph], lines 25(?), 32, 46, 48

[glyph] for plural strokes, line 59

[glyph] for [glyph], line 42

[glyph] for [glyph], line 3 (plene spelling)

[glyph] for [glyph], line 11

[glyph] for [glyph], line 45.

By contrast, an even larger number of errors involves the confusion of two signs whose shapes are more alike in hieroglyphs than in hieratic:

[glyph] for [glyph], line 47

[glyph] for [glyph], lines 4, 5

[glyph] for [glyph], lines 32, 34, 43; for [glyph], line 32

[glyph] for [glyph], lines 13, 48

[20] See Schenkel, *Frühmittelägyptische Studien*, pp. 62–64.

[21] Also found in Coffin Texts: *ECT* I 144c, 148a, 155c, 159f, 160f/i, 197f, 223d, 224c, 229c, 239h, 242d.

for , line 59

for , line 12

for , line 32; for , line 18

for , line 4

for , lines 5, 6, 31

for , line 20

for , line 48

for , line 6

for , line 10

for , lines 1, 5, 48, 54

for , line 32

Despite their apparent contradiction, both kinds of errors derive from a single original manuscript. This is clear from their distribution, as well as from the inherent unity of the texts as a whole. To have produced such errors, the original script must have been a blend of hieratic and hieroglyphs, the latter undoubtedly in cursive form. Many of the confusions that suggest a hieroglyphic original can be paralleled in the Pyramid Texts.[22] Those texts appear to have been transferred to the walls of the pyramids initially in a semicursive form, to serve as a guide for the eventual incision of the hieroglyphs themselves. Evidence for this is the frequent appearance of (in cursive, a simple horizontal line) for , also for and for the two short horizontal strokes determining *snwj*, "two."[23] Occasionally the cursive form of has been carved in error for the hieroglyph (Pyr 267*c* W, 286*d* W, 404*d* W, 478*a* W, 2084*b* N). The presence of a similar form in the original of B16C probably underlies the misreading of the determinative of *šʿ*(*t*) () as in lines 4 and 33.

The sum of internal evidence thus argues for an original document consisting of 73 + *x* columns of cursive hieroglyphs and some hieratic signs, written retrograde, and bearing the names of King Wahkare Akhtoy. Of the physical nature of the document itself there is less evidence. Three possibilities suggest themselves.

The reconstruction in Figures 3–4 shows the text laid out as if on the wall of a tomb, with columns of short spells separated by blank space from their titles at the bottom.[24] Moreover, the cursive form of the preliminary signs in the Old

[22] Sethe, *Pyramidentexte* IV §156.

[23] *Ibid.* In the first instance, compare B16 line 34 (*Ḏdwt*).

[24] Not all the titles of the original have been copied onto B16C, as shown by the blank field at the bottom of lines 22 and 26. For the insertion of a long spell (as cols. *6–*10), possibly without titles, in the midst of such columns, compare Nt 161–65.

Kingdom pyramids shows that the script of the original of B16C is not incompatible with such a medium. But the orientation of the signs in cols. *1–*73 does not coincide with the traditional location of the texts on the north wall (see Figs. 7–8); and in any case, the direct copying of the texts from the walls of a tomb to the sides of the coffin is highly improbable.

The possibility that the coffin of King Wahkare Akhtoy served as the original of B16C has raised some speculation, the more so in light of the passage in the Instruction for Merikare in which the king's father, whose name is lost, admonishes his son: "Do not disturb the tombs . . . I acted in this manner and the like came to pass."[25] While the identification of King Wahkare Akhtoy with Merikare's father has been generally discarded, the possibility remains of a spoliation of this sort, involving among others the tomb of Wahkare Akhtoy, was in the mind of the author of the Instruction. The likelihood that the plundered coffin could ultimately have come to serve as the model for *Nfrj*'s texts is a good deal more speculative. The link between the unknown resting place of the Heracleopolitan king and the Twelfth-Dynasty workshop that produced B16C involves too many assumptions about the geography, politics, history, and religion of the First Intermediate Period to be more than tenuous at best.

A simpler, and therefore more likely, hypothesis is that the texts on the head and foot of B16C were copied from a funerary papyrus (or leather roll) intended originally for King Wahkare Akhtoy; or better, that the scribe of B16C had access to the master from which the king's funerary texts were prepared.[26] The description of the original manuscript arrived at above belongs to a textual tradition already attested in the Ramesseum Dramatic Papyrus of the Middle Kingdom. The similarities between the two documents are numerous. The texts of both are arranged into retrograde columns; titles of the short ritual utterances are ruled off at the bottom of the column in which they occur. In the Ramesseum papyrus longer texts occupy full columns and occasionally intrude into the scenes below (lines 8, 46); the presence of a register of scenes or titles below the text may also explain some of the longer columns in the reconstruction of the original of B16C (cols. *40–*42, *64–*66, *73). Most importantly, the Ramesseum papyrus is written in a mixture of cursive hieroglyphs and hieratic, the kind of script most likely to underlie the scribal errors found in B16C.[27]

[25] See Lopez, *RdE* 25 (1973) 180–81, 188. The suggestion that *Nfrj* had usurped the king's own coffin is at variance with the evidence of the coffin itself: only in lines 3–11 does *Nfrj*'s name appear over an erased royal name. See von Beckerath, *ZÄS* 93 (1966) 16.

[26] Suggested by Georges Posener, review, *BiOr* 8 (1951) 170.

[27] The same features exist in the fragmentary funerary liturgy found together with the Ramesseum Dramatic Papyrus, published by Sir Alan Gardiner, "A Unique Funerary Liturgy," *JEA* 41 (1955) 9–17.

The Ramesseum Dramatic Papyrus preserves the accession ritual of Sesostris I; the original of B16C contained the funerary rituals of King Wahkare Akhtoy. Such a document is of the sort one would expect to find in the repertory of a funerary scriptorium. The existence of such master copies, intended originally for kings but re-used by commoners in the Twelfth Dynasty, can be deduced from the relationship between the texts in the pyramid of Unis and those in the Middle Kingdom tombs of Siese at Dahshur and Sesostris-ankh at Lisht. The Middle Kingdom texts are virtually verbatim copies of Unis; the reliance of all three on a common source is evident in the fact that mistakes corrected on the walls of the pyramid occasionally appear unemended in the later copies.[28] A close parallel for the situation represented on the head and foot of B16C also exists in the Twenty-first-Dynasty coffin of Butehamon, which reproduces the Eighteenth-Dynasty master for the Mouth-Opening Ritual of Amenophis I.[29] Its affinities with these documents places B16C, with its copy of the funerary rituals of King Wahkare Akhtoy, among the more important sources for the history and transmission of Egyptian religious texts.

This study is offered with respect and affection to Professor George R. Hughes. May it serve in a small way to honor the inspiration he has given to generations of his students.

[28] Pyr 30*a*, 33*a*, 37*c*, 39*c*, 59*c*, 115*a*, 118*a*, 257*c*, 262*a* S, 273*b* S, 367*b*, 407*b*. Uncorrected errors common to all three sources are Pyr 291*c* *sʿḥʿ.w* for *sjʿ.w*, the omission of subject in Pyr 303*a* (WS vs. Siese), Pyr 308*d* *sḏ* for *srwḏ*, Pyr 446*d* *ẖnm* for *ẖnmt.j*, and Pyr 482*c* *Jnwj* for *Jnwjt*.

[29] MOR document 4: see the MOR title and MOR 55A *t*. Otto, *Mundöffnungsritual* II 34–35, questions whether the title *wp(t)-rꜣ n Wsjr njswt (Ḏsr-kꜣ-Rʿw Jmn-ḥtp)|* signifies that Butehamon's text is a copy of the actual 18th-Dynasty manuscript or in larger terms that the New Kingdom ritual derives from that of Amenophis I. In fact, both may be true. The interpretation of *n* as the preposition "for" as against the genitive adjective is assured by other copies of the MOR title, and the king's name in MOR 55A *t* suggests that the original manuscript bore the king's name, for which that of Butehamon is elsewhere substituted. At the same time, the text of Amenophis I is the prototype of the New Kingdom ritual (*ibid*., p. 8); hence its selection by Butehamon for his own coffin.

TWO MONUMENTS OF THE FIRST INTERMEDIATE PERIOD FROM THE THEBAN NOME

Edward Brovarski

In a recent article[1] Fischer suggested that the Gebelein region belonged to Upper Egyptian nome 4 and not nome 3 as Vandier[2] thought. In support of his thesis, Fischer pointed out that two Gebelein stelae, Cairo 20001 and British Museum 1671, mention Thebes as the local capital.[3] Further support for Fischer's suggestion is provided by the coffin published here, Turin Supplement 13.268 (Figs. 9–10).[4] The coffin derives from Schiaparelli's excavations at Gebelein.[5] We translate its inscriptions as follows:

Left side.—An offering that the king gives Anubis, who is upon his mountain, lord of the sacred land, who presides over the god's booth, who is in the bandages, so that offerings may be invoked for the treasurer of the king of Lower Egypt and sole companion, the great overlord of the nome and overseer of priests, Ini.

Right side.—An offering that the king gives Osiris, lord of Busiris, so that offerings may be invoked for the one revered by the great god, the treasurer of the king of Lower Egypt and sole companion, the overseer of priests in the temple of Sobek, lord of Semenu.

[1] Henry G. Fischer, "The Nubian Mercenaries of Gebelein During the First Intermediate Period," *Kush* 9 (1961) 44, n. 2.

[2] Jacques Vandier, *Mo'alla, La Tombe d'Ankhtifi et la tombe de Sébekhotep* ("BdE" XVIII [1950]) p. 38.

[3] For the first stela, see Jacques Vandier, "La Stèle 20.001 du Musée du Caire," in *Mélanges Maspero, Orient Ancien* I ("MIFAO" LXVI [1934]) 137 ff. The second is published by Hans J. Polotsky, "The Stela of Heka-yeb," *JEA* 16 (1930) 194 ff.

[4] I would like to express my gratitude to Dr. Silvio Curto and to Dr. Anna Donadoni for permission to include Turin Supplement 13.268 here, in anticipation of its publication by Dr. Donadoni in a volume of the catalogue of the Turin Museum.

[5] For the Italian excavations at Gebelein, see E. Schiaparelli, "La Missione italiana a Ghebelein," *ASAE* 21 (1921) 126 ff., and G. Farina, "Notizie sugli scavi . . . a Gebelên 1930," *Aegyptus* 10 (1929) 291 ff.

A

B

FIG. 9.—Turin Supplement 13.268, left side (*A*) and right side (*B*)

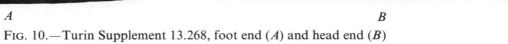

A B

FIG. 10.—Turin Supplement 13.268, foot end (*A*) and head end (*B*)

Foot end.—Ini. A beautiful burial in his tomb chamber of the necropolis, Ini.

Head end.—May he have a beautiful burial in the tomb chamber of the necropolis.

The title *ḥry-tp ꜥ3 n spꜣt* is so well attested that we read Ini's title "great overlord of the nome" with some confidence, despite the unorthodox writing of  for  . Nomes 2, 4, 6, and 7 of Upper Egypt almost without exception all write 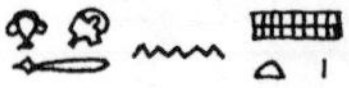 in Dynasties VI–VIII.[6]

Ini's title of *imy-rꜣ ḥm(w) nṯr m ḥwt-nṯr nt Sbk nb Smnw*, "overseer of priests in the temple of Sobek, lord of Semenu," is quite unprecedented. It is more common at such an early date to have *imy-rꜣ ḥm(w)-nṯr*, followed by the name of the deity in direct or indirect genitival construction.[7] An exception seems to be the title *imy-rꜣ ḥm(w)-nṯr m P Dp*, "overseer of priests in Pe and Dep" on a Sixth Dynasty monument in the British Museum.[8]

The writing of  on Ini's coffin indicates that this and not 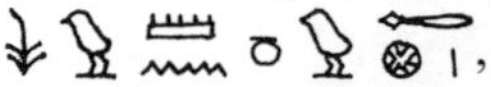, as Gardiner asserted,[9] is the earlier writing of Semenu. The town of Semenu was elaborately discussed by Kuentz,[10] who suggested that it was probably the ancient Crocodilopolis, the twin city of Pathyris (*Pr Ḥtḥr*) at Gebelein. Gardiner at first accepted[11] and then rejected this view, later equating Crocodilopolis with *ꜣIw-m-itrw*, supposedly an island near Gebelein.[12] He finally placed Semenu at Rizaqat.[13] Fischer has presented evidence, however, that identifies *ꜣIw-m-itrw* with Rizaqat.[14] The find spot of Ini's coffin at Gebelein suggests that Semenu was indeed at Gebelein, as Kuentz had asserted.

The Hathor of Pathyris was known as the "Mistress of the Two Rocks," a seemingly clear reference to the two parallel ridges, 164 feet apart, known as El-Gebelein, "the two rocks," which give the site its modern name.[15] The

[6] Henry G. Fischer, *Dendera in the Third Millenium B.C.* (Locust Valley, N.Y., 1968) p. 74, n. 307.

[7] *Ibid.*, p. 26.

[8] T. G. H. James, *Hieroglyphic Texts from Egyptian Stelae, etc.*, Pt. I (2d ed.; London, 1961) Pl. XXXV.

[9] Alan H. Gardiner, *Ancient Egyptian Onomastica* II (London, 1947) 20*. The determinative appears to be a combination of Gardiner Sign-List M 21 and W 24 and is, presumably, to be read *nw*, a complement to the last syllable of Semenu.

[10] Charles Kuentz, "Quelques monuments du culte de Sobk," *BIFAO* 28 (1929) 113 ff.

[11] Alan H. Gardiner, "Ramesside Texts Relating to the Taxation and Transport of Corn," *JEA* 27 (1941) 36.

[12] Gardiner, *Onomastica* II 20*.

[13] *Ibid.*, II 274*–75*.

[14] Fischer, *Kush* 9 (1961) 76, n. 80.

[15] Arthur E. P. Weigall, *A Guide to the Antiquities of Upper Egypt* (New York, 1910) p. 297.

temple of Hathor has been found on the summit of the lower and more easterly of the two ridges, and Gardiner has suggested that Pathyris was the name of the town surrounding the temple of Hathor.[16] Semenu may be represented by the ruins of an ancient town that lie under the northwest end of the eastern and at the foot of the western range.[17] As Griffith pointed out,[18] in the Late Period the two towns were closely connected and very friendly; their documents are mingled together in every find that has been made. But the earliest occurrence of Pathyris (*Pr Ḥtḥr*) is Pap. Reisner II, dating to early Twelfth Dynasty (reign of Sesostris I),[19] and Semenu is certainly the more ancient name for Gebelein. Though the temple on the eastern ridge dates back to the Third Dynasty,[20] the earliest mention of Hathor is in the cartouche of Nebhepetre Mentuhotep II in the Eleventh Dynasty.[21]

ʾIn is a well-known abbreviation for the name *ʾInỉ-ỉt.f*. Compare, for instance, Cairo statue 42005,[22] which is dedicated to *ʾInỉ-ỉt.f ꜥꜣ ms.n ʾIkw*, with a stela in New York[23] mentioning the same individual, but as *ʾIn ꜥꜣ ms ʾIkwỉ*. *ʾInỉ*, on the Turin coffin, may represent another variant of *ʾInỉ-ỉt.f*, just as *ʾIkwỉ* replaces *ʾIkw* on one of the monuments just noted.[24] If *ʾInỉ* is indeed hypocoristic for *ʾInỉ-ỉt.f*, it appears that we have in the owner of this coffin from Gebelein an ancestor of the Eleventh Dynasty Intefs of Thebes.

We have already noted that nomes 2, 4, 6, and 7 of Upper Egypt almost without exception all write *ḥry-tp ꜥꜣ n spꜣt*, "great overlord of the nome," in Dynasties VI–VIII. As late as the early Ninth Dynasty *St-kꜣ* at Elephantine uses the same form of the nomarch's title.[25] During the Heracleopolitan Period, however, the title becomes standardized into  + nome emblem. The

[16] Gardiner, *Onomastica* II 17* ff.

[17] Weigall, *Guide*, p. 297.

[18] F. Ll. Griffith *et al.*, *The Adler Papyri* (London, 1939) p. 64.

[19] William Kelly Simpson, *Papyrus Reisner II* (Boston, 1965) p. 44 (3).

[20] William Stevenson Smith, *A History of Egyptian Sculpture and Painting in the Old Kingdom* (London, 1949) pp. 137–38.

[21] Labib Habachi, "King Nebhepetre Menthuhotp: His Monuments, Place in History, Deification and Unusual Representations in the Form of Gods," *MDAIK* 19 (1963) Pl. XI*b*, Fig. 17.

[22] Georges Legrain, *Statues et statuettes de rois et de particuliers* I ("CCG" [1906]) 4–5.

[23] J. J. Clère and J. Vandier, *Textes de la première période intermédiare et de la XIe dynastie* ("Bibliotheca Aegyptiaca" X [Brussels, 1948]) p. 9, §14.

[24] It is possible, of course, that the terminal reed leaf in *ʾIkwỉ* replaces the seated man determinative; see Fischer, *Dendera*, p. 129, n. 571, p. 163 (*c*), n. 708. For comparable writings at El Kab, see Lepsius, *Denkmaeler* II, Pl. 117*q* as compared with Pl. 117*t*, references that I owe to the kindness of Dr. Henry G. Fischer. I know of no examples, however, where the replacement occurs with the feminine determinative.

[25] Fischer, *Dendera*, p. 74, n. 307, p. 130.

earliest of the Intef nomarchs known from Thebes is the Intef of Cairo stela 20009, who, Fischer thinks,[26] need not be later than the time of Ankhtify at Moʿalla. The form of the title on his stela is . Thus, on the basis of his title alone, Ini of Turin Supplement 13.268 might be considered to be earlier than this individual.[27]

The Intef of Cairo 20009 presents himself as loyal to his Heracleopolitan sovereign. On his stela, he is *mḥ-ỉb n nswt m rꜣ-ꜥꜣ gꜣw rsy, ỉwn ꜥꜣ sꜥnḫ tꜣwy.f*, "confidant of the king in a narrow southern doorway, a great pillar who causes his (that is, the king's) Two Lands to live." It would appear that it was not he who initiated the first Theban outbreak and fought with Ankhtify. Rather, the instigator was probably the *ʾInỉ-ỉt.f ꜥꜣ* who adopted the title "great overlord of Upper Egypt" and imposed his authority on Dendera.[28] That he was identical with the *ʾIn ꜥꜣ* of MMA stela 12.2.7 and the *ʾInỉ-ỉt.f ꜥꜣ* of Cairo statue 42005 has already been suggested by Fischer.[29] Since he was paid special reverence in later times, he was almost certainly the immediate predecessor of *Mnṯw-ḥtp ꜥꜣ*, who founded the Eleventh Dynasty and whose name was posthumously enclosed in a royal cartouche.[30]

One may wonder why Ini should have elected to reside at the southern extremity of the province he governed. Gebelein was a garrison town for Thebes and a colony for the Nubians employed as mercenaries in the struggles preceding Egypt's reunification.[31] That the border between the nomes of Thebes and Hieraconpolis was later a source of contention is clear from Ankhtify's choice of Moʿalla as a residence. Because he associates himself with the Heracleopolitan "King Kaneferre" at Moʿalla, Ankhtify has been thought a loyalist. But though he claimed royal or divine sanction for his action, Ankhtify had seized control of the nome of Edfu. Abydos, the old center of the Upper Egyptian administration, was hostile to Ankhtify on at least one occasion, and it was certainly through coercion that Ankhtify forced the council of the overseer of Upper Egypt, which sat at Abydos, to settle to Ankhtify's satisfaction an obscure matter involving his predecessor Hetepi (Vandier,

[26] *Ibid.*, p. 130, n. 575.

[27] The form  for the *ḳrs*-sign on the head end of the coffin, for instance, has parallels at Dendera (*ibid.*, p. 80 4) and Naqada (Henry G. Fischer, *Inscriptions from the Coptite Nome* ["Analecta Orientalia," Vol. 40 (Rome, 1964)] p. 9) that date to the transitional period between Dynasties VI and VIII.

[28] Fischer, *Dendera*, p. 129, n. 571.

[29] *Ibid.*, p. 203.

[30] *Ibid.*, and Labib Habachi, "God's Fathers and the Role They Played in the History of the First Intermediate Period," *ASAE* 55 (1958) 178–79.

[31] Fischer, *Kush* 9 (1961) 44 ff.

Mo'alla, inscr. II, β, 3–II, δ, 2). Ankhtify also claimed the office of commander of the army of Upper Egypt from Elephantine to Armant (inscr. VI, α, 4–5). Since Armant lay in the Theban nome, between Gebelein and Thebes, the attempt of the Thebans to regain control of the old religious center of the Theban nome[32] can be considered seditious only insofar as Ankhtify attempted to cloak his personal ambitions under the guise of loyalty to his Heracleopolitan master. Ankhtify's ambitious schemes may have been directly responsible for the first expansion of the Thebans and the eventual overthrow of the Heracleopolitan dynasty. His denial of grain to the Thebans and Coptites during the period of famine that plagued Upper Egypt can hardly have improved relations between the two camps.[33] The presence of the Theban nomarch Ini at Gebelein implies a traditional enmity between Upper Egyptian nomes 3 and 4, perhaps based originally on so seemingly trivial a matter as a border dispute, and provides the historical background for the events narrated in Ankhtify's tomb at Mo'alla.[34]

The earlier Heracleopolitan Neferkare, the third ruler of the Ninth Dynasty (Turin Canon IV, 20), is probably the "King Kaneferre" referred to at Mo'alla in the tomb of Ankhtify.[35] Two reigns precede his in the Turin Canon after the summary for the Old Kingdom (Turin Canon IV, 18, 19). If the great overlord of Upper Egypt *'Inỉ-ỉt.f* '3 was the opponent of Ankhtify of Mo'alla, then the floruit of the two Theban nomarchs who preceded him, Ini of Turin Supplement 13.268 and Intef of Cairo 20009, might well embrace those two preceding reigns, extending our knowledge of the origins of the Theban Intef dynasty to that age when Khety of Heracleopolis founded the Ninth Dynasty.

The stela illustrated in Figure 11, Boston MFA 04.1851, was purchased by Albert Lythgoe in Egypt in 1904 and is said to have come from Dra Abu l'Nagga.[36] The iconography and general style of the piece are unmistakable

[32] The Theban nomarch Ihy at the end of the Sixth Dynasty is "honored by Montu, Lord of Armant" (Percy E. Newberry, "A Sixth Dynasty Tomb at Thebes," *ASAE* 4 [1903] 97).

[33] Neither the Theban nor Coptite nomes are mentioned among the places that Ankhtify supplied with grain during a severe drought that plagued the Head of the South. Ankhtify supplied Edfu and *'Ỉ3t-ng3w* in the second Upper Egyptian nome and Elephantine and Ombos in the first, as well as his own cities of Hefat and Hormer. But he also sent Upper Egyptian barley to Dendera and Shabet in the Denderite nome, bypassing Thebes and Coptos (Vandier, *Mo'alla*, inscr. IV).

[34] This situation must be reconciled with the fact that the two stelae from Gebelein mentioned in note 3 speak of giving aid to Ankhtify's nome and city.

[35] William C. Hayes, "The Middle Kingdom in Egypt," in *Cambridge Ancient History* I (rev. ed.; Cambridge, 1964) chap. 20, p. 4.

[36] The Boston stela shows few of the most characteristic paleographic features of the Gebelein group (see Fischer, *Kush* 9 [1961] 79–80), a fact that may well support a Theban derivation. Two

and show the monument to belong to the group of stelae from Gebelein and Rizaqat discussed by Fischer in *Kush* 9 (1961) 44 ff. The stelae listed by Fischer are more or less contemporaneous with the Moʿalla inscriptions, but stylistically MFA 04.1851 bears the closest resemblance to two of the stelae that antedate Ankhtify of Moʿalla by a generation or so.[37] The two stelae are the stela of Hekaib, British Museum 1671,[38] and the stela of Merer in Cracow, MNK–XI–991.[39]

General Itety,[40] the owner of the Boston stela, is wearing a form of the *šndyt*-kilt, with a tab that widens toward the end. Such a kilt is frequently seen on Egyptians in the Gebelein stelae and very frequently in the tomb of Ankhtify, where Egyptian soldiers and laborers wear it, as do Ankhtify himself and his son.[41] At Gebelein the *šndyt*-kilt and a sash with a pendant piece appear to differentiate Egyptians from Nubians. The military associations of the kilt are legion, and it serves as an appropriate garb for General Itety. In most cases in the Gebelein stelae, however, the kilt is either plain or has a pleated panel. Itety's kilt is wholly pleated and is paralleled only on a Gebelein stela in Florence.[42] Ankhtify wears a similar but brightly striped *šndyt*-garment.[43]

The fillet worn by Itety also has military associations. On the British Museum stela it is worn by Hekaib and is part of the costume of two soldiers from Naqada.[44] A Nubian bowman in the tomb of Setka at Aswan also wears the fillet, which appears on a number of the Gebelein stelae listed by Fischer.[45]

---

paleographic criteria may point in the same direction. The vessel that replaces the *des*-jug (Gardiner Sign-List W 22) in the invocation formula on the stela recurs on two stelae from Thebes (Clère and Vandier, *Textes*, p. 1, No. 1; p. 5, No. 7). The city sign is also reduplicated exactly on the first of these. The *ẖkr*-sign takes a peculiar form on the Boston stela. Similar, if simpler versions of the same sign appear in stelae from Dendera (Fischer, *Dendera*, p. 136, Fig. 26). I would like to take this opportunity to thank Dr. William Kelly Simpson for permission to include here both MFA 04.1851 and Cairo 38673 and also for suggestions incorporated in the text.

[37] See Fischer, "Further Remarks on the Gebelein Stelae," *Kush* 10 (1962) 333–34.

[38] See note 3.

[39] Jaroslav Černý, "The Stela of Merer in Cracow," *JEA* 47 (1961) 5–9.

[40] Hermann Ranke does not seem to list the name Itety in his *Die ägyptischen Personennamen* I (Glückstadt, 1935).

[41] Fischer, *Kush* 9 (1961) 67, n. 52.

[42] Florence 7588, see Jacques Vandier, *Manuel d'archéologie égyptienne* II/3 (Paris, 1954) Fig. 290, and Fischer, *Kush* 10 (1961) 334. A Petrie photograph in the Oriental Institute files bears the number 10460.

[43] Vandier, *Moʿalla*, Pl. XL.

[44] Fischer, *Coptite Nome*, Nos. 16 and 27.

[45] Fischer, *Kush* 9 (1961) 45, Nos. 2, 3, 5, and p. 64, Fig. 5. The fillet is also worn by the owner of Leningrad stela 5633 (see Fischer, *Kush* 10 [1961] 334). The owner of the stela is named Hekaib

Courtesy Museum of Fine Arts, Boston

FIG. 11.—Boston MFA 04.1851

FIG. 12.—Cairo 38673

The figure of Itety's wife, Tekat,[46] resembles that of the other women depicted on the Gebelein stelae. The front lappet of her wig is indicated, however, a detail seen on no other of these women, and she alone among the ladies holds a flower. Three women on contemporary stelae from Naqada also hold a long-stemmed lotus before them,[47] and the mirror in its case likewise appears on two stelae from the latter site.[48]

While a number of late Old Kingdom stelae from Abydos take the form of atrophied false doors,[49] I know of only one other stela before the Middle Kingdom that reproduces the central niche of the false door together with the drum roll at its top. The example (Fig. 12) derives from Reisner's excavations at Giza and was found in the debris of Giza mastaba 2011. It was inscribed for "the inspector of the craftsmen of the royal *wꜥbt*, Ankhhaf," and has depictions of four of Ankhhaf's sons in recessed panels to either side of the central niche. The monument is now in Cairo and bears the number 38673.

Fischer has noted, in discussing the origin of Upper Egyptian stelae,[50] that both the central slab of the false door and the false door architrave may have influenced the development of stelae types in the late Old Kingdom and the Middle Kingdom. The Boston and Cairo stelae illustrated here may also have served as prototypes for the common Twelfth Dynasty stela with a niche in the center of its face.[51]

This study is offered as a token of gratitude to Professor Hughes and in admiration of his abilities as a scholar and teacher. I would like to join with the scribe of Papyrus Amherst III, who wished for his teacher that he might endure and have joy and delight. May you feel younger every day.

---

and has the interesting title "overseer of Nubians"(?). The *Wb* (III 301, 11) lists only the Late Period writing of for *ḫntyw*, "Nubians." Hekaib may have been in charge of a group of the Nubian mercenaries quartered at Gebelein. For the Leningrad stela, see the photograph in Boris Turaev, *List of a Collection Brought from Egypt in the Spring of 1909* (St. Petersburg, 1910) Pl. III, No. 1.

[46] For the name, which apparently means something like "the Torch," see Ranke, *Personennamen* I 431, 11. Ranke's source was Reisner's Giza mastaba G 2175. Photographs of the monument inscribed with the name are now in Boston and bear the Expedition numbers B 2038, 2039. The element *iḳr/iḳrt* is occasionally added to names from about the time of Ankhtify. The usage becomes more common in the Eleventh Dynasty (Fischer, *Dendera*, p. 131).

[47] Fischer, *Coptite Nome*, Nos. 28, 32, 35.

[48] *Ibid.*, Nos. 28 and 32.

[49] Henry G. Fischer, "The Cult and Nome of the Goddess Bat," *JARCE* 1 (1962) 8, n. 15.

[50] Fischer, *Dendera*, p. 61.

[51] See, for instance, Cairo 20526, William Kelly Simpson, *The Terrace of the Great God at Abydos* (New Haven and Philadelphia, 1974) Pl. 47 (ANOC 302).

SHESMU THE LETOPOLITE

Mark Ciccarello

In this essay the changing personality, role, and iconography of the god Shesmu are examined. Evidence is presented that suggests that Letopolis was the original home of this god.

Throughout all the documents that relate to Shesmu, from appearances in the Pyramid Texts to representations on the walls of the temples of the Greco-Roman period, he exhibits a dual personality. He can be a benevolent god, particularly to the dead, or he can be a very cruel god. Shesmu manifests these two sides of his personality by assuming a different role for each side. Through the Middle Kingdom the benevolent Shesmu is cast in the role of patron of the wine press, but at the beginning of the New Kingdom he exchanges this role for that of the ointment-maker par excellence. At every period, however, the cruel Shesmu is identified as a butcher. This division in the personality and role of the god is reflected in the iconography. Curiously, the good ointment-maker is the one that is often represented with the head of a lion, while the evil butcher is usually shown as completely anthropomorphic. We might have expected the opposite.

THE OLD KINGDOM AND THE PYRAMID TEXTS

Shesmu appears three times in the Pyramid Texts.[1] Some significant features of his personality and role are already well established at this date. Both sides of the god's personality and the corresponding roles are displayed in these passages. On the one hand, the friendly Shesmu brings wine for the dead king.[2] But in the "Cannibal Hymn," on the other hand, he acts as a butcher, cutting up the gods to be put into the cauldron.[3] This god's connection with wine is also illustrated by the fact that his name can be written ideographically by means of the hieroglyph for the wine press alone.[4]

[1] Kurt Sethe, *Die altägyptischen Pyramidentexte* (2 vols.; Leipzig, 1908–10) pars. 403*a*, 545*b*, and 1552*a*.

[2] *Ibid.*, par. 1552*a*. [3] *Ibid.*, par. 403*a*. [4] *Ibid.*, par. 403*a* (Unas version), 1552*a* (Pepi I version).

A scene of the grape harvest from the Saqqara mastaba of Ptahhotep further links Shesmu with viticulture. There a group of youths are throwing darts into the ground during a harvest game or ritual. The scene bears the label "shooting for(?) Shesmu" (*stỉ n Šsmw*).[5]

Other documents from the Old Kingdom add little to our knowledge of the personality, role, or iconography of Shesmu, but nevertheless do offer some interesting details. A priesthood of Shesmu appears to have existed at an early date, for fragments of a diorite bowl belonging to a "prophet" (*ḥm-nṯr*) of this god were found near the Step Pyramid.[6] Another early document worth mentioning is the curious scribal tablet found by Reisner at Giza, on which Shesmu is one of the gods listed.[7] Finally, two of the funerary foundations of Pepi II listed in his mortuary temple at Saqqara have theophorous names involving Shesmu.[8]

THE MIDDLE KINGDOM, THE COFFIN TEXTS, AND THE BOOK OF THE DEAD

During the Middle Kingdom a cult of Shesmu existed in the Faiyum region. Excavations at Harageh have unearthed a Twelfth Dynasty stele belonging to a man named Renefsonb. Shesmu happens to be one of the gods invoked in the *ḥtp-dỉ-nsw* formula that appears on this stele. Moreover, a black granite statuette of a man named Shesmu-hotep was also found at this site.[9]

[5] Norman de Garis Davies, *The Mastaba of Ptahhetep and Akhethetep at Saqqareh, Pt. I* ("Archaeological Survey of Egypt," Eighth Memoir [London, 1900]) p. 9 and Pl. XXIII.

[6] Cecil M. Firth and J. E. Quibell, *The Step Pyramid* (2 vols.; Cairo, 1935) p. 122,7 and Pl. 90,7. Three pieces of the bowl remain. Two of these pieces were published by Gunn ("Inscriptions from the Step Pyramid Site, III: Fragments of Inscribed Vessels," *ASAE* 28 [1928] 163 B. 8 and Pl. III, 5*a*,5). He believed erroneously that these two pieces joined one another, but in fact they were separated from each other by another piece. Cf. Raymond Weill, "Le Dieu *Ḫrty*," in *Miscellanea Gregoriana: Raccolta di Scritti pubblicati nel i Centenario dalla Fondazione del Museo egizio, 1839–1939* (Vatican City, 1941) p. 387.

[7] George A. Reisner, "A Scribe's Tablet Found by the Hearst Expedition at Giza," *ZÄS* 48 (1910) 113–14. See also Helen K. Jacquet-Gordon, *Les Noms des domaines funéraires sous l'ancien empire égyptien* ("BdE" XXXIV [1962]) pp. 259–63.

[8] Jacquet-Gordon, *Les Noms des domaines funéraires*, pp. 191–92, Nos. 49–50. Foundation No. 49 is named *Mr Šsmw ʿnḫ* [*Pp*]*ỉ*. Foundation No. 50 is named *Sʿnḫ Šsmw Nfr-kꜣ-Rʿ*.

[9] R. Engelbach and B. Gunn, *Harageh* (British School of Archaeology in Egypt, "Publications," XXVIII [London, 1923]) p. 29. Cf. Dimitri Meeks, "Génies, anges, et démons en Egypte," in *Génies, anges, et démons* ("Sources orientales" VIII [Paris, 1971]) p. 30 and n. 62; Jean Yoyotte, "Etudes géographiques, II: Les Localités méridionales de la région memphite et 'Le Pehou d'Héracléopolis,' " *RdE* 15 (1963) 105, n. 5.

The same characteristics that Shesmu had in the Old Kingdom remain with him throughout the Coffin Texts and the Book of the Dead. His good side is attested by a passage in the Coffin Texts in which he accompanies Sokar *ḫnty pḏw-š* in bringing provisions for the dead person;[10] later in the same spell these two gods are mentioned again as being part of the household help of the dead person in the beyond.[11] The cruel side of Shesmu is well illustrated by the part he plays in spells 473–81 of the Coffin Texts. These are the spells devoted to the theme of the net from which the dead person tries to escape. Various parts of that net are identified with parts of the bodies of different gods or with certain items of their accoutrement. The most common identification involving Shesmu equates the "peg" (*mḫsf*) of the net with his "calf" (*sbḳ*).[12] In these spells we also encounter the "cauldron" (*ktwt*), "knife" (*mds*), and "thighs" (*ỉwʿ.wy*) of Shesmu.[13] Various other passages in the Coffin Texts attest to the bloodthirstiness of this god.[14] Sometimes he is even assisted in his cruel endeavors by minor demons named the "Shesmus."[15]

Shesmu appears four times in the spells of the Book of the Dead.[16] In one of these spells he is said to offer the dead person the very best fowl for his meal.[17] Elsewhere he displays a less pleasant demeanor. Naturally enough we find him in spells 153*A* and 153*B*, which are descendants of the Coffin Text spells about the net. Here also the "peg" (*mḫsf*) is equated with the "calf" (*sbḳ*) of Shesmu,[18]

[10] *ECT* I 171*a*.

[11] *Ibid.*, p. 172*b*,*c*.

[12] *Mḫsf* = *sbḳ* in the following passages in *ECT* VI: 6*f*–*g*, 18*a*–*b*, 22*g*–*h*, 251, 27*g*, 30*h*–*j* (note that "Shesmu" is written with the sign 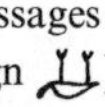); 35*i*, 44*c*, *h*. *Ḥsw* (meaning unknown) = *sbḳ* in 38*f*–*g* and 39*c*–*d*.

[13] "Cauldron" (*ktwt*) = "cauldron" (*wḥꜣ.t*) in *ECT* VI 32*g*–*h*. Here again "Shesmu" is written with the sign . In 8*d*–*e* the "cauldron" (*ktwt*) of Shesmu is equated with "woman" (*s.t*). Presumably this latter word was used by the scribe to indicate that a feminine noun belonged here, although the exact word had been lost. Compare the use of "man" (*s*), below. The "knife" (*mds*) of Shesmu = the "knife" (*ds*) in 32*e*–*f*. Again "Shesmu" is written by means of the sign . In 8*b*–*c* the "knife" (*mds*) of Shesmu = "man" (*s*). As noted above, "man" (*s*) is used to indicate the place of a masculine noun whose exact identity was unknown to the scribe. In 11*f*–*g* the "thighs" (*ỉwʿ.wy*) of Shesmu are equated with "oars" (*wsr.w*).

[14] See, for example, *ECT* I 123*b*, VI 179*h*. Cf. Jan Zandee, *Death as an Enemy* (Leiden, 1960) pp. 216–16.

[15] *ECT* V 396*b*,*d*.

[16] Spells 17, 153*A*, 153*B*, and 170, according to the numbering of Edouard Naville, *Das ägyptische Todtenbuch der XVIII. bis XX. Dynastie* (3 vols.; Berlin, 1886).

[17] Spell 170,6 (Pb). See Naville, *Das ägyptische Todtenbuch*, Pl. CXCI.

[18] Spell 153*A*, 7–8, 17–18, 25 (Pb). See Naville, *Das ägyptische Todtenbuch*, Pl. CLXXVII. In Papyrus Ryerson col. 151, 30 the "peg" (*mḫsf*) is equated with the "ring" (*dbn*) of Shesmu. See Thomas George Allen, ed., *The Egyptian Book of the Dead Documents in the Oriental Institute Museum* ("OIP" LXXXII [1960]) p. 277 and Pl. XLVIII.

while the "blade" (*š*‘.*t*) of the net is equated with his "knife" (*ḥsb*.t).[19] Finally, there is a new equation not found in the Coffin Text versions, in which the "finger" (*ḏb*‘) of Shesmu is equated with the "spool" (‘*ḏ*).[20]

In the famous spell 17 Re is called upon to rescue the dead person from a certain brutal god "who lassoes evildoers for his slaughter block, who cuts up souls." The ancient commentator on this passage identifies this god as Shesmu, the "mutilator" (*sỉꜣty*) of Osiris.[21]

THE NEW KINGDOM

Beginning with the New Kingdom the benevolent Shesmu assumes a new role, that of the ointment-maker. The mechanism behind this transference of roles is not hard to perceive. In ancient Egypt perfumes were extracted from fragrant substances by first soaking these substances in oil and then squeezing them in a sack, just as grape juice for wine was extracted from grapes.[22] It is easy enough to understand how Shesmu might have moved from the production of wine to the production of fragrant ointments, but the reason for this transference remains a mystery. We can say with certainty only that henceforth the good Shesmu devotes his energy almost entirely to the manufacture of ointments and essences, while his connection with wine is virtually forgotten. The first instance of Shesmu in this new role may be in a papyrus dating from the end of the Eighteenth Dynasty. In a broken context the following phrase appears: "Shesmu, the ointment-maker; *mrḥ.t*-oil is in his charge."[23] Similarly we find Shesmu in a hymn to the divinized *Mrḥ.t*-oil inscribed in the tomb of Sobk-Mose.[24] And the Harper's Song from the tomb of Neferhotep at Thebes

[19] Spell 153*A*, 26–27. See Naville, *Das ägyptische Todtenbuch*, Pl. CLXXVII. The word transliterated as *ḥsb.t* is written . *Wb* III 168, 5 cites only one example of such a word meaning "knife." This example comes from Book of the Dead spell 153*B*, 7 (according to Naville). There the *ḥsb.t* of Isis is equated with a "knife" (*š*‘.*t*). In Book of the Dead spell 153*A*, 9, however, this same *š*‘.*t* is equated with the 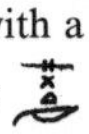 of Isis. Presumably 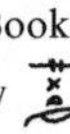 in spell 153*A*, 9 and in 153*A*, 26 should also be read *ḥsb.t*.

[20] Spell 153*B*, 5–6. See Naville, *Das ägyptische Todtenbuch*, Pl. CLXXVIII.

[21] Spell 17, 62–63. See Naville, *Das ägyptische Todtenbuch*, Pl. XXV.

[22] A. Lucas, *Ancient Egyptian Materials and Industries* (4th ed., rev. and enl. by J. R. Harris; London, 1962) p. 86.

[23] Ricardo A. Caminos, *Literary Fragments in the Hieratic Script* (Oxford, 1956) p. 36 and Pl. 13, sec. D, p. 2, l. 5.

[24] William C. Hayes, *The Burial Chamber of the Treasurer Sobk-Mosĕ from Er Rizeiḳāt* ("Metropolitan Museum of Art Papers," No. 9 [New York, 1939]) p. 20 and Pl. V.

(No. 50) says that the dead person is provided with ointment from the hands of Shesmu and clothing made by the craft of Tayt.[25]

An ingenious proposal to combine the cruel side of Shesmu's personality with his old role of patron of the wine press was advanced by Siegfried Schott in his publication of two illustrated papyri of the Ramesside period. Vignettes in these two papyri (Papyrus Berlin 3148 and Papyrus Turin 1781) show demons in the underworld holding nets that Schott has identified as wine presses. But instead of grapes in these wine presses there are heads. Schott believed that the cruel Shesmu put his wine press to work in the same way as these demons, squeezing blood from the heads of the condemned in the underworld just as he had squeezed juice from grapes.[26]

Schott's theory, however, cannot be reconciled with what we know about the personality and role of Shesmu. In the first place, wine is associated with the benevolent side of Shesmu's personality rather than the cruel side, as Schott would have it. In his cruel role the god is usually represented as a butcher. Furthermore, the notion that Shesmu would be involved with wine in a composition as late as the Ramesside period is not consistent with the fact that the shift in his roles appears to have taken place at the beginning of the New Kingdom.

Shesmu occurs in some neutral contexts in the mortuary temple of Seti I at Abydos. In a list of Memphite gods in the Ptah-Sokar room of the temple he is listed with the god *Ḥr-ḥry-rmn.wy.fy*.[27] Then in a scene in the Nefertem-Ptah-Sokar hall Seti I is shown offering bread to six gods, one of whom is Shesmu; this relief is probably the first pictorial representation of the god.[28] Finally, in another offering scene, located in the Gallery of the Lists, Shesmu is mentioned as a member of the Ennead of Ptah-Sokar-Osiris.[29]

The next pictorial representation of Shesmu occurs in the mortuary temple of Ramesses III at Medinet Habu. In one of the scenes depicting the Festival of

[25] Miriam Lichtheim, "The Songs of the Harpers," *JNES* 4 (1945) 198–9 and Pl. II, l. 10.

[26] Siegfried Schott, "Das blutrünstige Keltergerät," *ZÄS* 74 (1938) 88–93 and Pl. VI.

[27] Hermann Kees, "Eine Liste memphitischer Götter im Tempel von Abydos," *RT* 37 (1915) 67–68, 71, 75 col. 27, and 76 cols. 43–44.

[28] Auguste Mariette, *Fouilles exécutées en Egypte, en Nubie, et au Sudan* II (Paris, 1867), 85, middle. Mariette's is the only published drawing of this scene, but this book is hard to come by, and I have not been able to consult it. Cf. Bertha Porter and Rosalind L. B. Moss, *Topographical Bibliography of Ancient Egyptian Hieroglyphic Texts, Reliefs and Paintings* VI: *Upper Egypt: Chief Temples* (Oxford, 1939) 23, Nos. 207–8. According to A. Rosalie David (*Religious Ritual at Abydos* [Warminster, 1973] p. 178 [scene C]), in this scene the king offers bread to six gods, one of whom is "*Smsw* (sic) in the tomb."

[29] Auguste Mariette, *Abydos: Description des fouilles exécutées sur l'emplacement de cette ville* I (Paris, 1869) Pl. XLIV, col. 10.

Sokar, the king is shown burning incense before Khnum *ḫnty-ỉnb.w.f*, *Ḥry-rmn.wy.fy*, and Shesmu *ḫnty-pr-wr*.[30] In this scene Shesmu is shown as completely anthropomorphic. Gaballa and Kitchen, in their commentary on the festival, suppose that Shesmu's epithet *ḫnty-pr-wr* means that he was conceived of as being the guardian of Sokar's sanctuary.[31]

The first instance in which Shesmu can be connected with a lion may be in the text of a magical spell found on a statue of Ramesses III in Cairo (JdE 69771).[32] On line 13 of the posterior face of the statue (in Drioton's spell 7) the king is identified with Shesmu *mꜣty*, an epithet that Drioton translated as "lionceau."[33] If this interpretation is correct, it would be the earliest instance in which the helpful side of the god's personality is represented by the image of a lion.

THE LATE PERIOD

Most of the material found outside the temples deals with the benevolent side of Shesmu's personality. In these documents he is often depicted as an ointment-maker. For example, in a passage from the sarcophagus of Ankhnesneferibre, the manufacture of "the *tp.t*-oil of Re" is attributed to Shesmu. The last editor of the texts on this sarcophagus[34] overlooked this occurrence of Shesmu and transliterated the god's name as *Mḏd*, a transliteration that was adopted because the name is written  in this passage. As we see, here the hieroglyph of the warp stretched between two uprights (Gardiner AA 23–24) has been used instead of the usual wine press, an orthography that stems from the similarity of these two signs in hieratic.[35] This erroneous transliteration is by no means uncommon, and some earlier Egyptologists even referred to Shesmu as "Madj" or the like.[36]

[30] The Epigraphic Survey, *Medinet Habu, IV: Festival Scenes of Ramses III* ("OIP" LI [1940]) Pls. 196*C*, 220. See also G. A. Gaballa and K. A. Kitchen, "The Festival of Sokar," *Or* 38 (1969) 3–4, 49–51. The scene in question is called scene II in this study.

[31] Gaballa and Kitchen, *Or* 38 (1969) 50.

[32] Etienne Drioton, "Une Statue prophylàctique de Ramsès III," *ASAE* 39 (1939) 57–89. A parallel text to the spell in question is found in Papyrus Brooklyn 47.218.138. See Jean-Claude Goyon, "Un Parallèle tardif d'une formule des inscriptions de la statue prophylactique de Ramsès III au Musée du Caire," *JEA* 57 (1971) 154–59.

[33] Drioton, *ASAE* 39 (1939) 77, 78, n. *c*.

[34] C. E. Sander-Hansen, *Die religiösen Texte auf dem Sarg der Anchnesneferibre* (Copenhagen, 1937) p. 89, l. 225.

[35] Georg Möller, *Hieratische Paläographie* III (Leipzig, 1912) 34, No. 355, 46, No. 476.

[36] E.g., see Emile Chassinat, *Le Temple de Dendara* IV ("Publications de l'Institut français d'archéologie orientale du Caire" [Cairo, 1935]) 102. Similarly Shesmu goes by the name of "Mazed"

One of the benefits that the blessed dead are promised in the "Book of Traversing Eternity" is that they shall receive *mḏḥ.t*-oil from the hands of Shesmu.[37] Similar promises are expressed in Papyrus Rhind I, 5, 12 and Papyrus Vienna 19, 15.[38]

On those occasions when Shesmu is not associated with the actual production of ointments, he maintains a certain involvement with ointments by making use of them in embalming the dead. In Papyrus Rhind I, 3, 8 and II, 4, 4–5 Shesmu is represented as the god who prepared and wrapped the bodies of the deceased.

In other references Shesmu is completely divorced from ointments and functions as a helpmate to the dead only in a very general way. In the "Ritual for the Protection of the Bed," for example, Shesmu is invoked as the guardian deity during the twelfth hour of the night, a role that he also plays in the scenes of the "Hour-watchers" in the temples of Edfu, Dendera, and Philae.[39] Similarly, on the sarcophagus of Panehemisis in Vienna, a lion-headed Shesmu is described as pointing out to the dead the correct roads to take in the netherworld.[40] Perhaps the curious passage in the litany celebrating the purity of

---

in Ridolfo V. Lanzone, *Dizionario di Mitologia Egizia* (Turin, 1881–86) pp. 343–45. This matter is discussed by Bengt Julius Peterson, "Der Gott Schesemu und das Wort *mḏd*," *Orientalia Suecana* 12 (1963) 83–88. I cannot agree with his claim to have discovered, in Book of the Dead spell 17, another instance of Shesmu "hiding" under the *mḏd*-sign as in the passage from the sarcophagus of Ankhnesneferibre.

[37] Papyrus Vienna 29, l. 56. Parallel versions also give *mrḥ.t*-oil. See E. von Bergmann, "Das Buch vom Durchwandeln der Ewigkeit," *Sitzungsberichte der Kaiserlichen Akademie der Wissenschaften, Philosophisch-historische Classe* 86 (1877) 369–412. For other versions of this "book" see Jean-Claude Goyon, "La Littérature funéraire tardive," *Textes et langages de l'Egypte pharaonique: Cent cinquante années de recherches, 1822–1972* ("BdE" LXIV/3 [1974]) p. 76. Two further copies are to be found in Papyrus Oriental Institute Museum 25387, which is being edited by the author. Phillipe Derchain (*Le Papyrus Salt 825* [*B.M. 10051*]*: Rituel pour la conservation de la vie en Egypte* [Académie royale de Belgique, Classe des lettres et des sciences morales et politiques, "Mémoires" LVIII (Brussels, 1965)] p. 150) proposes that in this passage *mrḥ.t* should be translated "bitumen," rather than as some sort of oil.

[38] For Papyrus Rhind I, 5, 12 see Georg Möller, *Die beiden Totenpapyrus Rhind des Museums zu Edinburg* ("Demotische Studien," No. 6 (Leipzig, 1913). For Papyrus Vienna 19 see Ernst Ritter von Bergmann, *Hieratische und hieratisch-demotische Texte der Sammlung ägyptischer Alterthümer des Allerhöchsten Kaiserhauses* (Vienna, 1886) p. XI and Pl. VIII.

[39] Papyrus Cairo 58027, 3, 11. See M. Woldemar Golénischeff, *Papyrus hiératiques* ("CCG" [1927]) pp. 125, 127. Golénischeff has transcribed the god's name with diffidence as follows: . There are no photographs of this papyrus included in the volume, but the questionable sign could well be Shesmu's wine press. Golénischeff himself raised this possibility, but he rejected it in favor of the transcription given above.

[40] E. von Bergmann, "Der Sarcophag des Panehemisis," *Jahrbuch der Kunsthistorischen Sammlungen des Allerhöchsten Kaiserhauses* 1 (1883) 11.

Pharoah in Papyrus Berlin 13242, IVa, 10 should be included in this category. In this passage the purity of Pharaoh is equated with the purity of Shesmu in Edfu. The rest of the passage is not clear, but it seems to deal with the "back end" (*ḫpd*) of a *dšr*-fish.[41]

In the temple reliefs the number of pictorial representations of Shesmu increases substantially. The familiar split personality and double role of the god continues unchanged in these reliefs, and the lion motif becomes increasingly important as part of Shesmu's iconography. The occasional earlier portrayal of Shesmu as the benevolent lion-headed ointment-maker continues in the Greco-Roman period.[42] The lion motif also begins to appear in the orthography of the god's name. Sometimes Shesmu's name is written simply as a picture of a lion.[43] More often the name is determined by the picture of a seated god with the head of a lion.[44]

Not unexpectedly Shesmu the ointment-maker appears quite often in the inscriptions and reliefs in the so-called "laboratories" of the temples of Edfu and Dendera.[45] According to the "official" mythology, sacred ointments used in the temple service were prepared and stored in these rooms.[46] As the chief of

[41] Siegfried Schott, "Die Reinigung Pharaos in einem memphitischen Tempel," *Nachrichten der Akademie der Wissenschaften in Göttingen, Philologisch-historische Klasse*, 1957, No. 3, p. 61.

[42] E.g., see Emile Chassinat, *Le Temple d'Edfou* II ("MMAF" XI [1918]) 164, No. 5 and Pl. XLII*b*. For the spelling of the god's name in this passage see François Daumas, *Les Mammisis des temples égyptiens* ("Annales de l'Université de Lyon," troisième série: Lettres, fasc. 32 [Paris, 1958] p. 212, n. 8); Auguste Mariette, *Dendérah: Description générale du grand temple de cette ville* I (Paris, 1870) Pl. LII*b*; Chassinat, *Le Temple de Dendara* IV 102; François Daumas, *Les Mammisis de Dendara* ("Publications de l'Institut français d'archéologie orientale du Caire" [Cairo, 1959]) p. 243 and Pl. LXXXIII. For other references to Shesmu as a lion-headed god see Constant De Wit, *Le Rôle et le sens du lion dans l'Egypte ancienne* (Leiden, 1951) pp. 267–69. The curious fact that it is the benevolent side of his personality that was represented as lion-headed has already been noted by Dimitri Meeks ("Génies, anges, et démons," p. 70, n. 59).

[43] E.g., Marquis de Rochemonteix and Emile Chassinat, *Le Temple d'Edfou* I ("MMAF" X [1892]) 45.

[44] E.g., Chassinat, *Le Temple de Dendara* IV 107, lines 6–7.

[45] The "laboratory" at Edfu is the room labeled "Z" on the chart in Rochemonteix and Chassinat, *Le Temple d'Edfou* I, Pl. I. The texts of the scenes inscribed on the walls of this room were published by Chassinat (*Le Temple d'Edfou* II 189–230). For schematic line drawings of these scenes, see *Le Temple d'Edfou* II, Pl. XLIII*a–d*. For photographs of some of these scenes, see *Le Temple d'Edfou* XII ("MMAF" XXIX [1934]) Pls. CCCLXXXI–CCCCII.

At the temple of Dendera the "laboratory" is the room labeled "A′" on the chart in Chassinat, *Le Temple de Dendara* I, Pl. XLV. The principal publication of these scenes is Mariette, *Dendérah* I, Pls. XLVII–LIII.

[46] For the "laboratory" at Edfu see H. W. Fairman, "Worship and Festivals in an Egyptian Temple," *BJRL* 37 (1954–55) 169. Actually the production of the sacred ointments must have taken place outside the temple itself in some nearby workshops. Probably the "laboratory" was

production here, Shesmu is sometimes given the title "lord of the laboratory" (*nb ỉswy*).[47]

A favorite scene depicted on the walls of the staircases leading to the roofs of certain of the temples is a procession of gods bearing offerings for the New Year's Festival. An interesting feature of these scenes is that in some of these processions both the good ointment-maker Shesmu and the cruel butcher Shesmu appear, each one as a distinct god. The details of four of these processions are given below:

1. Temple of Hathor at Dendera, east staircase, east side: Following the first priest in this procession there is a lion-headed god carrying jars of ointment. Presumably this is Shesmu the ointment-maker.[48] Farther along in the same procession a human-headed figure carries pieces of meat. He is labeled "Shesmu, lord of the slaughterhouse of Horus. . . ."[49]

2. Temple of Hathor at Dendera, east staircase, west side: The first figure after the priests is a lion-headed god. He is called "Shesmu, lord of the laboratory. . . ."[50] Farther along the human-headed Shesmu appears, carrying pieces of meat that he has cut up. His label reads "Shesmu, lord of the slaughterhouse of Horus, chief of the slaughterblock, who hacks up the oryx, wild of countenance, who overthrows enemies, who slays all the beasts of the desert, mighty in his arm, who strikes down the rebel, who propitiates the heart of Hathor with what she likes."[51]

3. Roman mammisi at Dendera, staircase: Although the band of text above the procession mentions both forms of Shesmu, only the lion-headed ointment-maker is represented in the scene.[52]

4. Temple of Horus at Edfu, east staircase, left wall: In this procession the ointment-maker Shesmu is lion headed.[53]

As in the non-temple material, the good Shesmu may also appear as a generalized guardian deity, completely divorced from any association with ointments. As noted above, in the scenes of the "Hour-watchers" from the

---

used only for storage. Cf. François Daumas, *Dendara et le Temple d'Hathor: Notice sommaire* ("Publications de l'Institut français d'archéologie orientale du Caire, Recherches d'archéologie, de philologie, et d'histoire" XXIX [Cairo, 1969]) p. 40.

[47] E.g., Chassinat, *Le Temple d'Edfou* IV ("MMAF" XXI [1929]) 200.

[48] See Mariette, *Dendérah* IV, Pl. V.

[49] See *ibid.*, Pl. VII. [50] See *ibid.*, Pl. XIV. [51] See *ibid.*, Pl. XVI.

[52] See Daumas, *Les Mammisis de Dendara*, pp. 231, 243, and Pl. LXXXIII.

[53] See Rochemonteix and Chassinat, *Le Temple d'Edfou* I 565–66 and Pl. XXXVIII*k–l*. The New Year's Festival at the temple of Edfu and the role of this staircase procession in that festival are discussed in Maurice Alliot, *Le Culte d'Horus à Edfou au temps des Ptolémées* ("BdE" XX [1949]) pp. 389–411.

temples of Edfu, Dendera, and Philae, Shesmu is identified as the guardian of the twelfth hour of the night.[54] Similarly, Shesmu, "who overthrows his enemies," is one of the gods invoked in the "Book of the Protection of the Body," which is inscribed on the inner face, east side of the north end of the enclosure wall of the temple of Horus at Edfu.[55]

THE CONNECTION WITH LETOPOLIS

It is sometimes stated that the Memphite region was the original home of Shesmu.[56] A good number of documents concerning Shesmu support this theory.

From a very early period we have the above-mentioned diorite bowl belonging to a "prophet" (*ḥm-nṯr*) of this god.[57] This bowl was found at the site of the Step Pyramid, suggesting a connection between Shesmu and Saqqara, the necropolis of Memphis. Another connection with Saqqara can be inferred from the fact that in some passages from the Coffin Texts cited above Shesmu appears as the companion of Sokar, the patron of that necropolis.[58] A close relationship between Shesmu and the other gods of the Memphite region is implied by the nature of his three appearances in the mortuary temple of Seti I at Abydos, namely:

a) in a list of Memphite gods in the Ptah-Sokar room,
b) as one of six gods to whom bread is offered in the Nefertem-Ptah-Sokar hall,
c) as a member of the Ennead of Ptah-Sokar-Osiris in the Gallery of Lists.[59]

[54] Hermann Junker, *Die Stundenwachen in den Osirismysterien nach den Inschriften von Dendera, Edfu, und Philae* ("Denkschriften der Kaiserlichen Akademie der Wissenschaften in Wien, Philosophisch-historische Klasse," Vol. LIV [Vienna, 1910]) p. 124, No. 5.

[55] Chassinat, *Le Temple d'Edfou* VI ("MMAF" XXIII [1931]) 301; cf. Francis Abdel-Malek Ghattas, *Das Buch* Mk.t-ḥʿ.w "*Schutz des Leibes*" (Göttingen, 1968) p. 72.

[56] E.g., Hans Bonnet, *Reallexikon der ägyptischen Religions-Geschichte* (2d ed.; Berlin, 1971) p. 680. Often in the same breath it is alleged that Shesmu was the name of one of the decans; see *ibid.*; see also Dimitri Meeks, "Génies, anges, et démons," p. 30. However, the original name of the decan in question was probably "Crew" (uncertain transliteration). For an explanation of the process by which the wine press hieroglyph came to be used in the spelling of this decan see O. Neugebauer and Richard A. Parker, *Egyptian Astronomical Texts* I (London, 1960) 24; cf. *idem*, *Egyptian Astronomical Texts* III 161, No. 30.

[57] For this bowl see the references given in note 6, above.

[58] *ECT* VI 171*a*, 172*b–c*.

[59] For the three appearances of Shesmu in the Abydos temple see notes 27–29, above.

The pattern is continued in the reliefs from the mortuary temple of Ramesses III at Medinet Habu, where Shesmu plays a role in the festival of Sokar. In the particular scene where he appears, Shesmu is accompanied by *Ḥry-rmn.wy.fy* and Khnum *ḫnty-ỉnb.w.f*, both gods of the Memphite region.[60]

Thus, there is ample evidence to establish a relationship between the god Shesmu and the region of Memphis. But a closer examination of this evidence offers some hope of localizing this god's original home even more precisely. Certain indications point in the direction of Letopolis, capital of the second nome of Lower Egypt, at the northwest edge of the Memphite region.

Until now the suggestion that Shesmu originally came from Letopolis has been made only by Peter Kaplony, who cites a passage in the Pyramid Texts in which Shesmu is associated or identified with *Ḫrty*, the ram god of Letopolis.[61] This is the only instance of a close association between these two gods mentioned by Kaplony, but there are others. The diorite bowl mentioned earlier belonged to a man who was a "prophet" of a number of gods besides Shesmu, one of them being *Ḫrty*.[62] These same two gods are also linked by the evidence of the Old Kingdom scribal tablet from Giza, which lists Shesmu and *Ḫrty* one after the other in several columns.[63]

The evidence for Shesmu's connection with Letopolis is not limited, however, to his association with the god *Ḫrty*. A specific statement linking Shesmu to the area around Letopolis occurs in the reliefs of the mortuary temple of Seti I at Abydos; in the list of the members of the Ennead of Ptah-Sokar-Osiris, Shesmu's entry places him in a town called *ʾIst*.[64] Now this town is one of the cult places of Sachmet near Letopolis.[65]

Turning once more to the scenes of the Festival of Sokar at Medinet Habu, we note again that Shesmu is accompanied by Khnum *ḫnty-ỉnb.w.f*. This god happens to be a conflation of two different ram-headed gods, one being *ḫnty-ỉnb.w.f*, a specifically Memphite god, while the other is Khnum, who has strong connections with Letopolis.[66] The presence of this god adds a distinctly

[60] For the scene in the Festival of Sokar see note 30, above.

[61] Peter Kaplony, *Die Inschriften der ägyptischen Frühzeit* ("Ägyptologische Abhandlungen," Vol. 8/1 (Wiesbaden, 1963) p. 622; *idem*, "Der Titel *wnr(w)* nach Spruch 820 der Sargtexte," *MIO* 11 (1965) 160, n. 90. For *Ḫrty* see Bonnet, *Reallexikon*, p. 135; Weill, *Miscellanea Gregoriana*.

[62] For this bowl see the references given in note 6, above.

[63] For the scribal tablet see the references given in note 7.

[64] For the list of the Ennead of Ptah-Sokar-Osiris see note 29.

[65] On the town *ʾIst* see Serge Sauneron, "La ville ," *Kêmi* 11 (1950) 122–23; cf. Pierre Montet, *Géographie de l'Egypte ancienne*, Pt. I (Paris, 1957) 53.

[66] Gaballa and Kitchen, *Or* 38 (1969) 49, n. 9. Hermann Kees (*Das Priestertum im ägyptischen Staat vom Neuen Reich bis zur Spätzeit* ["Probleme der Ägyptologie" I (Leiden, 1953)] p. 33 and

Letopolitan flavor to the scene and may support the theory that Shesmu also originated in Letopolis.

Finally, the passage in spell 17 of the Book of the Dead in which Shesmu appears provides another hint of a connection between this god and the town of Letopolis. As we have noted above, the cruel god in this text, who lassoes sinners and beheads them, is identified by the ancient commentator as Shesmu. But this is only the preferred identification. Alternative proposals are also listed in the text following the name of Shesmu.[67] One of these alternatives is Horus of Letopolis, a variant that may indicate a Letopolitan origin for this portion of spell 17 and, with it, of Shesmu.

One of the principal deities of the region around Letopolis was Sachmet, who had several cult places in the area, one of them being the above-mentioned *ʾIst*. It has been suggested that Letopolis was her original home and that only later was she incorporated into the mythology of the Memphite area as the consort of its main god Ptah.[68] In a similar manner and possibly along with Sachmet, Shesmu may have been introduced into the greater pantheon of Memphis from the local pantheon of Letopolis. His connection with the gods and the necropolis of Memphis, at any rate, is fully established by the documents.

The fact that Sachmet was a lion goddess had a profound influence on a number of the lesser deities of Letopolis, who also assumed the form of a lion. Perhaps it was under the influence of Sachmet, for example, that the god *Ḫrty*, who was originally a ram god, could appear in later times in the guise of a lion.[69] It may be due to the same influence that Shesmu, also, could assume the form of a lion in later times.

---

n. 5) mentions Khnum *ḫnty wꜣr.f* as the god of the second (Letopolite) nome of Lower Egypt, who catches birds with a net. Perhaps this is the origin of Shesmu's connection with the net that was prominent in the Coffin Texts and the Book of the Dead.

[67] Book of the Dead spell 17, 65. See Naville, *Das ägyptische Todtenbuch*, Pl. XXV.

[68] Bonnet, *Reallexikon*, p. 643.

[69] Hermann Kees, *Der Götterglaube im alten Ägypten* (2d ed.; Berlin, 1956) pp. 79, n. 5, 137.

THE ORIENTAL INSTITUTE DECORATED CENSER FROM NUBIA

Carl E. DeVries

In giving honor to whom honor is due, it is fitting to pay academic tribute to one of the most personable and helpful figures in the ranks of Egyptologists. While scholarly excellence and human feeling are not necessarily natural concomitants, in George R. Hughes these qualities are combined to an unusual degree. Having been for many years engrossed in epigraphic work at Luxor, George became involved in the Nubian archeological campaign, first in epigraphy at Beit el-Wali and later in the digging at Serra East in the Sudan. The object discussed in this article came from the excavations directed by our mutual long-time friend and colleague, Keith C. Seele, and is one of the most significant finds from Egyptian Nubia.

This artifact (Field No. B–1728; Or. Inst. No. 24069) has come to be regarded by Nubiologists at the Oriental Institute and elsewhere as possibly the object carrying the oldest known sunk relief from ancient Egypt. Although the remaining surface is in relatively good condition, the object was found in several pieces and is incomplete. The function or purpose of the object is not certain, but it was probably a censer or lamp, and it will be referred to as a censer throughout the remainder of this article.[1]

During the 1963/64 season, the Oriental Institute Nubian Expedition excavated two A-Group cemeteries, designated L and W, on the east bank of the Nile, in the area of the village of Qustul. Of these, L was the more southerly and was excavated earlier, as the expedition moved northward from Adindan. It is thought that the two burial sites were more or less contemporary, but that Cemetery L represented a higher economic or social stratum of Nubia than did Cemetery W, for the graves in L were generally much larger and more complex in plan (usually having a roughly rectangular shaft, which served as a sort of

[1] I have previously presented two papers on the A-Group censers from Nubia. The first, on the general subject, was given at the annual meeting of the American Research Center in Egypt, at the State University of New York in Binghamton, November 4, 1972. The second, dealing more specifically with the decorated censer, was read at the 184th meeting of the American Oriental Society, at the University of California in Santa Barbara, March 28, 1974.

antechamber, with a burial chamber at the end of one of the long sides), and were furnished with more abundant, rich, and varied burial goods.

It may be noted, too, that the physical condition in which the two cemeteries were found was quite different. Cemetery W had only a shallow cover of wind-blown sand, and the graves themselves were not very deep. In spite of this, the graves had apparently escaped damage from both human and natural forces, and most of them gave the appearance of being undisturbed. Cemetery L, however, seems to have suffered all sorts of vicissitudes. Many of the objects were broken and widely scattered, as if some hurried, vindictive, or disappointed grave robber had been at work. Certainly the graves were much damaged by the action of water, whether by flooding from an unusually high Nile or, perhaps more likely, by a rare and extremely heavy rainstorm. The contents of many storage jars had been supplanted by water-laid material too hard to be removed by the tools we had at our disposal. In some cases the earth filling the graves was also much more solid than the surrounding soil into which they had been cut. It was necessary to use a pick in some graves and in the case of at least one burial chamber it was found advisable to cut away the overburden of original soil, which threatened to cave in on the workmen.

The pieces of the censer came to light on February 17, 1964. The object was the focus of interest and discussion at the time, and it was entered into the register with the following description by Dr. Seele:

> Limestone palette with deeply incised reliefs on side depicting three boats, one containing a baboon with standard in stern, with fish and plant in water, before which stands a man and a goat on hind legs, browsing; second boat containing a long-eared animal beneath a large bird; third boat containing a man, a cabin(?) and a standard; before the last a structure with elaborate door.

Calling the object a palette seemed a reasonable identification of its purpose at the time of its discovery. In both cemeteries we found an abundance of grinding-stones of various forms and uses. In the smaller, intact graves of Cemetery W a typical object was a small palette used for grinding malachite for cosmetic application. In Cemetery L there were also many larger grinding-stones, apparently intended for the grinding of grain. The largest and heaviest of these implements was oval in shape, and some of them bore a decoration in the form of a coil or "snake" pattern on the base.

Another type of grinding-stone found was somewhat cylindrical. Those made of relatively hard stone were often convex rather than straight along the vertical dimension. Somewhat similar in appearance were other artifacts made of a soft, very lightweight material (gypsum); the softness of the stone itself seemed to weigh against the proposal that these objects also were palettes or mortars, although this possibility should not be ruled out, for softer substances could have been ground on the prepared surface. On the upper surfaces of these objects characteristically there was cut a hollow or depression. Earlier excavations in Nubia, in the area of Faras, had produced similar objects and the excavators had taken them to be censers.[2] Some of the exemplars found in the Qustul area were blackened as if some substance had been burned in them. With the interest and cooperation of Dr. Philip E. Eaton of the Department of Chemistry at the University of Chicago, several of the specimens were submitted for appropriate testing. Although the results were not conclusive, there were indications that organic material had indeed been carbonized in the objects, and it was proposed that these objects, too, were really lamps or censers.

The repaired broken censer under discussion shows a general similarity to the cylindrical censers described above, but it also has some dissimilarities. It is of about the same size as most of them (8.9 cm. high, 15.2 cm. in diameter at the top, and 13.8 cm. in diameter at the base). The dimensions show that it has an outward taper from bottom to top, which is unusual for the censers. It is made of limestone, whose provenience is as yet unknown. The depression on the upper surface is deeper and the rim is wider than on the more ordinary forms. The hollow lacks any sure indication of either grinding or burning; notably absent is the carbon remarked upon above as typical of the others. The distinctive characteristic of this limestone censer is the sunk relief that covers its sides, although some of the others did have a modicum of decoration consisting of scratched or incised lines of geometric pattern, somewhat like that on the rim of this special piece.

We have from the outset regarded this object as having the same function as the other cylindrical objects. In a paper presented at the annual meeting of the American Research Center in the autumn of 1972 I reiterated this similarity of

[2] So identified by Cecil M. Firth. Said to be of sandstone. Cf. F. Ll. Griffith, "Oxford Excavations in Nubia," *Annals of Archaeology and Anthropology* 8 (1921) 9 and Pl. IV:3.

A. M. Blackman describes one from Cemetery 47 (Bugga [Boggaʿ]): "Limestone incense-burner(?), the depression in the top is fire(?) stained, decorated with incised lines," in George A. Reisner, *The Archaeological Survey of Nubia: Report from 1907–1908* (Cairo, 1910) I 277 and Pl. 64*h*.

Two are described in the final report of the Scandinavian Joint Expedition: from Serra East, Site 298.9:4 (p. 148 and Pls. 68 and 192:3); from Ashkeit, Site 332/17:3 (p. 172 and Pl. 85). Both are made of gypsum (calcium sulphate) or a mixture of gypsum and lime. Hans-Äke Nordström, *Neolithic and A-Group Sites* ("The Scandinavian Joint Expedition to Sudanese Nubia Publications," Vol. 3:1 [Uppsala, 1972]) pp. 119–20. Cf. T. Säve-Söderbergh, "Preliminary Report of the Scandinavian Joint Expedition: Archaeological Investigations between Faras and Gemai, November 1962–March 1963," *Kush* 12 (1964) 29 and Pl. III*a* (called a "stone lamp").

Another was found at Gezira Dabarose (Site AS 6–G–18, grave No. 42). See Hans-Äke Nordström, "Excavations and Survey in Faras, Argin and Gezira Dabarose," *Kush* 10 (1962) 58 and Pl. X*a*.

purpose and suggested that the unique relief could perhaps be accounted for by the aesthetic interest of the tomb owner, by some special individual use of the piece (it may have been used in the funeral services and then deposited in the grave), or perhaps even by the profession or craft of the tomb owner.[3]

It is interesting to trace the changes in the description and even in the suggested identification of this piece as they took place. In the office formerly occupied by Dr. Seele I found a description typed on the paper stock that is used for display labels in the museum:

This shattered ceremonial palette may turn out to be one of the most important objects ever discovered in Egyptian Nubia. Even the style of relief is noteworthy for it is possibly the earliest example of incised relief ever found in the Nile Valley. The composition depicts a river scene dominated by three boats with high prows and sterns, probably of the earliest Mediterranean type of sailboat: (1) A boat with hoisted sail, cabin with sloping roof, and steersman holding his oar approaches a niched structure on the Nile bank. Beneath the stern of this boat is a crocodile (head only preserved); (2) a much damaged boat containing an animal and a bird(?) with background of bending reeds; (3) a boat containing a large quadruped with long tail and claws and pointed ears, standing in front of a pole surmounted by a (damaged) standard, with fish and water plant beneath the prow; the boat appears to be faced by a man with uplifted left arm and by a goat standing on hind legs as if browsing on the tall vegetation, behind the goat a mooring stake fixed in the earth.

The style of the boats, the niched building, and the posture of the goat raise once more the vexed question of prehistoric Mesopotamian-Egyptian connections. However, the man, the fish, and the crocodile are unmistakably Egyptian. An identical type of sailboat is represented on a late Gerzean storage jar in the British Museum (which has other affinities with several of our objects from Nubia), while a less similar boat with high prow and stern occurs on the Narmer Palette. We are thus inclined to date this object and the grave in which it was found to the late Gerzean, or at latest to the predynastic period.

Although the date of the writing of that label is unknown, it is clear that at that time Dr. Seele still considered the object a palette. In his stimulating preliminary report, prepared originally for the conference on Nubian archeology at Cairo in the spring of 1971 and published posthumously in the *Journal of Near Eastern Studies*,[4] he made an entirely new attempt at identifying the function of this piece and suggested that it could perhaps have been a huge cylinder seal.

While every serious proposal must be given consideration, there are a number of arguments that would appear to rule out immediately any prolonged discussion of this identification. 1. The object bears on its upper surface the same

[3] In one tomb we found a huge stock of unfinished jewelry, which earned for L–19 the name "Tomb of the Jeweler." It is improbable, however, that the occupant of L–24 was a sculptor.

[4] Keith C. Seele, "University of Chicago Oriental Institute Nubian Expedition: Excavations between Abu Simbel and the Sudan Border, Preliminary Report," *JNES* 33 (1974) 1–43.

depression that is found on similar specimens; this must be regarded as a utilitarian feature. 2. The taper of the piece would make it impossible to impress the design on clay in a straight line. 3. The subject matter of the relief is very different from that of any sealings known from the archaic cemeteries, such as those at Sakkarah and Abydos. Typical sealings include the name of a king or serve as a royal identifying mark. The relief on this object shows a rather extensive scene and is representational rather than onomastic. 4. Most of the archaic seals must have been of relatively small diameter, because the sealings repeat the same motif a number of times. It would take a fairly large clay jar closure to accommodate the subject matter of a seal the size of our object.

Perhaps the most telling argument against the view that the censer may be a gigantic cylinder seal comes from the evidence of the seals found in our own A-Group burials. Part of an ivory cylinder seal (B–1313; Or. Inst. No. 23662) was found in L–17. A complete ivory cylinder seal (B–1504; Or. Inst. No. 23848), broken into two pieces, bears an incised design of essentially herring-bone pattern. This cylinder, from W–2, measures only 3.2 cm. in length and 1.4 cm. in diameter. The differences between these cylinder seals and our stone object are striking—in size, material, subject matter, and cutting technique of the decoration. If the cylinders are really seals, as designated, rather than beads or items with some function other than sphragistic, it seems virtually impossible that our large stone object should also be a seal.

It would therefore appear that we can rule out the possibility that this object was a cylinder seal, and our most probable identification would seem to remain that of a censer or lamp. Perhaps censer is the better suggestion, for the depression is quite shallow and could not have contained very much oil. A censer would have been used for only a brief period, and the burning of solid incense or aromatic oils was a common practice in ancient Near Eastern religions.

Dr. Seele also suggested that the cylinder may have been broken deliberately in an effort to preserve the seal from unauthorized use after the owner's death. Several arguments against this view may be advanced. In the first place, it seems unlikely that such an act would have been performed just before the tomb entrance shaft was filled. This object was the first thing we recovered from L–24; it was no longer in the grave chamber, where one would expect an item of personal use to have been deposited. In the second place, if the cylinder had been deliberately smashed by the persons in charge of the burial, one would expect that all of the pieces would have remained where broken. In view of the chaotic condition of this and most of the other tombs of Cemetery L it is difficult to conjecture much about the original position of many of the objects found in this tomb. As the first recorder of L–24 and the one who made the field notes about this piece, I am inclined to feel that the breaking of the object was not the work of the burial party, but probably the work of some later intruders, who may have thrown away some of the pieces of the article, so that they were not found in the grave. The Quftis and Illahunis we employed were extremely careful and conscientious, so it is reasonably certain that none of the pieces was overlooked in the process of excavation. Furthermore, the contents of many of the graves were methodically passed through a sieve so as to recover very small objects, such as beads.

At this point it may be well to comment briefly on the terminology used in connection with this relief and to examine the date of the earliest known sunk relief. In his description of the relief, Dr. Seele used the terms "incised" and "sunken" as interchangeable or synonymous. During my years in Luxor with the Epigraphic Survey I became accustomed to using the terms "raised" and "incised" to indicate the two types of relief with which we were concerned. In a private conversation some months ago, Bernard V. Bothmer suggested to me that we should standardize our terminology. The relief on our censer must be called "sunk" relief—relief in which the outline is cut away and the interior material cut down to uniform level.

The oldest sunk relief is generally thought to date to about the Fourth Dynasty.[5] Although this statement is several decades old, it is interesting to note the specific examples given by W. S. Smith:

> Possibly the earliest example of sunk relief proper is the granite block from Bubastis with the name of Cheops, but a curious variation of this type of relief is found in the decorations of Neferm'at and Atet at Medum, where the figures were hollowed out and filled with coloured pastes. The finished effect of these figures was very unlike sunk relief, but the actual technique differed little. This was not a popular form of work and was found again only in the hieroglyphs on the base of the statue of Hemyuwnuw. The earliest private example of sunk relief that I know is in the inscriptions in the mastaba of Prince Min-khaf (G 7430–7440) at Giza, probably of the reign of Chephren (Pl. 46). Possibly the use of sunk relief inscriptions in the granite casings of that king's temple may have made this type of work better known. At any rate, from this time on the use of sunk relief is fairly common, although it is ordinarily restricted to inscriptions on the outside of the chapel. It is probable that it was developed as an easier method than raised relief for dealing with decorations on hard stone, but it may also have been considered as a more protected form for exterior inscriptions.[6]

We come at last to what many will regard as the most interesting feature of this censer, the subject matter of the relief, which has been described several times above and which now must be considered in detail. It is extremely unfortunate that so much of the relief is missing; even if we had the piece intact

[5] *Ibid.*, p. 39.

[6] W. Stevenson Smith, *A History of Egyptian Sculpture and Painting in the Old Kingdom* (2d ed.; London, 1951) pp. 250–51.

there would be much room for speculation as to the representation, but the incomplete state of the relief increases the difficulties manyfold. What remains is of much curiosity and considerable ambiguity.

It appears to me that the reliefs represent one continuous scene, rather than several separate panels, for there are no scene dividers and the representation can be interpreted as a whole. Since there are three boats and only one building, I would suggest that the structure on the land is the unique or focal element. In view of what is known of later river processions, it is logical to surmise that the boats constitute a formal transport of that type. Inasmuch as the building appears to be the point to which or from which the procession is directed, it may be logical to assume that the structure would have more significance ideologically if it were the destination or goal toward which the boats are moving. In any case, if this is a procession, the direction of the boats indicates that the one containing the quadruped must be the last in line.

Another important consideration in connection with the representation is that there are no indications that any of the elements of the scene are in themselves unnatural or unreal, even though certain of the figures, such as the animal in the last boat, may be difficult to identify. The combination of some of the elements, however, is so unusual that we may judge that the scene cannot represent actuality. It is unlikely, for example, that any animal would be travelling alone in a boat on the Nile. Although the religious pigeonhole is the customary catchall of the archeological interpreter, in view of the overall religiosity of the ancient Egyptian, in this case it is quite natural to catalogue this scene as religious or perhaps mythological in character. If this interpretation is correct, we may then postulate that the structure is a shrine and that at least one occupant of one boat is a deity, probably in animal form. It is my opinion, therefore, that the scene depicts a riverine religious procession moving toward a shrine of niched architecture.

The nature of the scene brings us back to our conclusions concerning the function or purpose of our object. If the scene is religious in character it becomes even more likely that the object itself had some particularized religious association. This would be true if it were some type of censer, which could serve in a religious ceremony or as a votive object or both.

The study of this censer of necessity involves us in a number of questions regarding widespread cultural relations at a very early period, at the very beginning of historic times in Egypt. The niched panelling has been discussed often over the years, and the current prevailing opinion is still that this type of architectural construction or embellishment reflects a Mesopotamian origin. While it would not be amiss to recall the primitive shrines of Buto and Hierakonpolis, it is improbable that either of these can be linked to the central shrine of this scene. They merely confirm the fact that in Egyptian prehistory there were

FIG. 13.—View of the censer showing the niched building or shrine

FIG. 14.—View showing the first boat of the religious procession

shrines that may not have been far different in kind from the structure shown on this censer (see Fig. 13).

To the left of the remains of the shrine there is a large break. The next significant element is the first boat (see Fig. 14). Underneath the prow of the boat

FIG. 15.—View showing damaged portion with remains of the second boat

FIG. 16.—Another view of the damaged portion showing part of the second boat

are several kinds of vegetation. One variety has branches and was probably a leafed plant, while the other appears to be the matted growth or vegetable debris at the river's edge. A sprig of plant material is also shown under the prow of the third boat, while above boats two and three (and perhaps above the first boat

FIG. 17.—View showing details between the second and third boats, for example, a goat, a man, and a fish

also—all of the upper portion of the censer is broken away here) there are tall, arching, interlaced stems reminiscent of the reeds or papyrus growth native to shallow water, whether of marsh or river.

A striking omission in the depiction of the boats has parallels in the Gebel el-Arak knife handle, the Hierakonpolis wall painting, and generally in Gerzean pottery that shows river scenes: there is no indication of the water. By comparison, it is of interest to note that on the famous sailing vessel shown on the painted storage jar in the British Museum, BM35324, groups of water signs appear about the boat.[7] Whether this is a matter of artistic preference or an indication of some chronological pattern has not been determined, but it is a factor that should be kept in mind. The absence of such water signs on Gerzean pottery led Cecil Torr to propose that the boats shown on these pots were not boats at all but were forts with towers and other elements of defense.[8] In this conclusion he was followed to a degree by Victor Loret and others. But the finding of pottery models of ships of this type, and the general accumulation of evidence, has supported the original theory of Petrie that boats were intended.

Although the first two boats (especially the second) are much damaged, the

[7] See Björn Landström, *Ships of the Pharaohs* (Garden City, N.Y., 1970) p. 13 (Fig. 15), p. 14 (Fig. 18).

[8] Cf. Jean Capart, *Primitive Art in Egypt* (London, 1905) pp. 207–10, 217, n. 1; Landström, *Ships*, p. 13.

FIG. 18.—View of the censer showing the best preserved of the three boats with its animal occupant

third is perfectly preserved, and enough remains of the other two to give rise to much discussion as to their design and their place of origin. One cannot judge the intention of the artist, but it seems that the three boats are not identical in outline; the second boat is a bit different from the other two, having considerably more curve, less angularity of the stern at about the water line, just before the break in the stone.

The question of the origin of these boats is admittedly very difficult. Björn Landström, in his fine volume on ancient Egyptian ships, devotes much space to a comparison of representations of various types of prehistoric vessels. His conclusions are sensible, safe, conservative, and perhaps strictly correct: "We know far too little about pre-dynastic Egyptian ships, and almost nothing about contemporary foreign ships. No foundation exists on which to interpret these early testimonials in any direction."[9] Our boats, however, most closely resemble those that have come to be described generally as foreign, particularly Mesopotamian, especially when found in association with other cultural elements from that source. The nearest analogies are shown by the Gebel el-Arak knife handle, the Hierakonpolis wall painting, the slate palette of Narmer, and the British Museum storage jar BM35324.[10] Another boat of very similar outline

[9] Landström, *Ships*, p. 22.

[10] There are many reproductions that show these ships or boats. Perhaps most useful are line

appears on the historically important ivory label found at Negadeh bearing the name of Hor-Aha.[11] Landström refers to the label as a "bone plate" and believes that the carving "probably depicts a sun boat."[12]

In connection with the boat shown on the Gebel el-Arak knife handle, Landström points out that there are very similar hulls shown on the rock drawings of southern Egypt and Nubia: "We have here mainly vessels with straight high stems [misprint for sterns?], vessels of a type often designated as foreign (31, 35, 39, 40, 43). This naturally does not prove that the vessels on the knife handle and the black ship (cf. 17)[13] are not foreign, but the type undeniably occurred in Nubia."[14]

Although Landström is an authority on the history of boats and their construction, I am inclined to follow the judgment of those whose lifework has been in the field of archeology and the interpretation of ancient art. W. B. Emery, for example, says of the Gebel el-Arak knife handle and the Hierakonpolis painting, "In both these representations we have typical native ships of Egypt and strange vessels with high prow and stern of unmistakable Mesopotamian origin (Fig. 1)."[15]

To have only boats of "foreign" design on an object found in Egypt may be a different matter, so it is best to exercise some caution in interpreting our censer. Nevertheless, the appearance of these boats in association with the niched architecture, both of which are usually regarded as Mesopotamian in origin, hints strongly of widespread cultural relations throughout the Near East.[16]

We must return to the description of the first boat. This vessel is equipped with a simple pole mast and sail and with a cabin located toward the stern. Since

---

drawings, such as those in W. M. F. Petrie, "Egyptian Shipping," in *Ancient Egypt and the East*, 1933, pp. 11, 14; Landström, *Ships*, p. 14, Figs. 16–18; Capart, *Primitive Art*, p. 118, Fig. 91 (lower right), pp. 208–9, Figs. 162 and 163.

[11] W. B. Emery, *Archaic Egypt* (Baltimore, 1961) pp. 49–50 and Fig. 10. See also Emery, *Ḥor-Aḥa* (Cairo, 1930) pp. 110–11. For a full discussion of the ivory tablet, see Vladimir Vikentiev, "Les Monuments archaïques—I. La Tablette en ivoire de Naqâda," *Annales du Service des Antiquités de l'Egypte* 33 (1933) 208–34, with photograph and drawings, Pls. I–III.

[12] *Ships*, p. 25, Fig. 76.

[13] This boat is from the Hierakonpolis painting.

[14] Landström, *Ships*, p. 16.

[15] Emery, *Archaic Egypt*, pp. 38–39. Landström shows only one drawing of a ship from a Sumerian cylinder seal (*Ships*, p. 14, Fig. 21).

[16] For the "standard" view of the cultural influence of Mesopotamia on Egypt, see Henri Frankfort, "The Origin of Monumental Architecture in Egypt," *AJSL* 58 (1941) 329–58; Henri Frankfort, *The Birth of Civilization in the Near East* (Bloomington, Ind., 1951), esp. pp. 101–11; W. Stevenson Smith, *The Art and Architecture of Ancient Egypt* ("The Pelican History of Art" [Baltimore, 1958]) pp. 18–19.

the sail is hoisted, the boat should be traveling upstream, to the south. To the rear of the cabin is a man who is standing at the stern and is probably the steersman of the craft.

According to Björn Landström, the presence of a simple pole mast indicates that these boats were made of wood, not papyrus, for papyrus boats had a bipod mast, a fact that influenced boat construction down into the Old Kingdom. In his section on Egyptian traveling ships, Landström comments concerning ships of the Fourth Dynasty: "One of the ships (98) has a simple pole mast, and this is a perfectly unique piece of evidence before the Sixth Dynasty. The vessel in question is small, perhaps what we should call a boat, with no deckhouse and only one helmsman. All of the other sailing vessels have bipod masts."[17] His dating of Old Kingdom sailing vessels with simple pole mast to the Sixth Dynasty remains accurate and correct, for he is in error when he attributes his Figure 98 to the Fourth Dynasty. This example comes from the tomb of the dwarf Seneb[18] at Giza and is dated by Porter and Moss to "Middle Dynasty VI or later."[19] Earlier in his volume Landström comments that he believes that the bipod mast arose from its necessary and natural use on papyrus rafts, but that it was not required on wooden ships, such as those of the Old Kingdom. He states also, "The earliest pictures we have of sailing vessels (p. 13:14, 15, p. 16:31, 39) show only a single mast."[20] This is of some interest to us, for three of the boats he lists (13:15 and 16:31, 39) bear some resemblance to those on our censer. Of these, 13:15 is the painting on BM 35324, which is of the same form as ours but appears to be much larger.

There is an additional comment of moment to be made concerning the sail shown on the first boat on the Chicago censer. It is definitely a rectangular sail, with the long side vertical. Of his Figure 14 Landström comments that it has "something resembling a sail";[21] this sail is of somewhat irregular quadrilateral shape and it, too, has the long dimension vertical. Landström believes that sails during the Fourth and Fifth dynasties were trapezoidal in form, mounted horizontally with the shorter of the two sides below so as to prevent the sail from digging in when the ship heeled.[22] Placing the sail as on our first boat would probably have had a similar effect.

The cabin or deckhouse does not require comment, except that I may suggest

[17] *Ships*, p. 36.

[18] See H. Junker, *Giza* (Akademie der Wissenschaften in Wien, Philosophisch-historische Klasse, "Denkschriften," Vol. 71, No. 2 [Vienna and Leipzig, 1941]) p. 62, Fig. 14*b*.

[19] Bertha Porter and Rosalind L. B. Moss, *Topographical Bibliography of Ancient Egyptian Hieroglyphic Texts, Reliefs and Paintings* III: *Memphis*, Pt. 1, *Abû Rawâsh to Abûṣîr* (2d ed., rev. and augmented by J. Malek; Oxford, 1974) p. 101. W. Stevenson Smith dates the tomb of Seneb to "late in Dyn. V, if not Early Dyn. VI" (*A History of Egyptian Sculpture and Painting*, p. 57).

[20] *Ships*, p. 19. [21] *Ibid.*, p. 13. [22] *Ibid.*, pp. 43, 46.

that this may be a portable shrine being transported to the larger, more permanent, shrine, in similar fashion as the sacred bark and its accoutrements later traveled by river procession to various temples, for example, from Karnak to Luxor.

The man standing to the rear of the deckhouse is almost certainly the steersman. He is standing in a natural position, which here coincides with the later normal representation of the human figure in Egyptian art, with one foot placed before the other. The left, or rear foot, is clearly carved, while the right appears to merge with the object in front of the man. The buttocks are prominently shown, but this may be artistic license, error, or exaggeration.

The object before the man has been variously interpreted. It has been suggested that this is a *was*-scepter. It surely resembles such a scepter, although one may object that the two prongs at the base are not shown.[23] A stronger objection may be made on the basis of the context of the scene—a scepter does not fit the scene, an iconographic significance is doubtful here, and the value of a scepter as a phonogram also appears to be out of place in this artistic setting. It seems to me that the resemblance to a *was*-scepter is a coincidence, and that what is actually portrayed is the steering oar, with the hand and arm of the man holding it. This fits remarkably well with the scene as a whole, for if the boat is about to land in front of the shrine, and if the matted vegetation is an indicator of the shoreline, the steersman would lift his oar from the water and hold it in his hand as shown, his task successfully accomplished.

Under the stern of the first boat is a very realistically carved crocodile. To appreciate the detail of this fine sculpture one must hold the object in his hands or at least examine closely a good latex impression of this figure. The snout and especially the eye and the projection above the eye are done with almost phenomenal realism. This is one of the marks of a master sculptor and one of the details of the authentic Nilotic character of the scene. It is unfortunate that so much of the crocodile was lost in the damaged area.

There was something between the stern of the first boat and the prow of the second, but what remains is too sketchy for me to suggest any identification. The second boat is the most damaged of the three, and here conjecture almost gives way to imagination (see Figs. 15 and 16). I see what Dr. Seele described as a large bird and I think that even in the field there was general agreement that possibly a bird was represented. What I see reminds me of the primitive forms of falcons shown on the *serekh*s (palace facades) of the archaic sealings. If a falcon is portrayed here, it may be intended as the emblem of Horus. This may not fit well with our interpretation of the animal in the last boat, however, which may be the only divine figure shown in the procession.

[23] This is S 40 in the Gardiner Sign-List. Alan H. Gardiner, *Egyptian Grammar* (3d ed.; Oxford, 1957) p. 509. Variants in writing occur.

Dr. Seele's "long-eared animal" beneath the bird seems doubtful to me. If the creature in the last boat is to be regarded as a divinity, the pattern may be set for having only one such figure in a boat. The representation of an animal with long ears reminds one of the Seth-animal, which seems an improbable figure here. Furthermore, the size of the figure here would not be in proper proportion to the animal in the last boat, a factor that weighs against identifying these carved lines in the second boat as an animal. My suggestion is that the "ears" are the upraised arms of a man situated at the stern of the boat, comparable to the person in the first craft. What he may be doing is nearly beyond the realm of guessing, but if the only divine character in the scene occupies the third boat it is reasonable to postulate that the man in the second boat has turned to offer obeisance or to make some worshipful gesture toward the occupant of the last boat. This may also accord with the posture of the human figure shown on the river bank greeting the third boat. One can but deplore the poor condition of the sculpture of boat two.

Behind the second boat, fronting boat three, is an element that Dr. Seele logically took to be a mooring post (see Fig. 17). This is a reasonable interpretation, for the object is in the correct position at the prow of the boat and is certainly situated on the riverbank, being behind both the goat and the man, who also must be on the bank of the river and not far from the water. In aspect, however, it seems to me that this element more closely resembles the barbed harpoon, which became the phonogram *wʿ*.[24] As with the *was*-scepter, above, I do not see any reason for the presence of a harpoon, nor is a hieroglyph appropriate in this context. So, in spite of the sharp point at the upper end (so like a harpoon and so unfitting for the top of a mooring stake), the definite barb slightly below and to the left of the point, and the hint of a bit of rope attached to the barbed harpoon head, a mooring post seems the more plausible interpretation.

Immediately before the mooring post is a goat, standing on its hind legs and apparently browsing from the vegetation shown overhead. This is a common Near Eastern motif, with strong Asiatic affinities. Our example is particularly well cut. The goat is shown in very realistic fashion, and again the attention to detail and the excellence of the cutting of horns and ear is remarkable. The long twisted horns are like those of the species shown in the "Seasons" scenes of the Abu Gurob sun temple.[25]

To the left of the goat and in much smaller scale is the figure of a man who has his right arm at his side and the other arm upraised as if greeting or saluting the occupant of the last boat. To a large degree this figure is executed in accordance with what came to be the canon of Egyptian representation, with head

[24] The harpoon is T 21 in the Gardiner Sign-List (*ibid.*, p. 514); the mooring post is P 11 (p. 499).

[25] Cf. Smith, *A History of Egyptian Sculpture and Painting*, p. 180, Fig. 70.

shown in profile, shoulders squared as in the frontal position, and farther leg advanced before nearer one. There appears to be some depiction of the attire of this person, perhaps the end of a wide ribbon or sash worn about the waist.

Finally, there is the third boat and its affiliated elements (see Fig. 18). Beneath the prow of this craft there is a bit of leafy vegetable material, and below this a fish that may be using the vegetation for concealment or shade. This fish is quite definitely a Nile species.[26]

This boat is the best preserved of the three. It is represented with the prow tilted upward, as if the greater part of the weight of the animal in it is nearer the stern than the bow. This may be in part an artistic device, used in order to accommodate the fish in the space below the upraised prow. The element immediately behind the animal is generally taken to be a "standard," such as those ordinarily attributed to the boats on the Gerzean pottery. Most of the standard proper is missing, so that it is impossible to determine whether some emblem had been depicted. A less likely suggestion is that the element behind the animal is a mast, with the sail shown above its usual position because of the desire to represent the animal in greater size. The location of the element in the boat favors the interpretation that it is a standard.

A feature that sets this boat apart and may indicate the "religious" and "non-actual" character of the scene is the lack of any means of propulsion for the craft. There is no sail, nor oar, nor towrope, nor is a steersman shown, though perhaps it was intended that the boat should be towed.

The animal occupant of this boat is one of the most striking features of the entire relief, partly because its perfect preservation in the midst of so much damaged relief focuses attention on it at first glance, but mostly because of the mien of the creature and the fantastic presence of an animal as the sole occupant of a boat.

The identification of this animal may invite much discussion, for without a doubt there are uncertainties about it. The safest recourse is to call it a "quadruped," as Dr. Seele did in his preliminary report. It is desirable, however, if possible, to make more definite suggestions as to its identification, and so we shall be a bit more venturesome.

[26] Cf. Seele, second description, quoted above. My judgment is that the fish is not executed with the same accuracy as are the crocodile and goat. Because of the number and placing of the fins and the general aspect of the body, I am inclined to identify this fish as the *bûri* (Arabic; *Mugil cephalus*). This is K 3 in the Gardiner Sign-List, *Egyptian Grammar*, p. 477. See Ingrid Gamer-Wallert, *Fische und Fischkulte im alten Ägypten* ("Ägyptologische Abhandlungen," Vol. 21 [Wiesbaden, 1970]) pp. 14, 52–53, and Pls. I–II (Nos. 2, 3, 16, 25, 33, 36, 39, 45, 52, 53). Cf. also the fish models made of ivory, from the royal tomb at Nagadeh, in J. E. Quibell, *Archaic Objects* (Cairo, 1904–5) I 202–3, II, Pl. 41 (esp. 14030–14034). See Smith, *A History of Egyptian Sculpture and Painting*, Pl. A (upper right).

In the field, our first impression, as reflected in Dr. Seele's entry in the field register, was that the creature was a baboon. This was an overall impression, borne out by details such as the projecting forehead, the shape of the muzzle, and the hump above the shoulders, which may also hint at the existence of a kind of ruff. The primary objection to this identification is the pointed ears, a feature that does not seem to fit well with most animal species with the possible exception of some canines. Claws also seem to be rendered distinctly, but these may be only exaggerated portrayals of toes.

There are many models of baboons in Egypt from very early times, but most of them show the baboon in the squatting pose, which certainly was much easier for the sculptor to render than the standing position with the legs cut separately. Numerous baboon figurines were found at Abydos[27] and at Hierakonpolis.[28] The Abydos models were of various materials—ivory, "green glaze," limestone, and flint. Petrie comments that these figurines form a strange group and says that since a natural flint with some likeness to the head of a baboon was "placed with the rudest figures of baboons that we know, it seems that we have here the primitive fetish stones picked up because of their likeness to sacred animals, and perhaps venerated before any artificial images were attempted."[29] This statement of temporal priority of natural over man-made forms is open to question and does not lend itself to facile demonstration, but the incidence of baboon figurines does point to the prominence of that animal in early Egypt.

Petrie also remarked: "The resemblance of these baboons to those of the main deposit at Hierakonpolis of the age of Narmer should be noted."[30] The Hierakonpolis baboons are of limestone and faience and are, as Petrie says, quite similar to those from Abydos. Although different in posture from our animal, these models show the prominence of the forehead and the shape of the muzzle to good advantage, while several of the Hierakonpolis examples also show the "hump" of the shoulder that characterizes the animal on our censer.

One of the most interesting of the baboon figurines is that in Berlin, for it bears on its base the name of Narmer. H. A. Groenewegen-Frankfort comments: "The first historic monument, however—a baboon inscribed with the name of Narmer (Pl. X*c*) has both plastic articulation and coherence; it has, moreover, all the characteristics of later Egyptian sculpture—its cubism (though not yet pronounced), its frontality, its closed, static form."[31]

[27] W. M. F. Petrie, *Abydos* (London, 1902–3), Pt. I, 25 and Pl. LIII; Pt. II, 24, 27, 28 and Pls. I, II, VI, IX–XI.

[28] Barbara Adams, *Ancient Hierakonpolis* (Warminster, England, 1974) pp. 24–29, Pls. 18–23.

[29] Petrie, *Abydos*, Pt. II, 27.

[30] *Ibid.*, Pt. I, 25.

[31] *Arrest and Movement* (London, 1951) p. 24.

The best parallel for our animal is the model of the walking baboon from Abydos.[32] Except for the position of the tail, which in the figurine is carried behind rather than curved above the body, the resemblance to our sculpture is very close. Like the baboon on the Chicago censer, this model is done with great liveliness, as both Jean Capart and Petrie have noted.

The baboon that was venerated in Egypt and associated with the god Thoth is the Arabian or hamadryas baboon, native to northeast Africa and the Arabian coast of the Red Sea. With its long tail, doglike muzzle, and pronounced ruff, it resembles very closely the form shown on the censer.[33]

Only one other suggestion has been made concerning the identification of this animal. Bernard V. Bothmer voiced the idea that the animal may be a leopard or a panther. W. B. Emery gives several forms of panthers from seal impressions found at Sakkarah.[34] It seems to me that the shape of the head and muzzle, the pointed ears, and the carriage of the tail make this identification more unlikely than that of a baboon; besides, the animal on the censer just doesn't look feline to me, although this is a matter of personal impression. It may be argued, moreover, that if we should have a representation of a deity here, one might expect the baboon, an early form of Thoth, rather than the panther, which would be less appropriate as a religious symbol.

What is more, panthers and boats make an anomalous combination. Although baboons are seldom depicted with boats, there does exist a rare representation of a baboon standing on the prow of a boat under construction, while another (it may be a monkey—much of the figure is missing) is shown elsewhere in the scene. This is from the excellently decorated tomb of Nefer on the south side

[32] Petrie, *Abydos*, Pt. II, Pls. I, VII (86), and p. 25 ("simple but spirited work"). Cf. Capart, *Primitive Art*, Fig. 147 (center) and p. 186 ("the gait has been seized and rendered with much spirit").

[33] This baboon is usually called *Papio hamadryas*, but J. H. McGregor gives *Comopithecus hamadryas* (*Encyclopedia Americana* [New York, 1970] III 8).

I am indebted to one of the Oriental Institute Museum docents, Mrs. Ralph W. Burhoe, for informing me that a visitor to the museum casually commented that the animal on the censer is a hamadryas. Mrs. Burhoe did some checking in several sources and compiled a statement that she relayed to me by letter: "Papio Hamadryas: sacred baboon, sacred to the ancient Egyptians. Found in Arabia and N. E. Africa. Although two of the five species of Papio have short tails, Papio Hamadryas has a long tail. It and its relatives have dog-like muzzles and a shoulder ruff or hump. Their tails are carried in a characteristic arched manner, as in the illustration of the yellow baboon. The ears shown in the illustration are not too dissimilar from those on the 'censer-seal.' . . . I think you could feel reasonably confident in identifying the figure as a baboon."

Some lively scenes showing baboons are described by W. Stevenson Smith. These are from the reliefs of Unis and from the Cairo relief from the chapel of Tep-em-ankh (Mariette D 11) at Sakkarah (*A History of Egyptian Sculpture and Painting*, pp. 182, 187, and 342 [Fig. 225]). See also G. Maspero, *Le Musée égyptien* (Cairo, 1907) II, Pl. XI (cf. pp. 30–32).

[34] *Ḥor-Aḥa*, p. 86.

of the causeway of Unis at Sakkarah.[35] In his chapter on Egyptian amulets, E. A. W. Budge shows a baboon standing in a boat of archaic form and presenting the *wḏ3t*-eye to the moon god, Iaḥ.[36] Monkeys are often depicted in sailing vessels.[37]

The significance of identifying the animal shown on the censer lies in the association of the figure with some deity worshipped in ancient Egypt. We have already argued the possibility that the scene depicts a riverine religious procession and have stated that the figure may be a baboon that stands for Thoth, the god of wisdom and writing, the scribe of the gods. Thoth is often shown as an ibis-headed man, but even earlier he may have been represented in the form of a baboon.[38] Petrie states: "The oldest historic figures of gods are the baboons of Tehuti carved in diorite, which were found in the lower temple of Khafra, the granite temple at Gizeh. These have been left unheeded since they were found sixty years ago."[39] Petrie suggests, too, that the baboon may have been worshipped independently, before its association with Thoth.[40]

Thoth was one of the great deities in the Egyptian pantheon and is discussed in all of the standard works on Egyptian religion. One of the most concise statements regarding the worship of Thoth at an early period is given by W. B. Emery:

> Thoth, a moon god and patron of the sciences, was apparently worshipped as early as the First Dynasty, for the baboon (cynocephalus) was one of his sacred animals in conjunction

[35] A line drawing of this scene is given in Landström, *Ships*, p. 38, Fig. 103. It would appear that actual animals were intended and that they have no religious association.

[36] *Amulets and Talismans* (originally *Amulets and Superstitions*; New Hyde Park, N.Y., 1961) p. 141.

[37] For example, see the line drawings in Landström, *Ships*, p. 42, Figs. 109, 113, p. 43, Fig. 117. A photographic version of the scene shown in his Fig. 109 may be found in J. de Morgan, *Fouilles à Dahchour 1894–1895* (Vienna, 1903) Pl. XIX. This is from the tomb of In-Snefru-ishtef, which dates from the time of Snefru (see Porter and Moss, *Bibliography* [Oxford, 1931] III 235). De Morgan gives the name of the tomb owner as Snefrou-Ani-Mert-f.

[38] See Jaroslav Černý, *Ancient Egyptian Religion* (London, 1952) p. 21, quoted in note 40, below.

[39] W. M. F. Petrie, *Religious Life in Ancient Egypt* (Boston, 1924) p. 19. The original find was made by Mariette and fragments were found by Hölscher. See Uvo Hölscher, *Das Grabdenkmal des Königs Chephren* ("Veröffentlichungen der Ernst von Sieglin Expedition," Vol. 1 [Leipzig, 1912]) pp. 10, 42, 83.

[40] Petrie, *Religious Life in Ancient Egypt*, p. 80. Černý also comments: "Numerous small statuettes of baboons and a representation of this animal on an ivory label suggest that its cult dates from the beginning of Egyptian history; it may have been practised at Khmun (Hermopolis), where presumably it preceded the cult of the ibis of Thoth. The original reading of the name of this baboon god is uncertain; but later he was called Hedj-wer or Hedjwerew and interpreted as the "'Great White One' or 'Whitest of the Great Ones'" (*Ancient Egyptian Religion*, p. 21).

with Apis on two monuments dated to the reign of Udimu. The standard of Thoth also appears on palettes of the Predynastic period and a shrine of this god certainly existed in the time of Narmer.[41]

In summary, it appears that there may be an association between this deity and the animal shown so vigorously on the limestone censer from Cemetery L. The scene in sunk relief, perhaps the oldest example of that technique known from the Nile Valley, is the representation of a river procession involving the god Thoth in his form of a baboon; other deities may also have been participants in this procession. Coupled with these features is the question of possible foreign cultural relationships, a combination that makes the censer an object of widespread interest.

Described at the outset of this article as "one of the most significant finds from Egyptian Nubia," this censer is surely worthy of that designation and is an apt subject to be presented in honor of George R. Hughes and in memory of his friend and associate, Keith C. Seele. The censer will be the subject of much discussion in Nubiological and Egyptological circles for years to come.

[41] *Archaic Egypt*, p. 126.

SHIPWRECKED SAILOR, LINES 184–85

Mordechai Gilula

The story of the Shipwrecked Sailor is one of the most famous examples of ancient Egyptian literary art. It is a sketch, in very concise form, of the literary devices that were displayed more fully later on in the Stories of the High Priests of Memphis. But unlike the latter, which were written in a language closely resembling the colloquial idiom of the time (as is clearly evident from non-literary writings), the style used by the writer of this story is apparently a literary style. Although easily understood, it cannot serve as a representative model of Middle Egyptian sentence patterns, for it abounds in unusual and rare grammatical constructions (or "carefully chosen phraseology"[1]). One such construction appears to me to be the maxim that concludes the story—lines 184–85: *ỉn m rdỉt mw n ꜣpd ḥḏ tꜣ n sft.f dwꜣ(w)*. All translators more or less agree on the meaning of the sentence, illustrated here by the most recent English translation by W. K. Simpson: "Who gives water to the goose at daybreak when it is to be slaughtered in the morning?"[2] Although this translation (like many others) would appear to convey the meaning of the sentence to the general reader, it is phrased in such a way that it may leave the inexperienced student uncertain as to its construction. The first obscurity is found at the beginning of the sentence, which is not discussed by the current grammars.[3] I know from my own teaching experience that the way in which this sentence is commonly translated often leads the reader to the mistaken conclusion that it is a participial statement.[4] This misunderstanding has already been remarked upon by Erman, who suggested that if it were a participial statement, *rdỉ* should be expected and not *rdỉt*[5] (the required form is actually *dd*). He was also perplexed by the writing of the letter *m* and doubted whether *ỉn m*, as it is written here,

[1] Adolf Erman, *The Ancient Egyptians* (New York, 1966) p. 29.

[2] William Kelly Simpson, ed., *The Literature of Ancient Egypt* (New Haven and London, 1972) p. 56.

[3] The portion of the sentence beginning with *ḥḏ tꜣ* is cited by Gustave Lefebvre (*Grammaire de l'égyptien classique* ["BdE" XII (2d ed.; 1955)] § 386, p. 196).

[4] Alan H. Gardiner, *Egyptian Grammar* (3d ed.; London, 1957) §§ 373, 227,3.

[5] Adolf Erman, "Die Geschichte des Schiffbrüchigen," *ZÄS* 43 (1906) 24. See Gardiner, *Grammar*, §§ 373, 227,3; Kurt Sethe, *Das aegyptische Verbum im Altaegyptischen, Neuaegyptischen*

could be the interrogative "who," which throughout the text is written *n-m*. Such a writing of *m* is frequent, however, in Old Egyptian,[6] and all translators, including Erman, his doubts notwithstanding, have translated this sentence in the interrogative. If it is not a participial statement, the initial *ỉn* is a problem. One possible interpretation, which gives virtually the same meaning, is to take *ỉn* as the preposition that introduces the agent or the subject of the infinitive.[7] That is, instead of the usual construction **rdỉt mw n ꜣpd ỉn* N, "the giving of water to a goose by N," we have an inversion of the word order, possibly because of the interrogative *m*, "by whom is the giving of water to a goose?" In fact, an actual example of the normal construction of this kind is found in exactly the same context (see below). But since the suggested initial use of *ỉn* remains to be proved and no other example seems to be forthcoming, I should like to propose a second tentative solution.

If *ỉn* is not the agent indicator, it may perhaps be the preposition *n* in initial position. Although such a use is exceedingly rare, it cannot be rejected offhandedly. Two good Middle Egyptian examples of it are known: P. Kahun, Pl. XXXI, l. 8;[8] and Eloquent Peasant B1 79, in the compound preposition *ỉn mrwt*.[9] An Old Egyptian example is found in Edel.[10] Its meaning is "for," "because of," and when it occurs together with the interrogative *m* it can well be translated "to what avail," "why."[11] There is no other example of initial *ỉn-m*,[12] but other initial adverbial interrogatives, although rare, do occur.[13] One of these follows exactly the proposed pattern: *ḥr-m pꜣ nḥm tꜣ bꜣkt wnt*

und Koptischen (3 vols.; Leipzig, 1899–1902) II, § 753. A feminine participle (with *t*) is found occasionally, but only after feminine nouns.

[6] Elmar Edel, *Altägyptische Grammatik* ("Analecta Orientalia," Vols. 34 and 39 [Rome, 1955–64]) §§ 203, 1006; Lefebvre, *Grammaire*, § 679; *ECT* V 89*d*.

[7] Gardiner, *Grammar*, § 300.

[8] Cited in *ibid.*, § 148.5.

[9] *Ibid.*, § 181, p. 136, n. 16; see also § 164.

[10] *Grammatik*, § 757.

[11] One would expect *r-m*, "to what purpose," to be used in this meaning; but *r-m* (Gardiner, *Grammar*, § 496) generally has the connotation of a concrete attainable purpose, so that *n-m* is perhaps more suitable to express the abstract notion of futility. In Lebensmüde 103–29, *n-m* is generally translated "to whom"; there it can perhaps also be rendered "to what avail," "why." Other examples of *n-m* with different meanings can be found in Gardiner, *Grammar*, § 495.

[12] One possible example of *n-m* (not *ỉn-m*) having the proposed meaning may be Eloquent Peasant B1 201: *n-m tr sḏr r šp*. Usually translated "who sleeps until dawn?" it appears to me to make better sense when translated "why spend the night (i.e., wait) until morning?" that is, "what good is it to wait until morning to cross the river when to travel by night or by day is equally dangerous?" An example with an indisputable infinitive, however, would be more welcome.

[13] See Gardiner, *Grammar*, p. 405, n. 9 and *ECT* III 202; Edel, *Grammatik*, § 1119.

ḥnꜥ.ỉ rdỉ.tỉ n kỉỉ.[14] Peet's translation is "why has the female slave who was with me been taken away and given to another?"[15] Just as in the proposed analysis of the sentence under discussion, this sentence consists of an initial adverbial interrogative followed by an infinitive and its direct object. Although "distinctly tinged with the idiom of Late Egyptian,"[16] this text can be considered a good example of nonliterary Middle Egyptian. *Pꜣ* and *tꜣ* are not necessarily the Late Egyptian definite articles; they may, instead, be the Middle Egyptian anaphoric demonstrative article "this," which is required by the context. In our sentence—a maxim in a literary text—any kind of demonstrative would be out of place.

This tentative analysis of the first part of the sentence appears to me to be preferable to the usual analysis because, unlike the latter, it does not violate any proved grammatical rule, nor is there any evidence to contradict it. My translation of the first part of the sentence would be "why give water to a goose?" (literally, "to what avail is the giving of water to a goose?"), that is, it is useless and senseless to give water to a goose. This is also the spirit of the customary translation.[17]

The prevailing translation of the second half of the sentence is equally misleading. The words *ḥḏ tꜣ* are generally connected with the preceding line and translated "at dawn," "at daybreak." Faulkner[18] gives *ḥḏ tꜣ* the meaning "the land becomes bright," that is, "dawn." It is true that the words *ḥḏ tꜣ* can sometimes have the meaning of "dawn" or "morning,"[19] but the combination *ḥḏ tꜣ* is not a lexical unit. *Ḥḏ* is an adjective and a verb; *tꜣ* is a noun. Their juxtaposition results in a grammatical unit the construction and meaning of which vary according to the context.[20] In some cases the meaning "morning" or "dawn" seems to fit, particularly when preceded by a preposition;[21] in other

[14] T. Eric Peet, "Two Eighteenth Dynasty Letters: Papyrus Louvre 3230," *JEA* 12 (1926) Pl. XVII, lower part l. 2, opposite p. 70 (quoted by Gardiner, *Grammar*, p. 405, n. 9, as *ZÄS* 55 [1918] 85, l. 2).

[15] Peet, *JEA* 12 (1926) 71.

[16] *Ibid.*, p. 70.

[17] Gardiner, *Grammar*, p. 401, 2.

[18] Raymond O. Faulkner, *Concise Dictionary of Middle Egyptian* (Oxford, 1964) p. 181.

[19] *Wb* III 207–8.

[20] *Tꜣ ḥḏ* in the stative is found in Admonitions X 1. *Mk tꜣ ḥḏ* is found in *ECT* I 247*b*. *Tꜣ ḥḏ* after a possible *ḫr m-ḫt* appears in P. Westcar II 15. Another example after *ỉr m* is perhaps "Urk" III 34. A god by the name of *Ḥḏ tꜣ* is mentioned in *ECT* V 387*b*, 388*c*, and 398*i*.

[21] See, for example, Pyr 1334*a*: *ḏr ḥḏt tꜣ* (*ḏr sḏmt.f*), translated into English by Raymond O. Faulkner (*The Ancient Egyptian Pyramid Texts* [Oxford, 1969]) as "at dawn," but into German by Edel as "bevor die Erde hell werden wird" (*Grammatik*, § 736). *ECT* I 250*b* has an *r sḏmt.f* construction. Pyr 1807*c* has *m ḥḏ tꜣ* (*m*+infinitive). See also *Wb* III 207–8 and the references therein.

cases the meaning "eve," "the day (or evening) before" appears more suitable (see below). But to translate every occurrence of *ḥḏ* and *tꜣ* automatically as "morning," "dawn," or "eve" would be wrong; and it would be even more fallacious to render *ḥḏ tꜣ* as an adverbial ("at dawn," "in the morning") when it is not preceded by a preposition. The following features should be noted: (*a*) when not preceded by a preposition, *ḥḏ tꜣ* is found mostly in *sḏm.f* or *sḏm.n.f* constructions; (*b*) contrary to what might be assumed from most of its translations, it is always a main initial sentence, syntactically independent of the preceding one; (*c*) it is never preceded by *ỉw*; (*d*) it is always followed by an adverb or an adverbial phrase. This can mean only one thing—that it is an emphatic sentence. *Ḥḏ tꜣ* is found in the following types of sentences:[22]

I. *sḏm.n.f.*—Two patterns are distinguished here.

A. In one, the adverb *dwꜣw sp* 2, "very early," and the particle *rf* are integral parts of the sentence. This pattern is always followed by a main independent sentence, for example, Sinuhe B 248: *ḥḏ.n rf* (particle) *tꜣ dwꜣw sp* 2 *ỉw ỉw ỉꜣš n.ỉ.* In such sentences *ḥḏ.n tꜣ* has always been analyzed and translated as a temporal clause, "when dawn came and it was morning, I was summoned."[23] But *ḥḏ.n tꜣ* cannot be an adverbial clause, neither here nor in the sentences described below under IB, because initial finite verb forms such as the *sḏm.f* and *sḏm.n.f* are never adverbial in meaning unless introduced by a preposition, as for example, *ḫr m-ḫt sḏm.f*; *ḫr m-ḫt sḏm.n.f.*[24] Gardiner's "virtual clauses of time with verbal predicate" that *precede* the main clause[25] do not really exist. All sentences analyzed thus are clear cases of confusion between the *structure* and the *translation* of the sentence. The fact that such sentences may be readily translated as temporal (adverbial) clauses does not mean that they are such. They are, in fact, emphatic sentences, the adverbial "adjunct" of which is the grammatical, as well as the logical, predicate, and this adjunct should be stressed in the translation. Often it is difficult to translate such sentences literally into a modern European language; the best way is to reverse the roles of the elements in the translation and to render the *sḏm.f* or *sḏm.n.f* as a temporal clause even though it is not one in form.[26] Thus, while it is sometimes convenient to translate *ḥḏ.n tꜣ* as the adverbial "at dawn," this translation does not

[22] The discussion is of Middle Egyptian examples only. One or two 19th Dynasty references have been included, inasmuch as they rely on an earlier source and are important to the argument. Examples later than the 18th Dynasty can be found in part in the *Belegstellen* to *Wb* III 207–8. See also Karl-Heinz Priese, "Zur Sprache der ägyptischen Inschriften der Könige von Kusch," *ZÄS* 98 (1972) 122.

[23] Simpson, *Literature*, p. 71; see also Lefebvre, *Grammaire*, § 587*c*, p. 284; Gardiner, *Grammar*, § 212.

[24] Gardiner, *Grammar*, § 156; § 178, 4–6.

[25] *Ibid.*, § 212 and the references therein.

[26] H. J. Polotsky, *Collected Papers* (Jerusalem, 1971) pp. 49, 62 n. 1, and 78–79, esp. n. 19.

reflect the true nature of the sentence, which is not adverbial even "virtually." This is the explanation for the sentences described below under IB. The explanation does not account, however, for the sentences included in IA, which must be handled differently in translation. Their pattern is unique in its literal self-repetition. It occurs again in Hirtengeschichte 22–23: *ḥḏ.n rf tꜣ dwꜣw sp* 2 *iw ir mi ḏd.f*, and also in Hammamat 199 and *ECT* VII 36*r*. The particle *rf* is a mandatory element. It does not have a strengthening function but serves to connect the sentence with the preceding narrative. It indicates the resumption of the story in a new paragraph. This stereotypic sentence appears to have been an idiomatic literary phrase used to introduce a new section in a story.[27] The paucity of examples does not indicate that such a use was rare. On the contrary, its extensive use in Piankhi's victory hymn (only this time in the *sḏm.f*: *ḥḏ rf tꜣ dwꜣw sp* 2, "Urk" III 12, 30, 37, 40, 53) and also in Destruction of Mankind 34 may suggest a much wider use in Middle Egyptian. *Ḥḏ.n rf tꜣ dwꜣw sp* 2 is a complete sentence. The repeated adverb *dwꜣw sp* 2 (that is, *dwꜣw dwꜣw*, "very early") is the predicate of the emphatic *ḥḏ n tꜣ*. Since a second tense as a literary opening formula is rather unusual, it stands to reason that in this particular kind of sentence the emphatic form was automatically required because of the repeated adverb, in exactly the same way that *m dwn m dwn* in Late Egyptian under certain conditions necessitated a second tense.[28] A literal translation of this opening phrase, "it was very early when it dawned," would be awkward; therefore, in the translation I would connect the phrase with the following sentence and render one of them as temporal, even though syntactically they are two independent sentences. One possibility would be to make the first sentence adverbial (which, in fact, is done by all translators)—"when it was very early in the morning" (or, as suggested by Hintze [see n. 27], "on the next

[27] Fritz Hintze (*Untersuchungen zu Stil und Sprache neuägyptischer Erzählungen*, Vol. 1 [Deutsche Akademie der Wissenschaften zu Berlin, Institut für Orientforschung "Veröffentlichung," No. 2 (Berlin, 1950)] p. 11, n. 2) saw this formula as an extension of the *ḥḏ.n tꜣ* in Sinuhe B 20 and 129 and Carnarvon Tablet 14. These, treated below in B, are *not* narrative formulae. Hintze believed that the sentence in question, in all its variations, meant nothing more than "am nächsten Tage." So also did K. Sethe in his *Erläuterungen zu den ägyptischen Lesestücken* (reprint; Hildesheim, 1971) p. 131, re p. 82, l. 8 (see below, note 33). The Late Egyptian formula *ḫr ir m-ḫt tꜣ ḥḏ* 2 *n hrw ḫpr* is discussed by Hintze, *Stil und Sprache* I 15 ff. On p. 10 he dwells on the connection between this formula and P. Westcar II 15: [*ḫr m-ḫt*] *tꜣ ḥḏ* 2 [*n*] *h*[*rw ḫpr*].

[28] See Sarah Israelit-Groll, *The Negative Verbal System of Late Egyptian* (London and New York, 1970) p. 148, but also p. 77. Wolfhart Westendorf in his article "Zu zwei Tagesformeln der ägyptischen Literatursprache" (*ZÄS* 79 [1954] 65–68) has explained the second *dwꜣw* in *dwꜣw sp* 2 as a stative (old perfective) and translated *dwꜣw dwꜣw* as "als der Morgen morgte" or "als die Frühe früh war." Such an interpretation was rejected by Alan H. Gardiner (*Notes on the Story of Sinuhe* [Paris, 1916] p. 93) in favor of the now customary reading *dwꜣw dwꜣw*, "very early" (Faulkner, *Dictionary*, p. 310; *Wb* V 422). See especially *ECT* VI 314*f*: *dwꜣw sp* 2 *rʿ nb sp* 2, "very early every single day."

day," "on the next morning") "I was summoned." Perhaps a better solution would be to retain the emphasis in the first sentence by making the second one adverbial: "it was very early in the morning when the summons came to me." Thus Hirtengeschichte 22–23 quoted above would be translated: "it was very early in the morning when it was done as he said."

B. The second *sḏm.n.f* pattern is that of a normal emphatic sentence. The predicate (the stressed adverbial adjunct) can be any adverb or adverbial (circumstantial) sentence. The particle *rf* may or may not be present.

"Urk" IV 896, 4–8: (Tuthmosis III died and joined his god) *ḥḏ.n rf tꜣ dwꜣw ḫpr ỉtn wbn pt bꜣkꜣ.tỉ nsw bỉty ꜥꜣ-ḫprw-rꜥ sꜣ rꜥ [ỉmn-ḥtp] dỉ ꜥnḫ smnw ḥr nst nt ỉt.f.* Here *dwꜣw* is not the adverb "early" but rather the noun "dawn," "morning." The opening sentence is followed by three parallel adverbial clauses in the stative (old perfective), but only the fourth one is stressed. As mentioned above, such sentences are sometimes conveniently translated by rendering the first main sentence as an adverbial. It is not necessary to translate *ḥḏ.n tꜣ* here as a temporal, a better translation being "no sooner had the land become bright—dawn having broken, the sun having risen, the sky having brightened—than the king Amenophis II was established on his father's throne."

Carnarvon Tablet 14: *ḥḏ.n tꜣ ỉw.ỉ ḥr.f mỉ wn bỉk*, "no sooner had day dawned than I was upon him as though it were a falcon."[29]

Sinuhe B 129: *ḥḏ.n tꜣ (R)tnw ỉỉ.t(ỉ)*, "hardly had it dawned when Retenu (that is, the people of Retenu) came."

Sinuhe B 20: "I walked by night"[30] *ḥḏ.n tꜣ pḥ.n.ỉ Ptn*, it was as I reached Peten that day broke," or "I had barely reached Peten when day broke." *Pḥ.n.ỉ* is a circumstantial *sḏm.n.f.*

All these are examples of the emphatic *sḏm.n.f* used in past narrative passages. Later texts used the *sḏm.f* form in such passages.[31]

II. *sḏm.f.*—That this is an emphatic *sḏm.f* is indicated by the considerations mentioned above and also by the fact of its being a *sḏm.f* of an adjective verb.[32] It is always followed by a circumstantial clause or a prepositional phrase, its predicate. It is used to describe a general quality or a recurrent daily activity[33] stated by the predicate. *Ḥḏ tꜣ* in our passage also appears to me to be an

[29] A paraphrase of Gardiner's translation, *Grammar*, p. 160.

[30] Version C in Aylward M. Blackman, *Middle-Egyptian Stories*, Pt. I ("Bibliotheca Aegyptiaca" II [Brussels, 1932]) 12 is emphatic: *ỉrr.ỉ šmt r tr n ḫꜣwy*, "it was by night that I walked."

[31] E.g., *ZÄS* 28 (1890) 60: *ḥḏ tꜣ.wy ḥms.kwỉ ḥr wsrw*, "when the sun rose I had been seated at an oar"; see also *Belegstellen* to *Wb* III 207–8.

[32] H. J. Polotsky, *Etudes de syntaxe copte* (Cairo, 1944) p. 86.

[33] BD, chap. XV, l. 23 (Ani), E. A. Wallis Budge, *The Book of the Dead: The Chapters of Coming Forth by Day* I (London, 1898) 42. A difficult place is Sethe, *Ägyptische Lesestücke* (reprint;

emphatic *sḏm.f*, although a prospective one. Ever since its first translation by Golénischeff[34] it has been translated adverbially, "at daybreak," "in the morning." Sethe even believed it to be an expression for "Vorabend": "am Vorabend des Schlachtens sie morgen."[35] This interpretation of *ḥḏ tꜣ* had first been expressed by him earlier.[36] The passage mentioned there is now found in "Urk" IV 1860, 13: *sꜥḥꜥ ḏd ỉn nsw ḏs.f ḥḏ tꜣ n ḥb sd*. The translation "the erection of the *ḏd*-pillar by the king himself on the eve of the *ḥb-sd*" is correct in that the *ḏd*-pillar was indeed erected on the eve of the jubilee feast. It does not, however, represent the true structure of the passage, since the expression *ḥḏ tꜣ* is not necessarily adverbial. The rendering "on the eve of" happens to be suitable in the context because of the meaning of *ḥḏ tꜣ n* . . . , which is in all probability a prospective emphatic *sḏm.f* with the dative *n*. Its literal translation is "it is to (or, for) the . . . that the land will become (or, becomes) bright," that is, when morning comes something is supposed to happen, or some action is expected to take place. I believe there are two independent sentences here: (1) "The erection of the *ḏd*-pillar by the king himself"; this part of the sentence occurs independently also in "Urk" IV 1860, 9; and (2) "it is for the *ḥb-sd* that the sun will rise," that is, when morning comes the jubilee feast will begin, as everything is ready and prepared for the festival. *Ḥḏ tꜣ* is not adverbial in structure but can be rendered adverbially for the sake of a smoother translation. The expression *ḥḏ tꜣ n* (emphatic *sḏm.f* + dative *n*) is perhaps idiomatic, as it appears to have the same meaning also in the passage *ỉst ḥḏ tꜣ n smꜣ rmṯ ỉn nṯrt m sww.sn nw ḫntyt*.[37] This is a complete independent parenthetic informative sentence that is not a part of the chain of events. If the passage were omitted, the story would continue without interruption. It is clearly a new sentence, syntactically independent of its immediate contextual surrounding. It can neither be connected adverbially with the preceding sentence, nor be an initial temporal clause, because the following sentence *ḏd mdw ỉn ḥm n Rꜥ*, "then said the majesty of Re," has to be syntactically independent. Even if *ḏd mdw* has been written by mistake for *ḏd.ỉn ḥm n Rꜥ*, the *sḏm.ỉn.f* sentence, being a narrative continuative form, could not support a preceding temporal clause.

Hildesheim, 1959) p. 82, l. 8: *ḥḏ tꜣ ḥtp n dmỉ*, which Sethe analyzed as a "Temporalsatz (am nächsten Morgen)." *Ḥḏ tꜣ* can always be translated "on the next day," but that it is a temporal clause is highly questionable. The context is obscure and the meaning of the sentence is not clear.

[34] Accessible to me through Erman's quotation in *ZÄS* 43 (1906) 24.

[35] Kurt Sethe, "Bemerkungen zur Geschichte des Schiffbrüchigen," *ZÄS* 44 (1907) 87.

[36] *Idem*, *Beiträge zur ältesten Geschichte Ägyptens* ("UGAÄ" III [Leipzig, 1903]) p. 136, n. 2.

[37] A. de Buck, *Egyptian Readingbook* (2d ed.; Leiden, 1963) p. 125, "The Myth of the Destruction of Mankind," l. 10.

Because a night and dawn were still to follow before the goddess would get drunk and bungle her mission, the translation of *ḥḏ tꜣ* as "morning"[38] is inappropriate, but the meaning "the eve of" is acceptable. "It was the eve of the day on which the killing of mankind by the goddess was to have taken place. . . ."[39] Again this is possible because of the prospective emphatic nature of *ḥḏ tꜣ n* . . . , which in this case cannot in any way be considered a temporal clause.[40] Its literal translation (to paraphrase Wilson's translation in *ANET*, p. 11*b*) is, more or less, "It was for the slaughter of mankind by the goddess that the day was about to break." And this is exactly the meaning and structure of our sentence. *Ḥḏ tꜣ n smꜣ.sn* and *ḥḏ tꜣ n sft.f dwꜣ(w)* are not only built on the same pattern, but they also have the same meaning. The literal translation of our sentence should be "It is to its early slaughter that the day will break."

The construction of the first part of the sentence remains uncertain. I have proposed two tentative solutions. One is to interpret *ỉn* as the agent indicator in initial position, in reverse word order to the usual construction (represented by "Urk" IV 1860, 13: *sꜥḥꜥ ḏd ỉn nsw ḏs.f ḥḏ tꜣ n ḥb sd*). The other is to interpret *ỉn* in *ỉn m* as the preposition *n* in initial position. The meaning, however, is clearly conveyed by all translations.

In the second part of the sentence *ḥḏ tꜣ* does not mean "morning." *Ḥḏ tꜣ n* . . . appears to be an idiomatic expression in which *n* is a required preposition. It is a prospective emphatic *sḏm.f*, but, for convenience and for stylistic reasons only, it can be translated "on the eve of." Sethe translated this sentence "gibt man einer Gans Wasser am Vorabend, wenn man sie morgen schlachten will?" (literally, "am Vorabend des Schlachtens sie morgen").[41] The meaning is simply "what good is there in giving water to a goose just before it is killed?" and it was so understood by all translators.

[38] Erman, *The Ancient Egyptians*, p. 49: "Now it was the morning whereon the goddess purposed to slay mankind."

[39] The rest of the sentence "at the season (or, dates) of their faring upstream" is not clear and in the translation should perhaps be connected with the end of the preceding sentence, "then Re, the king of Upper and Lower Egypt, came together with these gods to see this beer—it was the day before the killing of mankind by the goddess was to have taken place—at the time of their faring upstream."

[40] An *ỉsṯ* + emphatic *sḏm.f* (most probably prospective) is found in Sethe, *Ägyptische Lesestücke*, p. 70, ll. 18–19.

[41] *ZÄS* 44 (1907) 87.

THE ROYAL SCRIBE AMENMOSE, SON OF PENZERTI AND MUTEMONET: HIS MONUMENTS IN EGYPT AND ABROAD

Labib Habachi

While Ahmed Fakhry was serving as Chief Inspector of Antiquities for Upper Egypt, it was reported to him in 1948 that some inhabitants of Khokha in the Theban Necropolis had succeeded in penetrating a tomb that was situated beneath their houses.[1] Upon inspecting it, he found that portions of its decorated walls had been sawn out. Steps were taken to punish the people responsible for the damage and also to prevent further desecration of the tomb. Enough remained in the tomb to suggest the importance of its owner, the royal scribe Amenmose, who is the subject of the present study.

Having become interested in the decoration of this tomb, in 1952 I obtained a small grant to clear the debris that filled the major portion of it. During the clearance a curious bust was brought to light, inscribed with the beginning of the name of the owner's father. This led me to search for other monuments inscribed with the name of the owner or the names of his parents. Apart from the tomb and the father's bust, I found that two monuments had already been attributed to Amenmose. Two more and also a bust of his mother had previously been published but had been wrongly assigned to a period later than that in which Amenmose actually lived. I was also able to add a statue of him, unknown before.

Realizing the importance of the tomb, I invited my friends George R. Hughes and Charles F. Nims to inspect it and to give me their invaluable advice. At Hughes's request Nims was kind enough to record the contents of the tomb

[1] Ahmed Fakhry, who was much interested in the Theban Necropolis, published the list of its tombs, from 335 to 367, giving the names of the owners, their main titles, their dates, the position of each tomb, and the scholar responsible for its discovery ("A Report on the Inspectorate of Upper Egypt," *ASAE* 46 [1947] 25–54; see pp. 37–45). With this list he completed numbering the tombs discovered in the Theban Necropolis up until 1936, following the Supplement by Reginald Engelbach (1924) to the Gardiner and Weigall catalogue published in 1913. I hope that more attention may be directed to the Theban Necropolis; in the last few years many of its tombs have suffered the same sort of damage as the tomb of Amenmose.

(photograph Nos. 10604–10612 of the Oriental Institute of the University of Chicago). Here, in discussing the monuments inscribed with the name of the owner and the names of his parents, I offer this study as a modest tribute to George R. Hughes, a great scholar and gentleman, whose help and friendship I have constantly enjoyed during the past thirty years.

1. The Tomb (No. 373 in the Theban Necropolis)

It is not my intention here to publish the tomb of Amenmose—neither time nor the scope of this *Festschrift* would allow that. The *Bibliography* by Porter and Moss, which lists every scene, whether published or unpublished, in all the tombs at the Theban Necropolis known at the time of the publication of the second edition in 1960 (Nos. 1–409), was the first work to describe each scene in the tomb of Amenmose, on the basis of the photographs taken by Nims. According to these descriptions, the scenes in the tomb show the owner adoring various divinities, especially those of the necropolis; some of the scenes also include hymns or representations from the Book of Gates. The tomb owner's name occurs many times as "Amenmessu," with the title of "scribe of the altar of the Lord of the Two Lands"; we learn that he lived during the Ramesside period and that the name of his father was Iny.[2] Subsequently, in an addendum, the period during which he lived was specified as the reign of Ramesses II, the name of his father was corrected to Penzerti, and that of his mother was given as Iny or Inty, that is, Mutemonet.[3]

There is no need to add to the description of the scenes except to say that the owner is also referred to by the simple title of "royal scribe" and that his mother is given the title *Šmʿyt n ʾImn*, "Chantress of Amun." Of special importance among the many divinities depicted or named in the tomb is Neit, whose name appears in the shrine at the end of the tomb. There she is invoked in an inscription carved on a scale larger than that of the other inscriptions (Fig. 19). We shall see below how this goddess was much venerated by Amenmose.

2. Bust of Penzerti (No. 171 in the new Luxor Museum)

The limestone bust of Penzerti is 37.5 cm. high, but originally it was nearly 50 cm. in height. It represents a man wearing a wig; his body is enveloped in a robe so that no arms are visible (Fig. 20). Whereas most such busts are uninscribed, ours bears the following inscription: "(1) Favored through Amun and Shu, the judge P[enzerti], (2) lord of the whole of Upper Egypt, (3) lord of

[2] Bertha Porter and Rosalind L. B. Moss, *Topographical Bibliography of Ancient Egyptian Hieroglyphic Texts, Reliefs and Paintings* I: *The Theban Necropolis*, Pt. 1, *Private Tombs* (2d ed.; Oxford, 1960) pp. 428 (plan), 433–34.

[3] *Ibid.*, Pt. 2, *Royal Tombs and Smaller Cemeteries* (1964) p. xvii, "Addenda to Volume I, Part 1, Errata."

the territory of Lower Egypt." The epithet in column 2 may refer to the god Amun, while that in column 3 may refer to the god Shu. Although only the first sign of the name of Amenmose's father is preserved, there is no doubt that this bust belongs to him, since it was discovered in his son's tomb.

One may ask where the bust was originally placed. The plan of the tomb[4] shows that on either side of the entrance to the second hall there is a niche. The one on the right contains two statues, while there is no record of anything having been found in the one on the left. This niche would have been the most likely place for the bust of Penzerti. The back of his bust is flat and has traces of plaster still adhering to it, showing clearly that at one time it had been attached to some architectural element.

3. Bust of Mutemonet (BM 1198)

The limestone bust of Mutemonet, similar to the one just described, represents a woman with the locks of Hathor (Fig. 21). Harry James, who was kind enough to examine this bust, sent me the following description: "It has a flat back, roughly finished, being approximately 19 cm. wide and 49 cm. high. We acquired it, by purchase, in Egypt in 1897, and, sadly, we have no information about its original provenance."[5] On the front of the bust is the inscription: "(1) Favored through Mut and Tefnut, the sistrum-bearer of Amun, Mut, and Khonsu, Mutemonet. (2) May Ptah give offerings in good veneration. (3) May the Beautiful-of-Face give offerings in good veneration." "Beautiful-of-Face" is one of several names for the god Ptah.

The bust was previously dated to the Twenty-sixth Dynasty,[6] perhaps because the inscription is so neatly carved. (A monument of Amenmose [No. 8, below] also shows very neat carving, which may explain why this monument as well had been attributed to a later period.) Inasmuch as the bust came from Thebes,[7] there is little doubt that it is a bust of the mother of Amenmose, who lived in Thebes. This bust may have stood in the same niche with the bust of Amenmose's father in the tomb of their son. In view of the fact that the bust represents his mother, I wrote to the authorities of the British Museum to give them its

[4] Porter and Moss, *Bibliography* I/1, p. 428. No inscription appears on the dyad to the right of the entrance (No. 9 in the plan) and it is hard to tell what persons it represents, but one of them must be Amenmose.

[5] Letter EA/8/01/75/AMK.

[6] British Museum, *A Guide to the Egyptian Galleries* (*Sculpture*) (London, 1909) p. 238.

[7] *Ibid.*; the owner's name and titles are also evidence of the Theban provenience of the bust. It is worth noting that Mutemonet is here described as "favored through Mut and Tefnut," who are the consorts of Amun and Shu, mentioned as favoring Penzerti on his bust. The fact that the two busts are almost the same size would seem to support the view that their owners were closely related to each other.

precise date, and I am glad to say that they agreed with me that it should be dated earlier than Budge had thought.[8]

Busts No. 2 and No. 3 resemble the many found by Bernard Bruyère in the village of Deir el-Medina, where the artisans who decorated the royal tombs in the Valley of the Kings used to dwell. These two busts differ from the busts found by Bruyère in that they were originally placed in a tomb rather than in a dwelling. Some other busts of this type, however, now dispersed in the collections of various museums, may also have come from tombs.[9] Bruyère, in calling such monuments "bustes de laraires," thought it possible that they represented deceased members of the family, but more often they appeared to him to be divinities specially revered by the common people.[10] J. Vandier d'Abbadie, however, stressed the fact that they were not divinities but mere mortals, or rather dead persons associated with the divine life.[11] That the busts were encountered in dwellings as well as in tombs, and that some of them were inscribed with the names of relatives who were probably dead, suggests that they did indeed represent deceased members of the family whom the survivors wished to commemorate.

4. Statue of Amenmose from the Karnak Cachette (CCG 42169, JdE 3672 in the Cairo Museum)

The statue of Amenmose from the Karnak Cachette shows the owner squatting with his knees up and his arms crossed on his knees; on the front of the statue is carved a smaller figure of the crocodile-headed god Sebk-re (Fig. 22). The owner is referred to as "the royal scribe Amenmessu (or Amenmessui), son of the judge Penzerti," and his mother's name is given as Mutemonet (or Inty), without any title. On the lap of the statue are inscribed the praenomen and nomen of Ramesses II, each preceded by the usual epithets. This is the only

[8] Harry James, letter EA/8/01/75/AMK.

[9] Jean Keith is preparing a corpus of such monuments, together with a study of their provenience. Her study should make it possible to determine why these monuments were erected and to understand their significance as a whole.

[10] "De toutes tailles, de matières différentes (pierre, terre cuite, argile crue, bois), ces bustes peuvent avoir été ceux des membres disparus d'une famille à qui les survivants gardent un culte tout spécial de souvenir; mais ils paraissent être plus souvent ceux des divinités particulièrement vénérés parmi la plèbe de la nécropole" (Bernard Bruyère, *Rapport sur les fouilles de Deir el Médineh* (*1930*) ["FIFAO" VIII/3 (1933)] p. 10; see also Fig. 3 on p. 11, where there is a view of fourteen such monuments discovered by him). J. Vandier d'Abbadie quotes Bruyère as having also said that these busts "ne représentent pas des dieux, ils représentent des mortels ou plutôt des morts associés à la vie divine comme en témoignent la perruque et le collier des initiés aux mystères d'après la mort" (in "A propos des bustes de laraires," *RdE* 5 [1946] 134).

[11] "Ces monuments auraient servi au culte des ancêtres"; *ibid.*, p. 135.

monument of Amenmose that specifies the king under whom he served. Following the praenomen the king is described as "beloved of Sebk-re, lord of Sumenu," while after his nomen he is characterized as "beloved of Sebk-re Appearing-in-Thebes." Inscriptions on the front of the statue and on the sides of the dorsal pillar (not shown) ask the god in his two forms to give offerings. On the rear of the dorsal pillar the owner is described as favored by the same god in his two forms. It is worth noting that on the sides of the dorsal pillar, just as in his tomb, Amenmose is entitled "royal scribe of the offering table of the Lord of the Two Lands."[12] Judging from this inscription Amenmose seems to have paid homage to Sebk-re in Sumenu,[13] one of the main cult centers of that god.

It is interesting that in half the inscriptions on this statue Sebk-re bears the epithet "Appearing-in-Thebes," an epithet resembling that given to Khonsu at Thebes, where he is almost always called "Khonsu-in-Thebes." Since it is known that Khonsu was also worshipped in Gebelein and Iomtru,[14] one may wonder whether he, as well as Sebk-re, may not have been introduced from their original cult places near Gebelein into the pantheon of Thebes when Thebes increased in importance during the Eighteenth Dynasty.

5. Statue of Amenmose from Qantir(?)

There is a small headless statue of Amenmose from Qantir in gray granite, of which the upper part is missing (Fig. 23). The height of this piece is 15 cm., including the pedestal, which measures 4 cm.; the width is 17 cm. It shows the owner seated on the ground with one knee raised and the other leg lying flat

[12] Georges Legrain, *Statues et statuettes de rois et de particuliers* II ("CCG" [1909]) 36–37, Pl. XXXIII. It should be noted that in Legrain's publication the two cartouches have been placed above the titles and epithets rather than to either side, as they appear upon the statue. The sign *mnw* in the place name Sumenu (Gardiner Sign-List T 1) has been consistently miscopied by Legrain as the wave *n*.

[13] At one time Sumenu was identified with Rizeikat (A. H. Gardiner, *Ancient Egyptian Onomastica* II [London, 1947] A. 330, 20* and note on 275*; see also William C. Hayes, *The Burial Chamber of the Treasurer Sobk-Mosĕ from Er Rizeiḳāt* ["Papers of the Metropolitan Museum of Art," No. 9 (New York, 1939)] p. 5), but now it is accurately fixed at some kilometers to the south, almost midway between Rizeikat and Gebelein, not far from the farm known as Awlad Mekky Dahamsha, in the vicinity of El-Mahamid El-Qibly. Recently a temple was found there with many monuments, some of which were reported to the Egyptian authorities, while others found their way to museums abroad; see Bernard V. Bothmer, "Private Sculpture of Dynasty XVIII in Brooklyn," *Brooklyn Museum Annual* 8 (1966–67) 74 ff. For the new discoveries at this place see Hassan S. K. Bakry, "The Discovery of a Temple of Sobk in Upper Egypt (1966–69)," *MDAIK* 27 (1971) 131–46. The presence at Rizeikat of some funerary monuments with the place name Sumenu may point to Rizeikat as having been at one time the cemetery of Sumenu.

[14] See Labib Habachi, "Amenwahsu Attached to the Cult of Anubis, Lord of the Dawning Land," *MDAIK* 14 (1956) 52–62. For Iomtru see Gardiner, *Onomastica* II, A. 331, 21* and 275*.

beneath it. Only a few signs remain of the inscription on the lap that continues on the top of the pedestal and ends on its front: "[The royal scribe Amen]mose, the blessed,[15] . . . , son of the judge Pen[zerti], . . . born of Iny." Though only a few signs are preserved of the names of Amenmose and his parents, enough remains to show that without question the statue is that of Amenmose.

I saw this statue in the shop of Abd er-Rahman es-Sadiq, an antiquities dealer in Hehia, who assured me that it had come from Qantir, not far from his town. If so, this means that Amenmose left a small statue of himself in a place now considered to have been the residence of the Ramessides, a place to which Ramesses II, his sovereign, devoted much attention.[16]

6. Statue of Amenmose from Memphis (Inv. No. 5749 in the Kunsthistorische Museum in Vienna)

Flinders Petrie discovered the torso of a statue of Amenmose (now in the Egyptian collection in the Manchester Museum) in his excavations in the Temple of Ptah at Memphis in 1910. He was able to show that it fits with the lower part of a statue, also found in Memphis, that was part of the viceregal collection sent to Miramar in 1855. The statue represents a man sitting on his legs on a cushion placed on a pedestal; his hands are on his lap, and in the left he grips a scribe's palette.[17]

Facsimiles of the inscriptions on the torso appear in Figure 24. These show that the owner is wearing a pendant above which there is mention of Ptah, Neit, and perhaps Re (*a*); on one shoulder is Neit (*b*), on the other Thoth (*c*). Below there is an inscription (*d*), continued on the belt (*e*), that reads: "The royal scribe Amenmose, the blessed,[18] son of the judge Penzerti."

The inscriptions on the lower part of the statue (Figs. 25–28) are more numerous and more interesting than those on the torso. Mainly they are concerned with the welfare of the owner, whose name appears here with his usual title of "royal scribe." The name itself, following the god's name, is written in two different ways, with the element *ms* rendered sometimes in the form of the sign representing three foxes' skins (Gardiner Sign-List F 31), sometimes in that of the figure of the child (Gardiner Sign-List A 17). Amenmose's name is usually followed by that of his father, though in one instance it is followed by that of his mother, inscribed as Iny. On the top of the lap is one invocation prayer

[15] This same writing of *mꜣʿ ḫrw*, "blessed," appears also on the torso of the statue of this man found in Memphis (No. 6, below).

[16] See Labib Habachi, *Tell ed-Dabʿa I; the Site in Connection with Qantir* (in press). I have spoken briefly on this question in my article, "Khatâʿna-Qantîr: Importance," *ASAE* 52 (1954) 479 ff.; cf. 558 ff.

[17] My warm thanks to Dr. Komorzynsky, director of the Kunsthistorische Museum, who was kind enough to have these photographed for me and gave me permission to publish them.

[18] See above, No. 5, Statue of Amenmose from Qantir, and note 15.

addressed to Ptah-Sokar-Osiris (*a*) and a second addressed to Neit (*b*), asking that they donate offerings on certain feasts (enumerated in *c*) for the welfare of the owner, whose name is found in the horizontal inscription at the top (*d*) and in the three columns of inscription below (*e*). On the front of the pedestal (*h*) is a prayer asking that all that appears on the offering table of Ptah may be enjoyed by "the royal scribe Amenmose, son of the judge Penzerti." In this inscription Ptah is referred to by his common epithet, "South-of-His-Wall." At the sides of this columnar inscription (*h*) the same prayer is addressed to "The Lord of Truth" (*i*) and "The Master of Ankhtaui" (*j*), both of these also being epithets of Ptah, the god of Memphis.

There remain the inscriptions that begin on the front and continue around the sides to the back. The ones on the front of the lap (*f* and *g*) are concerned with the ba, while those on the pedestal (*k* and *l*), meeting at the back, speak of the *showyt* or shadow and express wishes that Amenmose may be blessed in the Underworld. One of the inscriptions on the lap (*f*) reads as follows: "O Amenmose, the one of Tod, may it be well with thy ba, may thou be summoned on the *w*(ꜣ)*g*-feast, may the primeval waters be supplied to thee in Heaven. . . ." The other inscription (*g*), opposite, reads: "O Amenmose, the one of Tod, may it be well with thy ba, may the sweet breeze (be) at thy nose, may the breeze of the north come to thee. . . ." One of the inscriptions on the pedestal (*k*) reads: "May thou be justified, O Amenmose, with the ancestors in the Underworld, may thou be reckoned among those justified(?), may thou freely take thy place in the *Neshmet*-bark, (namely), the royal scribe, Amenmose." The inscription opposite (*l*) reads: "May thou be justified in the Necropolis, may thou reach the Underworld, may thou ascend to heaven among the divine souls, may thy *showyt* go to the place it likes as thou hast been on earth, (namely), the royal scribe, Amenmose."

On this lower part of the statue, as on the torso, while there is mention of Thoth and Ptah-Sokar-Osiris, it is the goddess Neit who appears to hold the position of great esteem. As Petrie says, "Neith seems to have been his personal devotion, as he bears her shuttle on his breast, his shoulder, and on both knees."[19]

Although some of the inscriptions on this statue have previously been copied,[20] in view of their importance I thought it worthwhile to provide facsimile copies of them here, with some improvements upon the earlier readings.

[19] W. M. Flinders Petrie *et al.*, *Meydum and Memphis* (*III*) ("British School of Archaeology in Egypt and Egyptian Research Account" XVIII [London, 1910]) p. 39 and Pls. XXX/2 and XXXI "Torso of Amen-Mes."

[20] S. Reinisch, *Die aegyptischen Denkmaeler in Miramar* (Vienna, 1865) Pl. XXVIII and pp. 228–29; Heinrich K. Brugsch, *Monumens de l'Egypte* (Berlin, 1857) Pl. XIII (lower); text *idem, Thesaurus Inscriptionum Aegyptiacarum* (Leipzig, 1883–91) pp. 239 f.

7. Statue of Amenmose in the British Museum (BM 137)

In the British Museum there is a headless statue of Amenmose in gray granite; the surviving part is 49 cm. high and 22 cm. wide (Fig. 29).[21] It was among the objects obtained from the Bonaparte Expedition under provisions of the Treaty of Alexandria in 1801, and in 1802 it was presented by King George III to the British Museum.

It is a statue of a kneeling man holding a sistrum.[22] At the beginning of the surviving inscription on the front (1) there is a bird, perhaps the *sꜣ*-goose, with the town determinative. If "Sais" is the correct interpretation of these signs, then it would be Neit, the mistress of Sais, to whom the following invocation was made: "May she give a good lifetime combined with health; may I join earth in peace on the West of Thebes, all my limbs being complete, in good condition, and prosperous, (2) on behalf of the ka of the royal scribe Amenmose, son of Inyt." On the other side, a god, rather than a king, is spoken of as the "(3) lord of the two tall feathers,[23] may he let me follow His Majesty during the daytime to see his beauty without (cessation) . . . (4) on behalf of the ka of the royal scribe Amenmose, son of the judge Penzerti."

On the back of the statue there are three columns of inscription of which the upper parts are missing, so that what remains is rather ambiguous in meaning: "(5) . . . with the royal scribe, Amenmose, son of the judge Penzerti. He is the worm(?)[24] of your body (6) . . . the royal scribe Amenmose, born of Inyt, weeping for the one who is in the Underworld, (7) . . . who is sad over the one who is against him, (namely), the royal scribe Amenmose, son of Penzerti, the man of Esna, whose mother is Iwnyt."

Although Budge had previously dated this statue to the period between the Twentieth and Twenty-second Dynasties,[25] James correctly dated it to the reign of Ramesses II on the basis of the same man's statue from the Karnak Cachette (No. 4, above).[26] Budge understood the name of the father to be Penzerti Iwny, but nowhere in the numerous inscriptions in which this name appears is it written so. The purpose of "Iwny" following the name was to indicate the man's home town, which seems to have been Esna.

[21] Harry James was kind enough to send me a description and views of the front and back of this statue, as well as hand copies of the inscriptions.

[22] The statue has been illustrated, but spoken of only briefly by Jean Jacques Clère in his "Propos sur un corpus des statues sistrophores égyptiennes," *ZÄS* 96 (1969) 1–4; see p. 3, n. 1 and Figs. 1 and 2 on Pl. I.

[23] *Wb* IV 425:12, 13. The two tall feathers are often pictured on either a god or a king.

[24] For "worm" see *Wb* V 451:6; in this inscription, however, the meaning is rather vague.

[25] Budge, *Guide* (*Sculpture*), pp. 207 f.

[26] In his description of the statue, James refers to tomb No. 373 and points out that the father

8. Statue of Amenmose from Tolemaita, Libya

The statue of Amenmose from Tolemaita, Libya, along with other Egyptian monuments, was found by Gennaro Pesce in the Palace of the Columns, the residence during the Roman Empire of the Roman magistrate in Tolemaita. The statue has been the subject of more than one study, the first being by Alan Rowe after he saw it during a visit to Tolemaita in 1943. According to him, "this statue is of dark brown stone; . . . It represents the royal [military] scribe . . . Shere-amen son of the judge . . . Pa-en-djerty and of the sistrum-bearer (musician) . . . Mut-em-int. The scribe, who was obviously posted at Ptolemais, was attached to the Ptolemaic army as is shown by the fact that he holds two standards each doubtless representing one of the divisions (or regiments) stationed in that town."[27]

The statue, of which the head, feet, and part of the legs are missing, is 55 cm. high and represents a man clad in a long dress, standing and holding in each hand a standard (Fig. 30). Between these standards and on the front of the garment is a vertical inscription in three columns: "(1) [May all that] which comes forth [from the offering tables] of Osiris, pre-eminent of the Westerners, and of Neit, mistress of Abydos, be for (2) the royal scribe Amenmose, son of the judge Penzerti, (3) (and for) the royal [scribe] Amenmose, son of the sistrum-player Mutemonet."

On the dorsal pillar there are two columns of inscriptions preceded by some signs common to the two. These signs (4) seem to be traces of the name of the owner that had probably been preceded by the words "royal scribe," his main title. Owing to the lacunae in the inscriptions their meaning is quite vague. One reads: "(4) [The royal scribe Ame]nmose, (5) he [adores] Neit, bringing joy(?) . . . in peace, raising . . . the mother of the father of gods in all peace. . . ." The other column is addressed to Osiris-Atum in the words: "(4) [The royal scribe Ame]nmose, (6) he adores Osiris-Atum, bringing . . . toward thee . . . he has come(?) to thee, O Bull of the Ennead. . . ."

Alan Rowe's study has been the subject of more than one review.[28] But the real study of the statue was that made by Giuseppe Botti in the publication by Gennaro Pesce of his excavation in Tolemaita.[29] It was Botti who recognized

---

must not be confused with the other Penzerti, mentioned in the Aswan graffiti; see British Museum, *Hieroglyphic Texts from Egyptian Stelae, etc.*, Pt. 9 (London, 1970) p. 59 and Pl. XLV, 2.

[27] Alan Rowe, *A History of Ancient Cyrenaica. New Light on Aegypto-Cyrenaean Relations. Two Ptolemaic Statues Found in Tolmeita* ("ASAE," Supplement 12 [1948]) p. 64 and Pl. XIV.

[28] E.g., Eberhard Otto, in *BiOr* 8 (1951) 28 f.; Claire Préaux, in *CdE* 25 (1950) 343 f.; and Jean Leclant, in *Revue des études anciennes, Bordeaux* 52 (1950) 337 ff.

[29] Gennaro Pesce, *Il "Palazzo delle colonne" in Tolemaide de Cirenaica* ("Monografie di Archeologia Libica" II [Rome, 1950]) pp. 70–71.

the owner's name as Amenmose, stating that he must have lived during the Nineteenth Dynasty. It was clever of him indeed to fix the date, for the neatness of the inscriptions, which resemble those on the bust of Mutemonet, might suggest a different date. Botti also pointed out the existence of two inscriptions carved on the shoulders of the statue, behind the standards. The one behind the standard of Osiris reads: "Hathor, mistress of the West, and chief of life," while the one behind the other standard reads: "[Anubis] who is above his mountain, pre-eminent of the divine booth."[30]

Thus we find four divinities mentioned—Anubis, Hathor, Osiris (conflated with Atum), and Neit. Osiris and Neit were the divinities to whom the statue was actually dedicated. On the front there is a prayer asking that the owner might profit from offerings coming from their offering tables, while on the back it is stated that he adores each of them. But more important is the fact that he is supporting two standards, one being that of "Osiris, lord of the Necropolis," the other that of "Neit, mistress of Sais." The former has on top the symbol of the Thinite nome or of Abydos itself, of which Osiris was the main divinity.[31] On the back of the statue Osiris is conflated with Atum, god of the setting sun. The Neit standard has at the top the uraeus, with the *Nt*-sign of the goddess appearing on the front.[32] It has often been suggested in descriptions of statues showing the uraeus that the *Nt*-sign on the chest of the cobra stands for the part that contains the poison. This sign seems to be the origin of the goddess's name, rather than the two arrows, as usually believed; the uraeus was the determinative of goddesses' names. Whether this be true or not, here, as on the statue from Memphis (No. 6) and on that in the British Museum (No. 7), it is the goddess Neit that has the place of greatest favor. Apart from the standard with her name and the wishes and prayers addressed to her, the *Nt*-sign hangs from the statue's neck. On one side of this sign is *Mert* of the south, and on the other side *Mert* of the north, each kneeling on the *nwb*-sign.[33] Neit and Osiris were worshipped in many places, especially in Sais. The standards held by Amenmose bearing their names reflect his zeal in worshipping them. These standards cannot be taken as the war standards of regiments named after the deities. War

[30] *Ibid.*, p. 71.

[31] Alan Rowe describes this standard as representing a lotus stem (*Ancient Cyrenaica*, p. 65), but it looks more like a papyrus stem. He does not identify the upper part of it as representing the Thinite nome or Abydos itself; for this symbol see Pierre Montet, *Géographie de l'Egypte ancienne*, Pt. II (Paris, 1961) pp. 99 f.

[32] Rowe depicts the standard as if almost all the upper part of it were broken off (*Ancient Cyrenaica*, p. 65, Fig. 11). For a possible appearance of the *Nt*-sign on the front of a uraeus see Bernard V. Bothmer, "More Statues of Senenmut," *Brooklyn Museum Annual* 11 (1969–70) 127, Figs. 2 and 5.

[33] See Hans Bonnet, *Reallexikon der ägyptischen Religions-Geschichte* (Berlin, 1952) p. 457.

standards are depicted differently and cannot be connected with the ones we have here. We must remember also that Amenmose never had a military career at any time.[34]

Although the inscriptions in the tomb of Amenmose, on the busts of his parents, and on his five statues do not add much to our knowledge about this man and his parents, it is clear that he was one of the important persons who lived during the long reign of Ramesses II. We know that high officials who lived during the prosperous days of ancient Egypt left monuments of themselves in various places in Egypt, and the monuments left by Amenmose had some significance in connection with the places where they originally stood.

Amenmose carved his tomb in the Theban Necropolis. In one place in this tomb, his name is followed by the words *n W3st*, "the one of Thebes," or "the Theban," perhaps to distinguish him from other persons bearing that popular name. His mother's name is inscribed in the forms Iny, Inty, and Mutemonet. Her name may also point to Thebes as her place of origin. His father's name, meaning "the one of Tod," points to his connection with the area to the south of Thebes. On the British Museum statue (No. 7), however, this name is followed by the place name *Iwny*, meaning "Esna." This may explain the son's devotion to the goddess Neit, whose cult was observed there.[35] On no monument of Amenmose, not even in his tomb, is there mention of any woman who may have been his wife. It therefore seems unlikely that he was ever married.

The statue from Karnak (No. 4) dedicated to Sebk-re was related on the one hand to Thebes, where this god was a member of the pantheon, on the other hand to Sumenu, one of his main cult centers.

Owing to the fragmentary state of the statue from Qantir (No. 5), we do not know whether there were more inscriptions than those giving the names and titles of Amenmose and his parents and whether any deities were mentioned.

The statue from Memphis (No. 6) makes mention of Ptah-Sokar-Osiris, the main god of that city, but also of Thoth, perhaps because the owner had "royal scribe" as his main title. The prominent position of Neit in the inscriptions on this statue, however, shows the special devotion of the owner to this goddess. While it is true that the goddess had a significant cult at Memphis,[36] hers could

[34] For military standards see John G. Wilkinson, *Manners and Customs of the Ancient Egyptians* I (rev. ed.; London, 1878) 188, and Raymond O. Faulkner, "Egyptian Military Standards," *JEA* 27 (1941) 12–18. Rowe says, "The standards of Neith and Osiris, *in the forms represented in the Ptolemais statue*, are unknown elsewhere" (*Ancient Cyrenaica*, p. 66).

[35] For the cult of this goddess in general see Dominique Mallet, *Le Culte de Neit à Saïs* (Paris, 1888), and Bonnet, *Reallexikon*, pp. 512 ff. For her cult in Esna see *Reallexikon*, p. 514.

[36] For her cult in Memphis see *ibid.*, p. 513.

hardly have been more important than that of Ptah-Sokar-Osiris, the main god of that city.

Amenmose's attachment to Neit can be seen also in the British Museum statue (No. 7). Although her name is missing on the surviving part of the statue, the name of Sais, her main place of worship, seems to be preserved. The fact that Amenmose is shown holding the sistrum suggests that he was adoring a goddess, in all probability Neit. The invocation on the other side of the statue may be addressed to the king or to a deity, perhaps Osiris. In our present state of knowledge it is difficult even to guess where this statue may have stood originally. It is clear, however, that the goddess Neit was favored by the owner.

The statue from Tolemaita (No. 8) seems to be of particular importance. Its discovery there raises the question whether that was where it originally stood, and, if so, what the relations were between Egypt and Libya during the reign of Ramesses II. Three scenes are known that show Ramesses II vanquishing the Libyans, and also some text that refers to such a defeat; this evidence is so vague, however, that one can never be certain that any hostilities actually did occur at that time.[37] At the time of the Second World War large blocks referring to the victory of Ramesses II over the Libyans were found at el-Alamein, which has a particularly strategic position.[38] More recently, stations from the reign of Ramesses II have been discovered on the west coast;[39] these, however, may have been erected as a precaution against the Sea People who had begun to threaten Egypt and who subsequently attacked it during the time of Ramesses III.[40]

[37] Two scenes are in Beit el-Wali Temple and the third in the Great Temple of Abu Simbel; see Wilhelm Hölscher, *Libyer und Ägypter* ("Ägyptologische Forschungen," Vol. 4 [Glückstadt, 1937; reprinted 1955]); he says that even from the texts referring to such hostilities it is not certain whether any did indeed occur during the reign of Ramesses II (p. 61). See also Etienne Drioton and Jacques Vandier, *Les Peuples de l'orient méditerranéen* II: *L'Egypte* (4th ed.; Paris, 1962) 425.

[38] For these blocks see Jasper Y. Brinton, "Some Recent Discoveries at el-Alamein," in *Bulletin de la Société Royale d'Archéologie d'Alexandrie* IX, No. 35 (1942) 78 ff., Fig. 6, and 163, Fig. 12; also Rowe, *Ancient Cyrenaica*, p. 7, Fig. 4.

[39] Labib Habachi, "Découverte d'un temple-forteresse de Ramsès II," *Revue du Caire* 33, No. 175 (1955) 62–65. In Zawiet Umm el-Rakham, at about 25 km. west of Mersa Matruh and 300 km. west of Alexandria, there was found a small temple with many stelae showing that a fortress had been built there. Also at Gharbaniyat, about 30 km. west of Alexandria, there was unearthed a column with the remains of what may have been a fortress; see Anthony De Cosson, *Mareotis* (London, 1935) pp. 127–28. Undoubtedly in el-Alamein there was also a third temple-fortress (see note 38, above).

[40] The mere fact that such fortresses were erected on the coast by Ramesses II may indicate that these people did threaten Egypt during his reign. But there is the even greater probability that they actually attacked Egypt. Jean Yoyotte in his study, "Les Stèles de Ramsès II à Tanis," *Kêmi* 10

Such being the case, one may ask whether Amenmose's statue was erected at the place where it was unearthed or whether it was taken there from another place in Egypt. It is true that some bodies tattooed with the *Nt*-sign have been found in Libya and that relationships between the goddess and this country have been attested since the Fifth Dynasty.[41] But one must remember that three more divinities are mentioned in the inscription on this statue of Amenmose: Osiris (conflated with Atum), Hathor, and Anubis. These divinities were adored in many places in Egypt, but especially in Sais. There Neit was the main divinity, followed in importance by Osiris and Atum, while Hathor and Anubis were also often encountered there. It is true that all these divinities are mentioned more often on monuments of the Twenty-sixth Dynasty, when Sais became the capital of all of Egypt, and in later dynasties. But Neit and Osiris already appear on monuments of the Nineteenth Dynasty, during the reign in which Amenmose lived.[42] The other divinities may also have had a cult at Sais; they were quite popular there in all the Pharaonic periods.[43] There can be no doubt that Amenmose, who was a fervent worshipper of Neit, erected the statue in question (and perhaps even the one now in the British Museum) in the place where the goddess had her main place of worship. The statue found in Tolemaita may have been moved there subsequently by one of the Ptolemies or by the Romans.

A phrase in Amenmose's tomb may explain how he came to leave several of his statues so far away from the place where he lived. On a cornice in the first hall, on the west wall to the right, is the conclusion of a damaged inscription (Fig. 31) that reads: *Sš-nsw rdỉ n nsw ḫntỉ r-prw, ʾImn-ms* (*ỉr n*) *ʾIny*, that can be rendered as: "The royal scribe, whom the king appointed(?) as head of the temples, Amenmose, (born of) Iny." This would suggest that he may have been an inspector of temples and may explain how he came to dedicate statues in different parts of Egypt.

(1949) 58–74, shows that these people did attack Egypt during the reign of Ramesses II; that is why he speaks of a military fleet; for further discussion see pp. 68 f. See also Rainer Stadelmann, "Die Abwehr der Seevölker unter Ramses III," *Saeculum* 19 (1968) 157 and n. 11; and Drioton and Vandier, *Les Peuples de l'orient*, p. 44c.

[41] For these relationships and the worship of Neit in Libya see Hölscher, *Libyer und Ägypter*, pp. 33–34 and 40.

[42] In his book, *Documents relatifs à Sais et ses divinités* ("BdE" LXIX [1975] 1–36), Ramadan El-Sayed published two monuments in the Louvre, both coming from Sais and dated to the Rameside period. The first is stela C.218, which mentions a hymn to Osiris; the second is statuette No. E 25.980, showing the goddess Neit.

[43] In Sais itself these divinities are shown on monuments of the Late Period; see *ibid.*, pp. 215–17 (Appendix B). There is no doubt that Atum was one of the main gods of Sais; see Labib Habachi, "Sais and Its Monuments," *ASAE* 42 (1943) 380–82.

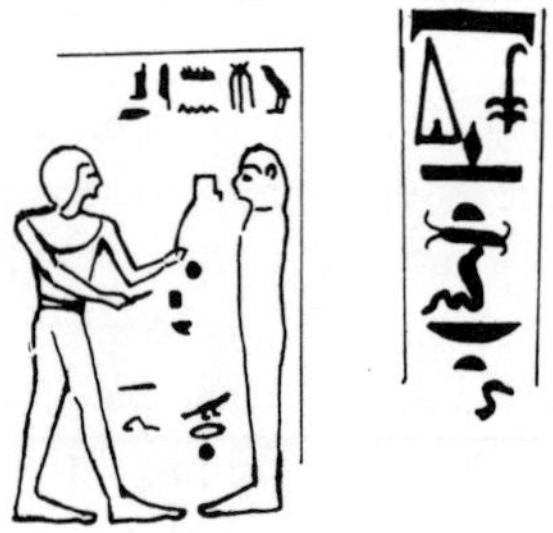

FIG. 19.—Inscription from Tomb 373 (Theban Necropolis) with invocation of Neit

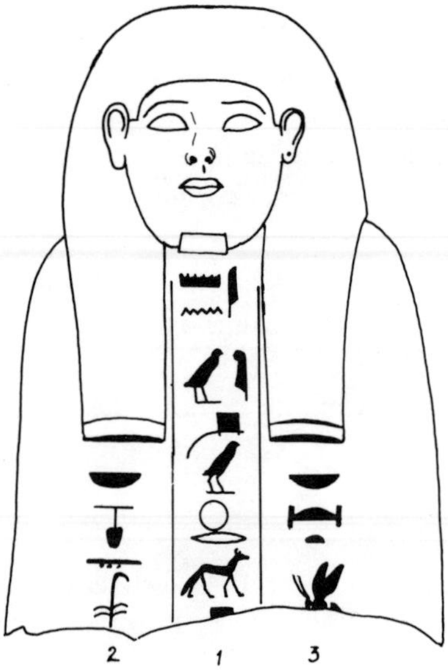

FIG. 20.—Bust of Penzerti

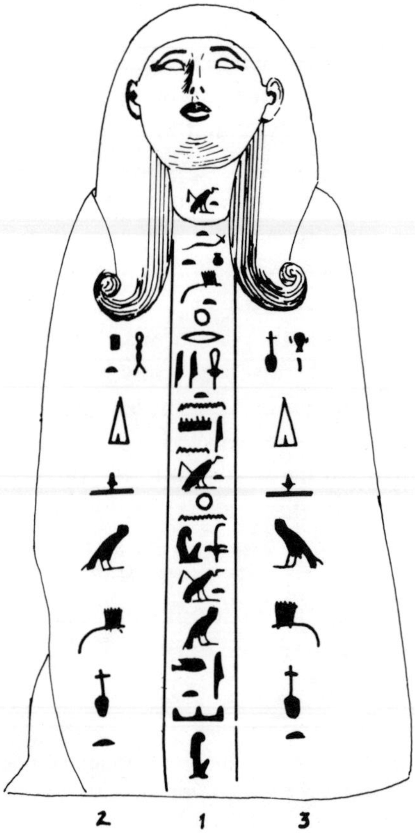

FIG. 21.—Bust of Mutemonet

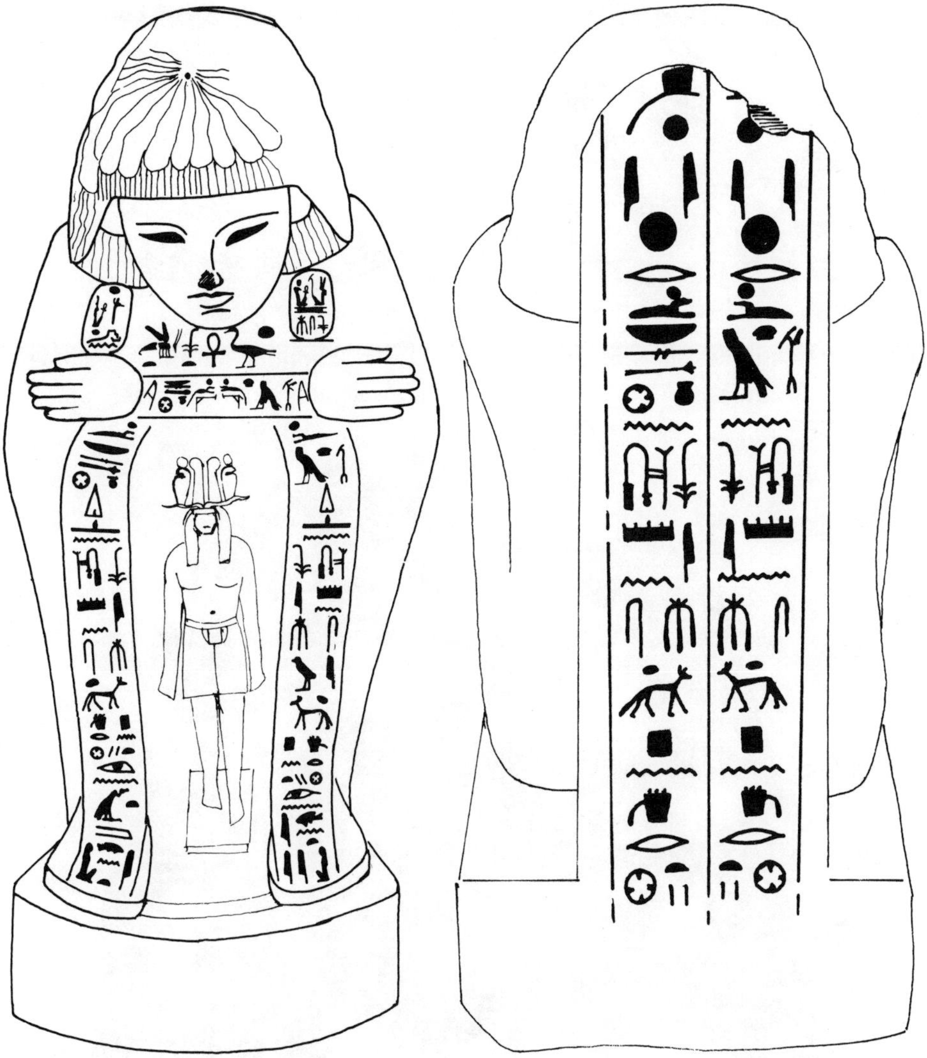

A *B*

Fig. 22.—Statue of Amenmose from the Karnak Cachette, front (*A*) and back (*B*)

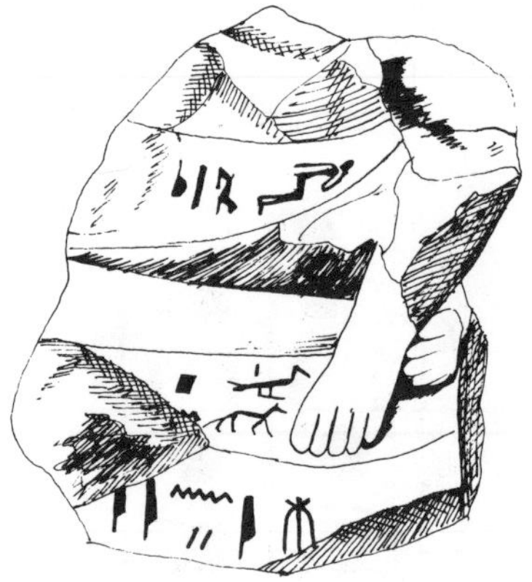

FIG. 23.—Statue of Amenmose from Qantir(?)

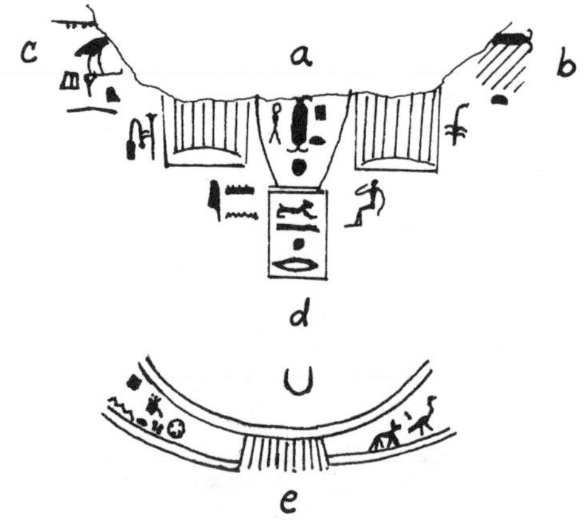

FIG. 24.—Inscriptions on torso of statue of Amenmose from Memphis

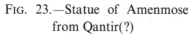

FIG. 25.—Statue of Amenmose from Memphis, top of lap

FIG. 26.—Statue of Amenmose from Memphis, front of lap (top) and left side (bottom)

FIG. 27.—Statue of Amenmose from Memphis, right side (top) and back (bottom)

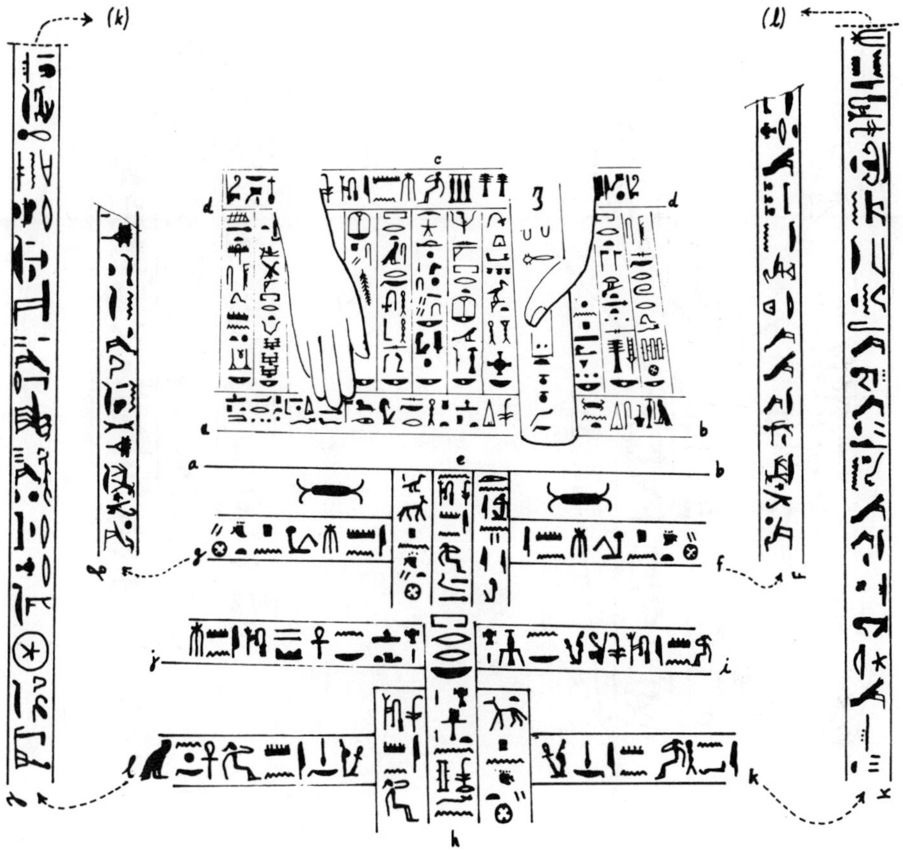

FIG. 28.—Inscriptions on statue of Amenmose from Memphis

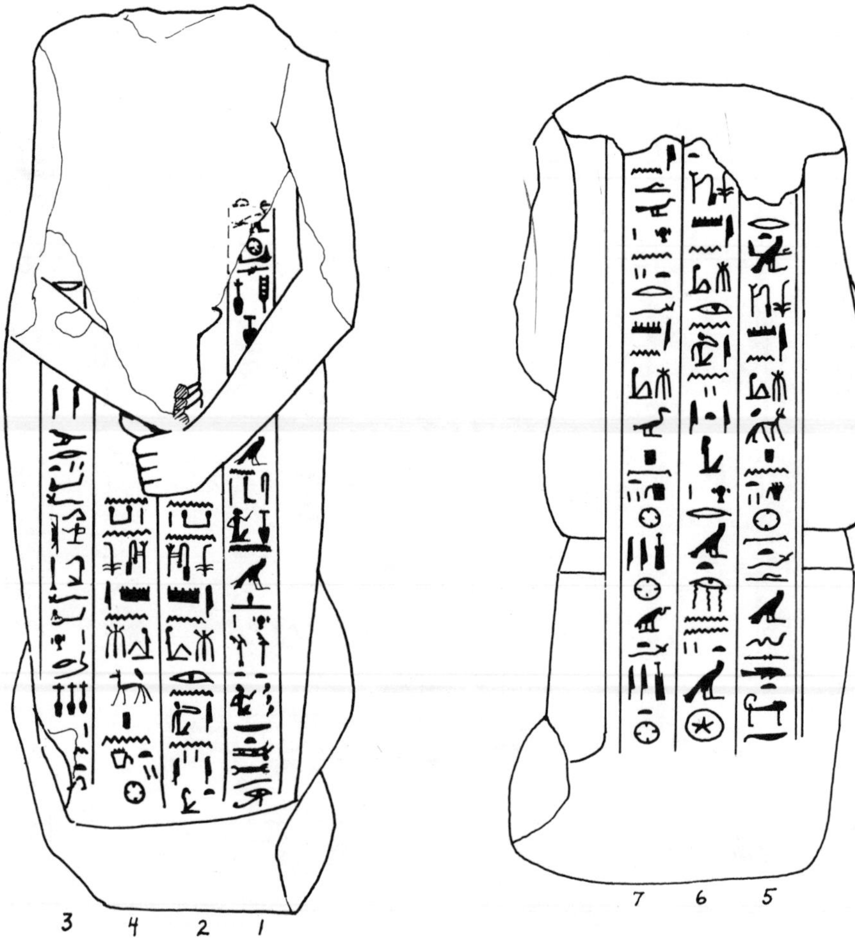

A B

FIG. 29.—Statue of Amenmose in the British Museum, front (*A*) and back (*B*)

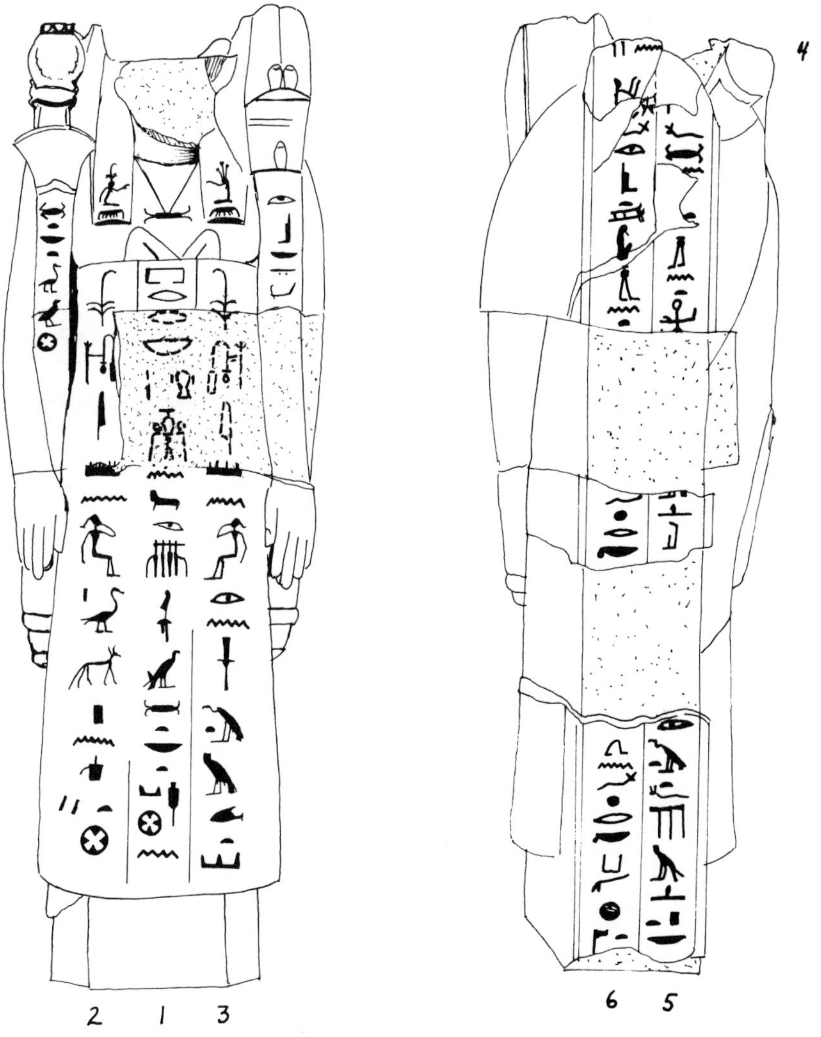

A *B*

FIG. 30.—Statue of Amenmose from Tolemaita, Libya, front (*A*) and back (*B*)

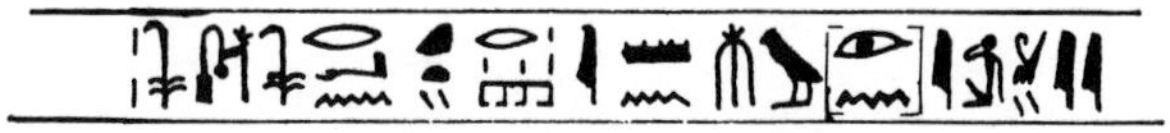

FIG. 31.—Inscription from Tomb 373 (Theban Necropolis) with title of Amenmose

THE DIALECT OF THE DEMOTIC MAGICAL PAPYRUS OF LONDON AND LEIDEN

Janet H. Johnson

Magical[1] apparently was found in Thebes, together with several other Demotic and Greek papyri,[2] all including either Greek or Demotic magical texts, or both, and dating from the third century of our era. It has been suggested that both Magical and the magical spells on the verso of one of these (Leiden I 384) were written by the same scribe.[3] Both texts could have been written elsewhere, brought to Thebes, and later buried there. It seems more likely, however, that the texts were actually written near where they were found. This assumption can be tested in two ways. First, the orthography, morphology, and grammar of Magical can be compared with those of a contemporary manuscript known to have been written in Thebes. Second, the dialect[4] in which Magical

[1] Published by F. Ll. Griffith and Herbert Thompson, *The Demotic Magical Papyrus of London and Leiden* (3 vols.; Oxford, 1921).

[2] Including Leiden I 384, Louvre 3229, Bibliothèque Nationale suppl. gr. 574, and probably BM 10588. They all come from the collections of Anastasi, on which see Warren R. Dawson, "Anastasi, Sallier and Harris and Their Papyri," *JEA* 35 (1949) 158–60.

[3] Janet H. Johnson, "The Demotic Magical Spells of Leiden I 384," *OMRO* 57 (1976; in press); F. Ll. Griffith, "The Date of the Old Coptic Texts and Their Relation to Christian Coptic," *ZÄS* 39 (1901) 82.

[4] It has long been assumed that Egyptian was split into different dialects well before Coptic. F. Ll. Griffith (*Catalogue of the Demotic Papyri in the John Rylands Library, Manchester* III [Manchester, 1909] 183) wrote, "From earliest times Egypt must have been the home of several dialects. It is so now that the language is Arabic: in ancient and more primitive times when communication was slower, the long course of the Nile valley, the Delta intersected and broken by rivers and marshes, the desert borders and Oases fostered dialect yet more." He also called attention to the passage in Anastasi I, of New Kingdom date, in which one scribe berates another for his poor compositions, all jumbled and confused, and says of his words:

Anastasi I, 28/6

st mỉ md.t n s ỉdḥw ḥnʿ s n ꜣbw

"They are like the words of a man of the marshes with a man from Elephantine."

Pre-Coptic dialectal study has been hampered not only because earlier stages of Egyptian did not write vowels but also because they regularly retained historical writings of words which did not reflect even consonantal changes. J. Vergote ("Les Dialectes dans le domaine égyptien," *CdE* 36

was written can be compared with the known dialects of Coptic, especially that of Thebes.[5] Both approaches confirm that Magical was written in Thebes by a scribe using the Theban dialect.

The analysis of the glosses and related dialectal information in Magical which forms the major part of this paper is based on a study done with George R. Hughes's encouragement and assistance as part of my doctoral dissertation. It was he who taught me Demotic and who awakened my interest in this field of Egyptology. He has always been extremely generous with his help, and I dedicate this article to him in what I hope is a fitting tribute to him as scholar, teacher, and friend.

[1961] 237–49) cited studies of Coptic and pre-Coptic dialectology, the latter on pp. 246–49. See also *idem*, *Grammaire copte* Ib (Louvain, 1973) 8–11. In earlier periods, as during the Coptic period, there was presumably one dialect which was the official dialect, but local peculiarities might appear in particular texts. In Demotic texts this is reflected also in the spelling of Greek names. "The considerable uniformity in the Graecized names of the Ptolemaic period from all parts of Egypt would seem to testify to the existence of an official dialect, although the local pronunciations are constantly seen to break through the skin of this official style" (Griffith, *Catalogue* III 184).

[5] The five major literary dialects are Bohairic (B), Fayumic (F), Sahidic (S), Subakhmimic (L), and Akhmimic (A). There are also a number of minor dialects; see Rodolphe Kasser, "Dialectes, sous-dialectes et 'dialecticules' dans l'Egypte copte," *ZÄS* 92 (1965) 106–15. Most modern students of Coptic dialectology or dialect geography have come to agree that B is a delta dialect, F the dialect of the Fayum, S the dialect of the northern part of the Nile valley, L that of the middle valley, and A that of the southern valley. See William H. Worrell, *Coptic Sounds* (Ann Arbor, 1934) Pt. II, chap. 1; Vergote, *CdE* 36 (1961) 242, Table 3; Paul E. Kahle, *Bala'izah: Coptic Texts from Deir el-Bala'izah in Upper Egypt* II (London, 1954) chap. 9; and Rodolphe Kasser, "Les Dialectes coptes," *BIFAO* 73 (1973) 78–91, although Kahle identified S as the dialect of Alexandria (*Bala'izah* I 256–57) and Kasser agreed (Rodolphe Kasser, "Les Dialectes coptes et les versions coptes bibliques," *Biblica* 46 [1965] 291–93). H. J. Polotsky ("Coptic," in *Linguistics in South West Asia and North Africa* ["Current Trends in Linguistics," Vol. 6, ed. Thomas A. Sebeok (The Hague, 1970)] p. 561) rejected this suggestion and returned to the older suggestion that S was native to Thebes. But the dialect of Thebes is known from nonliterary fragments found in the monastery of Epiphanius (H. E. Winlock, W. E. Crum, and H. G. Evelyn White, *The Monastery of Epiphanius at Thebes* [2 vols.; New York, 1926]; see also Worrell, *Coptic Sounds*, Pt. II, chap. 3). Dialect P (P. Bodmer VI, published by Rodolphe Kasser, *Papyrus Bodmer VI: Livre des Proverbes* ["Corpus Scriptorum Christianorum Orientalium," Vols. 194–95, "Scriptores Coptici," Vols. 27–28 (Louvain, 1960)]) is the literary equivalent; see Peter Nagel ("Der frühkoptische Dialekt von Theben," in *Koptologische Studien in der DDR* [Halle-Wittenberg, 1965] pp. 39–49), whose conclusions are accepted by Kasser (*BIFAO* 73 [1973] 81) and Polotsky ("Coptic," p. 561), although rejected by J. Vergote ("Le Dialecte copte P [P. Bodmer VI: Proverbes]: Essai d'identification," *RdE* 25 [1973] 50–57); Vergote would place dialect P between Memphis and Herakleopolis; on his arguments, see below, note 74. A comparison of Magical with the various Old Coptic texts would be valuable, but this is not attempted here because of the size limit on this article and because of the difficulty of the Old Coptic texts. In addition to the standard transliterations, the following will be used: in Demotic—-ꜥꜣ- for the group ꜥꜣ, "great," used as a vowel in the alphabetic script; in Coptic and Old Coptic—*g* for Demotic *g*; in Coptic—*ḏ* for Ϫ; *q* for Ϭ; *ẖ* for ⳉ (A) or ϧ (BP); in both (Old) Coptic and Greek, *e* and *o* are short vowels, *ē* and *ō* are long vowels.

A definitely Theban text of this late Roman period is the so-called Demotic Gardening Agreement, written on a pot found in excavations at Medinet Habu and published by Parker, who noted, "Palaeographically and grammatically the ostracon shows close agreement with the Demotic Magical Papyrus of London and Leiden."[6] Parker, in his notes to the text, frequently refers to the glossary of Magical, either to establish meaning or to parallel spelling. Perhaps the most striking similarity is the use of *ỉỉr.k* in place of *ỉw.k* as the second person masculine singular auxiliary.[7] Morphologically the two texts are very similar, although most of the forms are not distinctive.[8] Note the spelling *ỉr-rḫ* for the non-

[6] Richard A. Parker, "A Late Demotic Gardening Agreement," *JEA* 26 (1940) 84. This Gardening Agreement is a legal or semilegal document citing the duties and responsibilities of the owner and the gardener of a garden. Both the tenor of the composition and the carelessness of the scribe (see Parker's notes—for example, on B29, D18, and D24) suggest that it was written in the local dialect without literary pretensions.

[7] A usage shared with the other two Demotic magical texts found with Magical; see above, note 2. Magical has examples of *ỉỉr.k* for *ỉw.k* in the present tense, including circumstantials, relatives, and the progressive (Coptic first future); in the (third) future, including circumstantials and relatives; in the past tense when written nonhistorically *r*(-*ỉw*) plus subject plus infinitive, including a relative form thereof (see below); in the conditional, including the negative conditional; and in the conjunctive when written *n*(-*ỉw*) plus pronominal subject, rather than *mtw*. Leiden I 384 verso has an example in the negative future. (See the appropriate tables in Janet H. Johnson, *The Demotic Verbal System* ("SAOC" [in press].) The Gardening Agreement has examples of *ỉỉr.k* for *ỉw.k* in the circumstantial present (B31), present tense relative (B10), future (C7), future tense relative (A9–10), positive conditional (C10), and negative conditional (C9–10). The realization that not all forms written *ỉỉr.k* are second tenses eliminates some of the problems Parker perceived in his study of the Gardening Agreement. Thus in A8 *ỉỉr.k* need not be interpreted as "probably 2nd Present, marking the introduction of a new paragraph, with the meaning 'you have to, you shall' " (Parker, *JEA* 26 [1940] 91); it is simply a future with injunctive meaning. Similarly the example with second person feminine singular subject in C22 written *ỉỉr*, without the *.t* ending, corresponds to Mythus *r-ỉr* for *r-ỉr.t* (as Parker suggested, p. 104), and to Coptic *ere*. But the example in the Gardening Agreement is a circumstantial progressive form, not a second tense. It was used after the verb *ḫpr*, "to happen," where the circumstantial was normally used; see Johnson, *Demotic Verbal* (in press) and the example in Magical of a circumstantial progressive with noun subject following *ḫpr* (8/13–14).

[8] It may be significant that both scribes wrote the infinitive of *dỉ*, "to give," with a *y*-ending before a following dependent pronoun direct object. See *Magical*, glossary number 976 (16 examples) and Gardening Agreement A12, A18, B8, B19, C5, C11, and C13. Even more frequently, the scribe of Magical used the form written *dy* as a pronominal infinitive, followed by the suffix pronoun *f* as direct object (38 examples). The scribe of the Gardening Agreement twice used *dỉ*, without the *y*-ending, as the pronominal infinitive, followed by *f* as the direct object (A10 and A25). This *y*-ending is otherwise rare (e.g., in Hauswalt 3*a*/6, Poème satyrique, l. 73, and in Eugène Revillout, "Une famille de paraschistes ou taricheutes thébains," *ZÄS* 17 [1879] Pl. VI, doc. 23, ll. 1 and 2–3). The only example other than Magical cited by Wilhelm Spiegelberg (*Demotische Grammatik* [Heidelberg, 1925] par. 255) is an example in Rhind (glossary No. 363), which Möller (Georg Möller, *Die beiden Totenpapyrus Rhind des Museums zu Edinburg* ("Demotische Studien," Vol. 6 [Leipzig, 1913]) interpreted as a *sdm.f*.

indicative *sdm.f* of the verb "to know."[9]

There are two grammatical features in Magical and the Gardening Agreement which do not seem to occur in other Demotic texts.[10] Both wrote *r-ỉr*(*e*) for the conditional auxiliary with a noun subject,[11] whereas other Demotic texts used *ỉn-nꜣ*.[12] Both also occasionally used the relative converter *nty* to form past tense relatives or participles, whereas other Demotic texts used the historical relative and participial forms exclusively. Magical has examples of both participles and relative forms, with pronominal and nominal subjects, formed by prefixing *nty* to the nonhistorical past tense form written *r*(*-ỉw*) plus subject plus infinitive.[13] The Gardening Agreement has three examples of the participial form.[14] The most likely explanation of this construction is that the use of *nty* has been extended to the past tense by analogy with relative forms of other tenses. Such an extension has been assumed for the Coptic past tense relative *ntafsōtm*.[15] In noninnovative constructions the grammar of Magical is also consistent with that of the Gardening Agreement.

[9] Gardening Agreement B5–6, as a subjunctive after *dỉ*, "to cause." For the examples in Magical and a discussion of the various forms of *rḫ*, see Johnson, *Demotic Verbal* (in press).

[10] These are the only two texts, moreover, which seem to use the progressive freely. It is attested in Magical in main clauses and in circumstantial and relative forms (see *Magical*, glossary number 431 [1]), and in the Gardening Agreement in main clauses (B19, B33, C2, D5, D7–8, and D11) and in the circumstantial (C22–23). The last is written *ỉỉr*⟨*.t*⟩ *nʿ ỉr* and is used after the verb *ḫpr*, "to happen," for which reason it is identified as a circumstantial (see above, note 7, end). For a discussion of the qualitatives of the verb *nʿ*, "to go," see Johnson, *Demotic Verbal* (in press). It should also be noted that the verb *mtry*, "to be satisfactory, fitting," in B13, B16, and B35 cannot be a qualitative, as Parker suggested in his note on B13, because the qualitative was never used in the negative past (B13 and B35) or negative perfect (B16). The passive translation must come from an intransitive meaning of the verb.

[11] E.g., Magical V26/4–5 and Gardening Agreement A35 (*r-ỉr*), Magical 7/27–28 (*r-ỉre*).

[12] With pronominal subjects, the auxiliary *ỉw* was used. Thus the negative conditional clause in Gardening Agreement C9–10 written *ỉỉr.k tm wḫꜣ.w* is the standard form of a negative conditional clause, showing this scribe's substitution of *ỉỉr.k* for *ỉw.k*. There is no need to suggest an "erroneous omission of *ỉw.f ḫpr* ['If (it happens that)'] by the scribe," as Parker did in his note to C9. See Johnson, *Demotic Verbal* (in press). The use of the conjunctive immediately after *ỉw.f ḫpr* seems to be limited to Magical and the Gardening Agreement; see Parker in his note to B18.

[13] E.g., *nty r-ỉỉr.k ỉr.f* (5/14), *nty r pꜣ rʿ pꜣy.t ỉṯ dỉ* (12/26). The noun subject was deleted to form a participle; e.g., *nty r rḫ* (21/21). Magical also has an example where the form following *nty r* is not noun plus infinitive but the *sdm.f*, i.e., *nty r mtr pꜣ snf* (15/13). For further discussion of these past tense forms and their relatives, see Johnson, *Demotic Verbal* (in press).

[14] I.e., *nty r ḫpr* (A19), *nty r wṯ* (D5), and *nty r ỉy* (D10).

[15] Although Parker translated the example in A19 as a future (which it cannot be because in future relatives the subject is always expressed), he recognized that the examples in Column D are identical with the Magical examples and that they have past tense meaning in both texts. He correctly distinguished these forms from the perfect relative, which was written *nty ỉw wꜣḥ.f sdm*, but his

Thus, Magical and the Gardening Agreement reflect the same scribal tradition. The innovations they share may be the result of their late date more than of their geographical origin, but at the least the "paleography and grammar" of Magical do not contradict its suggested Theban origin. A more positive conclusion can be drawn from the study of the dialect of Magical.

Those who have attempted to determine the dialect used by the scribe of Magical have generally come to the conclusion that he was writing in one of the Upper Egyptian dialects. Rejecting Müller's statement that the glosses were in dialect F while the Demotic was *Untersahidisch* (A), or his later statement that the dialect used was between F and A, but nearer A, Griffith concluded that the glosses and the Demotic text were both written in one dialect and by one scribe.[16] Lexa, having decided that grammatical forms only rarely indicate dialect, turned to phonetic evidence, but studied only the Demotic, not the glosses in Magical. As a result, he concluded that Magical was written in an Upper Egyptian dialect, but not pure Upper Egyptian.[17] Haardt,[18] basing his study on the phonetics of both the Demotic and the glosses, concluded that most of Magical was in dialect S while almost all the rest was in A. With the publication of P. Bodmer VI (dialect P) and the identification of its dialect as Theban,[19] the suggested Theban origin of Magical can be tested by comparing all the distinctive dialectal features in Magical, phonetic and nonphonetic, with those of dialect P. Thus, the remainder of this paper is devoted to an analysis of such features in Magical and their comparison with the various Coptic dialects, especially P.

Since the most extensive, consistent, and most easily documented dialectal evidence in Coptic is phonetic,[20] the phonetic evidence in Magical is discussed first. This evidence includes a large number of words written phonetically, indicating both consonants and vowels, in glosses and ciphers. The glosses in Magical are written in Greek capital letters, with Demotic signs added for

identification of this last with Coptic *ntafsōtm* is less likely. In most Coptic dialects the perfect had died out and its meaning had been absorbed by the past tense, the latter derived from the indicative periphrastic conjugation *ỉr.f sdm. Ntafsōtm*, like the forms in Magical and the Gardening Agreement, was formed by prefixing the relative converter (*nt*) to the main clause past tense form (*afsōtm*). See Johnson, *Demotic Verbal* (in press).

[16] *Magical* I 9–10; see also below, note 38.

[17] František Lexa, "Les Dialectes dans la langue démotique," *Archiv Orientalni* 6 (1934) 162–63.

[18] "AK," pp. 24 ff.

[19] See above, note 5.

[20] See Worrell, *Coptic Sounds*, Pt. I, chap. 2; Walter C. Till, *Koptische Dialektgrammatik* (2d ed.; Munich, 1961) pars. 8–54; Kahle, *Bala'izah* I, chap. 3; Vergote, *Grammaire copte* I. The possibility that the differences between the dialects are merely orthographic has been noted by Kasser, *ZÄS* 92 (1965) 108; see also Polotsky, "Coptic," pp. 559–60. If the correspondences between the dialects

sounds not present in Greek. In some cases the glosses are added above Demotic words, including a few verb forms, thereby giving the pronunciation of the Demotic. Most commonly, however, what is glossed is a magical name—sometimes Egyptian, sometimes Aramaic,[21] but usually an unintelligible "abracadabra" word. Many of these same magical names are found not only in Old Coptic magical texts but in roughly contemporary Greek magical texts from Egypt as well.[22] The magical name was written in Demotic, usually using alphabetic signs, with the gloss added above. The correspondence between Demotic and gloss allows one to determine the pronunciation of the Demotic signs. Within the body of the Demotic text are found about ninety Demotic (or Greek) words spelled in cipher which occur elsewhere in the text in Demotic.

were completely regular, they might reflect different scribal traditions, rather than different pronunciations. But the occurrence of examples which do not fit the pattern indicates that these do represent actual differences of pronunciation.

The major literary dialects in Coptic show a few syntactic differences involving verbal auxiliaries. If a text includes one or more such grammatical variations characteristic of a particular dialect, it would suggest that the text was written in that dialect. There were also morphological differences between the different dialects; for example, the spelling of a qualitative form or the pronominal infinitive of a 3-weak verb might reflect the dialect used by the scribe who wrote the text. Finally, the lexicon of each of the dialects included vocabulary items not attested in some or any of the other dialects. However, the incidence of vocabulary is a very unreliable criterion by which to determine dialects. The majority of the Coptic texts preserved and published were written in one of two dialects, B or S. Thus the nonoccurrence of a word in the relatively smaller corpus of one or more of the other dialects may be due to the chances of preservation rather than to the actual loss of the word from the lexicon of the less well-attested dialect. If, on the other hand, a text uses a word known to occur in one of the minor dialects but not in S or B, this fact may be more significant. The most reliable dialectal evidence to be drawn from the incidence of vocabulary involves words for which some dialects used one of a pair of synonyms while others used the other. One must keep in mind, however, that there was much cross-dialectal influence. It was also a common practice, especially with literary texts, to translate from one dialect to another, during which process a scribe might retain in the translation vocabulary items of the original dialect. For these reasons, the evidence of vocabulary should be used only to reinforce other, more conclusive evidence, and not to contradict it. For the purposes of comparison between Coptic texts and Magical, allowance must also be made for the possible semantic development of a word between the time of Magical and that of the Coptic texts. For all of the above reasons the evidence of syntax, morphology, and the incidence of vocabulary will be discussed after the phonetic evidence. Since, as already noted (p. 105) it would appear that the scribe of Magical also wrote the Demotic magical spells on the verso of Leiden I 384, the distinctive dialectal features of that text will also be included in this study. But the glosses in Leiden I 384 verso involve only magical names, no Greek or Egyptian vocabulary, and therefore add no significant correspondences to those found in Magical. Thus, although Tables 2, 3, and 5 include items from the Leiden manuscript, this source is ignored in the discussion of the phonetic evidence which follows.

[21] E.g., Sabaoth, Adonai, Ba'al; see the list of glosses in Griffith, *Magical* III [113–36].

[22] For the Greek magical texts, including those found with Magical, see Karl Preisendanz, *Papyri Graecae Magicae: Die griechischen Zauberpapyri* (2 vols.; Leipzig, 1928–31).

This system of ciphers must have been developed for use in Greek texts, since, of the signs used, some are simply Demotic letters, for example, ϩ, ϭ, and ϧ, while four are inverted forms of Greek letters.[23] Although the latter might have been expected to conceal the value of the letter from either an Egyptian or a Greek, the former would have presented no difficulty at all to an Egyptian, while hopefully remaining a puzzle to a Greek.[24] Griffith was able to decode this cipher system and transliterate the words spelled in cipher into their Old Coptic equivalents.[25] Like the glosses, the ciphers indicated vowels. Thus these words as well as the words in the glosses provide useful phonetic information.

Many Greek words appear in Magical, sometimes in the glosses or ciphers, but more commonly in Demotic transliteration. Comparison between the original Greek spelling and the form actually used in Magical provides evidence of the pronunciation of the individual letters of the glosses and ciphers and of the Demotic letters themselves. After the phonetic system of the glosses has been studied, an attempt can be made to determine the Coptic dialect to which the spelling of the glossed Demotic words, including those used in magical names, most closely corresponds. Based on the evidence of correspondences between Demotic and glosses, and between Demotic and Greek, conclusions regarding the pronunciation of the Demotic signs can then be applied to nonglossed Demotic words and predictions made regarding the pronunciation of those words as well. However, since many Demotic words are written with ligatures or nonalphabetic signs, many of the Demotic words cannot be converted into Coptic even with the evidence derived from the glosses. After the phonetic system of the glosses and ciphers has been discussed, the scope of the present discussion will be limited to those Demotic words known from Coptic—both those actually spelled out in gloss or cipher and those whose actual pronunciation is only suggested by the correspondences between the Demotic and non-Egyptian scripts.

[23] See Haardt, "AK," pp. 15–16.

[24] The Egyptian signs used are the same signs for which the glosses also used the Demotic. Moreover, as Griffith noted (*Magical* III [108]), some signs are used only in Greek words and may indicate sounds which do not occur in Demotic; there is no special sign for the aspirate; and no distinction is made between *t* and *ḏ*, which an Egyptian could hardly have failed to distinguish. The concept of a purely alphabetic system seems more in accord with a Greek developer than an Egyptian. Furthermore, the ciphers were written from left to right, as noted by Wilhelm Spiegelberg (review of Griffith and Thompson, *Magical* II and III, in *OLZ* 12 [1909] 549). Although all the glosses in Magical are written from left to right, when writing the magical spells on the verso of Leiden I 384, the scribe began writing the glosses from right to left, immediately above the Demotic. But soon he switched and wrote them in the order in which they were to be read, i.e., left to right. See Johnson, *OMRO* 57 (1976; in press).

[25] See *Magical* III [105–7].

	Α	Β	Γ	Δ	Ε	Ζ	Η	Θ	Ι	Κ	Λ	Μ	Ν	Ο	Π	Ρ	Σ	Τ	Υ	Φ	Χ	Ψ	Ω
ⲁ	59																		1				1
ⲃ		8																					
ⲅ			6																				
ⲇ				4				1															
ⲉ	3				19		7		1										2				
ⲏ	1				2		15																
ⲑ								11										1					
ⲓ					2		1		16														
ⲕ			4							19											1		
ⲗ											23												
ⲙ												22											
ⲛ													28										
ⲟ														40									3
ⲡ															15								
ⲣ																30							
ⲥ						6											26						
ⲧ				1														11					
ⲩ																			17				2
ⲫ																				9			
ⲭ			1							1											6		
ⲯ																						1	
ⲱ														3									3
ϭ			1																				

TABLE 1
GREEK/OLD COPTIC CORRESPONDENCES

Table 1 gives the correspondences found in Greek words between the original Greek letters and those of the glosses or the ciphers, together called Old Coptic. The numbers in the table indicate the number of occurrences of each correspondence. As a glance at the table shows, there is a very strong correlation between the Old Coptic and Greek, indicating that the Old Coptic letters had been adopted with their Greek values.[26] The values of all the vowels show some variation, but only *e*/*ē* and *o*/*ō* show regular variation.[27] The only group of consonants that shows any appreciable variation is the velars. Half the time Greek *g* is written with a gamma, but a third of the time it appears as *k*, and

[26] As argued by Worrell for early Coptic, "We can take the spelling of Coptic very seriously. It represented at the beginning the sounds actually heard at that time. Were it not so, we should not have the different dialects, . . . , each with a consistent orthography; nor should we have the consistent misspellings of vulgar documents and of individual scribes. As long as Coptic was a spoken language the Copts . . . misspelled the school language in the direction of their actual local speech; or they gave up the school language and wrote frankly in their local speech" (*Coptic Sounds*, p. 4).

[27] For an explanation of this regular variation, see below. Notes on transliteration are given above, note 5, end.

numbers in *italic* indicate ciphers, numbers in roman indicate glosses

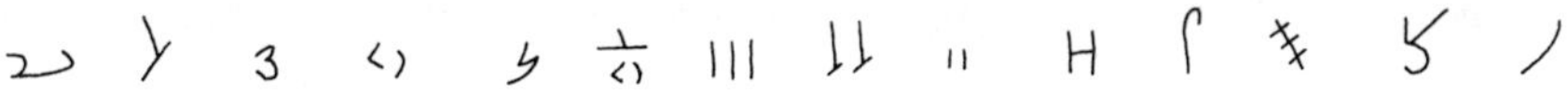

ⲁ	*1* 97	1		*4* 351/14	8		5		24		1			9
ⲁⲉ	*2* 3		*2* 6	*4* 1	*3*		*5* 7		*5* 133/10					
ⲏ	2		7				1		*1* 80/13	5				
ⲓ							*4* 258/10	2						
ⲓ̈							/2		/1					
ⲟ	2			2		*2* 99/8					*4* 10/1	1	1	
ⲩ									19/1		5			
ⲱ						105/11					3			
[illegible]						2					1	9		1
[illegible]											/1			
ⲁⲉ							3							
[illegible]									1					
ⲉⲓ							/2							
ⲟⲩ						1						*6* 91/2		10
ⲟⲓ									/1					

TABLE 2
DEMOTIC/OLD COPTIC CORRESPONDENCES (VOWELS)

there is one example each of *g* appearing as *x* and as *q*. Greek *k* is more consistent, only once being written *x* rather than *k*; but there is also one example of Greek *x* written as *k*. The same Greek word, μαγνης, has been glossed both *magnes* and *maknes*; here there is no difference in phonetic environment to account for the difference in correspondence. All this suggests that the scribe who wrote the glosses could hear *k* fairly accurately, but was not able to recognize *g* as reliably, often confusing it with *k*. It thus seems likely that in his native dialect the voicing distinction between *g* and *k* had been lost in part or in whole. Those instances where *g* is correctly written as gamma may indicate either that the distinction between *g* and *k* was retained in some words or

ϐ	124/15	5	2								
Γ											
Δ											
Ζ											
Κ											
λ											
Μ								125/5	3		5
Ν										120/8	13
Π				55/4	3	16	15				
Ρ											
C											
Τ											
Φ				2		1					
Χ											
ϥ			5								
ϧ											
ϩ											
[illegible]											
[ʿ]											
[illegible]											
ϭ											
3											
[illegible]											
[illegible]											

TABLE 3
DEMOTIC/GLOSSES CORRESPONDENCES

environments, or that the scribe knew that the Greek contained a *g* and therefore wrote the appropriate letter even though he could not hear the difference. It should be noted here that historical Egyptian *g* coalesced with some *k*'s in all Coptic dialects except dialect B, in which *g* and *k* usually remained distinct.

Tables 2–5 give the correspondences found between Demotic signs and the Old Coptic scripts. The numbers after a slash indicate the number of occurrences in Leiden I 384 verso. Table 2 presents all the vowel correspondences found, both those with the glosses and those with the ciphers. A majority of the Old Coptic vowels were written with Greek vowels. But the evidence presented in the table shows that the Demotic vowel system was different from the Greek. Both Demotic ꜣ and ʿ were almost always glossed *a*; in the overwhelming number of cases Demotic *y* is glossed *i*; and Demotic *w* is normally glossed *ou*, although about one-tenth of the examples appear as *o*. The Demotic sign [illegible] was most commonly glossed [illegible], but seems to have belonged to the *o*-family.[28] But Demotic -ꜣ- was split between Greek *o* and *ō*, while Demotic *e* appeared as *e* or

[28] As did [illegible] in Leiden I 384 verso.

ⲃ											
ⲇ											
ⲍ											
ⲕ											
ⲗ				101/6							
ⲙ	1										
ⲛ	2										
ⲡ											
ⲣ		73/15	6								
ⲥ										8	5
ⲧ											
ⲫ											
ⲭ											
ϥ											
ϧ									3		
ϩ											
ϫ											
[ʿ]					8	1					
ⲁ					8	2					
6								3			
3											
ꝺ											
Y					33	8	5				

TABLE 3

DEMOTIC/GLOSSES CORRESPONDENCES (*cont.*)

ē, the instances of *e* outnumbering those of *ē* about three to two. The same Demotic sign corresponded in some places to glosses with the Greek long vowel, in others to glosses with the Greek short vowel; thus the glossing reflects neither short vowels in closed accented syllables and long vowels in open accented syllables—a pattern which has been suggested for earlier stages of Egyptian on the basis of Coptic—nor long vowels in accented and short vowels in unaccented syllables. For example, Demotic *ꜣrmy-ʿꜣ-wt* is glossed *armioout* in V16/1 but *ꜣrmy-ʿꜣ-wth* is glossed *armiōouθ* in 5/20 and 16/10; *-ʿꜣ-rnw-ʿꜣ-rf* is glossed both *ornouōrf* and *ōrnouōrf* in 2/10; *b-ʿꜣ-el* may be glossed *boēl* (as in 7/8) or *bōēl* (as in 16/12). Also, Demotic *šfešfe*, written *šfe sp sn*, is glossed *šbešbē* in 29/6; and Demotic *ꜣrkhe* is glossed *arxe* in 17/18 and *ērxē* in 10/5. Thus the Demotic system seems to have distinguished only vowel quality, not quantity, even though some of the differences in quality may derive from original, or at least earlier, differences in quantity.[29]

[29] See Till, *Dialektgrammatik*, pars. 23 ff.; Vergote, *Grammaire copte* Ia, 19–43. Both Crum (*Epiphanius* I, chap. x) and Worrell (*Coptic Sounds*, Pt. II, chap. 3) referred to the interchange

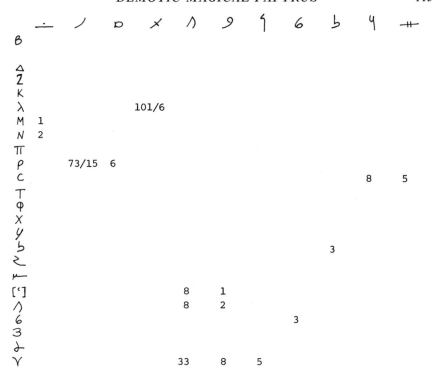

	<ıı	3ı	4	λ	3	σ	ᴍ	ϩ	ᓚ	ϧ	ıȷ	ʾ5
Β												
Γ						3	5					
Δ									2			
Ζ	3											
Κ	1					34	50/3	1/1				
Λ												
Μ												
Ν												
Π												
Ρ												
C	111/8	1	4									
Τ									89/3	30/1		
Φ												
Χ							3/1					
Ψ												
ϧ												
ϩ								11				
ϣ							1					
[ʿ]												
/)												
ϭ												
3				3	8							
ϯ											3	1
Υ												

TABLE 3

Demotic/Glosses Correspondences (*cont.*)

Some of the nonstandard correspondences occur in strictly limited environments or for some other reason call for comment. Two of the examples of Demotic *y* glossed *a* occur in the optative *my ỉr.y* glossed *mari* (as in 7/34), to which should be compared the gloss *ma* found in 1/11 and 1/18 where the imperative *my* is serving as a correction to a conjunctive form. However, *my* is also (15/15) glossed *maï*.[30] The other three examples of *y* glossed *a* all consist of the demonstrative adjective, that is, Demotic *pꜣy* glossed *pa* (as in 1/11). Most of the examples of Demotic *e* glossed *a* occur in the glosses *pa*, *ta*, and *na* to the Demotic possessive article (as in 1/26), possessive prefix (as in 8/16), or nominalized relative (as in 6/35). The nine instances where Demotic *r* is glossed

between *e* and *ē* and between *o* and *ō* as very common in nonliterary Theban Coptic. But Crum dismissed them as errors in orthography rather than facts of phonetic significance. Other Coptic instances of these interchanges are cited in Kahle, *Balaʾizah* I, chap. 8, pars. 22, 34, 44, and 61.

[30] The writing of final *i* with umlaut here and in *taï* for *dy*, "here" (17/20), corresponds to the examples in Leiden I 384 verso where final *y* was glossed *ï* rather than *i*.

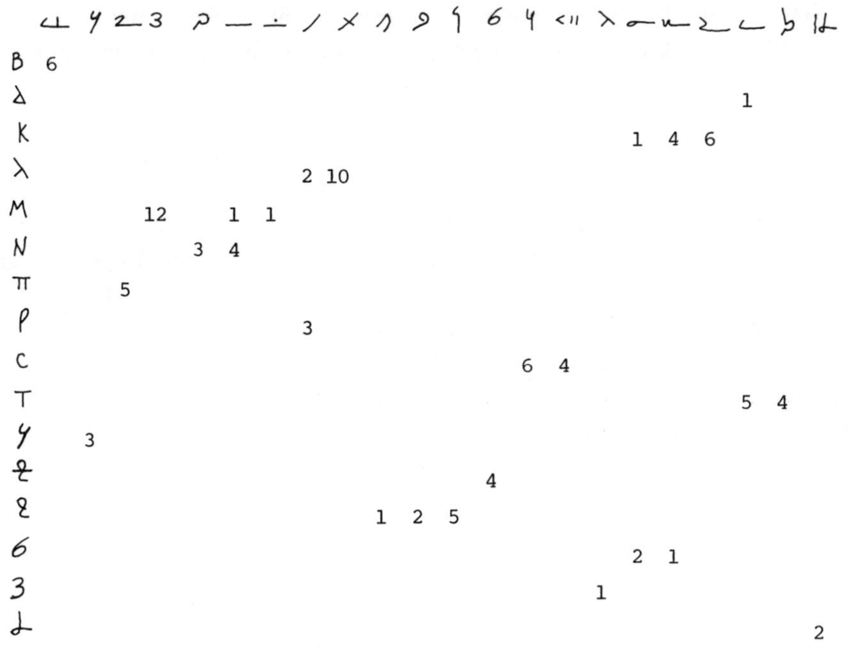

TABLE 4

DEMOTIC/CIPHER CORRESPONDENCES

a are especially noteworthy. In all but two cases,[31] the gloss *a* appears over an *r* with a syntactic function in the Demotic text. It is the gloss for the imperative prefix *r* twice in 1/5 (in *r-wn*) and once in 7/29 (*r-ỉry* glossed *ari*). The *r* of the relative form is glossed *a* in V16/3 (*r-ms* glossed *amsie*); the preposition *r* is so glossed in 1/8, in 9/23, and in V33/3, where *r-ḥr.y* is glossed *araei*. The vocalization of the relative *r* as *a* (both independently and in the nominalized relative forms mentioned above), and of the preposition *r* as *a* (especially in *r-ḥr.y* as *araei*) coincides exactly with the vocalization of A, L, and P. S, B, and F have *e* in each of these cases.

In every case where Demotic *e* is glossed *u*, the *u* is being used vocalically. No clear-cut environment for this correspondence was observed, although all examples occur in association with *r*, *l*, or an aspirated sound. Is there something about these sounds, perhaps, that changes the u-vowel to a vowel heard by the Egyptian as *e*?[32] Although this phenomenon does not appear in Coptic words

[31] 2/14 involves the alphabetic spelling of a Greek word; 10/30 the alphabetic spelling of the name of the god Anubis.

[32] See also cipher sign list No. 13, which has values of *h*, *e*, and *u*. This sign points to the same juxtaposition of *u* and *e* with what must be an *ĕ*-pronunciation. For the *h*-values of *u* see Table 3.

in any dialect of Coptic, the *e*/*u* interchange is one of the commonest misspellings of Greek words in Coptic.[33] Is it perhaps evidence of a change in the pronunciation of Greek upsilon from *u* to *e*?[34]

Other unusual vowel correspondences[35] occur so rarely and in such restricted environments that they should not deter one from using the normal correspondences in assigning vocalic pronunciations to the Demotic letters in question when these occur alphabetically in nonglossed words.

Tables 3 and 4 give the correspondences between consonants, Table 3 giving those found in the glosses, Table 4 those found in the ciphers. Most of the correspondences call for no comment. The following, however, are worth noting.[36] Five of the examples of — glossed *m* and both examples in the ciphers occur in the sequence *n* plus *p*; the pronunciation with *m* is that found in all dialects of Coptic. The one example of — glossed *m*, however, occurs before the word *grḥ*, where the pronunciation *m* is unexpected. The fact that *r* and *l* are not

[33] See, e.g., W. A. Girgis (in religion, Abba Pakhomius al-Muḥarrakî), "Greek Loan Words in Coptic, II," *BSAC* 18 (1966) pars. 7 and 18*a*; Kahle, *Bala'izah* I, chap. 8, pars. 25 and 59.

[34] I.e., fronting of the vowel. See the similar case of the pronunciation of the aspirates before *y*, below. In those cases where Demotic *w* has been glossed *u*, this is just an abbreviation for the normal *ou* and is not to be confused with *e* glossed *u*.

[35] One of the examples of Demotic ꜣ glossed *e* occurs in 29/10, where *hʿkyꜣ* is glossed *uakie*, probably corresponding to Greek ἁγια. Eight of the nine examples of *y* glossed *e* occur in contrast to *e* glossed *ē* (e.g., 27/8). The other example consists of the form *ỉỉry*, the second tense converter prefixed to a future form, glossed *ere* (7/1). The example of *w* glossed *a* (*nwstꜣr*/*nastor* in 2/17) is probably an error. The relatively large number of examples of cipher *e* corresponding to something other than Demotic *e* all involve ciphers 3–5 of Griffith's sign list (*Magical* III [105]). In several of these cases a Demotic ꜣ or ʿ corresponds to a Greek alpha in a Greek word written in the cipher script. It would thus seem that little reliance may be placed on the vocalization of these three cipher signs. The two examples of Demotic ꜣ glossed *o* may both be Egyptian words. In 20/29 *sꜣ* is glossed *so*, and in 7/33 *kꜣ* is glossed *qo*. Should these be compared to A and L *ă > *o* in word-final position? See Till, *Dialektgrammatik*, par. 26. The example of *r* glossed ϫ occurs in the Demotic word *mtr* glossed ⲘⲦϪ. Two of the three examples of Demotic *y* glossed *e* occur in the phrase *pꜣy ʿlw*. In 1/19 *pꜣy* is glossed *pae*; in 7/10 it is glossed *paei*. The other instance is the gloss *kae* over the second *ky* in the expression *mw ky pꜣ ky* in 7/14; the first is glossed *ki*. There is also an example of hieratic ϣ ꜥꜥ glossed *ē*. In Leiden I 384 verso, the examples of ⋂ glossed *o* and ıı glossed *oi* are dubious. The one example of ıı glossed *ï* is probably not complete. It is word-final and a third stroke has probably been lost, which would have made the original correspondence *y* with *ï*.

[36] The example of Demotic *s* glossed *k* is an error. To the three examples of Demotic *s* glossed *z* one should compare the examples quoted in Table 1 of Greek *z* appearing as *s*. To the correspondences listed in Table 3 should be added one example of ⲧ and two examples of ⲓ ⲭ glossed *s*. Aside from the correspondences within the *t*–*d*-family noted in Table 3 there are also two examples of ⌴, one example of Δ, and two examples of ʔ glossed *t*; and four examples of ⲇ glossed ϯ. Leiden I 384 verso has an example of *bh* glossed *b*.

	Γ	Δ	Z	Θ	Ξ	T	Φ	X	Ψ	ϯ
		1								
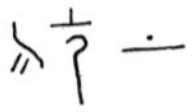		2								
		7								
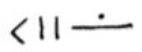			4							
	1									
	6									
				92/15						
		4		13		2				
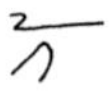							37/2			
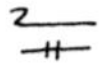									3	2
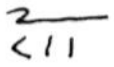									1	
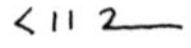									1	
									1	
							3			
								47		
								14/5		
					17/1					
					2					
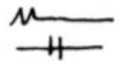					1/1			1		
								2		
								2		

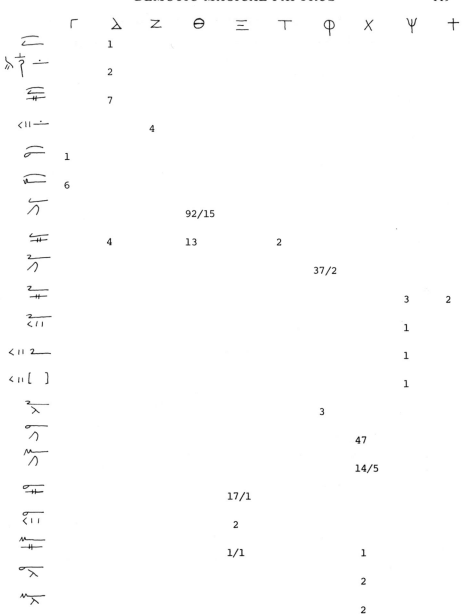

TABLE 5
DEMOTIC/OLD COPTIC CORRESPONDENCES

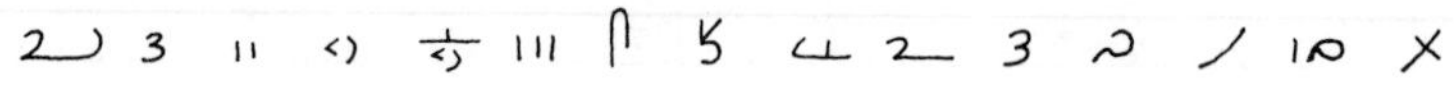

Α	12			46									1		
Β									9						
Γ															
Δ															
Є			7												
Η	1	1	27	1		1									
Θ															
Ι						15									
Κ															
Λ													2		16
Μ											20				
Ν												20			
Ξ															
Ο					7		9								
Π										15					
Ρ													19	1	1
Ϲ															
Τ															
Υ			2			1	9	1							
Φ															
Χ															
Ψ															
Ω					2		4	1							

TABLE 6

GREEK/DEMOTIC CORRESPONDENCES

interchanged[37] indicates that the scribe of Magical was not writing in the F dialect.[38] The three examples of *p*'s glossed φ and two of the three examples of *g* glossed *x* all immediately precede Demotic *th* glossed θ, where the one *h* serves as indicator of aspiration for both preceding letters.[39] A reliable indicator

[37] Only two examples are attested, both in the ciphers. The Egyptian words which are attested in F with *l* are here all spelled with *r*, e.g., *r.f*, "his mouth," is glossed *rof*, while *ỉrp*, "wine," is written *erp* in the ciphers.

[38] See Till, *Dialektgrammatik*, par. 20. This conclusion is in direct opposition to that of W. Max Müller ("Einige griechisch-demotische Lehnwörter," *RT* 8 [1886] 175), quoted by Griffith and Thompson (*Magical* I 10), that the glosses were written in Fayumic. His evidence was an example of glossed *l*. But, as Griffith pointed out, and also Haardt ("AK," p. 24, n. 3), the Demotic should not be understood as *r.w* but as the sign for *mr*, which appears in Coptic as *l* in such words as *lašane*; this evidence cannot be used to prove that the dialect was Fayumic. There are also two examples of h glossed *l*.

[39] See Herbert Weir Smyth, *A Greek Grammar for Colleges* (New York, 1920) p. 13. When two aspirated letters occurred together in Greek, only the second aspiration was heard.

A															
B															
Γ				2	6	3									
Δ							3		1						
Є															
H															
Θ							2	4	3						
I															
K				5	13										
Λ															
M															
N															
Ξ														2	1
O															
Π															
P															
Σ	2	2	21												
T							8								
Y															
Φ										2					
X					2							3	1		
Ψ											2				
Ω															

TABLE 6
GREEK/DEMOTIC CORRESPONDENCES (*cont.*)

of the B dialect is the presence of aspirated stops in certain environments.[40] This text gives no indication of such aspiration, which is evidence that the scribe was writing some dialect other than Bohairic.

The same conclusion is reached when the evidence of the *k*-family is studied.[41] Historical *g*, *q*, *k*, *d̲*, and *t̲* developed differently in dialect B than in any of the other dialects. All dialects except B differentiated between palatalized velar *ǧ* (old *t̲* and *d̲*) and palatal *q* (old *k*, *q*, and *g*). In dialect B all five had fallen together; *q* was the aspirated equivalent of *d̲*.[42] Since the scribe of Magical clearly distinguished between *g*, *k*, and *q*, on the one hand, and older *d̲* and *t̲*, on the other,[43] he was not writing in the Demotic forerunner of Bohairic.

[40] In a syllable before *b*, *l*, *m*, *n*, and *r*; before consonantal *y* or *w*; or immediately preceding the stressed vowel; see Till, *Dialektgrammatik*, par. 19 and Worrell, *Coptic Sounds*, Pt. I, chap. 2.

[41] In addition to the correspondences indicated in Table 3 there is one example of  glossed *k* and one of  glossed *q*.

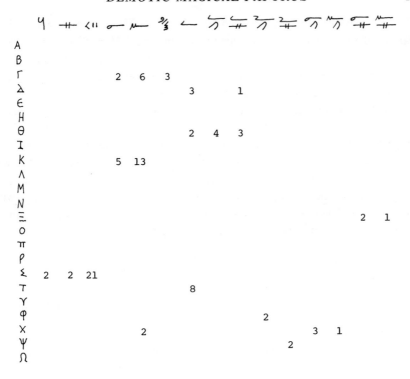

[42] See Worrell, *Coptic Sounds*, Pt. I, chaps. 2 and 3.

[43] Several of the words by which the equivalences between the alphabetic Demotic script and the

In contrast with this negative conclusion, a positive one can be reached by studying the distribution of the various *h*'s and the *š*.[44] Earlier *h* and *ḥ* both appear as *h*, and *š* appears as *š* in all Coptic dialects; *ẖ* appears as *h* in S, L, and F, and as *ẖ* in B, P, and A and the Ascension of Isaiah.[45] But by Coptic *ḫ* had undergone a split. Some *ḫ*'s became *h* in S, L, and F, *ẖ* in B, P, and A and the Ascension of Isaiah; the rest became *š* in S, L, F, and B, *ẖ* in A, ϣ̄ in the Ascension of Isaiah, and ⳋ in P.[46] The distribution and correspondence of the *h*'s and *š* in Magical indicate that the scribe of that text was distinguishing the same four groups as dialect P or Ascension of Isaiah.[47] A Demotic *š*, and only *š*, was glossed or appeared in cipher as *š*. Both *ḫ* and *ẖ* were written in glosses or cipher by using the appropriate Demotic sign; they never interchanged with either *h*/*ḥ* or *š*. The sound of *h*/*ḥ* was treated several ways in the glosses. It might consist of the Demotic sign for *h*; it might contain no overt transcription of the

glosses or ciphers were established are Egyptian words known from Coptic. All of these spellings show that the scribe was not using dialect B. Among these words are *kae* or *ki*—old *gy* (gloss), attested in B with *ḏ*, in the other dialects with *k* or *q*; *beq* (cipher), attested in B with *ḏ*, in S and F with *q*; *qemoul* (cipher), attested in B with *ḏ*, in Theban with *k*, in S, A, B, and F with *q*; *qenqlō* (cipher), attested in B with *ḏ*, in the other dialects with *q*; *ẖdan* (cipher), attested in S with *ḏ*, in B with *q*.

[44] In addition to the correspondences given in Tables 3 and 4, there are also two examples of *u* in the Demotic glossed *u* and two examples (27/20) where the gloss has been written in the line of the Demotic, and *h* has been glossed over the *x*. There is also one example of ʿ glossed ⳋ and one of ϭ glossed ⲋ. These latter two gloss one variant spelling of a Demotic letter into another spelling of the same Demotic letter. There are also two examples of ⊏⊐ glossed ʒ.

[45] On Coptic *ẖ*, see above, note 5, end.

[46] See Worrell, *Coptic Sounds*, Pt. I, chap. 6; Kasser, *P. Bodmer VI*, pp. XXI–XXII; Kahle, *Balaʾizah* I 205; Vergote, *Grammaire copte* Ib, par. 25; Kasser, *BIFAO* 73 (1973) 93.

[47] The glosses or ciphers which contain an *ḫ* are Egyptian words, and many of them appear in one or more dialects of Coptic. The evidence furnished by comparing the Demotic spelling of these particular words with their various Coptic spellings supports the conclusion that the dialect being used distinguished *ḫ* from *š*, as did dialects A and P. For example, *ḫate* (gloss), attested only in A (the other dialects use a synonym), spelled *ḫit*; *saḫe* (or *seḫe*) (cipher) spelled ⲤⲀⳋⲈ in P and *saḫe* in A, while the other dialects have *š*; and *ḫel* (cipher) spelled identically in A, while S, B, L, and F have *š*. Possibly ⳉⲱ (gloss) should be compared with A *ḫae* (S *ša*). In some other cases the word in question is not attested in the known corpus of A or P material, but the spelling in Magical differs from the spellings attested in the other dialects in the manner in which the A and P spelling would be expected to vary if the word were attested in A and P. For instance, ϭⲱï or ⲡⲋⲱï (gloss) contrasts with S *šōl*; *ḫdan* (cipher) has *ḫ* in contrast to S and B which have *š*; and *ḫatoul* (cipher), known only in B, where it is spelled *šaθoul*. The ciphers even include two spellings with *ḫ* of a word which in all dialects of Coptic is written with *h* (although the Demotic spelling includes *ḫ*): *ḏpoḫ* or *ḏpōḫ* for *ḏ*(*e*)*mpeh*. Note also ⲁⳉ (gloss), which is similar to (B) *iẖ*.

h/*ḥ*;[48] or, most commonly, it would be written *u*.[49] Thus the system of consonants used in the glosses and ciphers, and their correspondences with Demotic equivalents, indicate that the scribe was using P/Ascension of Isaiah or some similar dialect, and the vocalization presented above is consistent with this conclusion.

Table 5 gives the Demotic spellings of those Greek letters for which Demotic had no parallel, including Greek letters for which Egyptian had no equivalent (gamma, delta, zeta) and the Greek compound letters.[50] For Greek letters with no Demotic parallel the scribe of Magical sometimes tried to indicate the Greek sound by prefixing an *n* to an Egyptian letter with a similar pronunciation. Thus some gammas were indicated by *ng* or *nk*, some zetas by *ns*, and some deltas by *nt*.[51] But a glance at Table 3 will show that the scribe was not always this careful.

The Demotic equivalent of the Greek compound letters was, in most environments, simply the two parts of the Greek compound juxtaposed. There are, however, a fairly large number of correspondences between *ts* and *t*, *d*, or *θ*, *nts* and *d*, *pš* and *φ*, and *kš* and *x*. These spellings occur when and only when the letter in question is immediately followed by the vowel *i* (Demotic *y*, gloss *i*). If these letters are followed by any other vowel, by any consonant, or are word final, the normal correspondences are found, that is, *th* for *θ*, *t* for *t*, *ph* for *φ*.[52]

[48] This occurred if the Greek pronunciation of the gloss would automatically include aspiration. Examples with *r* include *ḥry* glossed *re*, *rhr* glossed *rr*, *hr* and *ḥr* glossed *r*; with vowels, *hrenwte* glossed *arenoute*, *he* glossed *ē*, and the examples in V12/7 of *yʿhw* glossed *iaō* (in contrast to V26/3 *yꜣ-ꜥꜣ-* glossed *iauō*) and *sʿbꜣh-ꜥꜣ-* glossed *sabaō*. There is even one example where *pꜣ ẖrd* is glossed *prat*. This treatment of aspiration is another indication that the glosses were intended for a Greek speaker.

[49] Griffith (*Magical* III [107]) has suggested that this gloss was a result of the fact that Greek *u*, when initial, was always aspirated. See also W. H. Worrell, "Popular Traditions of the Coptic Language," *AJSL* 54 (1937) 10, par. 32, who noted that Thebans called the letter *u ha*, "possibly because of some forgotten function." In *Le Mystère des lettres grecques* the letter *u* is called *he* (W. E. Crum, *A Coptic Dictionary* [Oxford, 1939] p. 467). In seven cases it was Demotic *he* which was glossed *u*.

[50] In addition to the correspondences found in Table 5 there is also one example of *ng* glossed *g*; one each of [Demotic], [Demotic], and [Demotic] glossed *θ*; one of [Demotic] glossed *φθ*; two of [Demotic] glossed *Ξ*; and one of [Demotic] glossed *Ξ*. One of the examples of *ps* is actually glossed ϥ. Leiden I 384 verso also has one example each of *nth* glossed *d* (dubious), *tꜣ*, "land," glossed *to*, *ps* glossed *ps*, and *g* glossed *x*. The example of *gs* glossed *x* is word final.

[51] Note also the dubious example in Leiden I 384 verso of *nth* glossed *d*. The use of *ng* or *nk* for *g* and of *nt* for *d* is found elsewhere in Demotic; see Spiegelberg, *Grammatik*, par. 11.

[52] The only exceptions to this rule, which was also noted by F. Ll. Griffith ("The Glosses in the Magical Papyrus of London and Leiden," *ZÄS* 46 [1909] 117–31), are one example of *khy* glossed

In addition, the example of *kss* for gloss *Ξ* appears before *y*, and the examples of *ps* glossed ϥ or + all have *y* following.[53] This phenomenon seems to be a clear case of conditioned allophonic variation, where different environments—in this case whether or not followed by *i*—produce different pronunciations of the same letter—in this case palatalization when followed by *i*.[54] That this allophonic variation was Greek appears from the presentation of the correspondences between Demotic and Greek in those Greek words spelled out in the alphabetic Demotic script; see Table 6.[55] In transcribing Greek words into Demotic the scribe of Magical likewise indicated palatalization when the following letter was an *i*. The only examples occur with Greek *d* or *θ*. Greek *d* was written *ts* in Demotic *ʿntsyke* for Greek ινδικη. Similarly, Greek *θ* was written *ts* in Demotic *psymytsy* for Greek ψιμυθιον, *epʿletsyʿ* for Greek επαληθευω, and *gꜣlꜣbꜣntsy* for Greek χαλκανθη (glossed *kalakanthi*). No other examples of *d* or *θ*, and no examples of *t*, are followed by *i*. None of the examples of Greek *Ψ* or *Ξ* were written with *š* since none were immediately followed by *i*.

This distribution shows that the Egyptian was hearing these allophonic differences in Greek words and suggests that the occurrences in the glosses stem from the same source. As in any case of allophonic variation, the native speaker of the language heard and perceived them to be the same sound, and thus wrote them with the same letter. But the speaker of a different language will often hear the differences between allophones as separate sounds.[56] If he then transliterates the allophones in the other language with a conscious effort to reproduce the exact sounds heard, he will write the different allophones differently. This

---

xi and two examples of *thy* glossed *θ(e)i*. Griffith's reference (p. 120) to a similar case in 18/36 is an error, since column 18 has no line 36. The only word in the ciphers in which *i* follows one of the letters with allophones in the glosses is the Greek word μη̄λακρητικα written *melakretikou*.

[53] Could this +, which occurs twice in one word, be an incomplete form of ϥ for *Ψ* followed by *i*?

[54] It is uncertain at this point whether the use of *s* after *t*, but *š* after *p* and *k*, indicates two slightly different modifications (Haardt "AK," p. 36), or whether *š* was used after *p* and *k* because *s* was already used with those letters to write Greek *Ψ* and *Ξ*.

[55] Here too the distribution of *g* and *k* suggests that the scribe heard no difference between them. He wrote either for both, although he used the Egyptian *g* about three times as often as the Egyptian *k*. The three examples of Greek *g* corresponding to Demotic  occur in three occurrences of the same Greek word πληγη. No attempt was made to distinguish *d* from *t*. The two examples of *θ* which are written with simple *t* in Demotic are both in Demotic versions of the Greek word θερμος. Could the aspiration in such close proximity to an *r* have been lost by the Egyptian?

[56] See Griffith, *Rylands* III 191, "A foreigner writes a word as he hears it pronounced, but a native writes it as it should be pronounced correctly."

is what the scribe of Magical did, because he needed to indicate the exact sounds carefully in order for the pronunciation of the magical names to be effective, and the allophones involved were not second nature to him or to his readers. Thus the Demotic scribe developed the system of *s* and *š* before *i* to ensure that the Egyptian speaker who recited the magical words would pronounce them correctly. Since the glosses were aimed at a Greek speaker,[57] they did not need to indicate the allophones, and with one single exception they do not. That one exception is the word *nwtsy*, which was several times glossed ⲚⲞⲨⲐⲒ, but once glossed *noutsei*, probably a direct transcription of the Demotic. This is probably the Egyptian word *ntr*, "god," Coptic *noute*,[58] which had become part of the group of incantation names drawn on by both Greek and Egyptian magical texts,[59] whose origin had been forgotten, and whose pronunciation conformed to Greek.

In addition to the general phonetic correspondences between the various scripts, the spelling of many Demotic words attested in Coptic indicates the dialect being used by the scribe. Those Egyptian words actually spelled out in either the glosses or ciphers can be compared directly with the corresponding spellings in the various Coptic dialects. When a word occurs only in the Demotic, but is spelled out rather than being written with ligatures or word groups, especially when one or more letters of the Demotic alphabetic script used in conjunction with the glosses has been added to the normal Demotic spelling of the word, it is assumed that the alphabetic signs were added to the Demotic spellings for the same reason that they were used in the magical names—to indicate the correct pronunciation.[60] On the basis of the general phonetic correspondences discussed above, the approximate pronunciation of these words can be determined and then compared with Coptic.

The most common addition was a word-final *e*—indicated by *ıı*, more rarely *ɜ*—immediately before the determinative.[61] Sethe thought the Demotic use of

[57] See above, note 48.

[58] Note also the example of *nwte* glossed *noute*.

[59] See above concerning magical names.

[60] This assumption seems justified since the alphabetic signs were added in consistent fashion and the dialectal conclusions reached using words so spelled are consistent with those reached on the basis of only Egyptian words fully spelled out in gloss or cipher. It should be noted that many of the words in the glosses or ciphers are words spelled identically in all dialects of Coptic, and so yield no information. Many Demotic words are still spelled historically, with no evidence of the actual pronunciation. Such words are not included here.

[61] There are 46 Demotic words written with this final *e* in Magical, in contrast to only six with a final *y*, in five of which the *y* was a consonant, not a vowel. What appears to be a *y*-ending plus determinative in *šmsy*, *<|||*, is more likely to be a mistake for the *s*, *<||*, with which this word was written correctly; see W. Erichsen, *Demotisches Glossar* (Copenhagen, 1954) p. 511.

this *e* was fortuitous and haphazard.[62] When the *e* was added to a feminine noun, however, it may easily be seen as an indication of the short vowel which, in Coptic, was the last remnant of the older feminine ending *t*.[63] Most of the masculine nouns to which the scribe of Magical added this final *e* also end in a final short vowel in at least one dialect of Coptic.[64] A good example of the distribution of this final *e* consistent with the appearance of a short final vowel in Coptic occurs in the word for vine. The absolute form of the noun is written *ꜣlle*, corresponding to spellings in S, A, L, and P with final *e*. But in the construct form *ꜣll šw* (S *elelšouōou*) there is no *e*. The scribe of Magical also consistently added the final *e* only to those verbs and in those forms which, in Coptic, appear with a final short vowel in at least one of the dialects.[65] The consistency with which the Coptic form corresponding to a Demotic word with final *e* also has a short final vowel suggests that the scribe of Magical, at least, was using the Demotic sign deliberately to indicate that the Demotic pronunciation also ended in a final short vowel. That this final short vowel was a final short *e* is indicated by the fact that, in the glosses, Demotic *e* in almost every case corresponds to *e*, whether stressed or unstressed,[66] and almost never to *i*, for which Demotic *y* was used, whether stressed or unstressed,[67] and that occasionally the Demotic word to which the final *e* was added was glossed, and the final *e* was glossed *e*.[68] In the Egyptian words appearing in the ciphers the final short vowel has been recognized as an *e* everywhere by Griffith. Many of the Egyptian words in the glosses also end with this final unstressed *e*. Of the glossed words ending in *i* which are recognizable as Egyptian words, only one uses this *i* as a final short vowel. In all the other examples the *i* was being used consonantally as *y*, as written in the Demotic. The one word written with final vocalic *i* is *nouθi* (or *noutsei*), which is also written once with final short *e*, *noute*. One of the major differences between the vowel systems of the different Coptic dialects is whether a final, nonstressed, short vowel appears as *i* (F and B) or as

[62] Kurt Sethe, "Die angebliche Bezeichnung des Vokals *ĕ* im Demotischen," *ZÄS* 62 (1927) 8–12.

[63] As in *ʿte.t*, *pẖre.t*, *pše.t*, *swre.t*, *snbe.t*, *tbe.t*.

[64] As in *ỉrpe*, *ỉrte*, *bʿe*, *bne*, *bre*, *bte*, *pke*, *fʿe*, *mne*, *mḥe*, *mste*, *nḥe*, *nge*, *rhwe*, *ḥnwḥe*, *ḥnke*, *skne*, *glme*, *kke*, *kwpre*, *kwke*, *kme*, *ṯse*, *ḏde*, Leiden I 384 verso *fʿe*. The number of nouns for which there is no Coptic parallel to the Demotic form with *e* is very small.

[65] See below. Note also that with a noun subject the periphrastic *sdm.f* of the verb *ỉr*, "to do," in any construction other than the indicative past tense was written *ỉre*, with a final *e*, corresponding to Coptic equivalents ending in *re*.

[66] As in *pꜣ sepe* glossed *psepe*.

[67] As in *tsytsyw* glossed *didiou*.

[68] As in the feminine noun *ẖytre.t* glossed ϭⲉⲓⲧ⳨ⲣⲉ; *nwte* glossed *noute*.

e (S, A, L, and P).[69] Thus the scribe of Magical was using one of the valley dialects rather than dialect B or F.

In addition, the scribe of Magical consistently added this final *e* where dialect A, and sometimes dialect L, add an epenthetic vowel *e*:[70] at the end of a word ending in a consonant or double vowel plus *b*, *l*, *m*, *n*, or *r*, and more rarely in *y* or *w*. The final *e* is especially common with the absolute infinitive. Examples from Magical include *hbrbre*, "to fall to pieces," *swne*, "to know," *kwpre*, a plant, *wtne*, "to pour," *hbke*,[71] "to wither," *skne*, "ointment," and perhaps *glme*, "dry sticks." Another example of the epenthetic vowel may be included in the partially destroyed gloss //ⲁ//ⲙⲉ over the verb *wḥm*, "to repeat." The addition of this vowel in Magical strongly suggests a connection between the dialect of Magical and dialects A and L, especially A, which has the identical innovation.

A comparison of the vowels of accented syllables in Coptic words shows a division of the dialects into two groups. S, B, and P generally have an *a* in words where A, L, and F have *e*; S, B, and P generally have an *o* where A, L, and F have *a*.[72] In the first case the evidence from Magical is mixed. Both cipher and Demotic *bel*, "eye," indicate A, L, and F; so do such cipher forms as *ietf*, "his eye," *set*, "tail," *ẖel*, "myrrh," and *šefe*, "swell." But the few words which appear in the glosses seem to indicate S, B, and P: *bal*, "eye," *nau*, "to look," *šaou*, "value," *taï*, "here"; so does the Demotic spelling *yʿl* for *eiel* (A), *(e)ial* (S), "glass, mirror." Dialect P spells the word for eye both *bell* and *bal*.[73]

But the evidence of the glosses, ciphers, and Demotic spellings of the *a/o* distribution all points to A, L, and F, not S, B, and P.[74] A few of the examples

[69] Elmar Edel ("Neues Material zur Herkunft der auslautenden Vokale -ⲉ und -ⲓ im Koptischen," *ZÄS* 86 [1961] 103–6) showed that in some L dialect texts both final short *e* and final short *i* are found, unlike the case in Magical.

[70] See Till, *Dialektgrammatik*, par. 51. Examples in the Theban ostraca are given by Crum, *Epiphanius* I 247.

[71] Here *e* shows that the metathesis seen in Coptic *hōqme* (L; not attested in A) has already occurred, producing the environment, *b/m*, which calls for the addition of *e*.

[72] See Till, *Dialektgrammatik*, pars. 24 and 34; for exceptions, see pars. 25–28 and 35–43. Of the Theban Coptic ostraca Crum states, "Far the most frequent of all vocalic peculiarities is the use of *a* in place of *o*. . . . *E* (often *ē*), in place of *a*, appears constantly" (*Epiphanius* I 237). See also Worrell, *Coptic Sounds*, pp. 101–2. The vowel pattern found in dialect P is discussed by Nagel, "Frühkoptische," par. 2.13 (to be taken with Polotsky's comments thereto, "Coptic," p. 561). See also the table in Kasser, *BIFAO* 73 (1973) 97.

[73] Kasser, *P. Bodmer VI*, glossary, p. 127.

[74] Nagel, "Frühkoptische," par. 2.13 on the distribution of the *a/o* vowel and par. 2.152 on final *a* are the two main paragraphs on the basis of which Vergote (*RdE* 25 [1973] 50–57) argued against Nagel's identification of the P dialect as Theban. But one must remember that the scribe of

from the glosses are: *san*, "brother," *spat*, "lip," *piatiate*, "the father of the fathers," *bal*, "outside," and *aou*(?), "and." In some cases Demotic spellings of a glossed word also indicate an *a*-vowel, for example, *pꜣ yʿm*/*piam*, "the sea" and *ꜣnk*/*anak*, "I." Examples spelled with *a* in the ciphers include *maou*, "water," *maout*, "dead," *ouamf*, "eating it," and *haite*, "hyena." Among the many words spelled in Demotic with an ʿ to correspond to A, L, and F *a* are *sʿl* and *šʿl*, "wick," *wlʿlʿ*, "to flourish," *dʿy.t* and *dʿe.t*, "wall," *gʿmgʿm*, "prevail," and *sʿr*, "scatter," while *ꜣbẖ*, "to forget" has ꜣ for *a*.

In both groups the S, B, and P spelling is innovative, that of A, L, and F archaic and conservative. Thus spellings with *a* (S, B, and P) for *e* (A, L, and F) are more diagnostic in determining dialect than the conservative use of *a* (A, L, and F) for *o* (S, B, and P); and the vowelling found in Magical also supports the conclusion that Magical was being written in P or a very similar dialect.[75]

The Egyptian words which appear in the glosses show no evidence of the aspiration of stops that is characteristic of dialect B.[76] Of the more than 15 examples of the group *tꜣ*, "land," in the magical names, only one is glossed *θō*, with aspiration; all other examples are without aspiration. Similarly *ṯꜣw* is

---

P was only trying to write his native dialect, while the "Thebanisms" in the later material from the monastery of Epiphanius are "localisms" which have crept into the writings of people trying to write in the S dialect. (Note the distinction by Worrell, *Coptic Sounds*, p. 4, quoted above, note 26.) This, plus several centuries of development between P and the texts from the monastery, accounts for the differences between dialect P and the forms which are called Th.

[75] In addition to the evidence already discussed, the spelling of some individual words (especially in the glosses) is most similar to that in dialects A or P. Since many of the words mentioned here do not occur in the corpus available for dialect P, more similarities between Magical and P might actually have existed. Specific examples include the gloss *op-* (cf. A *op-*); the gloss *nkē* and the Demotic spelling *nge* (A *nke*); Demotic *šʿš*(ʿ) (A *šašo*); Demotic *gbyr* (A *qbir*, P *kbir*; B uses *ḏaḏē*); Demotic *whe* (A *ouōẖe*); the imperative of *ḏd* written *rḏdys* and *eḏdys* (glossed *eḏïs*; A and L *aḏi*⸗ and *eḏi*⸗); Demotic *wʿyʿn*(ʿ)*y*(*ne*) (A and L *oua*(*e*)*ianin*); Demotic (*r*-)*nhe* (A, L, and P *anēhe*); Demotic *pꜣ sepe*/gloss *psepe* (S and A *psepe*); Demotic *bʿnyp* (S and A *banipe*); and Demotic *krʿ*(ꜣ)/cipher *klo* (S and A *klo*). Some of these words also occur in the ostraca from the monastery of Epiphanius with the same vowel as that indicated in Magical, e.g., *anehe* and *banipe* (Crum, *Epiphanius* I 236). In other cases the spelling is not distinctive, but A or P do include similar or identical spellings, for example, cipher *mkah* (S, A, and B *mkah*, P ⲙ̅ⲕⲁϩ), Demotic *spyr* (S, A, and L *spir*), and Demotic *ʿpe* (S, A, L, and P *ape*). The gloss *ma* over the conjunctive *mtw.k dỉ* is probably the imperative of the verb *dỉ* inserted as a correction; it corresponds to S, A, L, and P *ma*. But the imperative *my* is also glossed *maï*, identical with dialect F. The gloss ⲕⲟⲩⲓ̈ over Demotic *qwy* probably rules out B *kouḏi* or F *kouqi*, suggesting S, A, L, and F *kou*(*e*)*i* (P *k*[*oui*]?). Of the rare spellings in Magical which do not correspond to A/P, most are archaisms, e.g., gloss *iō*/cipher *eo* with final *o*-vowel, whereas A has final *ou*; retention of initial *i* in gloss *ïoh* (Demotic *yʿḥ*).

[76] See above concerning aspiration.

always glossed with *d* or *t*, never with *θ*, and *tꜣy* is glossed *ta*, not B *θa*. The word *sarpot*, "lotus," which appears in the glosses, is known only from B, but the B form shows aspiration while the gloss does not.

The evidence of the *h*'s is not as clear in the Demotic as in the glosses. The Demotic spelling *nwḏḫ*, "to sprinkle," with *ḫ*, however, certainly agrees with A, B, and P (*nouḏẖ*) as against the other dialects, which have *k* or *q* in this word. If *myḫ*(*e*) and *myš* are the same word (S *miše*, "to hit"), the Demotic spelling with *š* is unhistorical and corresponds to any dialect except A or P (*miẖe*). Similarly the spelling of the word for tooth as *šꜥl*, rather than historical *ḫl* (S *šol*, A *ẖal*) is unexpected. If the Demotic *hn* is a writing of S *hōn* (A *ẖnan*), "to approach," the confusion between *h* and *ẖ* is unexpected for A, B, and P. Should the spelling of cipher *paeiše* be compared with S *paiše*, a disease, which in an S^{A} text is written *paihe*, suggesting a possible derivation from *h*? These non-A or -P features all point toward the S dialect, as if the scribe were trying to write S forms, or, while copying an S manuscript, failed to make certain changes, or to reverse changes the S scribe had made.[77]

Two other words may be noted. The Demotic *mḥṱ*, "to seize," corresponds more closely to S and A *amahte* or L and P *emahte* than spellings without *t*, which occur in all dialects. The word *hantous*, "lizard" (cipher), is attested only in dialect B (*anθous*). The presence of *h* in the cipher when it is absent in the B form is paralleled by the cipher *haflele* corresponding to B *afleli*.[78]

The spelling of some verbs and verb forms is also diagnostic. The *t* found in the pronominal infinitive of 3-weak verbs in Magical[79] never appears in dialect B. Similarly, Magical, unlike S and F, has no *t* in the construct form of such 3-weak verbs as *šn*, "to ask." The spelling of some absolute infinitives with final epenthetic *e* indicates A, or to a lesser extent L. The evidence includes *wtne*, "to pour," and *swne*, "to know," attested with the *e* in dialects A and L; *hbrbre*, "to be confused," attested with the *e* only in dialect A; *blble*, "to blister," which is attested only in dialect S, where it is written without the *e*; and *qrmrme*, "to murmur," which is not attested in dialect A although it occurs in the other dialects, without the *e*. If attested, the A form of both *blble* and *qrmrme* would

[77] Griffith (*Rylands* I 184) suggested, "The historical conditions of the country throughout the Saite, Persian, and Ptolemaic periods point to the probability that the dialect, or one of the dialects, of Lower Egypt would take the lead amongst the educated and official classes." Klasens (referred to by Vergote [*CdE* 36 (1961) 247]), however, noted the mark of an Upper Egyptian dialect on all Demotic texts. Both Kahle and Kasser have suggested that already in pre-Coptic times dialect S was gaining in prestige as the literary dialect, and its use was spreading over all of Egypt. See Kahle, *Balaʾizah* I 242; Kasser, *ZÄS* 92 (1965) 109–11.

[78] B normally drops *h* before unstressed *a*.

[79] *ʾIn*, *ps*, *fy*, *mr*, *ms*, *ḥwy*, *ḥsy*, *st*, *šn*, *gm*, and *ṯꜣy*. For the spelling of the pronominal infinitive of *ỉr*, "to do," as *ỉyṱ*, note A and L *eet*⸗, L *eeit*⸗, P *aït*⸗.

have had the *e*. The only one of these words attested in dialect P is *swne* written *sooune*. The Theban ostraca have *saune*.

The spelling of the qualitative form *dỉ-ꜥlꜥyṱ*, "mounted," corresponds very closely to the A and L *talaeit*, as contrasted with B *talēout* or S and F forms without *t*. Likewise *ṯꜣy-ryṱ*, "lit," corresponds to S and L *ḏraeit* (not attested in A) rather than B *qrēout*. Thus *dỉ-kdyṱ*, "put around," corresponds to the spelling which would presumably have appeared in A and L if the word were attested in those dialects, rather than B *taktēout*. In P and the Theban ostraca the ending of such qualitatives is written *-oeit*.[80] In addition to these three qualitative forms, Magical includes examples of the qualitative of *ḥms*, "to sit," spelled *ḥmsṱ*. The *t* in the qualitative is attested only in A, L, and P, although forms of the qualitative without *t* are found in all five major dialects (but not P) and in Magical. The imperative of the verb *ỉr*, "to do," *r-ỉry*, is glossed *ari*, identical with the construct imperative *ari*⸍ in S, A, and B.[81] Thus the morphological evidence is consistent with the assumption that the scribe of Magical was using dialect P.

Since only one literary text is known in dialect P, that is, P. Bodmer VI, the range of vocabulary for comparison is very small. No significant overlap of vocabulary between P and Magical has been noted.[82]

The writing of some of the verbal auxiliaries in Magical does, however, indicate the dialect used by the scribe. He used the construction *n-drt* plus *sdm.f* to form a temporal clause, corresponding to the temporal in S, A, L, and P.[83] The historical spelling of the conjunctive prefix is *mtw* (|ꜥ\), the first person singular of which is glossed *nta* in one place, with *n* for *m*.[84] The rare spellings in Magical using *n-ỉỉr.k* or *n-st* correspond to the younger forms such as *nk* found in all Coptic dialects except B, in which the *t* was always retained, and A, which also dropped the *n*. The scribe of Magical used a group identical with the conjunctive prefix glossed *nta* to write the terminative, indicating the presence of an *n* in that prefix, unlike B and A *šatef*.[85] The (cipher) vocalization of the *sdm.f* in the aorist with *e*, in *mtes* or *mtef*, corresponds to A, L, and F. The conditional auxiliary *r-ỉre* introduced by the scribe of Magical for use with

[80] See Nagel, "Frühkoptische," p. 43, par. 3.42.

[81] And see the imperatives of *ḏd*, discussed above, note 75.

[82] But such words as *ḥnwḥe*, "to be afraid" and *ḥte.t*, "threshing-floor," are attested only in dialect A.

[83] See Till, *Dialektgrammatik*, par. 265; Kasser, *P. Bodmer VI*, glossary, p. 141, *n̄tar*.

[84] In Coptic both the conjunctive and the independent pronoun, which was written with the same Demotic group as the conjunctive, have *n*, not *m*.

[85] Till, *Dialektgrammatik*, par. 260.

noun subjects is perhaps a phonetic spelling of that auxiliary. Since *r* corresponds to *a* and the spelling *ỉre* indicates an ending *re*,[86] a pronunciation *are*, as in B and A, seems indicated. In one instance the scribe of Magical used the conditional particle, which he wrote *šʿne*, resembling S, B, and F *šan* more than P, A, and L *ša*.[87] The *e* at the end almost resembles the epenthetic *e* added after some letter combinations, including final *n*.[88] If this one example of the conditional particle has been borrowed from another dialect, it may indicate an early attempt to adapt this element, not native to the dialect, to P, A, and L pronunciation, a method which was later abandoned by P, A, and L scribes in favor of the standard *ša* found in Coptic texts. This might well be another example of borrowing, or translation, from S.[89] The perfect tense, *wꜣḥ.f sdm*, is freely used in Magical. Its descendant, *hafsōtm*, is found in P, A, L, and F.[90] In the other dialects the perfect has coalesced with the past.[91] The participial forms derived from *wꜣḥ.f sdm* occur in P and in the Theban ostraca.[92] The example of the relative form of the negative aorist written *nty ỉw my.s* would at first glance seem to indicate that this form was being pronounced **etemys*, a pronunciation found in none of the Coptic dialects. However, the glossing of the imperative *my* as *ma*[93] suggests that the spelling *nty ỉw my.s* is an attempt to indicate the pronunciation *etemas*, identical with P, A, and L (*ma*).[94] Perhaps the clearest indicator is the innovative spelling of the vetitive, which is written *bn*, identically with the negative existence particle *bn*, Coptic *mn*. The only Coptic dialects that use *mn* for the vetitive are P and A; the other dialects all use the form *mpr*, from Demotic *m-ỉr*, the historically attested form, which is also occasionally used in Magical.[95]

Thus all the dialectal features in Magical support, or are consistent with, the conclusion that Magical was written in a dialect identical with or very similar

[86] See above, note 65.

[87] Till, *Dialektgrammatik*, par. 334; Kasser, *P. Bodmer VI*, p. XXVII, 7.

[88] See above concerning the addition of an epenthetic *e* by the scribe of Magical.

[89] See above, note 77.

[90] See Walter Till, *Achmîmisch-koptische Grammatik* (Leipzig, 1928), pars. 132*b* and 236*b*; Till, *Dialektgrammatik*, par. 262; Kahle, *Balaʾizah* I, pars. 150 ff.; and the two examples in P. Bodmer VI spelled *hisōtm* (see Kasser, *P. Bodmer VI*, p. XXVII, 12).

[91] On the historical development of the Demotic past and perfect into Coptic, see Johnson, *Demotic Verbal* (in press).

[92] See Nagel, "Frühkoptische," par. 3.43, and Crum, *Epiphanius* I 249 and 251.

[93] See discussion following p. 116.

[94] Till, *Dialektgrammatik*, par. 250; Kasser, *P. Bodmer VI*, glossary, p. 134.

[95] See Till, *Dialektgrammatik*, par. 244; Kasser, *P. Bodmer VI*, glossary, p. 136. An example also occurs in the Theban ostraca; see Crum, *Epiphanius* I 149.

to P, although including a few features found in S or A. This in turn substantiates the original assumption that the text of Magical (and Leiden I 384 verso) was actually written in Thebes, where it was found. Since the Demotic text of Petubastis Vienna, from the first century of our era, shows definite F characteristics,[96] it seems valid to conclude that, certainly in the Roman period, different dialects, the forerunners of the various dialects found in Coptic texts, were used by different scribes, presumably in different geographical parts of the country, although the use of one, standard, literary dialect was also widespread.[97]

[96] See Lexa, *Archiv Orientalni* 6 (1934) 165. He also assigns tentative dialect identifications to several other Demotic texts.

[97] See above, note 77.

THE SHORTEST BOOK OF AMDUAT?

Leonard H. Lesko

An unusual unpublished papyrus in the Lowie Museum of Anthropology at the University of California, Berkeley, is the subject of this short study in honor of Professor Hughes.[1] This papyrus, numbered 5–267, is part of a group (264–268) that was a gift of Mrs. P. A. Hearst, who acquired it somewhere in Egypt, probably in Luxor. The University received this gift in 1905 in a tin box marked "mummy cloth." It was noted that the cloth was "covered with papyrus which, however, was not inscribed or the writing has been entirely effaced." The fact that the papyrus was in fact inscribed was not discovered until sixteen years later, when H. F. Lutz separated the cloth from the papyrus. There are no records to show whether Lutz attempted to identify the texts he uncovered.

There were portions of at least three almost complete pages of papyri in the wrappings, but there appears to be no connection between them. Two of them contain Chapters 146 and 149 from the Book of the Dead, while the third, which is the subject of this paper, has a very abbreviated version of the "Book of That Which Is in the Netherworld" (Amduat). The three pages were evidently prepared for different people originally, since portions of the names and titles of the owners of each survive on them.

With these papyri there were several leather braces bearing the embossed figures, names, and titles of King Osorkon II and of the god Amon-Reʿ. The folded-over insides of two of the leather straps are clearly visible on the accompanying photo since these still adhere steadfastly to the papyrus. The braces are worth noting for the information they seem to provide concerning the provenience and date of these Late Period papyri. Since the papyri were discovered inside the linen wrappings only in 1921, it does seem that both the braces and the papyri were included in the wrappings originally. It is doubtful, however, that the papyri of three different people would have been included in the mummy wrappings of a person buried with royal trappings during the Twenty-second Dynasty. More likely the papyri were collected and used, perhaps reused, for magical purposes in wrapping a mummy of somewhat later date. The braces as well could have been included in this later burial without their having been

[1] I am grateful to the staff of the Lowie Museum for permission to publish this papyrus and for providing the photograph.

linked to the owners of any of the papyri. If, on the other hand, there is a connection between any of the papyri and the braces, perhaps it is only with the page under consideration here, since this one alone has the leather straps so integrally involved with papyrus, linen, and resin.

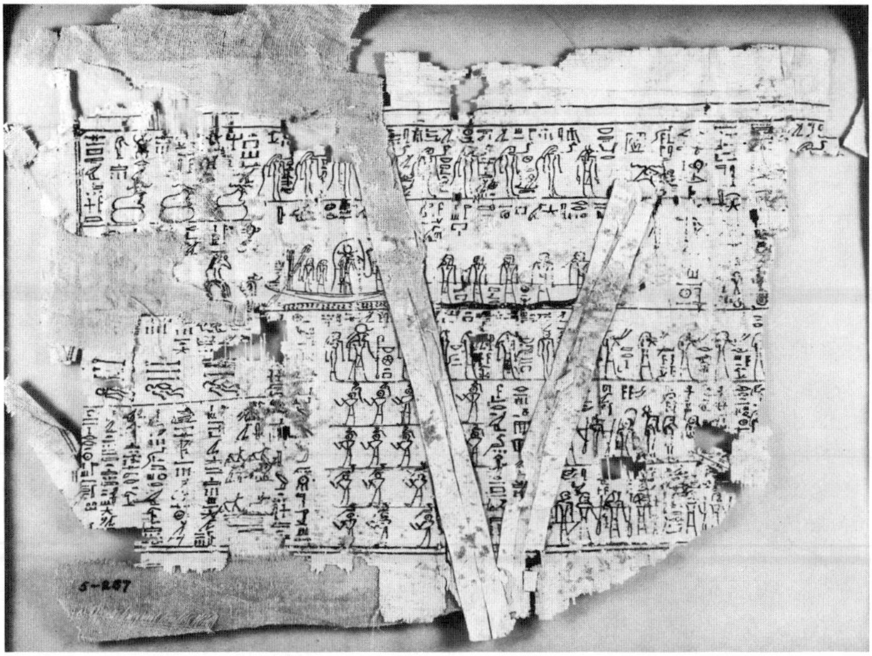

FIG. 32.—Amduat papyrus in the Lowie Museum of Anthropology, University of California, Berkeley

This small Amduat papyrus (Fig. 32) measures 36 cm. in length and 26 cm. in width. It is inscribed only on the recto. The cursive hieroglyphic is mostly in retrograde with only black ink used. The papyrus is light colored, but there are some darker spots that consist of dried resin. These spots are more prominent on the actual papyrus than on the photo, which was taken with infrared film. There are also places where the ink and some portions of one or both layers of papyrus have been lost because they adhered to the linen wrappings that faced the papyrus. Unfortunately most of the owner's name was lost in this way.

The upper right-hand portion of the papyrus (containing the horizontal signs to the *m*-owl above the head of a woman with a snake at her neck) does not belong in this position, having been misplaced when the papyrus was mounted between panes of glass. The fragment does belong at the top, but left of center and partly behind the leather strap. When the glass panes were recently separated, a few more signs on this fragment were revealed, but these proved to be of no great help in completing the text at that point. The other loose fragment in the upper right-hand corner has no writing on it at all, and the fragment at the upper left (with the legs of a bird facing left) probably belongs to a different papyrus.

An important question is how much is missing from the right side of the papyrus. Originally I decided that there would have been at least another page equal to this in size, and I thought that this would have contained some portions of the missing hours of the book of Amduat, especially the Fourth, Seventh, and Eighth. I am no longer convinced of this, since there seems to be little conformity with the standard arrangement into the hours as we know them from either the long or short versions of Amduat,[2] and there is also the strong argument that what predominates here is the Twelfth Hour and this should be near the end of the book, which in a normally retrograde text would be to the right. In any case this question will probably be answered if or when other parts of this text are found or when other of the very short versions known to be in museums are published.[3]

There are some exceptional features to be noted in this abbreviated Amduat. One is that there is no clear division into three equal registers. Another is that there are evident lapses from the retrograde writing that are not found in the longer versions. And a third is that there are individuals and groups of beings represented here that are unknown from other published versions.

There are several problems with the text that I have been quite unable to resolve. This very garbled text is being presented here partly to show a heretofore unpublished and generally unknown near-ultimate stage in the degeneration of the most important book of New Kingdom mortuary literature and partly to offer something to which others might be able to add by using material available to them.

The upper right-hand portion of the papyrus (disregarding the small misplaced fragment) contains three vertical rows of cursive hieroglyphs. The signs are slightly larger than those on the rest of the page and here generally face left. They reach down to the middle of the papyrus in spite of the fact that the line that divides the central part of the upper portion of the papyrus into two registers

[2] Cf. Erik Hornung, *Das Amduat. Die Schrift des Verborgenen Raumes* ("Ägyptologische Abhandlungen," 7 and 13 [Wiesbaden, 1963–67]).

[3] Cf. Gustave Jéquier, *Le Livre de ce qu'il y a dans l'Hades* (Paris, 1894) pp. 27–34, and Alexandre Piankoff, "Le Livre de l'Am-Duat et les variantes tardives," in *Ägyptologische Studien*, ed. O. Firchow ("Deutsche Akademie der Wissenschaften zu Berlin, Institut für Orientforschung Veröffentlichung," No. 29 [Berlin, 1955]) pp. 244–47.

extended originally to the right and was not erased satisfactorily. Portions of the first two lines are legible, and these apparently identified the person for whom the papyrus was made: "Provide[4] protection for Osiris[5] [. . .] p-n-Ḫnsw[6] of[7] the ⸢pure place⸣ (of) the prophet, he who is in his[8] month, that he may make ⸢lasting jubilation⸣.[9] . . ."[10]

The upper register continues with a mummified ram deity with the name "Djebis"[11] above. The name is followed by a *nṯr*-sign and also a seated figure within a *ḥwt*-sign, so perhaps this should be read "Djebis-ḥwt-nṯr" or "Djebis of the Temple."

Next there is a jackal-headed standing human figure with the title "Lord of the Necropolis." A kneeling jackal-headed figure with this name is known from the First Hour of the long version of Amduat.[12]

Eight female beings with snakes at their necks follow. These beings regularly occur in the Twelfth Hour, but none of the names here correspond to the names that appear in the other versions. The only name that I recognize from elsewhere is "Mistress[13] of Slaughter," and the only others that I would venture to translate are "She who makes great what is unknown (or sealed)," and "She[14] who goes forth in the day."

The text above these figures is probably intended as a major heading for the scene of the Twelfth Hour of Amduat. It appears to be a garbled version of the text over the twelve towline-pullers in the middle register of the Twelfth Hour, but perhaps it can be read: "Born is this god in the land. Every day is in his hands. What they bear . . . ."[15]

[4] Either an imperative or the infinitive "providing."

[5] Up to this point the text apparently reads from right to left.

[6] The only suggestion I can offer for the reconstructed name is an unknown Pa-shep-en-Khons. This would be the male counterpart of the known name, Ta-shep-en-Khons.

[7] Or "in," if *n* is an error for *m*.

[8] There appear to be traces of an *f* facing left. Note that what follows apparently faces right again.

[9] The *mn* is fairly clear at the top of the third line. For the traces before this I am only guessing at some form of either *ḥʿi* or *hy-hnw*.

[10] There are more traces but not enough upon which to base a reconstruction.

[11] Cf. *Dbj-nṯr* and *Ḏbb-nṯr* from the Third Hour (No. 195) in Hornung, *Das Amduat*, Pt. II, p. 65.

[12] No. 25, *ibid.*, pp. 13–14.

[13] There is no feminine *t*, but the figure is female and she is also known from the Ninth Hour (No. 635); cf. Hornung, *ibid.*, p. 156.

[14] Again the feminine *t* is omitted.

[15] At the end of this we can add the misplaced fragment from the right side. After the *m*-owl the fragment also has , but this is not much help.

At the upper left are three mummiform rams that perhaps resemble the ram from the middle register of the Ninth Hour. What the "East" goes with is uncertain even though the signs around it are reasonably clear. The last five vertical columns over the rams are again not in retrograde and we can read: "They summon their secret forms which are in it."

In the second register the central scene is of the bark of the ram-headed sun-god being dragged by at least five human figures standing on a great snake. The horizontal heading is again from the Twelfth Hour and begins with: "[The na]me of the cave (of) the door of this city." This is followed by legible characters whose disposition and translation are uncertain. Three of the pullers have unknown names.

Left of this scene are a large upraised snake's head and a ram's head on a stele(?). These possibly combine a few elements from the second register of the First Hour. A heading has, "upon it this great god."

Below this in the third register are three drowned ones of Duat corresponding to those regularly shown in water (rather than below water signs) in the Tenth Hour of Amduat.

Next are two longer vertical rows of mostly illegible hieroglyphs that refer to "the crew which is in the ⌜city⌝ . . . when this god appears."

To the right of this in the middle register is a female figure facing right, and in front of her is a hawk-headed deity with sun disk and scepter who is labeled "Lord of Duat." His figure here is more in keeping with what we would expect of this deity than what we find in the regular versions of the Twelfth Hour (No. 837).

The rest of this register has various named deities with an untranslatable heading and also some adoring figures, again from the Twelfth Hour. Among the names are "Mistress[16] of Eternity" from the Twelfth Hour (875) and *Mḥy*, possibly "Drowned One," from the Tenth Hour (746).

The longest text on the page is from the very important Fifth Hour of Amduat, and this occurs in retrograde at the lower left-hand corner.

> "The name of the cave of this god is 'West,'
> the secret ways in the west, the doors,
> the holy place of the Land of Sokar.
> The flesh[17] and the body as first forms of appearance.
> ⌜May our . . . be⌝ at a time with
> this great god in this peace, ⌜after we praised
> the might . . .⌝."

Below the last column of this text are at least four jackals, and in the center

[16] Again with no *t*.

[17] *Ḥʿw* instead of the usual *iwf*; cf. Hornung, *Das Amduat*, Pt. II, p. 93, n. 10.

of the bottom register are more than fourteen standing beings facing left with snakes upon their heads. These figures appear masculine but should be compared with the female figures with similar snakes in the bottom register of the Tenth Hour. The heading to their right says, "The names of the gods . . . 'Uraei who drive away the storm.'"

The lower right-hand corner of the page has two registers with beings in a variety of forms facing right. Many of these hold oars like the rowers of the Ninth Hour in the longer versions. One being with a unique representation and name is "Horned One" from the Fifth Hour (No. 352), and the two figures to his right look like they belong to the middle register of the Sixth Hour.

Indeed, it seems most likely that a text such as this represents an extreme abbreviation of the known versions of the Book of Amduat rather than a deliberate and meaningful adaption of that text. My attempts at reasonable translation proved futile, and I have come to the conclusion that when this was drawn up the texts were probably no longer supposed to be read. Perhaps the texts were considered superfluous to the purpose of this document, which seems to have been to represent this famous guide to the beyond in summary form, or merely to give a general impression of it. The recognition of various elements of the book is perhaps as much as was intended originally and probably all that should be attempted now.

THE NAUCRATIS STELA ONCE AGAIN

Miriam Lichtheim

The understanding of the Naucratis stela of Nectanebo I had been hampered by its orthographic peculiarities. After these difficulties had been resolved by the successive labors of Maspero, Erman, Sethe, Piehl, Kuentz, Posener, and Gunn, it seemed as if Gunn's translation, published in 1943, represented a more or less definitive rendering of the text, except that two additional corrected readings were contributed by H. de Meulenaere in 1959.[1] As far as I know, no further comments on the stela have appeared since then. A recent reading of the text has convinced me, however, that the crucial part of the decree, the passage in which the king's donation to the temple of Neith is specified (lines 8–10), has all along been mistranslated and misunderstood.

All translators and commentators have followed Erman's interpretation, according to which the king's donation consisted of "1. der Zehnte, der im Hafen *Ḥnwt-ḥnt* von allem vom griechischen Meer her Importierten erhoben wird, 2. der Zehnte, der in Naukratis von allem dort Fabrizierten erhoben wird."[2] Yet while affirming his belief in the correctness of this interpretation, Erman admitted a certain uneasiness in the face of the "vagueness" of the Egyptian phrasing and the lack of clarity of the key terms. He proposed to read *wꜥ ꜥ* 10 for what in fact is written as *wꜥ m* 10 and wondered why this term rather than *r*-10 was used. He pointed to the uncertain meaning of the noun *ỉšty*. And, most important of all, he observed that the two relative clauses, *nty tw ḥsbw* and *ntt tw ḥsbw*, cannot be connected with "ein Zehntel" because their antecedents are the "imported" and the "fabricated" goods. In short, Erman was aware that the

[1] Bibliography: G. Maspero, "Une Stèle de Nectanébo II," *CRAIBL* 27 (4th series; 1899) 973–95 and in E. Grébaut, *Le Musée égyptien* 1 (Cairo, 1890–1900) 40–44 and Pl. XLV; Adolf Erman and Ulrich Wilcken, "Die Naukratisstele," *ZÄS* 38 (1900) 127–35; Karl Piehl, "La Stèle de Naucratis," *Sphinx* 6 (1903) 89–96 and *idem*, "Plagiat ou non?" *ibid.*, 182; Kurt Sethe, "Zur Erklärung der Naukratisstele," *ZÄS* 39 (1901) 121–23; Charles Kuentz, "Sur un passage de la Stèle de Naucratis: La Lecture du signe [hieroglyph]," *BIFAO* 28 (1929) 103–6; G. Posener, "Notes sur la Stèle de Naucratis," *ASAE* 34 (1934) 141–48; Battiscombe Gunn, "Notes on the Naukratis Stele," *JEA* 29 (1943) 55–59; Günther Roeder, *Die ägyptische Götterwelt* (Zurich, 1959) pp. 86–94; H. de Meulenaere, "Zwei Bemerkungen zur Naukratisstele," *ZÄS* 84 (1959) 78–79; Hellmut Brunner, *Hieroglyphische Chrestomathie* (Wiesbaden, 1965) Pls. 23–24.

[2] Erman and Wilcken, *ZÄS* 38 (1900) 131.

wording of the key phrases was not in harmony with his conclusions. He tried to account for these discrepancies by attributing the "Unklarheiten" to the insufficient knowledge of the classical language on the part of the "Hierogrammaten."

Erman's interpretation was universally accepted, and thus the notion that the Naucratis stela offered firm evidence for the existence of a 10 per cent customs levy and a 10 per cent tax on trades, both collected at Naucratis in the reign of Nectanebo I and perhaps also earlier, became an axiom cited in all handbooks and history books, and wherever Egyptian trade and taxes were discussed.[3]

Let us now read the passage:

Ḏd.ỉn ḥm.f: ỉmỉ dỉ.tw wꜥ m 10 nb m ḥḏ m ḫt m mḏḥt m ḫt nb pr m wꜣḏ-wr ḥꜣw-nbw m ỉšty nb nty tw ḥsbw ỉr pr-nswt m nỉwt ḥnwt rn.s; ḥnꜥ wꜥ m 10 nb m ḥḏ m ỉḫt nb ntt ḫpr m pr-mryt ḏd.tw n.s kꜣrṯ ḥr spt ꜥnw ntt tw ḥsbw r pr-nswt r ḥtpw-nṯr n mwt.ỉ Nt r km ḏt.

The literal rendering is:

His majesty said: "Let there be given one in 10 (of) gold, of silver, of timber, of worked wood, of everything going out on the sea of the Greeks, of all the ⌜goods⌝ (or: being all the ⌜goods⌝) that are reckoned to the king's domain in the town called Ḥenwe; and one in 10 (of) gold, of silver, of all the things that come into being in Pi-emroye, called ⟨Nau⟩cratis, on the bank of the Anu, that are reckoned to the king's domain, to be a divine offering for my mother Neith for all time."

Observe first that the scribe both times wrote *wꜥ m* 10 *nb*, and not *wꜥ* 10 *m nb*. It is possible that this was done for graphic reasons and that he did indeed mean *wꜥ* 10 *m nb*. Sethe read it as *wꜥ* 10 *m nb*, but also concluded that the original meaning would have been "one in 10."[4] Whichever way one reads it, the meaning is "one in 10" or "one-tenth," and not "the tenth" or "the tithe." Observe how Sethe shifted from "ein Zehntel" to "das Zehntel"!

As for the word *ỉšty*, despite lingering doubts it is probably merely a graphic variant of *ỉšt*. Even if it is not a mere variant of *ỉšt*, its meaning can hardly have

[3] E.g., Hermann Kees, *Ägypten* ("Kulturgeschichte des alten Orients" 1 [Munich, 1933]) p. 255: "Für das Delta mit seinem 10%igen Einfuhrzoll auf alle Waren vom Ägäischen Meer, der vorwiegend den griechischen Handel über Naukratis belastete, zeigt uns noch im 4.Jh.v.Chr. die Naukratisstele Nektanebos' I. die gleichen Verhältnisse. Auch diese fiskalische Steuer tritt der König, sogar zusammen mit der aus Naukratis einkommenden Gewerbesteuer von gleicher Höhe auf alle Betriebe, bei seinem Regierungsantritt an den Neithtempel von Sais ab." And most recently Wolfgang Helck in his article "Abgaben und Steuern," in *Lexikon der Ägyptologie* I, ed. Wolfgang Helck and Eberhard Otto (Wiesbaden, 1975) col. 6: "Hierzu gehören auch die zehnprozentigen Abgaben von Naukratis vom Hafenumschlag wie von der Produktion, die Nektanebis I. vom Staat an den Tempel der Neith von Sais überträgt."

[4] *ZÄS* 39 (1901) 122.

differed significantly from "goods," for the parallelism between the two periods, with their relative clauses, is very pronounced.

Third, the two relative clauses need to be looked at very closely. As Erman had observed, the clause *nty tw ḥsbw ỉr pr-nswt m nỉwt ḥnwt rn.s* and the corresponding clause *ntt tw ḥsbw r pr-nswt* do not refer to *wʿ m* 10 *nb* (etc.) but belong to *ỉšty nb* and *ỉḫt nb*, respectively. Now what is the meaning of imported goods "that are reckoned to the royal domain in Ḥenwe" and locally made goods "that are reckoned to the royal domain"? The location of Ḥenwe is unknown. Being connected somehow with Naucratis, it may have been the harbor quarter, or perhaps a nearby site where there were storehouses. Erman rendered the passage with a sense of uncertainty: "von jedem . . . , das man versteuert(?), an den Fiskus in der Stadt, die *Ḥnwt-ḥnt* heisst." Gunn translated: "all goods(?) which are reckoned to the King's Domain in the city called Ḥenwe," and explained in a footnote: "I.e. on which the king's taxes are levied."[5] The seeming ambiguity of the phrasing is due to our ignorance of the underlying situation. Does "goods reckoned to the royal domain at Ḥenwe" mean imports which, on arrival, were sorted and assessed for taxation? Or does it mean goods which, having been assessed on the basis of the tax law, were being forwarded to the royal treasury? In the first case, "goods reckoned to the royal domain" would mean "taxable goods." In the second case it would mean "taxed goods."

The second alternative appears to me the more likely in view of the terms used and in view of what I envisage to have been the real-life situation. But whichever of the two meanings applied, the main point remains the same. It is that the text says specifically that *of* all the imported goods "that are reckoned to the royal domain" and *of* all the locally manufactured goods "that are reckoned to the royal domain" the temple of Neith is to receive one-tenth. In other words, the literal reading of the text shows that the king is not granting the Neith temple the proceeds of a 10 per cent tax on imports to Naucratis, nor the proceeds of a 10 per cent trades tax levied on goods manufactured at Naucratis. Rather, *the king grants the temple one-tenth of all the goods that are taxed (or, taxable) at Naucratis on the basis of a customs tax and a trades tax, both taxes being levied at unspecified rates of taxation.*

Even if "taxable" rather than "taxed" goods was meant, the text neither states nor implies that the king was diverting his tax revenue to the temple. And in no way is it indicated at what rate of taxation that revenue accrued. The difference between "taxed" and "taxable" goods would be one of quantity and manner of collecting the revenue. If the temple were to receive one-tenth of the "taxable" goods, it would be getting its share in a transaction parallel with the king's taking his share, whereas the more natural reading "taxed goods" implies that

[5] *JEA* 29 (1943) 58.

the temple gets a 10 per cent share of the royal tax revenue after it has been collected.

As far as I know we do not possess a single Egyptian document prior to the Ptolemaic era in which a rate of tax assessment is stated directly.[6] Even so relatively certain a figure as the standard grain delivery of five sacks per arura of land, which probably represents total yield rather than tax or rent, has been obtained indirectly by calculation from lists of receipts, rather than directly from formal statements. Is this absence of officially recorded rates of taxation due merely to the massive loss of Egyptian texts? I suspect that there were reasons for not recording tax rates in the permanent form of decrees. In any case, the Naucratis stela, as hitherto interpreted, stood out as an exception.

This is not to say that the figure of 10 per cent was not often employed in assessing a tax, a contribution, a deduction, or a fee. It was probably quite common. One well-known example of the use of this figure is the statement by Ramses III in the Great Harris Papyrus that he did not, as other kings had done, remove one-tenth of the temple personnel in order to draft them into the army (P. Harris I 57, 8–9). Is it a mere accident that the practice of drafting one-tenth of the temple personnel is known only negatively through a disclaimer?

In Ptolemaic documents there are occasional references to rates of tax assessment. On the Rosetta Stone, for example, Ptolemy Epiphanes is thanked for having freed the temples of the tax of one artaba for every arura of sacred land (line 30).

The Famine Stela[7] is often cited alongside the Naucratis stela as alleged evidence for a customs tax assessed at the rate of 10 per cent. Kees, for example, formulated the claim thus:

"Mit dem Besitzrecht über Unternubien war die Erhebung eines Zehnten Durchgangszoll auf alle Handelsartikel aus dem Sudan, Gold, Elfenbein, Hölzer (vor allem Ebenholz) und Minerale verbunden, der dem Chnumtempel zustehen sollte."[8]

This view is maintained in the already cited recent article by Helck, "Abgaben und Steuern" (col. 6): "Auch auf der Hungersnotstele beträgt der Durchgangszoll bei Elephantine 10%." On the other hand, H. Brunner in his article "Die Hungersnotstele"[9] summarized the royal donation as follows:

[6] The presently known Egyptian records dealing with revenues and taxation have been worked over assiduously by a number of scholars, and the results are now expertly summed up in Helck's article "Abgaben und Steuern" cited above, note 3.

[7] Published in P. Barguet, *La Stèle de la famine à Séhel* ("BdE" XXIV [1953]).

[8] *Ägypten*, pp. 106 and 255. See also Kees's more elaborate statement in his later work, *Das alte Ägypten, eine kleine Landeskunde* (Berlin, 1958) pp. 182–83.

[9] Hellmut Brunner, "Die Hungersnotstele," in *Kindlers Literatur Lexikon* III (Zurich, 1967) cols. 2255–56.

"Zum Dank dafür erlässt der König am nächsten Morgen ein Dekret, worin er alle Menschen, die in dem von Elephantine bis Takompso reichenden Gebiet des Dodekaschoinos wohnen, dem Chnum(-tempel) unterstellt und ein Zehntel aller Einkünfte dieses Gebietes, vor allem an Bodenschätzen, ebenfalls dem Gott überweist."

Thus, according to Brunner, the decree of the Famine Stela assigns to the Khnum temple one-tenth of all the revenue that the king derives from the region, while according to Kees and Helck the king relinquishes to the temple customs dues of 10 per cent on Nubian imports and a variety of local revenues that had also been taxed at the rate of 10 per cent.

Barguet's edition of the Famine Stela has greatly advanced the understanding of this very difficult text. A number of uncertainties remain, but I believe that a close reading of the passage dealing with the royal donation (lines 23–30) yields the following results:

The king declares that he grants (*ḥnk*) to the Khnum temple the entire region of the Dodekaschoinos. This sweeping declaration is clearly hyperbolic, for it is immediately qualified by a series of specific grants that define the limits of the donation. What is actually granted is enumerated in the following order:

(1) All the harvests, or harvest dues (*šmw*) of those who till the fields of the Dodekaschoinos are to be given to the temple.

(2) The king will take (*šdỉ*) one-tenth of the catch of the fishermen, fowlers, and hunters. It is not stated that he will collect this amount in order to give it to the temple, but this seems to be the intended meaning. The king's own share is then unspecified.

(3) The temple is to receive a regular supply of animals for the daily sacrifices. A lacuna occurs here that makes it impossible to determine whether a 10 per cent figure stood here. Barguet did not think so and restored the lacuna as *r ꜣw*, "entirely."

(4) Nubian products imported from Khent-ḥen-nefer, consisting of gold, ivory, ebony, and other goods, are to be given to the temple. The sentence begins with a group of three signs that had been read as *dỉ r*-10. On the basis of this reading Kees and others had arrived at the notion of 10 per cent customs dues relinquished by the king in favor of the temple. Barguet, however, did not admit this reading. According to him the third sign is not the numeral 10, but rather the determinative of the sack, and the whole group is to be read as *ʿrf*, "sack." I am not convinced that Barguet's reading is the correct one, because the sentence dealing with Nubian imports then lacks a verb unless it is attached to the preceding sentence dealing with sacrificial cattle, as Barguet indeed took it to be. But if so attached, the sentence becomes excessively long and combines too many disparate elements. If the reading *dỉ r*-10 is maintained, it nevertheless does not follow that the king is relinquishing to the temple a 10 per cent royal

tax on Nubian imports. It merely follows that he grants the temple one-tenth of his Nubian tax revenue.

(5) No official is to give orders "in these places" or to take anything away.

(6) One-tenth of all that the mine and quarry workers produce and one-tenth of all the products made by the various craftsmen connected with the mining operations is to be given to the temple. Again there is no indication that the king's revenue consisted of 10 per cent of these products, but only that he grants the temple a 10 per cent share. Since the king owned all mines and quarries except where he had ceded mining rights to a temple, it would be strange indeed if his revenue were here listed as a mere 10 per cent of the output.

Thus, the Famine Stela does not provide evidence for a 10 per cent tax on Nubian imports in Ptolemaic times. At best it indicates that the authors of this pseudepigraphon attributed to the king the intention of assigning to the Khnum temple a 10 per cent share of his Nubian trade revenue along with a 10 per cent share of other revenues derived from the Dodekaschoinos. That is to say, the summary of the royal donation given by Brunner is correct, while the conclusions drawn by Kees, Helck, and others need to be revised.

As regards the several Greco-Roman hieroglyphic inscriptions in which the Dodekaschoinos is donated to Isis of Philae,[10] two of these mention the grant of "one-tenth of everything that comes from Nubia." Here, too, the phrasing suggests a grant of one-tenth of the royal revenue rather than the ceding to the temple of revenue obtained from a 10 per cent tax.

I append a complete translation of the Naucratis stela. The encomium to the king is metrically composed and its rhythms are underlined by assonances. The decree itself is written in prose, a prose whose deliberate cadences show that even at this late date the ancient literary language was handled with skill.

(1) Year 1, fourth month of summer, day 13 of the majesty of Horus, Strong-armed; King of Upper and Lower Egypt; Two Ladies, Who benefits the Two Lands; Gold-Horus, Who does the gods' wish; Kheperkare, Son of Re Nekhtnebef, ever-living, beloved of Neith, mistress of Sais; good god, Re's image, Neith's beneficent heir.

She raised his majesty above millions,
Appointed him ruler of the Two Lands,
Placed her uraeus upon his head,
Captured for him the nobles' hearts,
Enslaved for him the people's hearts,
And vanquished all his enemies.

Mighty monarch guarding Egypt,
Copper wall (3) enclosing Egypt,

[10] The references will be found in Kurt Sethe, *Dodekaschoinos das Zwölfmeilenland* ("UGAÄ II/3 [Leipzig, 1901]) pp. 3 and 16.

Powerful one with active arm,
Sword master who attacks a host,
Heart afire at seeing his foes,
Heart-gouger of the treason-hearted.
Who does good to him who's loyal,
They can sleep till daylight,
Their hearts full of his good nature,
And they stray not from their paths.
Who makes green all lands when he rises,
Who sates every man with his bounty,
All eyes are dazzled by seeing him,
Like Re when he rises in lightland,
Love of him sprouts in each body,
He has granted life to their bodies.

Whom the gods acclaim (5) when they see him,
Who wakes to seek what serves their shrines,
Who convokes their prophets to consult them,
On all the functions of the temple,
Who acts according to their words,
And is not deaf to their advice.
Right-hearted on the path of god,
Who builds their mansions, founds their walls,
Supplies the altar, heaps the bowls,
Provides oblations of all kinds.
Sole god of many wonders,
Served by the sun disk's rays,
Whom mountains tell their inmost,
Whom ocean offers its flood,
Whom foreign lands bring (7) their bounty,
For he rests their hearts in their valleys.

His majesty rose in the palace of Sais, and set in the temple of Neith. The king entered the mansion of Neith, and rose in the Red Crown beside his mother. He poured a libation to his father, the lord of eternity, in the mansion of Neith. Then his majesty said:

"Let there be given one in 10 (of) gold, of silver, of timber, of (9) worked wood, of everything going out on the sea of the Greeks, of all the ⌜goods⌝ (or: being all the ⌜goods⌝) that are reckoned to the king's domain in the town called Ḥenwe; and one in 10 (of) gold, of silver, of all the things that come into being in Pi-emroye, called ⟨Nau⟩cratis, on the bank of the Anu, that are reckoned to the king's domain, to be a divine offering for my mother Neith for all time (11) in addition to what was there before. And one shall make one portion of an ox, one fat goose, and five measures of wine from them as a perpetual daily offering,[11]

[11] Gunn's rendering "And let them be converted into one portion of an ox, etc." creates the impression that the entire donation would yield only the modest daily offering of one portion of an ox, one goose, and five measures of wine.

the delivery of them to be at the treasury of my mother Neith. For she is the mistress of the sea; it is she who gives abundance.

"My majesty has also commanded to preserve and protect the divine offering of my mother Neith, (13) and to maintain everything done by the ancestors, in order that what I have done be maintained by those who shall be for an eternity of years."

His majesty said: "Let these things be recorded on this stela, placed in Naucratis on the bank of the Anu. Then shall my goodness be remembered for all eternity." On behalf of the life, prosperity, and health of the King of Upper and Lower Egypt, Kheperkare, Son of Re Nekhtnebef, ever-living. May he receive all life, duration, and dominion, all health and joy like Re forever!

PAPYRUS HARKNESS

Thomas J. Logan

It is a great pleasure to make available in honor of Professor Hughes one of the longest Demotic religious texts still in existence.[1] It was Professor Hughes who introduced me to Demotic, a language that possesses a literature that can be both highly entertaining and humorous yet is almost completely ignored by the standard surveys of ancient Egyptian literature.

In 1931 Edward S. Harkness gave a papyrus to the Metropolitan Museum of Art, and it was accessioned as MMA 31.9.7. Papyrus Harkness measures 136.5 cm. × 24.5 cm. and consists of six columns, i to v on the recto and vi on the verso (Figs. 33–44).[2] The columns range between 32 (col. v) and 38 lines (col. i); in addition there are several intralinears, and columns ii through v measure between 26.5 cm. (col. v) and 29.5 cm. (col. iii) in width (col. vi on the verso is shorter). To accommodate column vi the papyrus was turned over, so that line 1 of column vi is on the opposite side of the papyrus from the first line of column v, the top side being the same for both recto and verso. The papyrus was then rolled up beginning with column v of the recto on the inside; the verso, with its vertical fibers, is the exterior of the roll.[3] Thus when the papyrus was completely rolled the blank portion of the verso was on the exterior. The papyrus roll was then turned 90 degrees and an "address" was written on the exterior with the roll held in a horizontal position.

[1] Surpassed in size only by the famous Papyri Rhind and Louvre E. 3452. Photographs of the papyrus were made available to Prof. Nathaniel J. Reich and Dr. B. H. Stricker, who kindly supplied the museum with a tentative reading of the name of the owner of the papyrus and with the date of her death. I would like to thank Dr. Karl-Theodor Zauzich and Prof. Janet H. Johnson for further suggestions concerning the readings of the personal names. In addition, Dr. Stricker pointed out the importance of the contents of the papyrus as an independent religious composition.

[2] There are faint traces of Demotic signs on the left-hand side of the verso (now blank) and the right-hand side of the recto (col. i and part of col. ii). The area that was used as a palimpsest is darkened as a result of the erasure, and in places, the erasure is incomplete. This has caused some uncertainties in the readings of certain signs in cols. i and ii.

[3] It was customary to have the vertical fibers on the outside of the roll for they would be compressed and buckle if rolled up inside; see Jaroslav Černý, *Paper and Books in Ancient Egypt* (London, 1952) p. 10.

Unfortunately the outermost layer has suffered some damage, but enough traces of the address survive (the preserved traces would fit the mother's name) to show that no columns preceded column i. Using the minimum and maximum widths of the other columns of the recto to restore the original width of column i from its present width of 26 cm. to between 26.5 and 29.5 cm., one can estimate the original width of the papyrus to have been between 137 and 140 cm. or between 0.5 and 3.5 cm. longer than now preserved.

Address on verso (scale 1:1)

The papyrus was mounted in 1931 between two sheets of glass in a metal frame. In the fall of 1975 the papyrus was consolidated and mounted[4] under an ultraviolet-resistant Plexiglas (UF 1) with an acid-free rag-board backing by Madeleine Braun under the direction of the Egyptian and Conservation Departments of the Metropolitan Museum of Art.

The papyrus was written in a clear and competent hand that can be dated paleographically to the early Roman Period and can be more precisely fixed from column vi (verso), line 32, which gives the date of death of the owner of the papyrus Tanꜣwerow as

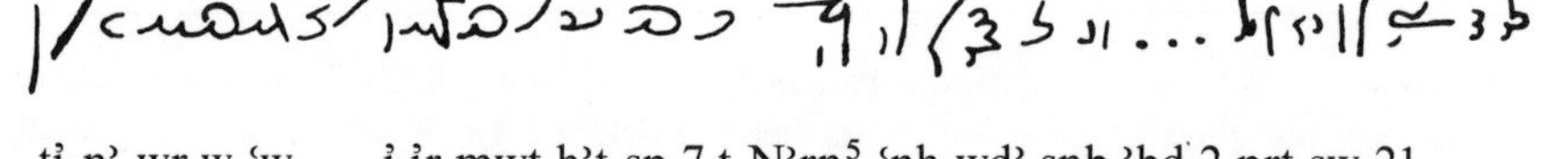

tỉ-nꜣ-wr.w-ʿw . . . ỉ.ỉr mwt ḥꜣt-sp 7.t Nꜣrn[5] ʿnḫ wḏꜣ snb ꜣbd 2 prt sw 21
"Tanꜣwerow, . . . who died in the seventh year of Nero, L.P.H., the twenty-first day of Mekhir."

The provenience of the papyrus is not known. It was purchased in Cairo in 1922 together with a linen cloak, an armband, and a cap with side-lock, all belonging to a Setem priest's costume dating from the Roman Period (MMA 31.9.4–6). The papyrus and the priest's costume were said to have been found

[4] This process had not been completed when this article was submitted and the photographs are of the papyrus before consolidation.

[5] Written .

together, but unfortunately, as Winlock points out,[6] we are dependent upon the dealer's veracity for this. If the information is true, then it may be supposed that the papyrus and costume came from a *Massengrab* or that the costume was used by the priest during the funeral ceremony and then placed in the tomb at the completion of the burial.

The papyrus was written for the woman (col. v, ll. 26–27)

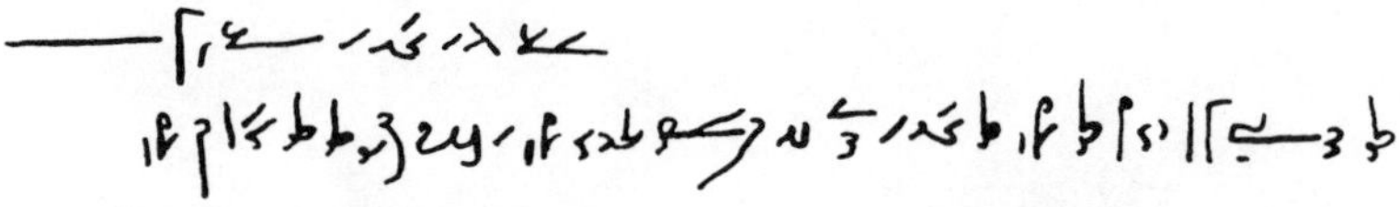

Ḥwt-ḥr Tỉ-nꜣ-wr.w-ꜥw tỉ Ḥr sꜣ Tꜣy.f-nḫṱ.t r.ms Tỉ-tw-tp(?)
"the deceased Tanꜣwerow the daughter of Hor the son of Tefnakht, born of Tatetep(?)."[7]

A variant to this (col. iii, l. 14) is

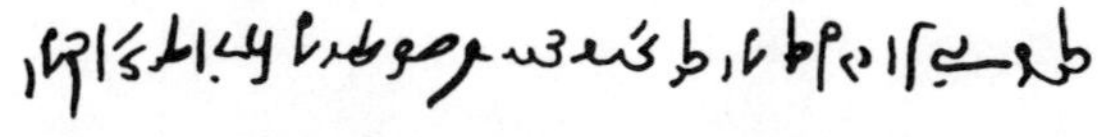

Tỉ-nꜣ-wr.w-ꜥw tỉ Ḥr sꜣ Tꜣy.f-nḫṱ.t mwt.s Tỉ-tw-tp(?)
"Tanꜣwerow the daughter of Hor the son of Tefnakht, her mother Tatetep(?)."

Her father was the scribe who wrote the papyrus (col. v, l. 30)

r.sẖ Ḥr sꜣ Tꜣy.f-nḫṱ.t pꜣy.s ỉt
"written by Hor the son of Tefnakht, her father."

The content of the papyrus is funerary in nature. It is an independent composition concerned with the transition between this life and the next. Since Demotic funerary texts comprise a surprisingly small corpus,[8] Papyrus Harkness is an important contribution to this class of literature. With this in mind it was felt desirable to call attention to this papyrus.

[6] H. E. Winlock, "The Costume of an Egyptian Priest," *BMMA* 27, No. 8 (August 1932) 186 with n. 3. In 1931 an inscribed linen was also given to the museum by Harkness, but Winlock rightly rejects the possibility that it was found together with the Setem priest's costume and papyrus since the records show that it was not acquired in the same lot.

[7] The reading of the sign  is problematic. In these name formations a theophorous element is expected after *ΠΕΤΕ-* or *ΤΕΤΕ-*; see Wilhelm Spiegelberg, *Aegyptische und griechische Eigenname aus Mumienetiketten der römischen Kaiserzeit* ("Demotische Studien" I [Leipzig, 1901]). Yet the sign does not suggest the name of any deity. Rather it resembles the sign found in *-nw*, *Nw.t*, *tꜣ*, *dr.t*, etc., as well as in *tp*. The reading *tp*, "the first," has been chosen by analogy with the *wr.w*, "the great ones," and *ꜥw.(w)*, "the important ones," that appear in the daughter's name.

[8] See J. C. Goyon, "La Littérature funéraire tardive," in *Textes et langages de l'Egypte pharaonique, Hommage à Jean-François Champollion* ("BdE" LXIV/3 [1974]) pp. 74 ff.

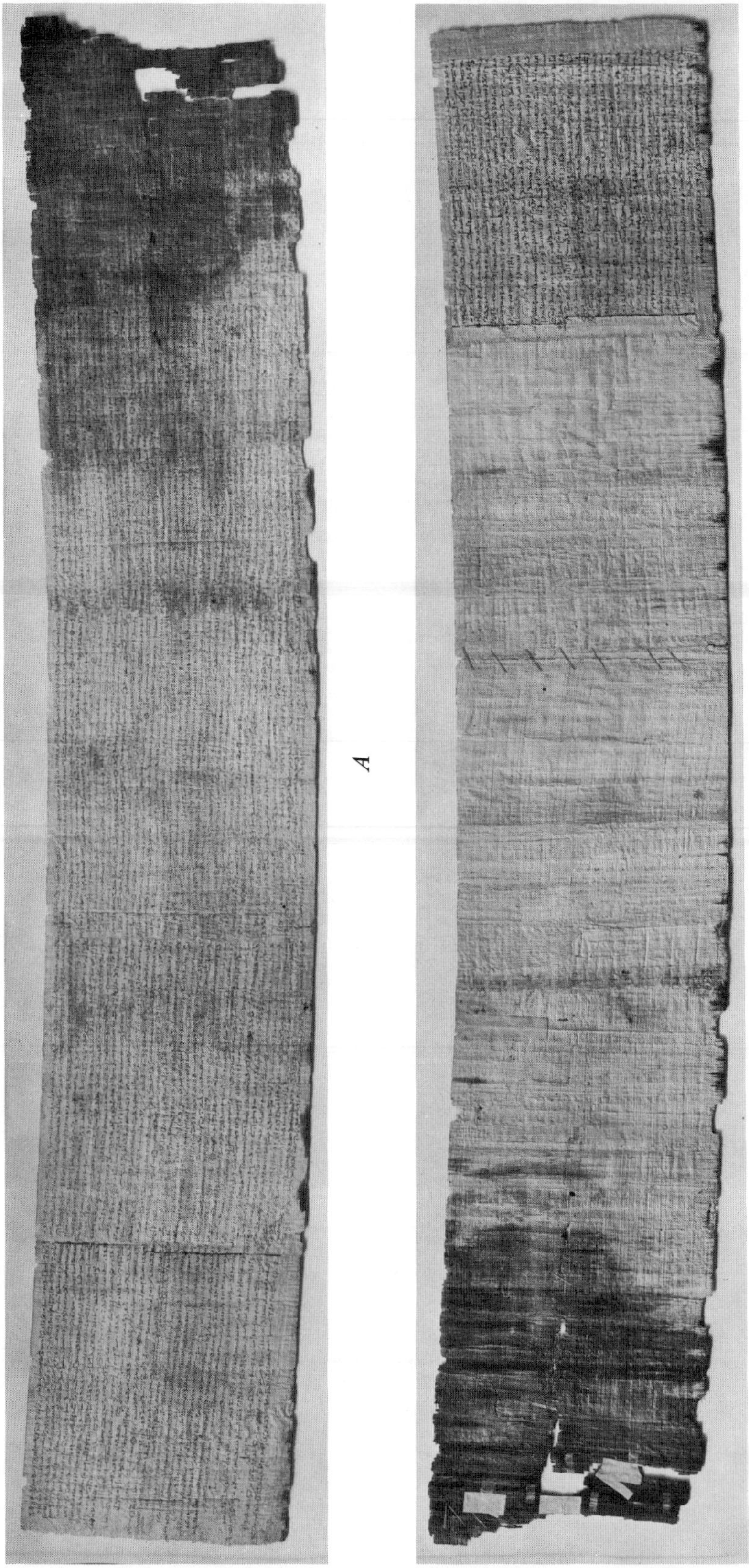

A

B

FIG. 33.—Papyrus Harkness, recto (*A*) and verso (*B*)

FIG. 34.—Infrared photograph of Papyrus Harkness, col. i

FIG. 35.—Papyrus Harkness, col. ii

FIG. 36.—Tracing of col. ii

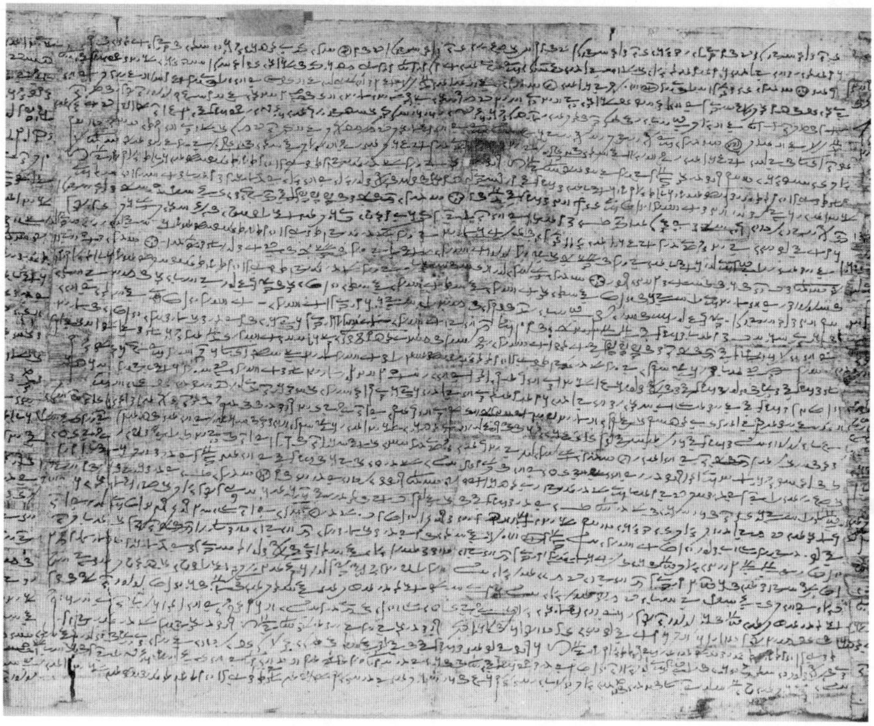

FIG. 37.—Papyrus Harkness, col. iii

FIG. 38.—Tracing of col. iii

FIG. 39.—Papyrus Harkness, col. iv

FIG. 40.—Tracing of col. iv

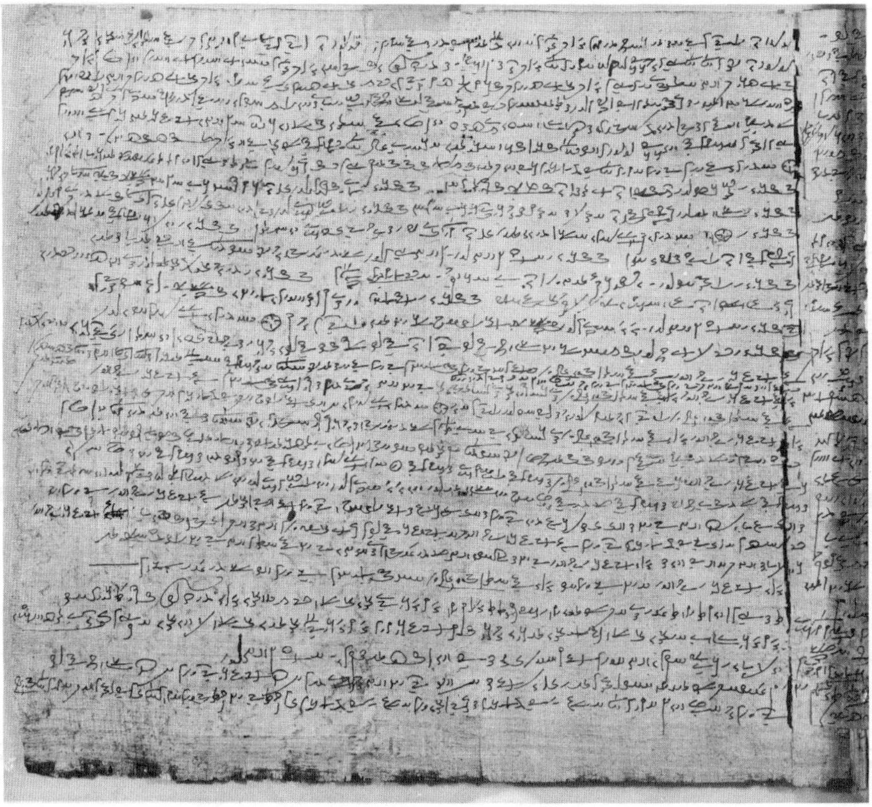

FIG. 41.—Papyrus Harkness, col. v

FIG. 42.—Tracing of col. v

FIG. 43.—Papyrus Harkness, col. vi, verso

FIG. 44.—Tracing of col. vi

ON THE ACCESSION DATE OF AKHENATEN

William J. Murnane

Familiar evidence sometimes yields new dividends. In the present instance, I hope the results will interest George Hughes on the occasion of his jubilee.

Although dated documents from the reign of Akhenaten are not scarce, they provide no clear indication of when his regnal year began. Redford has suggested that Akhenaten came to the throne in the month of I Proyet, possibly I Proyet 8, when the oath concerning the boundaries of Akhetaten (in the "Later Proclamation") was renewed.[1] This conclusion rests, first, on the calculated date for the accession of Amenophis III (in II Shomu)[2] and, second, on a hypothetical figure of seven months (supposedly in the original text of Manetho's lost *History*) as the length of his final year of rule.[3] Reexamination of this material raises a few doubts, but it also yields some revealing facts.

The opening of the "Later Proclamation" on most of the boundary stelae is dated IV Proyet 13 in year six (thus S, U, and A).[4] The date of R was probably the same, but the day number is broken, leaving only 10+x; stela Q has the variant "IV Proyet 14," and on N the date is "regnal year eight, I Proyet 13."[5] These variations are probably due to error, for on all accessible copies the occasion is defined as "the day when his Majesty, L.P.H., was manifest upon the span, upon the great chariot of electrum . . . going in a southerly direction; halting by his majesty, L.P.H., on his chariot in the presence of his father, *The Aton*, upon the southeastern mountain of Akhetaten."[6]

[1] Donald B. Redford, "On the Chronology of the Egyptian Eighteenth Dynasty," *JNES* 25 (1966) 121–22.

[2] *Ibid.*, pp. 120–21; see now Charles Cornell Van Siclen III, "The Accession Date of Amenhotep III and the Jubilee," *JNES* 32 (1973) 290–94.

[3] W. Helck, *Untersuchungen zu Manetho und den ägyptischen Königslisten* ("UGAÄ" XVIII [Berlin, 1956]) p. 67.

[4] Norman de Garis Davies, *The Rock Tombs of El Amarna* V ("Egypt Exploration Society Archaeological Survey of Egypt" XVII [London, 1908]) Pl. XXVII, l. 1 (unless otherwise specified, the numbering of stela S will be followed here).

[5] *Ibid.*, Pl. XXIV.

[6] *Ibid.*, Pl. XXVII, ll. 5–6, 8–9.

Greater diversity is found on the various copies for the date ascribed to the repetition of the oath. The version of stela A is lost here, but S, N, and R are dated to "regnal year eight, I Proyet 8." B and U have "regnal year six, I Proyet 4," and F (after Petrie's copy) seems to have "I Akhet 4"![7] It might appear that these dates each refer to a different occasion, but this seems unlikely. The writing of the date on B is uncertain;[8] and while the U version is preserved (), it, also, is ambiguous.[9] The variant on F could not be checked because the location of the stela was lost after Petrie noted it.[10] As in the case of the "Later Proclamation," however, all copies seem to agree on the nature of the occasion, which was "when One was in Akhetaten, when Pharaoh, L.P.H., arose and was manifest upon the great chariot of electrum, and beheld the stelae of the Aton which are on the mountain, as the southeastern boundary of Akhetaten."[11] Here, too, there are differences: stela B omits the great chariot and refers to the stelae on the mountain "as the southern boundary of Akhetaten,"[12] while F speaks of stelae on "the east mountain as the south(?) boundary."[13] Despite these variations, it is plain that all versions stem from a single master copy. The events described in each case can hardly reflect separate visits to each group of stelae, for F is on the western side of the Nile, and B can by no stretch of the imagination be described as occupying the southern boundary of the heretic capital.[14] We are not dealing, then, with several repetitions of the oath made at different times, but with one action, performed when the king visited the stelae emplaced on the southeastern boundary of the city on I Proyet 8 in regnal year eight.

Further dated material is preserved on stelae A and B, the two northern monuments on the western side, which alone, of all the boundary stelae, possess a colophon which occupies the lower portion of each tablet. The purpose of the record is clearly set forth in the opening section: "regnal year eight, IV Akhet, ⌈last day⌉: oath which the king, etc., pronounced at the establishment of the stelae wh[ich are on] the boundary of Akhetaten," followed by a brief restatement of the city's limits.[15] The colophons also mention that there were then

[7] *Ibid.*, Pl. XXVIII, l. 25; cf. pp. 33–34, n. 14.

[8] "Only probable agreement" with S is noted for the central portion of the date on B (*ibid.*, Pl. XXVIII, l. 25); for further garbling of the text of B, see *ibid.*, Pl. XXVII, l. 9.

[9] *Ibid.*, Pl. XXV, ll. 23–24.

[10] Davies, *El Amarna* V 20, n. 1.

[11] *Ibid.*, Pl. XXVIII, l. 26.

[12] *Ibid.*, (B, l. 21).

[13] *Ibid.*, p. 34, n. 3.

[14] See map, *ibid.*, Pl. XXXIV.

[15] *Ibid.*, Pl. XXXIII.

three stelae on the west bank of the Nile (necessarily, A, B, and F), and since A and B are only 3.5 kilometers apart, it seems plausible that these were the stelae that Akhenaten visited on that date. Each of the colophons, moreover, starts on a new line, whereas the "repetition of the oath" begins, in all copies, in the middle of a line and is obviously a continuation of the main text. This fact may not prove that the colophons were added later, as an afterthought, although it does suggest this. But the position of these two subsidiary texts at least indicates that the royal visit they commemorate took place after the "repetition of the oath" recorded above.[16] In other words, the oath was repeated in year eight, on I Proyet 8, and the king attended the formal "unveiling" of stelae A and B on IV Akhet ⌜30⌝. Since between these two dates there was no year change (and thus no accession date), and since there are only eight days left to the regnal year, Akhenaten must have become king between the first and the eighth days of I Proyet.

This interval, small as it is, might be narrowed still further if we could place the two preserved dates from regnal year twelve in their proper order. We know that on II Proyet 8 of this year a "parade of foreign tribute" was celebrated at El Amarna,[17] and it now appears that the disputed hieratic docket on Amarna letter No. 27 is to be read "[regnal year] twelve, I Proyet 5 (or 6)," instead of "[regnal ye]ar two, ..."[18] Unfortunately, it does not seem possible to establish any secure relationship between the two dates. It was once believed that EA 27 referred to the funeral of Amenophis III, and upholders of a long coregency identified this occasion with the festivities (supposedly celebrating Akhenaten's accession to sole rule) at El Amarna.[19] Knudtzon's "great festival for *mourning*" has since been abandoned in the light of modern lexicographic

[16] Compare, for instance, the Elephantine stela of Amenophis II, with the main text dated to year three and the colophon to year four ("Urk" IV 1288–99).

[17] Davies, *El Amarna* II ("Egypt Exploration Society Archaeological Survey of Egypt" XIV [London, 1905]) Pl. XXXVII; *ibid.*, III (Vol. XV [1905]) Pl. XIII.

[18] J. A. Knudtzon, *Die El-Amarna-Tafeln* I ("Vorderasiatische Bibliothek" II/1 [Leipzig, 1915]) 240–41. See now Cord Kühne, *Die Chronologie der internationalen Korrespondenz von El-Amarna* ("Alter Orient und Altes Testament," Vol. 17 [Neukirchen-Vluyn, 1973]) pp. 43–44, n. 205, p. 44, n. 207. The reading of the day number is Černý's. On the basis of a photograph of the docket on EA 27 (kindly sent by Dr. Steffen Wenig), I would agree that the traces suit "10"; see Georg Möller, *Hieratische Paläographie* II (Leipzig, 1909) 60, No. 665. In the hieratic of the New Kingdom, *sp* never has a tail when part of *ḥꜣt-sp*, and in other contexts a tail does not appear earlier than the Nineteenth Dynasty, and then infrequently, mostly in ligatures: *ibid.*, p. 36, Nos. 403 and 403*B*; cf. Mounir Megally, *Etudes sur le Papyrus E. 3226 du Louvre* III: *Considérations sur les variations et la transformation des formes des signes hiératiques dans le Papyrus E. 3226 du Louvre* ("BdE" XLIX [Paris, 1969]) Pls. XIII (*k–l*), XIV (*a–b*), XXIX (*j–l*).

[19] Thus, for instance, Cyril Aldred, *Akhenaten, Pharaoh of Egypt—A New Study* (London, 1968) pp. 114–16.

research,[20] but although the supposed funeral goes with it, we are still in the dark as to the real significance of the occasion. The conventional view has the Mittanian messengers returning *from* a festival celebrated by the Egyptian king. This could be the "parade of foreign tribute," which would yield an interval of nearly eleven months (II Proyet 8 through I Proyet 5 or 6) during which the regnal year did not change, and the king's accession would fall between I Proyet 6 and 8. The last seventy years have witnessed great advances in our understanding of the language of the Amarna letters, however, and these advances have resulted in a radical change in both the time and the place ascribed to the "great festival": now the messengers are seen traveling *to* a feast, which is to be celebrated in Mittani![21] This, if it be so, tells us nothing about what might have been happening in Egypt: the delivery of EA 27 might still have followed the "parade of foreign tribute," but the order of events could have been the reverse, in which case, the accession would fall between I Proyet 1 and 5/6. About all that can be said is that the day on which EA 27 received its hieratic docket (I Proyet 5 or 6) was a working day at the Egyptian chancery, and thus probably *not* the anniversary of the accession.

In sum, Akhenaten came to the throne within the first eight days of I Proyet, with Redford's proposed I Proyet 8 as likely a day as any. The wider results of this determination, I am afraid, are not too clear. If we could be sure that Amenophis III reigned no more than seven months out of his last regnal year, the fact that his son came to the throne seven months after his father's accession day would imply that he succeeded upon his father's death, with no room for a coregency. The sole authority for this figure, however, is one manuscript of Eusebius[22] in which Josephus' account of Manetho's text is quoted—not a very reliable source! Our problem, in dealing with the fragments of the *History*, lies not so much in selecting that version which accords best with the Egyptian sources[23] as in determining the figure (right or wrong) that Manetho transmitted. There are already enough discrepancies in the various accounts of what

[20] A. Leo Oppenheim, ed., *The Assyrian Dictionary*, Vol. 8 (Chicago and Glückstadt, 1971) 375; Wolfram von Soden, *Akkadisches Handwörterbuch* I (Wiesbaden, 1965) 478.

[21] Thus Kühne, *Chronologie*, p. 44, n. 205; this interpretation is supported by William L. Moran in private correspondence with the writer.

[22] Georg Friedrich Unger, *Chronologie des Manetho* (Berlin, 1867) pp. 78, n. 3 (top), and 157, n. 26.

[23] The highest regnal dates for Amenophis III are preserved on two jar labels from the palace at Malqatta, being the first and second epagomenal days (the birth[day]s of Osiris and Horus) in his thirty-eighth regnal year; see William C. Hayes, "Inscriptions from the Palace of Amenophis III," *JNES* 10 (1951) Fig. 11, Nos. 143 and 143*A*; for the sequence and writings of these dates see references *ibid.*, p. 87, n. 83, especially Ost. Cairo 25515, recto iii 26–iv 4 (J. Černý, *Ostraca hiératiques* I ["CCG" (1935)] 11*) and Ost. DM 158, ll. 1–5 (Černý, *Catalogue des ostraca*

Eusebius says Josephus said he saw in Manetho;[24] and the preserved text of Josephus himself gives the figure of thirty-six years, five months.[25] Anyone who chooses to rely on any of these versions does so, I would suggest, at his peril. For the present, we can say that Akhenaten came to the throne on a date that was seven months into his father's regnal year. Whether he became king at the death of Amenophis III, or after a coregency of undetermined length, is a question that goes beyond the modest scope of this study.[26]

---

hiératiques non-littéraires de Deir El Médineh II ["DFIFAO" IV (1937)] Pl. 35). If II Shomu 1 is the accession date of Amenophis III (Van Siclen, *JNES* 32 [1973] 294), his surviving monuments attest a reign of thirty-seven full regnal years, plus ninety-two days.

[24] Eusebius *apud* Syncellus: "36 years (in another copy, 38 years)" (W. G. Waddell, ed., *Manetho* ["Loeb Classical Library" (London, 1940)] p. 115); Eusebius/Armenian version: "28 years" (*ibid.*, p. 117).

[25] Josephus *Contra Apionem* I.15, 16.96: "36 years and 5 months" (*ibid.*, p. 103); Theophilus *Ad Autolycum* III.20, copies Josephus here, giving also "36 years and 5 months" (*ibid.*, p. 109), with some corruption for other kings in the dynasty.

[26] A case for a short coregency is made by the writer in *Ancient Egyptian Coregencies* (in press).

RAMESSEUM SOURCES OF MEDINET HABU RELIEFS

Charles F. Nims

To George R. Hughes, friend and colleague for nigh half a century

In the preface to *Medinet Habu* VI, George R. Hughes calls attention to "the fact that Ramses III patterned his mortuary temple after that of Ramses II, but on a smaller scale," and demonstrates that the astronomical ceiling in the Royal Mortuary Complex of the former could have been copied only from the astronomical ceiling in the second hypostyle hall of the Ramesseum.[1] Seventy years ago James Henry Breasted recognized that the "Blessing of Ptah" at Medinet Habu[2] derived from a similar text from the time of Ramses II.[3] Whether or not this text and others on the east face of the first pylon at Medinet Habu had as their direct source the face of the similar pylon at the Ramesseum cannot now be determined, as the latter has collapsed.

The Ramesseum parallels to some of the scenes and inscriptions in Medinet Habu are shown in the publications of the latter. The depiction of the sons of Ramses III appearing on Plate 109 apparently was suggested by a similar scene from the earlier temple shown on Plate 127*A*.[4] The relief of the games shown in

[1] The Epigraphic Survey, *Medinet Habu* VI, pp. x f.

Plate numbers used hereafter refer to the Epigraphic Survey, *Medinet Habu*, I–VIII ("OIP" [1930–70]). The plates are numbered consecutively through the volumes, thus: I ("OIP" VIII) Pls. 1–54; II ("OIP" IX) Pls. 55–130; III ("OIP" XXIII) Pls. 131–92; IV ("OIP" LI) Pls. 193–249; V ("OIP" LXXXIII) Pls. 250–362; VI ("OIP" LXXXIV) Pls. 363–482; VII ("OIP" XCIII) Pls. 483–590; and VIII ("OIP" XCIV) Pls. 591–660.

[2] *Medinet Habu* II, Pls. 105–6.

[3] James Henry Breasted, *Ancient Records of Egypt* (Chicago, 1906) IV, §§ 132–35. For comments on the derivation of the text, see William F. Edgerton and John A. Wilson, *Historical Records of Ramses III* ("SAOC," No. 12 [1936]) pp. 119 f. Another copy of the text, not noted in this discussion and still unpublished, is on the south face of the west tower of the ninth pylon at Karnak; see Bertha Porter and Rosalind L. B. Moss, *Topographical Bibliography of Ancient Egyptian Hieroglyphic Texts, Reliefs and Paintings* II (2d ed.; Oxford, 1972) 181 (541).

[4] See also Edgerton and Wilson, *Historical Records*, pp. 136, 137, n. 7*a*; John A. Wilson, "Ceremonial Games of the New Kingdom," *JEA* 17 (1931) 212 and n. 1; and Harold H. Nelson in *Medinet Habu Reports* ("OIC," No. 10 [1931]) p. 38.

the drawing, Plate 111, bottom, and in a photograph, Plate 112, was copied from the Ramesseum. A fragment of the relief from the latter temple was set in the wall at Medinet Habu in recent times. Originally this block was longer at the left; the end was cut off to make it fit.[5] The match is not exact, as the figures on the Ramesseum relief are slightly larger than those in the Medinet Habu scene.

The Medinet Habu Calendar was in greater part copied from that at the Ramesseum.[6] There is some slight evidence that the frieze above the Medinet Habu Calendar was copied from or was influenced by the similar frieze at the Ramesseum.[7]

The extant reliefs of the Min Feast at the Ramesseum are shown on Plates 213, 214, and 215*A*; the comparable scenes at Medinet Habu are on Plates 203, 205, 207, and 201. The differences are minor; they appear to arise from careless copying, the variation in available space, stylistic changes, and, of course, such revisions in content as were necessary to fit the reign of Ramses III.[8] Two epigraphic notes are necessary. In the Ramesseum reliefs (Pl. 213) there are three short inscriptions that are omitted in the Medinet Habu copies—lines 2–3, 21–22, and 54. In ancient times lines 21–22 were covered with plaster, probably before the copy was made. The word *ꜣšꜥ*, on Plate 213, line 1, just above line 38, appears in earlier copies as *mšꜥ*. This incorrect reading was caused by a small break in the stone, extending downward from the beak to the breast of the vulture, and touching the body of the bird. This break gave the hieroglyph the appearance of the owl when viewed from any distance.[10]

In seeking to determine what other reliefs at Medinet Habu may have been copied from the Ramesseum, one must remember that the earlier temple was about 20 per cent larger than the later one in its ground dimensions. Moreover, much of the preserved structure of the Ramesseum corresponds to parts of Medinet Habu that have been destroyed. Those sections of the two temples that are similarly preserved include a considerable number of reliefs from which comparisons can be made.

[5] Pl. 127*B*.

[6] Pls. 187–90; see *Medinet Habu* III, p. ix.

[7] The only known parts of the Ramesseum frieze adjacent to the calendar are shown on Pl. 189, blocks 35, 38. On the former block the seated god has only one foot; this could correspond to Pl. 574*D*, where the god is Ptah. The second Ramesseum block could correspond to the overlapping area of Pl. 574*D–C*.

[8] *Medinet Habu* IV, p. vii.

[9] *Wb* II 156.15, *Belegstellen*, 2, p. 232.

[10] This is only one example of many showing the necessity of a close-up observation to insure accuracy.

Ramses III used the rear face of the first pylon of Medinet Habu for accounts of his military exploits, just as Ramses II used the equivalent space at the Ramesseum for his. The long account of Year 8 of Ramses III was carved on the front face of the north tower of the second pylon at Medinet Habu; the parallel wall at the Ramesseum seems to have been occupied by the famous battle poem of Ramses II. The rear face of this pylon at the Ramesseum, on the other hand, shows battle reliefs below the scenes of the Min Feast, as does the lower register of the east wall of the first hypostyle hall south of the axial doorway, while in Medinet Habu the corresponding walls have religious scenes.

In addition to the almost identical reliefs in the two temples that have been noted above, there are other instances that show the dependence of the Medinet Habu wall decorations on those of the Ramesseum. In determining these, I have used my own notes, made while a staff member of the Epigraphic Survey of the Oriental Institute, and also photographs in the files of the Institute in Chicago, supplemented by Helck's publication of the ritual texts from the Ramesseum.[11]

The passage through the first pylon of the Ramesseum is partially preserved and that of Medinet Habu is complete. The scenes that appear at Medinet Habu (Pl. 246 I*A*, *B*) have the same deities as in the corresponding positions in the Ramesseum,[12] but not the same texts (*Ram*, p. 11). The scenes shown on Plate 247*A*, *B*, and *F*, *D* have the same deities, the same ritual acts, and the same titles of the acts[13] as occur at the Ramesseum (*Ram*, pp. 6 f., 11 f.). The vertical inscriptions and the figures of the deities on the west faces at either side of the doorways are the same in both temples (Pl. 251, *Ram*, pp. 14–17).[14]

In the north side of the second court of the Ramesseum there are preserved eight polygonal columns, with engaged Osirid figures facing the court, four on the east and four on the west. I have checked the scenes on each of three other sides of these columns with those similarly placed at Medinet Habu, comparing the deity, the ritual act and title, the crown worn by the king, and the additional inscriptions. The columns on the east have three scenes on each of the sides, a total of 36. Of these, 25 scenes show the same deity in both temples; the other similarities in such scenes are tabulated below.

[11] Wolfgang Helck, *Die Ritualdarstellungen des Ramesseums* I ("Ägyptologische Abhandlungen," Vol. 25 [Wiesbaden, 1972]); abbreviated as *Ram*.

[12] The Ramesseum parallel to Pl. 246 I*B* shows "Ptah who hears prayer." At Medinet Habu, "Ptah . . . who hears prayer" is in the passage through the Eastern High Gate, Pl. 608.

[13] The scene on Pl. 247*A* has no title; that on Pl. 247*G* has both incense and water in the ritual act and title.

[14] Helck (*Ram*, p. 14) notes that the Medinet Habu reliefs here are copied from the Ramesseum. The Ramesseum parallel to Pl. 251*L* has the figure of *Sỉꜣ* behind Thoth, as at Medinet Habu.

	Plate[15]	*Ramesseum*[16] Column	Page	Same ritual act[17]	Same crown on king	Same inscriptions[18]
Column 16	266*A*,b	15 S,b	49	X	X	
	266*B*,m	15 E,m	47	X		
	266*B*,b	15 E,b	47	X		X
	267*A*,m	15 N,m	45	X		
	267*A*,b	15 N,b	46	X	X	
Column 17	267*B*,m	14 S,m	42	X		X
	267*B*,b	14 S,b	43	X		
	268*A*,m	14 E,m	40	X	X	X
	268*A*,b	14 E,b	40			
	268*B*,t	14 N,t	37	X	X	X
	268*B*,m	14 N,m	37	X	X	
	268*B*,b	14 N,b	38			
Column 18	269*A*,b	13 S,b	35			
	269*B*,m	13 E,m	32		X	
	269*B*,b	13 E,b	32	X		
	270*A*,b	13 N,b	31			
Column 19	270*B*,t	12 S,t	27		X	
	270*B*,m	12 S,m	27	X	X	X
	270*B*,b	12 S,b	28			
	271*A*,t	12 E,t	24	X	X	
	271*A*,m	12 E,m	25	X		
	271*A*,b	12 E,b	26	X		
	271*B*,t	12 N,t	22			
	271*B*,m	12 N,m	22	X	X	X
	271*B*,b	12 N,b	23	X	X	

In 18 of the 25 scenes showing the same deity in both temples the ritual act depicted is the same; in 11 of them the king wears the same crown. But the accompanying inscriptions are alike in only six of the scenes, and even then only in part. The greatest total number of similarities occurs on the northernmost column in the row (Medinet Habu Column 19, Pls. 270*B*–271*B*, and Ramesseum Column 12); here the deities are identical in all instances, the ritual acts in six, and the king's crown in five.

A peculiarity in both temples is the bottom scene on the north side of the north column, where the king is "giving the house to its Lord." This scene

[15] For the Medinet Habu and Ramesseum columns, "t" is the top scene, "m" the middle, and "b" the bottom.

[16] For Ramesseum columns, "S" is the south side, "E" the east, and "N" the north.

[17] In several cases at the Ramesseum the title of the ritual act is either lost or was never written, though the act depicted is the same.

[18] In the cases tabulated, only some of the inscriptions are the same at Medinet Habu as in the Ramesseum.

should be next to the axial aisle, as it is on Medinet Habu Column 32 (Pl. 260*A*). Apparently the scribe who laid out the designs at the Ramesseum reversed the order of scenes, placing this scene at the wrong end of the four northern columns, and the mistake was copied at Medinet Habu. No earlier temple with similar scenes is known, so that the error cannot be traced to a time earlier than the Ramesseum.

Though the scenes on the columns on the east sides of the second courts in the two temples are often unlike, those on the columns on the west sides—Medinet Habu Columns 24–27 (Pls. 279–82) and Ramesseum Columns 23–20 (*Ram*, pp. 58–80, starting with Column 20)—are almost completely identical in the elements compared. In only one case is the identity of the deity different (Pl. 281*C*, lower and Ramesseum Column 21 N, lower) and in one case the royal crown (Pl. 280*B*, lower and Ramesseum Column 22 West, lower). In all scenes the ritual acts are the same. The scenes on the south face of Medinet Habu Column 27 (Plate 282*A*), however, appear in reverse order as to the upper and lower position from the same scenes on the south face of Ramesseum Column 20. Many of the inscriptions in the scenes on Medinet Habu Columns 25 and 26 (Pls. 280*A*–281*C*) are identical throughout with the inscriptions in the same scenes on Ramesseum Columns 22 and 21.

The fact that two-thirds of the deities and half of the ritual acts in the 36 scenes on the eastern row of columns in the second courts of the two temples are identical and that the 24 scenes on the western columns are almost completely identical is evidence of the dependence of the decorators of Medinet Habu on the Ramesseum as the source of their material. There are, however, some interesting differences in detail.

In the Ramesseum the title of the scene is often followed by *ỉr.f dỉ ʿnḫ*; the suffix *f* is invariable whether the deity is male or female. In Medinet Habu, however, when the phrase is used in connection with a female deity, it always reads *ỉr.s dỉ ʿnḫ*. Thus in the Ramesseum the subject of the verb *ỉry* is the monarch, as it had been in earlier inscriptions, while in Medinet Habu the subject of the verb is the deity.[19]

In the Ramesseum inscriptions the writing of "his father" in the titles of ritual acts is usually *t/f*; I have noted only two exceptions—once as *t/f*/determinative/*f* (*Ram*, p. 80) and once as *t/f*/determinative (*Ram*, p. 157). In Medinet Habu, however, in the titles of ritual acts on all columns and in most places elsewhere, "his father" is written *t/f*/stroke/*f*.[20]

[19] See also Charles F. Nims, review of *Kings at Karnak*, by Gun Bjorkman, in *JNES* 34 (1975) 76.

[20] The spelling *t/f* in the titles of scenes is rare in Medinet Habu. I have noted the following: Pls. 227*A*/2, 319*B*/1, 345*B*/1, the titles in all scenes in Pls. 442–44 (Room 16), 496*A*/1, 536/1, and the titles in the offering scenes in the High Gate, Pls. 617–19, 623. In historical inscriptions and in inscriptions written horizontally, "his father" is often written *ỉ*/*t*/stroke/*f*.

In the scenes on the columns of both temples the goddess *Wꜣḏyt* often appears above the head of the king. In the Ramesseum she has the wings and body of a vulture, but the head of a cobra. In Medinet Habu, where this goddess is shown in such a position, however, both on the columns and elsewhere, she always has a vulture's head.[21]

At the Ramesseum only three of the round pillars on the terrace remain; on each there are two scenes side by side. The corresponding pillars at Medinet Habu also have two scenes, but with a different division of the space used. The right scene on Column 29 at Medinet Habu (Pl. 375*D* 1–3) has the same two deities before the king and the same ritual act as appear in the right scene on the comparable column at the Ramesseum (Column 48, *Ram*, pp. 86 f.), but shows an additional deity, a goddess, behind the king. Medinet Habu Column 31 has in the left scene (Pl. 266*C* 1–2) the same ritual act but only one of the two gods who appear in the left scene on Ramesseum Column 46 (*Ram*, pp. 83 f.). The right scene on Column 31 at Medinet Habu (Pl. 376*D* 1–3) shows essentially the same ritual act, the same deities before the king, and the same inscriptions that appear in the corresponding scene on Ramesseum Column 46 (*Ram*, pp. 82 f.), but again shows an additional goddess behind the king.

At the Ramesseum a portion of the west wall of the second court south of the axial doorway has been preserved with a number of scenes in whole or part (*Ram*, p. 94, diagram). At Medinet Habu in the corresponding places (Pls. 287*B* [the parallel at the Ramesseum is only partly preserved], 288*A*, *B*, 290*B*, 291) the scenes with ritual acts are identical with those at the Ramesseum (*Ram*, pp. 94–98), but have different texts except for the names of the deities, the titles of the ritual acts, and apparently one divider between scenes (Pl. 288*A*, l. 5; *Ram*, p. 97). The procession of princes at Medinet Habu (Pl. 299) is in the same relative position below the religious scenes as it is at the Ramesseum (*Ram*, pp. 98 f.), but only at Medinet Habu are there cartouches separating the figures.

On the other face of this wall, the east wall of the first hypostyle hall, there are, at Medinet Habu, four scenes in the upper register (Pls. 311, 312), all of which have the same deities, the same crowns on the king, and in all but the scene on the left the same ritual acts as have the corresponding scenes at the Ramesseum (*Ram*, p. 99, diagram, scenes 104–8, texts, pp. 100–3), but again the accompanying texts are different except for the vertical line at the left end of the scenes (Pl. 311*A*, l. 6, *Ram*, p. 103). Of the west wall of the first hypostyle hall at Medinet Habu there are preserved only the lower courses, showing the feet of the princes in procession (Pl. 348*A*, *C*), in the same position as those of the princes in the corresponding scene at the Ramesseum (*Ram*, pp. 133, 143).

[21] In a different type of representation of *Wꜣḏyt* and *Nḫbt*, both goddesses are shown as winged cobras, Pls. 349 and 351.

The speech of Amon-re (Pl. 448, ll. 2–6) that appears in the scene with the persea tree in the mortuary suite in Medinet Habu has its only parallel known to me in a similar scene at the Ramesseum, on the north side of the west wall in the room with the astronomical ceiling, where the words are spoken by Atum (*Ram*, p. 168). The speech of Thoth in this scene at Medinet Habu (ll. 8–12) may have been the same as the speech of Thoth in the Ramesseum depiction, where only a few words have been preserved (*Ram*, p. 168).

As noted at the beginning of this article, the astronomical ceiling in the second hypostyle hall of the Ramesseum was the source of the astronomical ceiling in the Royal Mortuary Complex at Medinet Habu. The positions of some of the representations of the northern constellations were altered in the latter, however, though the rest of the ceiling follows that of the Ramesseum.[22] A small fragment of another astronomical ceiling at Medinet Habu, almost certainly from the second hypostyle hall there, shows the same altered arrangement of the northern constellations.[23] Apparently the scribe who copied the extant astronomical ceiling at the Ramesseum used this copy, with the alterations, for both ceilings at Medinet Habu.

This evidence of the copying of the Ramesseum reliefs by the scribes who planned the reliefs in Medinet Habu shows that a large number of the ritual scenes in the latter temple had their origin in the scenes in the former and occupied the same relative positions in both temples. In the Calendar, as Nelson notes, "Mistakes which occur in the earlier version were copied slavishly in the latter,"[24] and the same is true of the Min Feast. In other scenes changes were made in some instances but not in others. Very often the texts that accompany the scenes at Medinet Habu do not follow the Ramesseum versions. In a few instances the texts were changed so as to make them suitable for the later temple, but for the most part the changes are in the short texts beginning *dỉ.n.ỉ n.k*, with the following words different in the reliefs at Medinet Habu from those in parallel reliefs at the Ramesseum. This suggests that some copyists did not bother to copy fully these short trite sentences.

Because of the incomplete state of preservation of the two temples, it will never be possible to determine to what extent the nonhistorical reliefs at Medinet Habu were dependent on the Ramesseum reliefs, but it seems probable that the dependence was much greater even than the present evidence shows.

[22] O. Neugebauer and Richard A. Parker, *Egyptian Astronomical Texts* III (Providence, 1969) pp. 26 f.

[23] *Ibid.*, pp. 27 f.; *Medinet Habu* VI, Pl. 477.

[24] Harold H. Nelson and Uvo Hölscher, *Work in Western Thebes, 1931–33* ("OIC," No. 18 [1934]) p. 26.

THE SOTHIC DATING OF THE TWELFTH AND EIGHTEENTH DYNASTIES

Richard A. Parker

Recently Ronald D. Long has taken modern scholars to task for placing uncritical and undeserved reliance upon the earliest Sothic dates as firmly establishing the chronological setting of the Twelfth and Eighteenth Dynasties.[1] His point is that when these dates were first published—the Eighteenth-Dynasty date in 1873 and the Twelfth-Dynasty date in 1899—scholars debated them vigorously and reached no certain conclusions; but over the years the hypotheses proposed have come to be taken as facts now so firmly accepted that they are used as secure checks against other Near Eastern chronologies, as well as against carbon-14 dating.

Long examines all the known Sothic dates, seven in number, but his strictures are reserved essentially for the first and second in time. Thus in his conclusion he states:

> The two remaining Sothic dates are subject to serious doubt. Admittedly, they seem to fit the Sothic pattern and coordinate with the other dates. Have chronologists, however, juggled the reigns and figures in order to reconcile the evidence? To a certain degree this has definitely occurred. The Sothic date in Dynasty XII cannot be assigned to any one pharaoh until the papyri are made available for investigation. The identification of the Ebers papyrus hieratic cartouche, still the subject of speculation, will probably never be firmly and solidly resolved.[2]

Let it be admitted at once that it would be easy to document Long's thesis that over the years what first appeared as a qualified statement about a historical event may have undergone a gradual transition to an unqualified statement. But how well has Long made his present case? Have modern Egyptologists really gone so far astray as he claims? Since his charges have appeared in such a reputable journal as *Orientalia* these are important questions that require answers.

[1] A Re-examination of the Sothic Chronology of Egypt," *Or* n.s. 43 (1974) 261–74.

[2] *Ibid.*, p. 274.

THE ILLAHUN DATE

In 1899, on the basis of two papyrus fragments found in the precincts of a temple at Illahun, Borchardt proposed that together, one before and one after the event, they confirmed a heliacal rising of Sirius on the sixteenth day of the fourth month of the second season (the eighth month of the Egyptian civil year) of the seventh year of a pharaoh whose name appeared on neither fragment. They were nevertheless to be assigned to Sesostris III because their handwriting was the same as that found on other fragments of a temple register for years five to nine, securely dated to Sesostris III.[3] This conclusion by Borchardt, according to Long, has been uncritically accepted by his successors so that present-day studies take it as an unequivocal fact, instead of the mere supposition that it really is.

Long argues (1):

> The truth is that no name of a ruler, not even a partial cartouche, or any other evidence of a pharaoh is to be found in the Illahun papyrus. Thus, year seven could apply to almost any pharaoh of Dynasty XII—a dynasty which was 200 years long.

and (2):

> Thence, the assignment of both fragments to Sesostris III is based on an assumption. In fact, the fragments may belong to two different pharaohs. Any doubt as to the Sesostris III arrangement or desire to read the hieratic itself is hindered and frustrated by the fact the papyri have not as yet been published.[4]

Taken together these seem strong arguments, quite sufficient to invalidate the accepted chronology for the Twelfth Dynasty and leave that dynasty floating in a range of two hundred years, plus or minus. Unfortunately for Long, however, he committed the cardinal sin for a scholar of not having gone back to the original sources. Had he done so, he never would have made such a sweeping statement for his first point.

There were two finds of papyri at Illahun (Kahun). The earlier, in 1889, was published in 1898 by F. Ll. Griffith under the title *Hieratic Papyri from Kahun and Gurob*.[5] The second find, still unpublished, was made in 1899. In quantity of papyri the second was some seven to eight times larger than the first. Both finds were made in the precincts of the pyramid temple of Sesostris II, who evidently founded the town of Illahun when he built his pyramid. From neither

[3] Ludwig Borchardt, "Der zweite Papyrusfund von Kahun und die zeitliche Festlegung des mittleren Reiches der ägyptischen Geschichte," *ZÄS* 37 (1899) 99–101.

[4] *Or* n.s. 43 (1974) 265.

[5] "The Petrie Papyri" (London, 1898).

find has there come to light any papyrus dated to a pharaoh earlier than Sesostris III. Besides him there are papyri dated to Amenemhet III and Amenemhet IV (though none to Queen Sobek-nefru, the last of the dynasty), and to two of the earliest pharaohs of the Thirteenth Dynasty, Sekhem-Reʿ Khu-tawy (the third ruler)[6] and Sekhem-ka-Reʿ (the fourth).[7] Moreover, had Long checked Borchardt's 1899 article, he would have found that the first papyrus fragment, announcing the forthcoming heliacal rising of Sothis, was a letter addressed to "the staff of the temple of Sekhem-Sesostris, justified, of Anubis . . . , of Sobek . . . ." The staff in question was that of the mortuary temple of Sesostris II, deceased, and no amount of wishful thinking can ascribe the fragment to a pharaoh prior to Sesostris III, the immediate successor of Sesostris II. The only other possible candidates to whom the fragment might be assigned, then, would be Amenemhet III and Amenemhet IV, since neither Queen Sobek-nefru nor the early rulers of the Thirteenth Dynasty reigned for as long as seven years. In view of these considerations the possible range for the Sothic date is immediately reduced from Long's two hundred years to less than ninety.

Is the argument based on paleography substantial enough to assign the fragment to one of the three above-named pharaohs? Edgerton, in an article from which Long quotes in an effort to make his first point, had this to say about Borchardt's assignment of the date to Sesostris III:

> This statement was printed after Borchardt had devoted a considerable amount of study to the originals of these and the related papyri in Berlin and, presumably, to the photographic facsimiles of those in London. The claim that he could recognize an individual handwriting is inherently plausible and has never, as far as I know, been challenged by anyone who has seen the originals. It has been endorsed by Möller and by Scharff. In any such case the personal equation must weigh heavily. Until Borchardt's, Möller's, and Scharff's identification is questioned, after examination of the originals or sharp photographs, by some equally high authority on Middle Kingdom hieratic, I am compelled to accept the identification as a fact.[8]

Although Long neither quotes nor counters this decision by Edgerton, by his silence and his call for the publication of the papyri as the only real possibility of judging the validity of Borchardt's conclusion he appears to suggest that the

[6] Following Griffith, I had, in "The Beginning of the Lunar Month in Ancient Egypt" (*JNES* 29 [1970] 220), erroneously taken Sekhem-Reʿ Khu-tawy to be the first ruler of the Thirteenth Dynasty. Jürgen von Beckerath (*Untersuchungen zur politischen Geschichte der Zweiten Zwischenzeit in Ägypten* ["Ägyptologische Forschungen," Vol. 23 (Glückstadt, 1964)] pp. 30–36) has shown that he is actually the third. This does not invalidate my argument, since according to von Beckerath the first three rulers of the dynasty ruled only about eight years in all.

[7] Georg Möller, *Hieratische Paläographie* I (2d ed.; Leipzig, 1927) 13.

[8] William F. Edgerton, "Chronology of the Twelfth Dynasty," *JNES* 1 (1942) 307–8.

paleographic evidence is too dubious to serve as the decisive factor in the acceptance of such an important date, and his own conclusion, as we have seen, is that it is "subject to serious doubt."

I do not, of course, agree with Long, since some years ago, in a study of the various Egyptian calendars, I attempted to fix the date of the Twelfth Dynasty by combining Edgerton's calculated date for the seventh year of Sesostris III as 1870 B.C. ± *ca.* 6 years with the dates of certain lunar events as given in the civil calendar for the reigns of both Sesostris III and Amenemhet III.[9] All the data I could assemble fitted together nicely to establish 1872 B.C. as the correct seventh year, and from this fixed point the other reigns of the Twelfth Dynasty could be worked out. In the years since 1950 I have not seen any evidence to challenge the validity of this date for Sesostris III.

Let us assume with Long, however, that paleography by itself is too weak a reed to support such an important conclusion. The problem then sets itself in this fashion: There are three pharaohs to one of whom the Sothic date for Year 7 must be assigned—Sesostris III, Amenemhet III, or Amenemhet IV. As we have just seen, a completely acceptable solution can be proposed for Sesostris III. Can the other two candidates be ruled out by any other means than the argument from paleography? I believe that to be possible in both cases, again by the combination of the Sothic date and the various lunar data available.

The most important of the lunar data comes from the reign of Amenemhet III. It is the Illahun temple account (Berlin Museum, Pap. 10056, verso) that lists alternate months of phyle-priests according to the lunar year and thereby provides a sequence of twelve dates (one emended) for the beginnings of lunar months over the civil/regnal years 30 and 31. There is no question of ascribing these dates to any pharaoh other than Amenemhet III since the phyle-leader, Meket's son Nekhtisonb, is mentioned both in the Berlin papyrus and in Pap. Kahun IV 1, in the latter in association with a Year 40 which must be ascribed to Amenemhet III.[10] On the assumption that the Sothic date belonged to Sesostris III, the twelve lunar dates for years 30/31 of Amenemhet III were calculated as having occurred during 1813–1812 B.C.; ten of the twelve papyrus dates are the same as those calculated on the basis of this assumption.

Here it is necessary to interject a few words about the repetitive character of Egyptian lunar dates.[11] In short, since 25 Egyptian years have almost exactly the same number of days as 25 lunar years (309 lunar months), any lunar date would have to repeat itself after 25 years. A single date might conceivably be

[9] *The Calendars of Ancient Egypt* ("SAOC," No. 26 [1950]) Excursus C.

[10] *Ibid.*, § 330 and see also Parker, *JNES* 29 (1970) 217–20.

[11] A full discussion appears in Richard A. Parker, "The Lunar Dates of Thutmose III and Ramesses II," *JNES* 16 (1957) 39–40.

repeated after 11 years (one day late) or after 14 years (one day early), depending on the accuracy of the observations. This hazard can be ruled out when a sequence of several dates is involved, and that is the peculiar importance of Pap. 10056. We can state with great certainty that years 30/31 of Amenemhet III fell either during 1813–1812 B.C., or else 25 or 50 years earlier.

At this point a digression becomes necessary. We have noted above that Edgerton gave a possible range for the Sothic date of IIII *prt* 16 as 1870 B.C. ± *ca.* 6 years—that is, from 1876 to 1864 B.C. The earlier date assumed the point of observation to be Heliopolis (latitude 30.1°) and the *arcus visionis* B (the necessary height for visibility of the star above the sun, calculated with the sun in the horizon) to be 9.5°. The later date had Illahun (lat. 29.2°) as the point of observation and B as 8.6°.[12] Edgerton added that even these limits might be too narrow and were subject to future verification. One comment can be offered immediately. Edgerton attacked the Sothic date as though it were a solitary example, without taking into account any of the later discussion by Greek writers of the phenomenon known to them as the Sothic cycle, and as though the heliacal rising of Sirius itself had to be actually observed every year for the proper celebration of the festival. And yet the Egyptians of the Twelfth Dynasty must have been just as aware as those who lived at the time of the Decree of Canopus under Ptolemy III Euergetes that the festival of *prt Spdt* normally fell for four years on the same day of the civil year and then moved to the following day. Nor must we forget that the date with which we are concerned was announced in a letter to the temple staff, some days before the festival. Now such a letter would hardly have been written in Illahun, where the official could have addressed the staff directly. It is much more likely that he was in either Memphis or Heliopolis and writing the forecast from there.[13]

Before going further with this point we must review the various years—tropical, sidereal, Julian, Gregorian, and Egyptian—that play a role in our problem. The *tropical* or *solar* or *natural* or *astronomical* or *equinoctial* year is the period that it takes the sun's center to pass from one equinox to the same equinox again; it has a mean length of 365.24220 days (365 days, 5 hours, 48 minutes, 45.5 seconds). This is the year that all calendar years try to match. The *sidereal* year is the time in which the sun's center passes from the ecliptic meridian of a given fixed star to the same meridian again; its length is 365.25636 days (365 days, 6 hours, 9 minutes, 9.54 seconds). The difference between the

[12] Edgerton, *JNES* 1 (1942) 309.

[13] One control of the forecast could very well have been the star clocks still in use in the Twelfth Dynasty. Sirius, as a decanal star, was preceded in the clock by other decans whose heliacal risings would mark the end of the twelfth hour of the night 10 days or 20 days before that of Sirius. See O. Neugebauer and Richard A. Parker, *Egyptian Astronomical Texts* I: *The Early Decans* (London, 1960) chap. 3.

two is .01416 of a day, or 20 minutes, 24.04 seconds per year. The *Julian* year is a calendar year of 365.25 days and represents an attempt to keep in synchronism with the tropical year. That it does not quite do so resulted, as we know, in the *Gregorian* reform and a mean year very close indeed to the length of the tropical year. Nevertheless it is the Julian year, projected backward, that has remained the one in use for dates in ancient history and for astronomical calculations. Another calendar year is the *Egyptian* civil year, consisting of only 365 days. Being 1/4 day shorter than the Julian, it moved forward against the latter so that any given coincidence of dates would have been repeated for four years but then again only after 1460 Julian years (= 1461 Egyptian years).

Now from Censorinus[14] and coins of Antoninus Pius[15] it is safe to conclude that in the years A.D. 139 to 142 Sirius rose heliacally on I *ꜣḫt* 1 Egyptian, corresponding to July 20 for A.D. 139 and July 19 for A.D. 140 to 142. From this anchor in time it would be quite simple to calculate the place of the yearly heliacal rising of Sirius in the Julian calendar if only that star were a fixed one whose position did not vary for long periods of time and so could be measured by the sidereal year. Unfortunately for simplicity, Sirius is not a fixed star but one with a motion of its own. Its year, measured from one heliacal rising to the next, is itself not constant in length, though throughout the millennia of Egypt's history it has always been very close to that of the Julian year. It was Theodor Oppolzer who, in 1884, first calculated the length of the Sirius year, and it was Eduard Meyer in 1904 who applied it. According to Meyer's figures, in 4231 B.C. the Sirius year was 365.2498352 days long, in 3231 B.C. 365.25 (exactly the length of the Julian year), in 2231 B.C. 365.2502291, and by 231 B.C. 365.2508804.[16]

Over the years these values have been slightly refined. The most recent study of the Sothic cycle was made by Ingham in 1969.[17] With Memphis as the point of observation and a constant *arcus visionis* of 9° he calculated four cycles, between −4226 (4227 B.C.) and +1591. The intermediate cycles began after 1458 years, in −2768; after 1456 years, in −1312; and after 1453 years, in +141. The final cycle was 1450 years long. His first mean cycle year was thus 365.25025 days long and the last one 365.25164 days long, to be compared with those of Eduard Meyer. Ingham, on the plausible assumption that the *arcus visionis* might have been smaller in the past than it is today because the sun and

[14] *De die natali*, chap. 21.

[15] Ludwig Borchardt, *Die Annalen und die zeitliche Festlegung des Alten Reiches der ägyptischen Geschichte* ("Quellen und Forschungen zur Zeitbestimmung der ägyptischen Geschichte," Vol. 1 [Berlin, 1917]) pp. 55–56.

[16] Eduard Meyer, *Aegyptische Chronologie* (Berlin, 1904) p. 14.

[17] M. F. Ingham, "The Length of the Sothic Cycle," *JEA* 55 (1969) 36–40.

Sirius were then farther apart in azimuth, also calculated the cycles for an *arcus visionis* beginning at 8° and increasing linearly to 9°. On this basis the first cycle became 1456 years in length, ending in −2770; the second ended in −1316, after 1454 years; the third in +136, after 1452 years; and the last in +1585, after 1449 years. The corresponding increase in the mean Sothic year for the first cycle was to 365.25051 days and for the last cycle to 365.25181 days.

After this somewhat lengthy and arid discussion we are now in a position to check Edgerton's range of years for the Sothic date of the Twelfth Dynasty. Taking Censorinus' +139 as the starting point, we reach the beginning of the preceding cycle by adding to it 1453 years (B of 9°) and 1452 years (B variable), with results of −1314 and −1313, respectively. For the next earlier cycle we add 1456 years to −1314 and 1454 years to −1313, with results of −2770 and −2767. Now from I *ꜣḫt* 1 to IIII *prt* 16 there are 225 days and from IIII *prt* 16 to the following I *ꜣḫt* 1 140 days. To allow for possible errors in observation we use the rounded figure of four years to one day (a cycle of 1460 years) and arrive at 900 years for the first interval and 560 for the second. From −2770 we take 900 for a lower limit of −1870; to −1314 we add 560 for an upper limit of −1874. Between these limits must have fallen the first year of the four in which our Sothic date must occur if the *arcus visionis* was constant at 9°. For a variable B we take 900 from −2767 for a lower limit of −1867, and add 560 to −1313 for an upper limit of −1873. To allow for both eventualities we combine these limits and arrive at −1874 as the upper and −1867 as the lower limits, with both extremes highly unlikely because the Sothic cycle, whether B was fixed or variable, was in fact shorter than 1460 years. The first year of four in which our date must have fallen then has to come between 1875 B.C. and 1868 B.C., with 1865 B.C. as the latest year possible.

Now Amenemhet's thirtieth year has to be either 1813 B.C., 1838 B.C., or 1863 B.C. His seventh year would then necessarily be either 1836 B.C. or 1861 B.C. Only the last comes at all close to the calculated range, and it is four years later than the latest possible extreme. The conclusion is secure. The Sothic date cannot belong to Amenemhet III. The date of 1872 B.C. already arrived at for Sesostris III, however, fits comfortably within the limits and involves neither of the extreme figures.

There remains to be considered the assumption that the Sothic date belongs to Amenemhet IV. Can he be excluded on astronomical grounds? This cannot be done simply by setting Year 30 of Amenemhet III back one more lunar cycle, to 1888 B.C. This would make his Year 40 1878 B.C. and it would be easy to work out a Year 7 for his successor within the range of 1875–1865 B.C., with allowance as well for the known coregency between the two.

There is, however, another possible line of attack. In the ninth year of one of our three pharaohs there was celebrated a *wꜣg*-feast on II *šmw* 29. If this feast belonged to Amenemhet IV, it is easily fitted into a chronology that assigns the Sothic date to Sesostris III.[18] The chronology breaks down, however, if the Sothic date be assigned to Amenemhet IV. The *wꜣg*-feast with which we are here concerned is a movable one, determined by the original lunar calendar. In this calendar it always falls in the first month of the year, *tḫy*, and most usually on the thirteenth day of the month, two days before the *tḫy*-feast on the day of full moon.[19] Now from IIII *prt* 17 (on the assumption that by Year 9 the rising of Sothis had dropped back one day) to II *šmw* 29 there are 72 days. In the original lunar calendar the feast of the rising of Sothis, also called *wp rnpt* (Opener of the Year) had to fall in the twelfth month of the year (named *wp rnpt*), and only if the feast fell in the last 11 days of the month was the following month intercalary. Therefore the maximum number of days that could go by between *prt Spdt* and the *wꜣg*-feast and still have the feast occur in the first month of the next year, *tḫy*, would be the 11 days of *wp rnpt* (if that month had 30 days), plus the 30 days of the intercalary month of *Ḏḥwtyt*, plus the number of days in *tḫy* that would have gone by up to the day on which the feast fell. At the very latest this day in *tḫy* could be only day 27, since the feast of *tḫy* followed that of *wꜣg* by two days and had to fall within the month it named. But these total at most only 68, and not 72 days.

By the same calculations as outlined above, both Sesostris III and Amenemhet III can be eliminated as pharaohs to whom the *wꜣg*-feast on II *šmw* 29 might be assigned. For these two pharaohs the results of the calculation could prove even worse. Since both preceded Amenemhet IV, the date of *prt Spdt* would have had to be even earlier for them than IIII *prt* 16, if that date be ascribed to Amenemhet IV.

We are left with only one possible solution to the problem of fitting Sothic date, lunar dates, and *wꜣg*-feast date with one another in an astronomically sound arrangement.

The Sothic date of Year 7 must belong to Sesostris III and fall in 1872 B.C., Year 30 of Amenemhet III must fall in 1813 B.C., and Year 9 of Amenemhet IV must fall in 1790 B.C.

When I first proposed this solution in 1950 I wrote: "In the chronology of the second millennium B.C. there is no such thing as absolute certainty, but I submit that there is strong probability that it is correct." Although we may still not have absolute certainty, the probability is now much, much stronger.

[18] Parker, *Calendars*, §§ 336–37.

[19] *Ibid.*, §§ 182–85.

THE EBERS PAPYRUS DATE

Heading a table of correspondence between calendars on the verso of the famous medical papyrus Ebers is a date that is commonly accepted by modern scholars as recording a rising of Sothis on III *šmw* 9 in Year 9 of Amenhotep I. On the basis of early debate in the years between 1870 and 1890 by such scholars as Brugsch, Smith, Ebers, Eisenlohr, Lepsius, Goodwin, Naville, and Chabas (together with a misinterpretation of an opinion by Edgerton in 1937) over the correct reading of the name in the cartouche, Long has concluded that not only is the year still doubtful but, as already quoted above: "The identification of the Ebers papyrus hieratic cartouche, still the subject of speculation, will probably never be firmly and solidly resolved."

In 1890, however, Erman in his study of Papyrus Westcar subjected the reading of the name to thorough analysis and comparison with other hieratic documents and demonstrated conclusively, at least to the satisfaction of every competent scholar since his time, that the pharaoh in question must be *Ḏsr-kꜣ-Rꜥ*, Amenhotep I.[20] This judgment was specifically upheld by Möller in his monumental *Hieratische Paläographie* (1st ed. 1908, 2d ed. 1927) in these strong terms (p. 20): "Dass dieser name *Ḏsr-kꜣ-Rꜥ* (= Amenophis I) zu lesen ist, hat *Erman* (Westc. II, 56 ff.) in über jeden Zweifel erhabener Weise beweisen." At the same time he confirmed the reading Year 9, which comparative paleography had already put beyond dispute.

Against this weight of opinion Long could bring only two sentences from an article by Edgerton. "We must return, then, at least provisionally, to the view that the heliacal rising of Sothis occurred on the ninth day of the eleventh month in the ninth year of Amenhotep I. I do not claim that this view has been established with absolute certainty; new evidence may compel us to reconsider the question at any time.[21] What Long does not quote is the very next sentence, which reads: "For the present, however, Borchardt has conspicuously failed in his effort to upset the traditional translation of the text." But what Borchardt was trying to upset was not the name *Ḏsr-kꜣ-Rꜥ* nor Year 9 nor III *šmw*. His new interpretation and what was most successfully combatted by Edgerton was taking "ninth day of the month," *psḏ*, to be "day of the new moon," *psḏntyw*. As Edgerton wrote: "I cannot discern any difference whatever between the two publications in the form of the numeral 9 in l. 2, the only sign whose exact form

[20] Adolf Erman, *Die Märchen des Papyrus Westcar* II ("Mittheilungen aus den Orientalischen Sammlungen," VI [Berlin, 1890]) 56–60. Long erroneously ascribed these pages to Ebers as representing a second reversal of opinion by him (Long, *Or* n.s. 43 [1974] 267, n. 19).

[21] William F. Edgerton, "On the Chronology of the Early Eighteenth Dynasty (Amenhotep I to Thutmose III)," *AJSL* 53 (1937) 192.

concerns us here."[22] Whatever doubt lingered in Edgerton's mind was surely because of the repetition of the same sign with the following eleven months in the table of correspondence with no adjustment for the epagomenal days. This doubt might be justified to some degree if the list of months against those of the civil year was that of a fixed or Sothic year, always beginning on the day of the heliacal rising of Sothis. We now know, however, that the first column lists the months of the original lunar year. Properly it begins with the month of *wp rnpt*, the last month of the year and the one in which the rising of Sothis, *prt Spdt*, must be kept so that the lunar year remains in correct relation to the natural year. From the date of the Sothic rising was then projected the series of "day nine" in the civil calendar months, merely to serve as a guide to the physician, who must have dispensed his prescriptions with concern for the correct lunar month, which he could easily determine by checking to see into which month any "day nine" of the current civil month might fall.[23]

The one element of uncertainty in the Ebers dating—and with this Long does not deal—is the place of observation. The papyrus was found at Thebes, and Thebes was then the capital of the Empire. It is known that the heliacal rising of Sirius is visible one day earlier for each degree of latitude that one moves southward in Egypt. Thus Hornung, in his recent study, has the Sothic date falling in 1544–1537 B.C. if the observation point is Heliopolis, and in 1525–1517 B.C. if it is Thebes.[24] The latter date has been attracting much support of late, and Hornung himself suggests 1527–1506 B.C. as the most likely years for the reign of Amenhotep I.

In any event we can paraphrase Edgerton and state that for the present Long has conspicuously failed in his effort to upset the traditional translation of the text and the solidity of the first Sothic dates as well.

ADDENDUM I. SOME REMARKS ON THE DATES IN THE DECREE OF CANOPUS

Having charged Long with neglect of scholarly duty, it is only fair that I admit to the same failing myself. For years now, along with others, I have been taking the date of the Decree of Canopus, Year 9 of Euergetes I, I *prt* (Tybi) 17, and the date of *prt Spdt* on II *šmw* (Payni) 1 as necessarily falling in the same year,

[22] *Ibid.*, p. 190, n. 5.

[23] Parker, *Calendars*, §§ 188–218.

[24] Erik Hornung, *Untersuchungen zur Chronologie und Geschichte des Neuen Reiches* ("Ägyptologische Abhandlungen," Vol. 11 [Wiesbaden, 1964]) pp. 20–21.

238 B.C., the one on March 7 and the other on July 19.[25] Yet one has but to read any of the three texts—Greek, Demotic, or hieroglyphic—to learn that the festival had already been celebrated in Year 9.[26] The simple explanation is that the Decree's events were dated not by the Egyptian calendar, with Year 9 beginning in I *ꜣḫt* (Thoth) 1, but by the Macedonian regnal year that began before Thoth 1 and consequently overlapped parts of two Egyptian calendar years. In all three versions, be it noted, the Macedonian month and day are given first after the year and are followed by their equivalent in the Egyptian calendar.

The most recent and thorough discussion of the chronology of the period is that by A. E. Samuel.[27] He has shown—conclusively, in my opinion—that the first year of Euergetes I was a very short one, with his accession falling on Dios 25 (= IIII *ꜣḫt* [Choiak] 7) and his second year beginning on Dystros 24 (= I *šmw* [Pachons] 4).[28] By Egyptian reckoning his Year 1 would run to the end of the epagomenal days and Year 2 would begin on Thoth 1, with a consequent lag of some four months. Further calculation would show that Year 9 (Macedonian) should begin on Dystros 24 in 239 B.C., certainly before *prt Spdt* on II *šmw* (Payni) 1, so that festival would indeed have already been celebrated by the date of the Decree proper, though still in Year 9.

With July 19, 239 B.C. thus established for the Sothic date, other questions arise. From Censorinus we have placed *prt Spdt* on I *ꜣḫt* 1 in A.D. 139 (July 20) and A.D. 140–42 (July 19). Assuming a constant four-year cycle back to the Canopus Decree we have 95 days from II *šmw* 1 to I *ꜣḫt* 1 representing 380 years. Now 380 years before A.D. 139 is 242 B.C. and 239 is then the last year of the quadrennium, after which, in 238, the rising would fall on II *šmw* 2. But one purpose of the Canopus Degree was to have, at four-year intervals, a sixth epagomenal day in order to keep the rising of Sothis on II *šmw* 1. The date of the Decree, however, means that for the year of its publication the epagomenal days were already past, though it was exactly to these that the sixth day should have been added. The conclusion must be that 239 B.C. was not the last year of a quadrennium and that to some degree observation still controlled the date of *prt Spdt*.

[25] Richard Parker, "Sothic Dates and Calendar 'Adjustment,' " *RdE* 9 (1952) 103; *idem*, review of *Untersuchungen zur Chronologie und Geschichte des Neuen Reiches*, by Erik Hornung, in *RdE* 19 (1967) 186, n. 1.

[26] Tanis stela, Greek, l. 39; Demotic, l. 38; hieroglyphic, ll. 19–20. This was brought out long ago by G. H. Wheeler, "The Chronology of the Twelfth Dynasty," *JEA* 9 (1923) 198.

[27] *Ptolemaic Chronology* ("Munchener Beiträge zur Papyrusforschung und antiken Rechtsgeschichte," Vol. 43 [Munich, 1962]).

[28] *Ibid.*, pp. 95–96.

We have seen from the recent calculations of Ingham (see above) that the Sothic cycle between −1314 and +139 was 1453 years long. Over the whole length of the cycle, then, there must have been seven triennia, one of these occurring roughly every two centuries. Thus one triennium should have fallen between the Canopus Decree and A.D. 139. The result would be that the normal quadrennium at the time of the Decree would be 241–238 B.C. and there would be no conflict between II *šmw* 1 as the rising in 239 B.C. and a sixth epagomenal day in 238 B.C.

I see no problem in reconciling the idea of a sixth epagomenal day with earlier observations of the annual rising of Sothis. It is true that for two centuries at a time the event did move by one day every four years and it is also true that in 238 B.C. the Egyptians had been using a 25-year lunar cycle for probably more than a century and were thus accustomed to the idea that lunar festivals could be fixed without the need for observation.[29] It must have been thought possible to establish a cycle for Sothis. But the truth of the matter is that the sixth epagomenal day was never actually introduced into the calendar. We must conclude that corrective observation of the rising of Sothis continued to remain the rule, and this had the effect of retarding the date by one triennium in the Ptolemaic Period.

ADDENDUM II. YEAR 8 OF SEKHEM-KA-REʿ

Between the completion and publication of this essay I came across the results of Hintze's reexamination of the Nile inscriptions at Semna, as reported in a private communication to Barbara Bell and incorporated by her in her study "Climate and the History of Egypt: The Middle Kingdom."[30] Hintze has found new high dates of Year 13 for Amenemhet IV and Year 8 for Sekhem-ka-Reʿ, who may be either the second or fourth ruler of the Thirteenth Dynasty. A Year 13 for Amenemhet IV does not affect any argument made above and in that light may be disregarded. A Year 8 for Sekhem-ka-Reʿ, however, raises a possibility that must be examined. Could the Sothic date of Year 7 be his? This assumption would place him in a situation exactly similar to that of Amenemhet IV (see above). It would indeed be possible, by setting Year 30 of Amenemhet III back another lunar cycle of 25 years to 1913 B.C., to fit his Year 7 into the range of 1875–1865 B.C. Assuming roughly 15 more years for Amenemhet III, 13 for Amenemhet IV, 4 for Sebeknefru, 2 for Khu-tawy-Reʿ, and 7 for Sekhem-ka-Reʿ (41 years in all) would bring us to 1872 B.C. However, the occurrence of

[29] Parker, *Calendars*, chap. 2.

[30] *AJA* 79 (1975) 229, n. 11.

the *wꜣg*-feast of Year 9 on II *šmw* 29 raises exactly the same problem with respect to Sekhem-ka-Reʿ as it does with respect to Amenemhet IV. Even on the assumption that Sekhem-ka-Reʿ had a Year 9 not yet attested, the gap in days between IIII *prt* 16 and II *šmw* 29 would be just too great. And what was true for the predecessors of Amenemhet IV would be just as true for those of Sekhem-ka-Reʿ. In fact, the gap could only be greater. The conclusion that the Sothic date must belong to Sesostris III has thus not been weakened in any way by Hintze's findings.

OF MYTH AND SANTORIN

Robert L. Scranton

Plato, epitome of Hellenic intellect, tells in the beginning of his *Timaeus* about how Solon, wisest of his forebears, went to Egypt to learn from the sages there. On one occasion, when Solon was speaking to the Egyptians about the Hellenic traditions of earliest times—the Flood, and the First Man—the Egyptians interrupted to say that the Greeks were little aware of the facts of earliest bygone times and proceeded to tell him their own account of primeval man and even of the achievements of the Athenians themselves in a time totally unknown to the uninformed Greeks. Among these accounts was one of the war conducted by the Athenians against a powerful invader whose home was in Atlantis, a vast continent in what is now the Atlantic Ocean. In the *Critias*, Plato purports to give their highly detailed and circumstantial account of this land of Atlantis—its topography, the design of its chief city, its people and their constitution. In particular, the city was in a great plain, in the center of a series of concentric canals, joined by another canal to the sea. The city was fantastically splendid and luxurious, the land fabulously rich and beautiful, the people highly sophisticated and wise. These Atlantians had conquered all the territories of the western Mediterranean and were moving eastward against Greece and Egypt when the Athenians defeated them and drove them back to their home beyond the Pillars of Hercules. "And afterwards there occurred violent earthquakes and floods, and in a single day and night of rain all your warlike men in a body sank into the earth, and the island of Atlantis disappeared and was sunk into the ocean" (*Timaeus*, 25*E–D* [Jowett]).

The story has, of course, evoked an enormous amount of speculation based on the assumption that it is an essentially accurate account of an authentic historic event—that there did physically exist at one time a territory marked by at least many of the features that Plato attributes to Atlantis; that this territory did sink beneath the surface of the sea; and that the facts about it were preserved in oral tradition, or even in written records, and were available to Plato, and perhaps also to Solon. Most recently the story has been related to the eruption in the fifteenth century B.C. of the volcanic peak of Thera, or Santorin.[1] This eruption was more tremendous than any other such eruption known

[1] See, *inter alia*, A. G. Galanopoulos and Edward Bacon, *Atlantis* (New York, 1969); A. N.

in human experience and had direct and indirect consequences of the most critical sort, including the fatal crippling of Minoan civilization in Crete and, of course, the destruction of all life on the island itself and the literal disappearance of a large part of the original island. Remains of the dwellings of those who were living at the time on the part of the island that survived have recently been freed of their covering of volcanic ash; they are as well preserved as the remains of Pompeii and do represent brilliantly a highly sophisticated and splendid culture. Oceanographic scientists have taken profiles of the sea bottom within the caldera and around it and have even detected what they, or some of them, have taken to be indications of encircling canals. This broad configuration of circumstances—the cataclysmic destruction of a prosperous civilization and the sinking or annihilation of a substantial mass of land in the remote past of Aegean history—has led some people to say in effect that Santorin was the historical reality represented by Plato under the name "Atlantis."

Against the idea that the story is authentic history is, for one thing, the fact that it seems to have been known only to Plato (or at least that it has been mentioned by no other known author than Plato). There are, to be sure, other stories about Atlantians and Atlas, but one would hardly recognize them as the Atlantians of Plato. In any case, to be objective, one has to consider the possibility that the story may have been an invention of Plato's for his own dramatic purposes, like the myth of Er in the *Republic*, or the mythic vision of the cosmos in the *Phaedo*, or like Xenophon's (or Prodicus's) "Choice of Herakles." These stories, too, contain highly circumstantial details of description and narration that no one would be inclined to take as "historical." Some, perhaps many, of the details of these stories may indeed have been drawn from nature or tradition, but in their context they belong to a fictitious world, designed to convey some philosophic meaning. So, too, even if Plato's account of Atlantis is mere fiction, there may be details taken from nature, history, or other fiction. I myself[2] have tried to show that the concept of the city surrounded by concentric canals may have been suggested by such arrangements in the Copaic Basin (which, too, was on occasion flooded with water), and the idea of the cataclysmic destruction may indeed have been suggested by some tradition of the annihilation of Santorin, with or without any of the atmosphere of glory and romance.

Thus, while we recognize the authentic historicity of the eruption of Santorin and its consequences and can believe that some elements of tradition may be

Kontaratos, *Anadrome sten proistoria tes Santorines* (Athens, 1970); D. L. Page, *The Santorini Volcano and the Desolation of Minoan Crete* ("Papers of the Society for the Promotion of Hellenic Studies," Supplement 12 [London, 1970]); S. N. Marinatos, "Late Minoan Thera," in *Prehistory and Protohistory* (London, 1974) pp. 220–30; and *idem*, *Some Words about the Legend of Atlantis* (Athens, 1971).

[2] "Lost Atlantis Found Again," *Archaeology* 2 (1949) 159–62.

present in the fabric of Plato's story, most people would be inclined to think that his account of Atlantis is his own invention. Nevertheless, the possible relation of the eruption of Santorin to Plato's story does lead us to consider the other side of the question: If the eruption of Santorin was of such unparalleled magnitude, so tremendously catastrophic, we might properly wonder whether the tradition of this eruption might not indeed have been preserved somehow among the Greeks, whether in the story of Atlantis or not.

Here it may be useful to try to distinguish certain terms and categories of "tradition." Leaving aside written records, which scarcely count as a factor in the traditions from the Bronze Age Aegean, we are left with the oral tradition. This can include: fiction—stories invented by poets and handed down orally through the generations; folk tale, which we might define for convenience as fictitious stories invented anonymously for entertainment or to transmit folk wisdom on various matters; legend, or recollections of historic events; and "myth." "Myth" is a word widely and variously used,[3] sometimes defined quite narrowly, sometimes quite loosely—so loosely even as to include all of the other categories just set forth. But in the present context let us, if only arbitrarily, agree to understand the term as referring exclusively to an account of natural phenomena understood as animated by numinous power—by an energizing force with a degree of humanlike will and quasi-intelligence. With this definition of "myth," however arbitrary, let us first try to explain it further by some illustrations, if only for the particular purposes of the immediate discussion.

Among the more elaborate illustrations would be certain cult myths, such as that of Eleusinian Demeter and Persephone. Here we have the narrative of Persephone, who was stolen away by Hades and carried off to the underworld. Demeter, her mother, sets out in search of her, and finally the hiding place of Persephone is discovered, and she is brought back to the world of the living, though only after she has performed an act that compels her to return to the underworld for six months out of each year. Meanwhile, Demeter has passed by the palace of the king of Eleusis, where she is pitied and helped in her distress, and has been given the task of caring for the young prince Triptolemos. In appreciation, she undertakes to make him immortal by certain fearsome rites, in the course of which she is discovered and interrupted, so that Triptolemos becomes only partly immortal. But somehow she succeeds in imparting to him the secrets of the successful cultivation of grain, and perhaps of other mysteries as well; he in turn passes the secrets on to his successors, and indirectly to people at large, through the rites of the "mystery cult" of Demeter at Eleusis.

At the other extreme, there is a multitude of tales known to us with only a bare minimum of narrative incident—the encounter of some hero with such creatures,

[3] Cf. recently G. S. Kirk, *Myth—Its Meaning and Function in Ancient and Other Cultures* ("Sather Classical Lectures," Vol. 40 [Berkeley, 1970]), esp. pp. 172–251 and in particular 226–51.

usually monstrous, as the Hydra, Gorgons, Harpies, or simple allusions, with no narrative at all, to nymphs, naiads, oreads, and so forth.

As these beings and their stories have come down to us, they have been colored and romanticized by the literary treatment given them during the Hellenistic and Roman periods, but there can be no doubt that in early times they existed, in the minds of the Greeks, in a more vital way. It is clear from a few examples, and fully plausible with regard to most, that some of the monstrous creatures, as well as some of the more recognizably anthropomorphic ones, were the local spirits or numinous presences of some locality: Thus, the Graiai ("Old Sisters, gray from birth," with one eye among them) gave their name to the locality from which comes our word "the Greeks"—"Graikoi." Moreover, one is at least encouraged to consider the hypothesis that among the primitive inhabitants of the Aegean all nature was felt to be alive—not only what we ourselves recognize as *animate* nature, but what we think of as *inanimate* nature as well. If this be true, then, not only animals and plants, but rivers and rocks and the weather were perceived by the Greeks to be all animated with numinous force or power, and it was this power that energized the occurrence of natural events. The vitality in the grain, the vitality in the earth were conceived as numinous forces. These forces were designated by words (it is not irrelevant that in Greek these have gender), and, as the phenomena of planting, harvest, storage of seed, and so forth were described and became part of the ritual by which men—as on the instruction of Triptolemos—undertook to influence the events, the words came to take on personalities and to become the names of "gods" and ultimately the dramatis personae of romantic tales. So, too, with the phenomena of springs and the sea, the weather, the sun, and all else.

All these interpretations are widely familiar, though not universally accepted in all details. But they are one step toward an interpretation of certain aspects of the poet Hesiod that is not entirely commonplace and leads on toward Santorin. Hesiod, in his *Theogony*, appears most superficially simply to be describing a family tree, a genealogical table of the gods and other divine powers. But a little beneath this he seems to be assembling a hodgepodge of theological and mythological and legendary material and trying, as we say, "to make sense of it." We can detect, perhaps, the effort to bring together into one rational system several theological and metaphysical systems otherwise known in his time as separate from each other. He tries to show how all divine beings —numinous forces—had emerged from a single source and how all the mythic narratives, many of them previously separated, belong to one connected mythic cosmic structure and "history."

In the *Theogony* one of the most vivid and dramatic episodes is that concerning what we call the Battle of the Gods and Giants, or the Titanomachy, ostensibly an Olympian conflict between Zeus and the gods of his generation against his father Cronus and the gods of *his* generation, the Titans. The story has it that the first pair of divinities were Heaven (Uranus) and Earth. They had several sets of children, of which those pertinent to this context are three: one set comprised the three Cyclopes—Brontes, Steropes, and Arges (the Thunderer, the Lightener, and the Vivid One); the second consisted of the three Giants—Cottus, Briareos, and Gyes (whose names elude confident translation); the third was composed of the Titans—Cronus, Rhea (his mate), Ocean, and others. All of these children Uranus had tried to dispose of in some way at their birth, hiding the Giants, in particular, in the inmost recesses of the earth, until Cronus plotted with Earth against his father and overcame him and brought them back. Then Cronus and Rhea proceeded to have their own brood of children, Zeus and the other Olympians. In the struggle that ensued between Zeus and the Olympians on the one hand and the Titans on the other, Zeus enlisted on his side the Giants (and perhaps also the Cyclopes). And then came the battle:

The boundless sea rang terribly around, and the earth crashed loudly; wide Heaven was shaken and groaned, and high Olympus reeled from its foundation under the charge of the undying gods, and a heavy quaking reached dim Tartarus and the deep sound of their feet in the fearful onset and of their hard missiles. So, then, they launched their grievous shafts upon one another, and the cry of both armies as they shouted reached to starry heaven; and they met together with a great battle-cry.

Then Zeus no longer held back his might; but straight his heart was filled with fury and he showed forth all his strength. From Heaven and from Olympus he came forthwith, hurling his lightning: the bolts flew thick and fast from his strong hand together with thunder and lightning, whirling an awesome flame. The life-giving earth crashed around in burning, and the vast wood crackled loud with fire all about. All the land seethed, and Ocean's streams and the unfruitful sea. The hot vapour lapped round the earthborn Titans: flame unspeakable rose to the bright upper air; the flashing glare of the thunder-stone and and lightning blinded their eyes for all that they were strong. Astounding heat seized Chaos: and to see with eyes and hear the sound with ears it seemed even as if Earth and wide Heaven above came together; for such a mighty crash would have arisen if Earth were being hurled to ruin, and Heaven from on high were hurling her down; so great a crash was there while the gods were meeting together in strife. Also the winds brought rumbling earthquake and duststorm, thunder and lightning and the lurid thunderbolt, which are the shafts of great Zeus, and carried the clangour and the warcry into the midst of the two hosts. An horrible uproar of terrible strife arose: mighty deeds were shown and the battle inclined. But until then, they kept at one another and fought continually in cruel war.

And amongst the foremost Cottus and Briareos and Gyes insatiate for war raised fierce fighting: three hundred rocks, one upon another, they launched from their strong hands and overshadowed the Titans with their missiles, and hurled them beneath the wide-pathed earth, and bound them in bitter chains when they had conquered them by their strength for all their great spirit, as far beneath the earth as heaven is above earth; for so far is it from earth to Tartarus.[4]

There is another account, very similar and at least as vivid, that appears also in the *Theogony* a few lines farther on, when Hesiod tells us:

But when Zeus had driven the Titans from heaven, huge Earth bare her youngest child Typhoeus of the love of Tartarus, by the aid of golden Aphrodite. Strength was with his hands in all that he did and the feet of the strong god were untiring. From his shoulders grew an hundred heads of a snake, a fearful dragon, with dark flickering tongues, and from under the brows of his eyes in his marvelous heads flashed fire, and fire burned from his heads as he glared. And there were voices in all his dreadful heads which uttered every kind of sound unspeakable; for at one time they made sounds such that the gods understood, but at another, the noise of a bull bellowing aloud in proud ungovernable fury; and at another the sound of a lion, relentless of heart; and at another, sounds like whelps, wonderful to hear; and again, at another, he would hiss, so that the high mountains re-echoed. And truly a thing past help would have happened on that day, and he would have come to reign over mortals and immortals, had not the father of men and gods been quick to perceive it. But he thundered hard and mightily: and the earth around resounded terribly and the wide heaven above, and the sea and Ocean's streams and the nether parts of the earth. Great Olympus reeled beneath the divine feet of the king as he arose and earth groaned thereat. And through the two of them heat took hold on the dark-blue sea, through the thunder and the lightning, and through the fire from the monster, and the scorching winds and blazing thunderbolt. The whole earth seethed, and sky and sea: and the long waves raged along the beaches round and about, at the rush of the deathless gods: and there arose an endless shaking. . . . A great part of huge earth was scorched by the terrible vapour and melted as tin melts when heated by men's art in channeled crucibles; or as iron, which is hardest of all things, is softened by glowing fire in mountain glens and melts in the divine earth through the strength of Hephaistos. Even so, then, the earth melted in the glow of the blazing fire.[5]

It is commonplace to recognize in these accounts the color of the spectacle of a volcanic eruption—some have suggested that it was an eruption of Mt. Aetna[6] —but in the present context one cannot fail to be struck by the thought that they could at least equally well be describing the eruption, the "titanic eruption" of Santorin itself. Nor does it damage the hypothesis to recall that there seems to be a basis for suspecting that there were in fact two eruptions of Santorin, some fifty years apart.[7]

[4] *Theogony*, trans. Hugh Evelyn-White, in *Hesiod, the Homeric Hymns and the Homerica* ("Loeb Classical Library" [Cambridge, Mass., 1954]) lines 678 ff.

[5] *Ibid.*, lines 820 ff.

[6] *Ibid.*, p. 141, n. 1.

[7] Marinatos, "Late Minoan Thera," in *Prehistory and Protohistory*, p. 229.

The serious point of this essay, however, is not merely to consider whether Plato's "myth" of Atlantis or Hesiod's "myth" of the Battle of the Gods and Giants in fact represent some tradition of the eruption of Santorin. If we can entertain the hypothesis that Hesiod is indeed reporting such a tradition, the point is rather to consider in terms of what concepts the tradition was inspired and understood by those who handed it on. Are we dealing with a story of anthropoid gods in conflict, derived perhaps from the Near East[8] but colored by Hesiod with details from factual reports of a natural phenomenon such as Pliny's description of the eruption of Vesuvius—just as we might suppose that the canals in Plato's description of his Atlantis were suggested to him by a fragmentary tradition of a long-ago city surrounded by canals, or that his story that Atlantis was submerged in the sea may have been suggested to him by another random tradition of Santorin (or by the evidence of the Copaic Basin)?

Or, is Hesiod recording a true myth, complete in its own terms—that is, an oral tradition of the Santorin eruption conceived in a genuine mythic understanding of the natural phenomenon? Perhaps one should suppose that those who had seen and survived the eruption told about it actually as, for the most part, Hesiod writes, in terms of the wind, sea, and fire in a conflict of dimensions beyond human comprehension, objectively alive with all the human qualities of rage, fear, violence, and ruin, superhuman in scale but not in kind—a conflict of numinous forces. In other words, that the account of the natural event was an account of natural "things" acting in a human way—an account of the action of numinous forces inherent in the natural things, in which the understanding of the event was not as one of physical action and reaction, but rather of willful forces that were the essence of the physical things.

This distinction may have a deeper significance—that is, that the tradition was not one of independently self-existing "gods" manipulating physical substances, but rather of the natural substances themselves acting by virtue of their inherent numinous will. Even though we might suppose that in Hesiod's time these understandings may have become more "objectified" in terms of "gods," that is, in the form of more concrete, anthropomorphic personalized images, it may be that the newer understanding or "objectification" was less pervasive than we sometimes think. In several places Hesiod speaks of what we might call "non-persons," though the inclination of editors to print their names with capital letters tends to color the concept for us. At the beginning of his survey

[8] Cf. Hans Güterbock, "The Hittite Version of the Hurrian Kumarbi Myths: Oriental Forerunners of Hesiod," *American Journal of Archaeology* 52 (1948) 123–34. J. W. Mavor, Jr. (*Voyage to Atlantis* [New York, 1969] pp. 133–38) reports conversations with Edward Loring and A. G. Galanopoulos in which the Santorin eruption is discussed in relation to Near Eastern myths and Hesiod, but the presentation is as uncritical as is that of the whole thesis of Atlantis itself, with no clear explanation that is reasonable or convincing.

Hesiod says that "Verily at the first chaos came to be, but next wide-bosomed earth, the ever-sure foundation of all the deathless ones who hold the peaks of snow Olympus, and dim tartaros in the depth of the wide-pitted earth, and love, fairest among the gods . . . from chaos came erebus(?) and black night, but of night were born air and day."[9]

If we capitalize Chaos, Earth, Tartaros, Love, Erebos, Night, Air, Day, the passage has quite a different ring.[10] And it is true that when he speaks of something "being born" of something, or something "begetting" something, we tend to think of this in terms of humanlike procreation. But the Greek commonly thinks of things as "being generated" or "generating themselves," and we ourselves can speak of "rage born of frustration" without deifying or personifying either.

Again, Hesiod says: "And night bare hateful doom and black fate and death, and she bare sleep and the tribe of dreams . . . and abhorred strife bare painful toil and forgetfulness and famine and tearful sorrows, fightings, battles, murders, disputes . . .," etc., etc.[11] When written with capital letters and in a language in which nouns have gender, these notions tend to be conceptualized as poetic personifications. On the hypothesis here being advanced, one would suppose that while the Greeks certainly did feel something willfully alive in all these concepts, just as even we sometimes perceive a personal quality in them, they were not thinking of the "person" as distinct from the phenomenon.

In general, then, the point to be made is that Hesiod, acting as an encyclopedic, systematic theologian and researcher into the history of religion and philosophy, encountered mythic material (in our particular sense) of many ages

[9] *Theogony*, lines 116 ff.

[10] Capitalization would of course not have been used in the early manuscripts, however the concepts were understood. But modern scholars in general seem to tend to use capitals and to understand the concepts as persons, or at least "personifications." M. L. West in his *Hesiod's Theogony* (Oxford, 1966) seems to allow that those in immediate question might be "abstractions" derived from earlier "daimones," referring to Hermann Usener, *Götternamen* (Bonn, 1929) pp. 364–75. For more recent discussions see J. Blusch, *Formen und Inhalt von Hesiods individuellen Denken* (Bonn, 1970). See also two articles by T. B. L. Webster, "Personification as a Mode of Greek Thought," *Journal of the Warburg Institute* 17 (1954) 10–21, and "Language and Thought in Early Greece," *Memoirs and Proceedings of the Manchester Literary and Philosophical Society* 94 (1952/53) 16–38. In these Prof. Webster is discussing the "personifications" of certain kinds of abstractions, chiefly in classical Greek literature, in a way that comes close to what I am trying to suggest, and superficially seems quite close. But I believe that he is thinking in terms of literary modes and, indeed, "habits of thought" as they appear and develop in Greek literature as it is preserved to us, whereas I am trying to suggest that there is also an element that stems from religious and metaphysical understandings current prior to the earliest known Greek literature, that indeed persisted in later times; and that this element endows the "personifications"—or many of them—with a degree of objective reality in their own right.

[11] *Theogony*, lines 211 ff.

and many levels and was trying to organize and rationalize it all. In this he has perhaps preserved to us some hitherto inadequately noticed evidence for "mythic" material existing far earlier than his own time. And he has done so at a level that Plato himself says (*Timaeus* 22 *C–D*) was called to the attention of Solon by the Egyptian sages when they reminded him of the story of Phaethon (the word means "the [agent doing the] shining"), the "son" of Helios (the sun), who had yoked his father's steeds in his father's chariot and, because he was unable to control them, burned up all that was on earth and was himself destroyed by a thunderbolt. Of this story the Egyptians explained: "this is said in the form of a myth, but really [it narrates] the aberration of the [things that are] moving around the earth and through the heavens, and the destruction of things on earth by great heat, which happens at long intervals."

PASHED, THE SERVANT OF AMON: A STELOPHOROUS FIGURE IN THE ORIENTAL INSTITUTE MUSEUM

David P. Silverman

This article is a tribute to George R. Hughes, professor emeritus of the Oriental Institute, on the occasion of his seventieth birthday. It is a privilege to have been his student.

The figure of Pashed (Fig. 45) has been part of the collection of the Oriental Institute Museum (OI 13700) since 1928, when it was purchased in Egypt by James Henry Breasted.[1] Although it has been discussed previously in regard to its style,[2] there still remains some ambiguity about its dating; moreover, the inscription on the stela has not yet been published. The piece is carved limestone with traces of paint still remaining on much of the surface. Its dimensions are 32 cm. × 13 cm. × 21.5 cm.

In discussing this piece, Vandier at one point suggested that it belonged to the reign of Amenhotep III, though he remarked on the exceptional attitude of the figure; Pashed inclines slightly forward, whereas most stelophorous figures sit upright.[3] Later in his study, however, he suggested that Pashed belonged to the Ramesside period, although he pointed out that the long unified skirt worn by Pashed, which is more typical of the period prior to the reign of Amenhotep III, is quite rare afterward.[4] Other characteristics, such as the wide eyes, provide no certain dating, but can occur both during the Ramesside period and earlier. The wig, not discussed by Vandier, is not at all common.

[1] I would like to thank John A. Brinkman, director of the Oriental Institute, for permission to publish both OI 13700 and 13701. For the hand copies of the inscriptions, I would like to thank Mr. Raymond Johnson; for the photograph in Fig. 46, Mr. Albert Leonard.

[2] J. Vandier, *Manuel d'archéologie égyptienne* III: *Les grandes époques, la statuaire* (Paris, 1958) pp. 472–94 and Plate volume, Pl. CLX, 1.

[3] *Ibid.*, pp. 472–73.

[4] *Ibid.*, p. 494.

The name Pashed would seem to be in accord with Vandier's second choice, since this name occurs primarily during the Ramesside period.[5] It is not yet possible, however, to identify the owner of OI 13700 with any other bearer of the same name, since neither the title borne by the Oriental Institute piece, *sḏm ꜥš n Jmn* "servant of Amon," nor the name of "his sister, his beloved, the mistress of the house, *ꜣst m-ꜥ.(j)*" can be associated with any other Pashed.[6] There are, however, two fragments of a stela (OI 13701) in the Oriental Institute (Fig. 46), purchased by Breasted at the same time as the figure of Pashed, and this stela belonged to a Pashed. Below is the translation of the fragments:

I (1) Osiris, foremost of the West, (2) great god. (3) Giving praise to the lord (4) of Abydos, (5) kissing the ground (6) for Onnophris. (7) I give praise to you every day. (8) His sister[a] . . . (9) Dedicated by Pashed.

II (1) Nefertari[b] (2) His son (3) (His?) daughter *Mwt-nfr(t)*[c]

Commentary:

[a]The remaining parts of the headband and flower indicate that a woman had been pictured, despite the apparent presence of *sn.f* rather than *snt.f*.

[b]See Tosi and Roccati, *Stele*, p. 249, where Nefertari is referred to as the wife of Pashed. See also Bruyère, *Rapport*, 1923–24, Tomb 323 (pp. 84–86). Unfortunately our stela provides no familial relationship for her.

[c]See Bruyère, *Rapport*, 1923–24, p. 83, where *Mwt-nfrt* is referred to as a wife of Pashed. It is less likely that the *sꜣ* before *Mwt* is an element in a name.

Given the circumstances of their appearance, it is possible that these two pieces belong to the same Pashed as OI 13700. If one considers the amount of activity in Deir el Medineh, both before and during 1928, and the frequent appearance of the name Pashed in that area, it is likely that these pieces in the collection of the Oriental Institute may also have a similar provenience and dating.[7]

[5]See the references provided by Hermann Ranke, *Die ägyptischen Personennamen* I (Glückstadt, 1935) 119, No. 13. See the occurrences of the name in the Theban area in Bertha Porter and Rosalind L. B. Moss, *Topographical Bibliography of Ancient Egyptian Texts, Reliefs and Paintings* I/1 (2d ed.; Oxford, 1960). See also Mario Tosi and Alessandro Roccati, *Stele e Altri Epigrafi di Deir el Medina* ("Catalogo del Museo Egizio di Torino" I, 2d series [Turin, 1972]) pp. 245–46, where all the occurrences listed of the name Pashed are from the Nineteenth Dynasty. Bernard Bruyère, *Rapport sur les fouilles de Deir el Médineh*, 1922–51 ("FIFAO" I/1; II/2; III/3; IV/3, 4; V/2; VI/2; VII/2; VIII/3; X/1; XIV–XVI; XX; XXI; XXVI [1924–53]) also lists several occurrences of the name, and these date either to the Nineteenth Dynasty specifically or to the Ramesside period more generally. These references indicate that the name Pashed is post-Eighteenth Dynasty.

[6]See the indices of names and titles given by Tosi and Roccati, *Stele*, pp. 245–46 and by Bruyère, *Rapport*. The title most commonly associated with Pashed is *sḏm ꜥš m st mꜣꜥt*. Neither index includes the name *ꜣst m-ꜥ.j*, nor does Ranke, *Personennamen*.

[7]See Bruyère, *Rapport* ("FIFAO" XXI [1952]) pp. 79–80, where it is pointed out that Chicago's

The inscription on the stelophorous figure (Fig. 45*A*) appears to support the later date. It was H. M. Stewart who suggested that this type of funerary statuette evolved in the Eighteenth Dynasty owing to the need to accommodate longer and longer inscriptions, the texts of which were primarily sun hymns.[8] Such hymns began as prayers inscribed directly on the figure of the worshipper. When more space was needed for an inscription, a stela was added that provided a good surface for text and could be enlarged as necessary. In some cases, the stela was the most prominent element of the statuette. Most of these stelae had texts dealing with the sun, and the devotion to Re during this period can also be seen in funerary texts, which, as Stewart has already pointed out, often contain prayers to Re.[9] There are in fact several *ḥtp-dj-nswt* formulas of the Eighteenth Dynasty that include sections concerning Re. It appears that the text inscribed on the stela before Pashed belongs to this class rather than to the class of solar hymns, although most inscriptions on stelophorous figures belong to the latter category.[10]

There are parallels to the inscription that appears on the stela of Pashed (see Fig. 47), but none of them come from inscriptions on stelophorous figures, and each of them dates to the Eighteenth Dynasty.[11] They do not supply evidence that would date Pashed to the same period; on the contrary, the misspellings and errors in the Pashed text indicate that it was a later copy and condensation of an earlier original composition.

---

excavations at Medinet Habu also provided pieces produced by artisans from Deir el Medineh. Bruyère (*ibid.*, p. 78) also notes that a stela from Theban Tomb 359, Inherkha, was purchased from a Luxor dealer in 1932 by K. Seele two years after the opening of that tomb.

[8] H. M. Stewart, "Some Pre-ʿAmārnah Sun-Hymns," *JEA* 46 (1960) 84 and "Egyptian Funerary Statuettes and the Solar Cult," *Bulletin of the Institute of Archaeology, University of London* 4 (1964) 165–70. See also *idem*, "Traditional Egyptian Sun Hymns of the New Kingdom," *ibid.*, 6 (1967) 29–74. For a more recent study of the hymns to the sun, see Jan Assmann, *Liturgische Lieder an den Sonnengott* ("Münchner Ägyptologische Studien," Vol. 19 [Berlin, 1969]).

[9] Stewart, *JEA* 46 (1960) 84.

[10] See the examples collected by Stewart, *Bulletin of the Institute of Archaeology, University of London* 6 (1967) 45–70 and Assmann, *Liturgische Lieder*, pp. 376–77.

[11] The parallel texts are excerpted from Wolfgang Helck, *Urkunden der 18. Dynastie* ("Urk" IV/18 [1956]) pp. 1519–21. See also a discussion of some of the stelae in Alfred Hermann, *Die Stelen der thebanischen Felsgräber der 18. Dynastie* ("Ägyptologische Forschungen," Vol. 11 [Glückstadt, 1940]). For a study of the *ḥtp-dj-nswt* formulas of the Eighteenth Dynasty, see Winfried Barta, *Aufbau und Bedeutung der altägyptischen Opferformel* ("Ägyptologische Forschungen," Vol. 24 [1968]) pp. 107–38.

A *B*

FIG. 45.—Stelophorous figure of Pashed OI 13700, front (*A*) and three-quarter view (*B*)

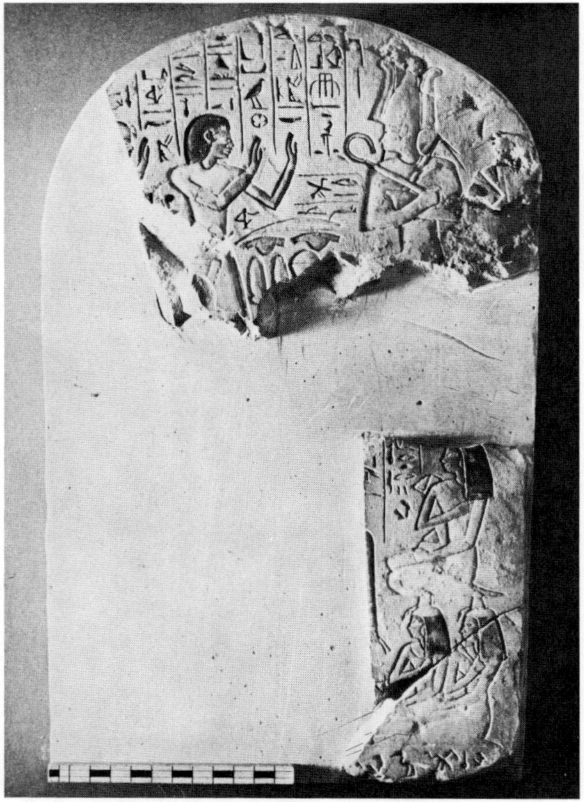
A

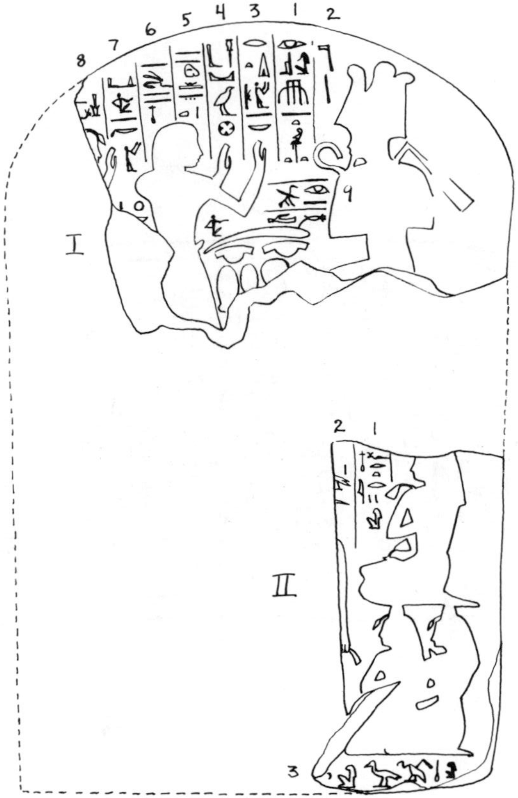

B

FIG. 46.—Stela OI 13701, photograph (*A*) and inscription (*B*)

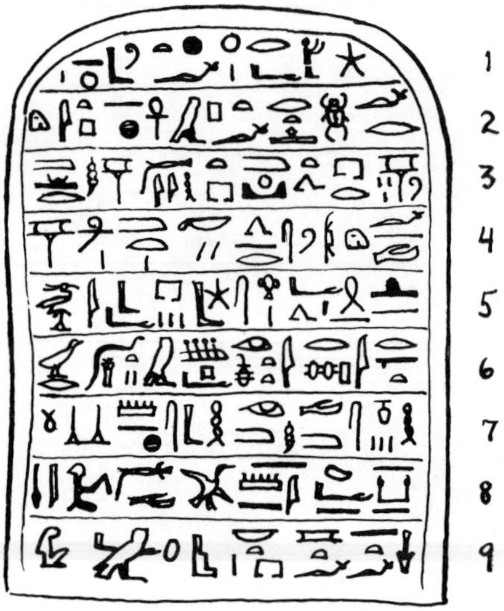

Inscription on stelophorous figure
of Pashed OI 13700

(1) Adoring Re when he rises (2) until he sets in life, breathing (3) the breezes, going forth[a] from the horizon, the north wind being pleasant[b] to (4) the nose, escorting[c] Sokar[d] in the necropolis,[e] (5) without being repelled[f] at the portals [of the Netherworld],[g] being exceptionally well supplied [with][h] (6) wine and milk and being in receipt of oil, unguent, (7) eye paint, sweet things, clothing, and linen (8) for the ka of the servant of Amon, Pashed, true of voice, (9) and his sister, his beloved, the mistress of the house, *ꜣst m-ꜥ.j*.

Commentary (refer to Fig. 47):

[a] Although *t* is written in our text as well as in one of the parallels, it is omitted in another. It is possible that the participle *pr*, rather than the infinitive, was meant.

[b] The parallels have *nꜣw n mḥt*.

[c] Both extant parallels write *šms.f*.

[d] Neither Sokar nor Re (above, line 1) is written with a god determinative, although all of the parallels use it. Note also the spelling of Sokar as *Srk*. The same spelling also occurs on a Middle Kingdom stela in the Cairo Museum, JdE 47927.

[e] For the spelling of *R-sṯꜣ*, which may be a later writing, see W. Spiegelberg, "Miszellen," *ZÄS* 59 (1924) 159–60.

[f] It would also be possible to translate, "There is no repelling . . . ." One parallel corresponds to our text, while another has *nn šnꜥ.tw.f*, "He will not be repelled."

[g] Our text apparently omitted *n dwꜣt*, which appears in the parallels.

[h] The parallels consistently write *bꜥḥj jm m* while our text omits the adverb and the preposition, spells *bꜥḥj* with 𓉔 rather than with 𓎛, and inserts what appears to be a misplaced adverbial *r ꜥꜣt* (Edward F. Wente suggested the reading). The text appears to be

garbled here, but there is a slight possibility that the sign in question might be , in which case we could read either *rdj.tw* or *rdjt*. The translation of the former would be, "There is an abundance; wine and milk will be given," while the latter would be, "The giving of wine and milk overflows." Owing to the use in the parallels of *m* after *bꜥḥj* (in all cases) and *šsp* (in most cases), it is likely that the two words should be understood to be the same form.

Although Vandier suggested two possible dates for this statuette, it would appear that the later date, the Ramesside period, is the more likely one. There are several uncommon characteristics that the piece exhibits: the zigzag curls of the wig; the forward incline of the figure; the long, one-piece skirt; and the use of a funerary prayer rather than a solar hymn on the stela; all of these point to the later date. During the Eighteenth Dynasty, a time when this type of statuette was regularly being made, it is unlikely that such an unconventional piece would have been produced. It is more plausible to assume that the standardized elements would have been replaced by new and, in some cases, unprecedented substitutions as the result of a later interpretation of an earlier model. The abridged inscription, with its misspellings and errors, supports this suggestion, and the name Pashed, which is attested primarily in the Nineteenth Dynasty, also points to a later dating. Finally, although it may be purely coincidental, a stela bearing the same name as that of the owner of OI 13700 came into Breasted's possession at the same time.

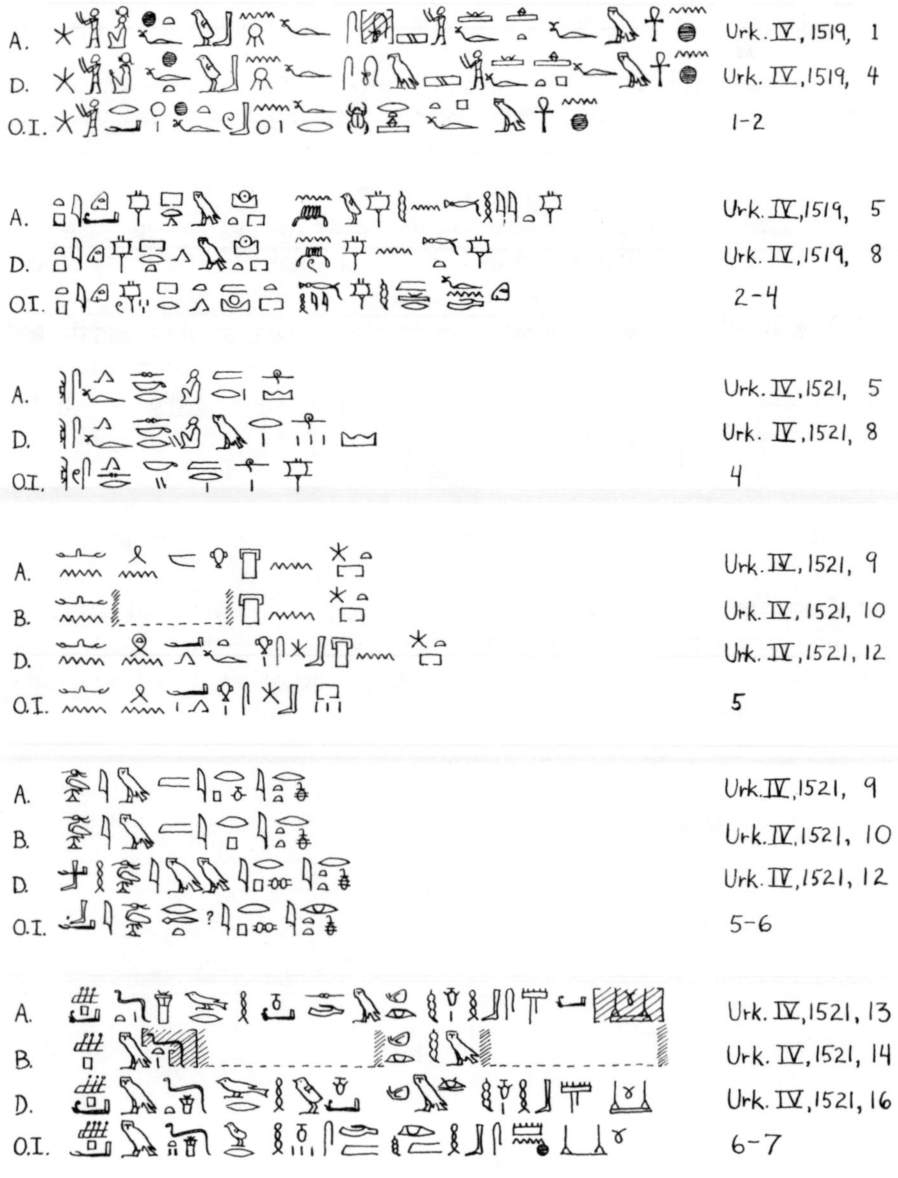

FIG. 47.—Parallel versions of inscription on stelophorous figure of Pashed

CAIRO OSTRACON J. 72460

Elizabeth Thomas

If my understanding of George Hughes is correct, he would prefer a puzzle on his seventieth birthday rather than a problem solved. Therefore Cairo Ostracon J. 72460 is presented with my best wishes for the years to come.[1]

As Černý's note on the upper left of his transcription indicates, the 11 by 13 cm. flake of limestone bears a complete text, except at the beginning of verso 1–2. To judge by the photograph, the blank area on the verso is rough and presumably was intentionally skipped by the scribe. With regard to the transcription, Janssen suggests that the hieratic signs following *pꜣ* in recto 4 and those at the beginning of verso 2 are to be read 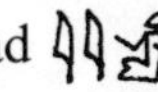, and that those omitted between *pꜣ* and *ỉmy-r* in recto 6 are probably to be transcribed as 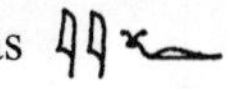. Wente believes the dot under the *wr*-bird in recto 6 may represent the seated man, .

According to the accession records of the Cairo Museum, the general provenience of this ostracon is the Valley of the Kings, from the excavations of Theodore Davis. Specifically, a comparison of "marqué 8" (the number is circled) with similar designations in Černý's *Ostraca hiératiques* strongly suggests that 72460 was found by Howard Carter, working for Davis, in 1902:[2] in January–March "a few ostraca" were discovered near the anonymous tombs 28 and 21, and "many ostraca and broken fragments, some dating from the XIX–XXth dynasty" were discovered in the vicinity of tomb 36 (Maiherperi);

[1] The Cairo Museum has generously permitted publication of the photographs of the ostracon. The Griffith Institute has permitted publication of Jaroslav Černý's transcription of it. I would like to express appreciation to these institutions and also to Dr. A. K. Selim for forwarding the photographs and accession information from the Museum records, to Mr. and Mrs. J. Dorman, Dr. J. Málek, Miss H. Murray, Dr. G. Bryce, Miss H. Phillips, Prof. J. Johnson, Prof. E. Wente, and especially to Dr. J. J. Janssen for criticism and textual emendations that are individually credited below. Černý refers to J. 72460 in *A Community of Workmen at Thebes in the Ramesside Period* ("BdE" L [1973]) pp. 82–84. He cites no similar texts and no ostraca in the same hand. My limited search has disclosed neither.

[2] Jaroslav Černý, *Ostraca hiératiques* I ("CCG" [1935]) 127, Index VI, "Provenance des ostraca." In this index circled numbers occur as "marqués" of ostraca only under "campagne de 1902"; the ostraca bearing numbers 1, 2, 3, 7, and 10 are credited to the excavations of Theodore Davis, the other two (18 and 37) to the excavations of Georges Daressy.

A

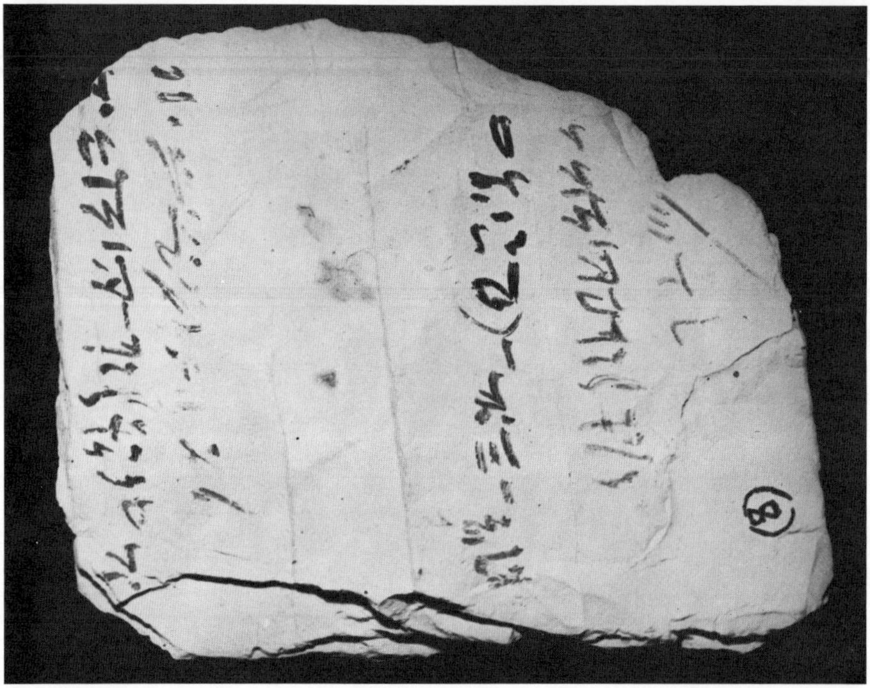

B

FIG. 48.—Cairo Ostracon J. 72460, recto (*A*) and verso (*B*)

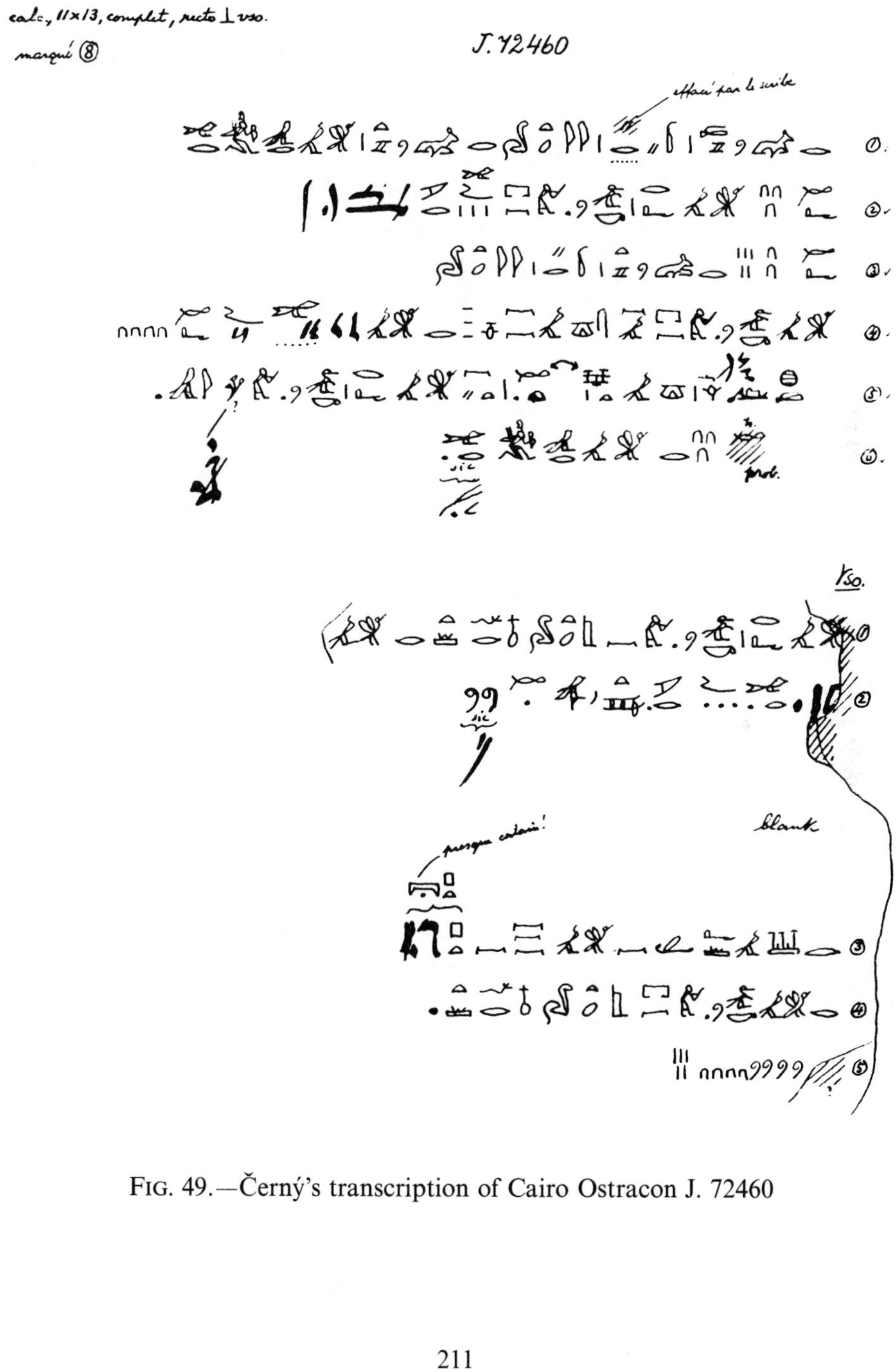

FIG. 49.—Černý's transcription of Cairo Ostracon J. 72460

then from November to April, 1903, "many hieratic ostraca" were found in the *wadi* below tombs 19, 20, and 43 (Montuherkhepeshef, Hatshepsut, and Thutmose IV).[3] Thus the provenience of 72460 is probably the area of tombs 28, 21, or 36, or possibly below 19–20.

The date of the inscription according to the Cairo Museum records is the Twentieth Dynasty, but the paleography suggests the Nineteenth Dynasty.[4] And a date in the reign of Ramesses II, which Wente believes likely, is supported by internal evidence and probably by the paleography of two contemporary letters from Lower Egypt, inscribed on papyrus—P. Leiden I 360 and 368.[5]

Overall the text is concerned with perhaps eight unidentified "sites" that the provenience appears to place within the Valley of the Kings or in its general vicinity. An approximate translation is as follows:

recto:
1. From *Tr*(*t*)*yt* [*A*] to the "Generalissimo"[6] [*B*],
2. 30 cubits (15.693 m.),[7] [⌈and to⌉] the tomb[8] of the Greatest of Seers Meryatum [*C*],
3. 25 cubits (13.0775 m.). From *Tr*(*t*)*yt* [and? to?]
4. the tomb of the oils [*D*] to my (*pꜣy.ỉ*) Greatest of Seers[9] [*C*], 40 cubits (20.924 m.).
5. Downstream (north) on the northern path [*E*] on which lies the old[10] tomb [*F*],
6. 30 cubits (15.693 m.) to his (*pꜣy.f*) Generalissimo [*B*].

verso:
1. [From?] the tomb of Isisnefert [*G*] to the
2. [tomb of?] my (*pꜣy.ỉ*) Greatest of Seers Meryatum [*C*], 200 cubits (104.62 m.).
3. From the end (bottom?) of the Water of the Sky [*H*]
4. to the tomb of Isisnefert [*G*],
5. 445 cubits (232.7795 m.).

[3] Howard Carter, "Report on General Work Done in the Southern Inspectorate," *ASAE* 4 (1903) 45–47 and 176–77.

[4] See Georg Möller, *Hieratische Paläographie* II (Leipzig, 1909); Jaroslav Černý, *Catalogue des ostraca hiératiques non littéraires de Deir el Médineh* I–V ("DFIFAO" III–VII [1935–51]) and *idem, Ostraca hiératiques*.

[5] See the photographs published by J. J. Janssen, "Nine Letters from the Time of Ramses II," *OMRO* 41 (1960) Pls. III and XIV. This reference was given to me by Martha Bell.

[6] The title so translated by Edward F. Wente, *Late Ramesside Letters* ("SAOC," No. 33 [1967]) p. 3, with reference to Herihor; cf. K. A. Kitchen, *The Third Intermediate Period in Egypt* (Warminster, 1973) pp. 16–19.

[7] Taking the cubit to be 52.31 cm.; see Howard Carter and Alan H. Gardiner, "The Tomb of Ramesses IV and the Turin Plan of a Royal Tomb," *JEA* 4 (1917) 136; cf. 52.3 cm. in Sir Alan Gardiner, *Egyptian Grammar* (3d ed.; London, 1957) par. 266, 2.

[8] *Pꜣ r-ʿ bꜣk*, "'the work-in-progress,'" according to Černý, *Community of Workmen*, pp. 81–85; also otherwise applied and abbreviated *pꜣ bꜣk*.

[9] The readings *pꜣy.ỉ* and *Wr-mꜣw* are Janssen's, as again in recto 6 and verso 2 (*pꜣy.f*, *pꜣy.ỉ*). Personal communications are the source of all Janssen references unless stated otherwise.

[10] The reading, "*ỉs*, as usual in ostraca," is Janssen's interpretation.

A, *Tr*(*t*)*yt* (*Ṯr*(*t*)*yt*), is apparently related to a willow divinity. Is it here a cult place and/or the tree itself, perhaps planted near a *ghafîr*'s hut as is the palm tree today? The willow was evidently associated with the desert necropolis because this tree was sacred to Hathor in her aspect of guardian of the West and the tomb. Funerary wreaths made from its leaves are common and were found, for example, on the royal mummies in the Deir el-Baḥri cache as well as on the mummy of Tutankhamon.[11]

B, *pꜣ* (*pꜣy.f*) *ỉmy-r mšꜥ wr*, "the (his) Generalissimo," logically indicates the tomb of Ramesses II, although there is no proof of this. In 1960 Janssen had "a strong impression" that "'the general'" mentioned in Leiden Letters 360 and 368 "could not be anybody else than Ramses II."[12] This view was not supported in his following study of P. Leiden I 350 verso.[13] He has not "come across another indication of that kind," nor would such an identification constitute actual proof in our text. However, the large tomb of Ramesses II was surely in process of being erected, along with those of his wife and son, if 72460 was indeed inscribed during his reign, and it could hardly have been overlooked by our scribe. Further, the tomb of this king is perhaps indicated by the possessive *pꜣy.f* in recto 6. Such a relationship of Meryatum, to whom the pronoun must refer, to "his Generalissimo" is especially likely if the latter is Ramses II, for the prince is called a charioteer as well as a son of Ramesses.[14]

C apparently occurs three times as the tomb of *Wr-mꜣw* Meryatum, the son of Ramesses and Nefertari discussed under *B* above.

D is probably a small robbed and/or unfinished and unused tomb that served as a storehouse for *sgnnw* that were to be used, at least in part, in greasing "candles"[15] plaited from rags similar to those of the "bundles" placed on two occasions in tomb 49.[16]

E in this *gebel* is surely "northern path," rather than "narrow road" or the

[11] See M. Ludwig Keimer, "L'Arbre *ṯr.t* est-il réellement le saule égyptien (*Salix safsaf* Forsk.)?" *BIFAO* 31 (1931) 177–234, especially in the section entitled "Guirlandes en feuilles de saule égyptien," pp. 197–202.

[12] Janssen, *OMRO* 41 (1960) 45–46.

[13] *Idem*, *Two Ancient Egyptian Ship's Logs*, Supplement to *OMRO* 42 (1961) 19–20.

[14] The most recent discussion of Meryatum is found in the following reference given to me by Janssen: Mohamed I. Moursi, *Die Hohenpriester des Sonnengottes von der Frühzeit Ägyptens bis zum Ende des Neuen Reiches* ("Münchner Ägyptologische Studien," Vol. 26 [Munich and Berlin, 1972]) pp. 64–68, 158, 170; also see Černý, *Community of Workmen*, p. 82.

[15] See Černý, *Community of Workmen*, p. 84, and *idem*, *The Valley of the Kings* ("BdE" LXI [1973]) pp. 43–54, especially 44–45.

[16] Graffito 1282 in J. Černý, *Graffiti hiéroglyphiques et hiératiques de la nécropole thébaine* ("DFIFAO" IX [1956]); my interpretation in my revision of *The Royal Necropoleis of Thebes* (Princeton, 1966; 2d ed. in preparation) is in disagreement with Černý's "garments" and his proposed date of this tomb (*Community of Workmen*, p. 15).

like.[17] Proceeding north for 15.693 m. from an unknown starting point (*C*??), one reaches *B*, the Generalissimo, after passing "the old tomb" (*F*) to the right or left, east or west, on the way.

F, "the old tomb," was presumably excavated in the Eighteenth Dynasty, though it seems unlikely that it was one of the open shafts noted by John Romer on the *gebel* above the Valley of the Kings.[18] Was *F* left incomplete and open, or was it simply evident but inaccessible in the early part of the Nineteenth Dynasty?

G is surely the tomb of Isisnefert. If, as we believe, the text was inscribed during the reign of Ramesses II, she is certainly his queen and the mother of Merneptah.[19] Otherwise, she is probably a daughter of Ramesses II and the wife of Merneptah.[20]

H must be a prominent waterfall on the desert side of the Valley of the Kings, granted that the tomb of Isisnefert is located here, where the runoff from the high *gebel* is greatest; the maps and photographs at my disposal suggest the stretch extending from the cliffs above tomb 36 (Maiherperi) to those just beyond tomb 15 (Seti II). The specific site is possibly above tomb 13 (Bay?), where the terrain may allow the two or more cascades that *pḥ*, "(the) end," perhaps implies.[21]

As yet waterfalls are attested only in the Valley of the Queens and in the West Valley. Graffiti 3012–13 are found below the cascade at the end of the first *wadi*. The older, 3013, may be translated literally as follows: "Year 62, 4 Shemû, Day 23, this day going down to look at the Water of the Sky," the high year date indicating the reign of Ramesses II.[22] Graffito 3012 is identical except in its

[17] See, for example, James Henry Breasted, *Ancient Records of Egypt* III (Chicago, 1906) 137, § 307, and John A. Wilson, in James B. Pritchard, ed., *Ancient Near Eastern Texts Relating to the Old Testament* (2d ed.; Princeton, 1955) p. 255.

[18] Romer (personal letter dated June 25, 1974) has "found a few more shaft tombs above the Kings' Valley which seem unrecorded and of early XVIII dynasty date." He says that the tomb placed in this general area on the recent map of the Valley of the Kings (J. Černý *et al.*, *Graffiti de la montagne thébaine* I ["Centre de Documentation et d'Etudes sur l'ancienne Egypte" (Cairo, 1969–71)] Pl. IV) is also a shaft tomb. Presumably all of these tombs will be published by Romer in his study of tombs of this period (in preparation).

[19] See Černý, *Community of Workmen*, p. 82.

[20] See Henri Gauthier, *Le Livre des rois d'Egypte* III ("MIFAO" XIX [1914]) 106–7, 125, 421; and Janssen, *OMRO* 41 (1960) 32 and *idem*, *Two Ancient Egyptian Ship's Logs*, p. 26.

[21] See J. Félix *et al.*, *Graffiti de la montagne thébaine* II (1970–71) plans 37–38. The area of tomb 36 is found in plans 15 and 34–35; the cascades south of tomb 32 in plan 74 probably lack the height and slope required for maximum effect.

[22] As first stated in Černý *et al.*, *Graffiti de la montagne thébaine* I, p. XVIII, and supported by the facsimile in *ibid.*, III (1970–72) Pl. CLXXXV, but contrary to "Year 2" in the transcription, *ibid.*, IV (1970–73) 154. For the precise location of the text see Félix *et al.*, *ibid.*, II, plan 22.

date, "Year 4 of Baenre [Merneptah], 1 Shemû, Day 27."[23] Graffito 1736, inscribed on the cliff wall about 140 m. beyond the tomb of Amenhotep III in the West Valley, states simply that the scribe Amennakht and his three middle sons were "at," *r*, the Water of the Sky in Year 2, 4 Shemû, Day 25.[24] The relative age of the sons suggests the reign of Ramesses IV or V.[25] Finally, Graffito 2868 presumably records a fourth downpour, again dated in a Year 2, 4 Shemû, but on Day ⌜4⌝,[26] when *sḏm-ʿš* Amenpahapy[27] and his brother, *sš*, "went down to look at the water from the Water of the Sky." This text was inscribed in a grotto on the south side of the outflow from the Bibân el-Molûk.[28]

Did a rare cloudburst and perhaps a first visit to the royal necropolis with "his" Meryatum inspire the author of Cairo Ostracon 72460? The opening phrase of his first two sentences, "From *Trtyt*," suggests that the scribe was seated near the proposed willow while he jotted down the distances apart of the tombs and landmarks within his range of vision, tombs and landmarks that are presently lost or unidentified. For us his text is like a pirate's chart to buried gold, full of clues that we cannot interpret. Our search might begin with the ostracon itself, to confirm or emend the readings proposed here; with an attempt to confirm or deny the proposed identification of *pꜣ ỉmy-r mšʿ wr* with the tomb of Ramesses II; and with an intensive topographical investigation within the

[23] See Černý *et al.*, *ibid.*, III, Pl. CLXXXIV and *ibid.*, IV 154. For the precise location of the text see Félix *et al.*, *ibid.*, II, plan 22. A partial parallel to *mw n pt* is the *mw nw pt* of Anastasi II 2,4 and IV 6,9; it is interesting since the reign is also that of Merneptah.

[24] My reading of the facsimile, Černý *et al.*, *ibid.*, III, Pl. XV; that of the transcription (*ibid.*, IV 14) is "Day 24." For the precise location see Félix *et al.*, *ibid.*, II, plan 85. The site and part of the transcription are also published by C. Desroches Noblecourt in "Les Temples de la Nubie submergée et la rive gauche de Thèbes," *Le Courrier du CNRS* 9 (July 1973) 35.

[25] See Černý, *Community of Workmen*, pp. 339–46; Userhat (Graffito 2061) should be added to the table, p. 346. Černý believes that Amennakht was "Scribe of the Tomb" from Year 16 of Ramesses III to Year 6 or 7 of Ramesses VI.

[26] "Day 4" is read in the transcription, Černý *et al.*, *Graffiti de la montagne thébaine* IV 128; in the facsimile (*ibid.*, III, Pl. CLXV) two vertical strokes are followed by two horizontal lines. For the exact location of the text see Félix *et al.*, *Graffiti de la montagne thébaine* II, plan 125.

[27] An Amenpahapy occurs in Cairo Ostraca 25607, 25650, and 25660, which Černý in *Ostraca hiératiques* I 37, 49, and 52 dates respectively to the first half of the Twentieth Dynasty, to the Twentieth Dynasty, and to the beginning of the Twentieth Dynasty.

[28] Of course, only heavy downpours on the high desert could have caused appreciable cascades in the *wadi*s or outflows from them, but the rain could also have been general, as it probably was in 1819 (Giovanni d'Athanasi, *A Brief Account of the Researches & Discoveries in Upper Egypt* [London, 1836] p. 15) and positively in November 1916 (Carter, Griffith Institute Notebook G, I. K. 21). Probably only the high desert was affected in the early 1800's (Giovanni Belzoni, *Narrative of the Operations and Recent Discoveries* I [2d ed.; London, 1821] 124) and in October 1918 (Carter, Griffith Institute Notebook G).

Valley of the Kings and perhaps in the surrounding area. Within the *wadi* the first objectives should probably be the location of the waterfall, at least a superficial examination of the high shaft tombs, and then ideally the clearance of tomb 5. This tomb, now undetectable, lies about 35 m. down and across the outflow from the tomb of Ramesses II. It is definitely related to this king by the occurrence of his cartouche on an entrance lintel.[29] Also, it lies, if only coincidentally, roughly 235–45 m. below tombs 36 and 13 (Maiherperi, Bay?).

[29] Burton's copy and his sketch plan of this large unusual tomb (BM 25642, 19) are reproduced in Thomas, *Royal Necropoleis*, Fig. 14, p. 120; for discussion with references see pp. 149–50 and Index; cf. Edward F Wente, "A Prince's Tomb in the Valley of the Kings," *JNES* 32 (1973) 228.

A CHRONOLOGY OF THE NEW KINGDOM

Edward F. Wente and Charles C. Van Siclen III

As field director of the Epigraphic Survey of the Oriental Institute from 1949 to 1964, Professor George R. Hughes made significant contributions in the study and recording of monuments of considerable importance to historians of ancient Egypt. His remarks concerning the triumphal reliefs of Shoshenq I reflect the considered judgment of one who has worked intimately with the basic source material.[1] While his appraisal of the chronological implications of these reliefs might be regarded as overly cautious,[2] it is clear from what he has to say on the subject that Shoshenq I's accession cannot be fixed in time as firmly as some would aver.[3] The outline of the chronology of the New Kingdom that we propose here is in part made possible because of Professor Hughes's perceptive comments regarding the significance of the Bubastite reliefs for the chronology of the Twenty-second Dynasty. We present this essay on the occasion of his seventieth birthday as a token of appreciation to an outstanding teacher and genial colleague.

Chronologists have often made liberal use of Manetho's history of Egypt, as recorded in various excerpts; in particular, Wolfgang Helck's ingenious attempt at reconstructing the original Manetho[4] has influenced the recent work of some scholars.[5] It cannot be denied, however, that the important Eighteenth Dynasty is somewhat confused in the surviving excerpts from Manetho's history, and it has become something of a parlor game to try to reconcile Manetho's kings and the lengths of their reigns with ancient Egyptian data. Because of the extreme difficulties presented by that portion of Manetho that treats the New Kingdom,

[1] In The Epigraphic Survey, *Reliefs and Inscriptions at Karnak* III: *The Bubastite Portal* ("OIP" LXXIV [1954]) Preface.

[2] Cf. Kenneth A. Kitchen, *The Third Intermediate Period in Egypt (1100–650 B.C.)* (Warminster, 1973) p. 73, n. 360.

[3] See Edward F. Wente, review of Kitchen, *Third Intermediate Period* in *JNES* 35 (1976) 275–78.

[4] *Untersuchungen zu Manetho und den ägyptischen Königslisten* ("UGAÄ" XVIII [Berlin, 1956]).

[5] E.g., Erik Hornung, *Untersuchungen zur Chronologie und Geschichte des Neuen Reiches* ("Ägyptologische Abhandlungen," Vol. 11 [Wiesbaden, 1964]), and to some extent Donald B. Redford, "On the Chronology of the Egyptian Eighteenth Dynasty," *JNES* 25 (1966) 113–24.

TABLE 1

CHRONOLOGY OF THE NEW KINGDOM

EIGHTEENTH DYNASTY

Ahmose I	1570	1546		
Amenhotep I	July 1551	(March) 1524		
Thutmose I	March 1524	(October) 1518		
Thutmose II	October 1518	(May) 1504		
Thutmose III	May 1504	March 1450		
Hatshepsut	1503/1498	1483		
Amenhotep II	November 1453	1419		
Thutmose IV	1419	(May) 1386		
Amenhotep III	May 1386	1349		
Akhenaton	1350	1334		
Smenkhkare	1336	1334		
Tutankhamon	1334	1325	Alternative	
Aye	1324	1321	(1324–	1319)
Haremhab	1321	1293	(1319–	1291)

NINETEENTH DYNASTY

Ramesses I	1293	1291	(1291–	1289)
Sety I	May 1291	(September) 1279	(1289–	[September] 1279)
Ramesses II	September 1279	(July) 1212		
Merenptah	July 1212	(May) 1202		
Amenmesse	May 1202	(December) 1199		
Sety II	December 1199	October 1193		
Siptah	October 1193	1187		
Tausert	1193	1185		
Interregnum	1185	1185/4		

TWENTIETH DYNASTY (KITCHEN SEQUENCE)

Setnakht	1185/4	(March) 1182
Ramesses III	March 1182	April 1151
Ramesses IV	April 1151	(September+) 1145
Ramesses V	(September+) 1145	(October) 1141
Ramesses VI	October 1141	(January) 1133
Ramesses VII	January 1133	(November+) 1127
Ramesses VIII	(November+) 1127	(June) 1126
Ramesses IX	June 1126	October 1108
Ramesses X	October 1108	(April) 1098
Ramesses XI	April 1098	1070

TWENTIETH DYNASTY (VON BECKERATH SEQUENCE)

Setnakht	1185/4	(March) 1182
Ramesses III	March 1182	April 1151
Ramesses IV	April 1151	(September+) 1145
Ramesses V	(September+) 1145	(October) 1141
Ramesses VI	October 1141	(March+) 1134
Ramesses VIII	(March+) 1134	(January) 1133
Ramesses VII	January 1133	(June) 1126
Ramesses IX	June 1126	October 1108
Ramesses X	October 1108	(April) 1098
Ramesses XI	April 1098	1070

the chronology that we are proposing relies as little as possible upon data supplied by the excerpts or by modern interpretations of them.

Similarly we are avoiding reference in this discussion to the estimated ages at death of the pharaohs of the New Kingdom, whose mummies have occasionally been considered in chronological reconstructions.[6] Recently, Professor James E. Harris of the University of Michigan has re-examined the royal mummies, and members of his team of investigators have proposed some revised estimates of their ages at death.[7] In particular, the kings of the Eighteenth Dynasty appear to have died at younger ages than previously supposed. Because of possible uncertainties in these estimates, our revision of the chronology of the New Kingdom refrains from referring to the royal mummies. We might mention, incidentally, that whereas there has been an overall reduction in the estimated ages at death of members of the Eighteenth Dynasty royal family, the mummy of Thutmose IV, according to recent estimates, is that of a man older than previously thought. This increase in the age of one king may be significant.

In view of uncertainties still surrounding an absolute chronology of Western Asia, synchronisms between Egypt and the rest of the ancient Near East had best be excluded at the outset from immediate consideration. Only after the chronology of the New Kingdom has been reconstructed on the basis of Egyptian evidence alone should one seek to make correlations with other chronologies.

The revised chronology presented here does take into consideration a factor that has generally been neglected by chronologists: evidence pertaining to the royal jubilee. It is a remarkable fact that those pharaohs of the New Kingdom who reigned thirty or more years all celebrated their Sed-festivals according to a set scheme. The first jubilee began in regnal Year 29 and concluded in Year 30.[8] It has been claimed that certain kings, like Thutmose I and II, celebrated a jubilee earlier in the reign, but such claims often rest upon misinterpretation of iconographic evidence. If, for example, one finds a scene depicting Thutmose II running with flasks of water, one must not conclude rashly that in this scene he is necessarily celebrating a Sed-festival,[9] for such a ritual act is not confined to the royal jubilee.[10] The evaluation of evidence pertaining to the Sed-festival

[6] E.g., Claude Vandersleyen, *Les Guerres d'Amosis, fondateur de la XVIIIe dynastie* (Brussels, 1971) pp. 195–200.

[7] See James E. Harris and Kent R. Weeks, *X-raying the Pharaohs* (New York, 1973) chaps. 4–5, for some very preliminary estimates.

[8] See Charles Van Siclen, "The Accession Date of Amenhotep III and the Jubilee," *JNES* 32 (1973) 290–300.

[9] As, for example, Redford, *JNES* 25 (1966) 118, with n. 38.

[10] See Hermann Kees, *Der Opfertanz des ägyptischen Königs* (Leipzig, 1912) chap. 2, and *idem*, "Nachlese zum Opfertanz des ägyptischen Königs," *ZÄS* 52 (1914) 64–69.

is for the most part adequately discussed by Erik Hornung and Elisabeth Staehelin.[11]

In the Rosettana Decree there occurs the expression κυρίου τριακονταετηρίδων, and a demotic papyrus contains the words *ḥb n ḥ3t-sp* 30, "Festival of Year 30," as a designation of the royal jubilee.[12] There is thus a certain tradition that the jubilee conformed to a thirty-year principle that determined the celebration of the first jubilees of the long-reigning Thutmose III, Amenhotep III, Ramesses II, and Ramesses III. If one denies the general validity of such a thirty-year principle during the New Kingdom, then the question arises just how these four great kings knew in advance that they would have lengthy reigns. Why did they not celebrate their first Sed-festival at some point earlier in their reigns? That a thirty-year principle did indeed exist in the New Kingdom is suggested by the Late Egyptian mythological story, "The Tale of the Two Brothers," which has to do with certain aspects of the royal succession. At the conclusion of the tale we read: "His (that is, the king's) elder brother was brought to him, and he appointed him crown prince in the entire land. He ⟨spent⟩ thirty years as king of Egypt. He departed from life, and his elder brother acceded to the throne on the day of death."[13] One function of the Sed-festival was the renewal of kingly vigor so as to avoid just such a death after thirty years of rule.

According to William Kelly Simpson a thirty-year principle seems to have been operative also in the Twelfth Dynasty; at least there is no firm evidence to the contrary.[14] More recently Hornung and Staehelin have concluded that historic jubilees were generally celebrated in the thirtieth year of rule.[15] There are two notable exceptions to this generalization: Hatshepsut and Amenhotep IV (Akhenaton). Hatshepsut's first jubilee was celebrated in Year 16 of her joint rule with Thutmose III; and Amenhotep IV's took place around his fourth regnal year at Karnak, before he changed his name to Akhenaton and moved to Amarna.[16] While Hornung and Staehelin assume that Hatshepsut calculated

[11] *Studien zum Sedfest* ("Aegyptiaca Helvetica" I [Geneva, 1974]).

[12] See Franz J. Lauth, *König Nechepsos, Petosiris, und die Triakontaëteris* ("Sitzungsberichte der Bayerischen Akademie der Wissenschaften, Philosophisch-historische Abteilung," No. 2 [Munich, 1875]) pp. 89–144.

[13] Alan H. Gardiner, *Late-Egyptian Stories* ("Bibliotheca Aegyptiaca" I [Brussels, 1932]) p. 29, ll. 7–10; cf. Hornung and Staehelin, *Studien zum Sedfest*, p. 84.

[14] "Studies in the Twelfth Egyptian Dynasty: I. The Sed Festival in Dynasty XII," *JARCE* 2 (1963) 59–63.

[15] *Studien zum Sedfest*, pp. 80–85.

[16] Some scholars, like Cyril Aldred ("The Beginning of the El-ʿAmārna Period," *JEA* 45 [1959] 32) and Donald B. Redford ("Reconstructing the Temples of a Heretical Pharaoh," *Archaeology* 28/1 [1975] 18), tend to place Amenhotep IV's first jubilee in Year 2, but we are inclined to believe

the date for her Sed-festival by reckoning from the accession of her father Thutmose I,[17] it is equally plausible that her jubilee occurred twenty-nine years after his death or her theoretical accession in Year 1 of Thutmose II.

In the case of Amenhotep IV one is dealing with a most unusual reign during which the king's association with the Aton is constantly stressed. As we know from jubilee scenes in the tomb chapel of Kheruef from the time of Amenhotep III, a culminating point in the traditional Sed-festival was the apotheosis of the king identifying him with the sun-god.[18] It seems very likely that Amenhotep IV's premature celebration of the jubilee served to inaugurate what was to last throughout his reign: his oneness with the Aton. Indeed it is probable that Amenhotep IV's Karnak Sed-festival was a joint festival of the king and the god. Some have supposed that subsequent historic jubilees were held at Amarna, but there is really no positive evidence to support this view. On the Karnak jubilee *talatat* and at Amarna there is evidence for a high priest of the living king.[19] This is extraordinary. Might not one suppose that Akhenaton's reign itself was a sort of perpetual jubilee, as expressed in the following words: "The Ruler is born like the Aton, enduring unto eternity like him in celebrating the million jubilees that the living Aton decreed for him"?[20]

Other instances of alleged anticipatory celebration of the jubilee are those of Amenhotep II, Thutmose IV, and Merenptah, as well as of two kings who ruled after the New Kingdom: Osorkon II and Psamtik II. For the first two of these kings, Amenhotep II and Thutmose IV, the early celebration of their jubilees is predicated upon the fact that the length of each of their reigns was supposedly established at less than thirty years. This established length, however, reflects merely the highest preserved dates of each king and a possible interpretation of the Manethonian tradition, but no facts are currently in evidence that limit the length of the reigns of either of these two kings to less than thirty-five years. Although these kings did celebrate jubilees, it cannot be demonstrated that they were anticipatory celebrations.

---

that this date is somewhat too early; cf. Jan Assmann, "Palast oder Tempel?" *JNES* 31 (1972) 151, n. 54.

[17] *Studien zum Sedfest*, p. 54.

[18] See Ahmed Fakhry, "A Note on the Tomb of Kheruef at Thebes," *ASAE* 42 (1943) Pl. XL and pp. 494–95, and Edward F. Wente, "Hathor at the Jubilee," in *Studies in Honor of John A. Wilson* ("SAOC," No. 35 [1969]) p. 90.

[19] See Donald B. Redford, "Studies on Akhenaten at Thebes: I. A Report on the Work of the Akhenaten Temple Project of the University Museum, University of Pennsylvania," *JARCE* 10 (1973) 86, and Hermann Kees, *Das Priestertum im ägyptischen Staat vom Neuen Reich bis zur Spätzeit* ("Probleme der Ägyptologie" I [Leiden, 1953]) pp. 84–85.

[20] Maj Sandman, *Texts from the Time of Akhenaten* ("Bibliotheca Aegyptiaca" VIII [Brussels, 1938]) p. 73, ll. 6–7.

In the case of Merenptah, the length of his reign is certainly below the requisite thirty years (see below), but the attribution of a jubilee to his reign is itself open to question. The main evidence rests in Papyrus Bologna 1094, which is dated to Merenptah's Year 8.[21] Within that papyrus are two passages that refer to preparations for the celebration of a second jubilee.[22] The first of these is attributed to an official of what is presumably the temple of Merenptah at Memphis,[23] and it would seem that the jubilee referred to is that of Merenptah. But little confidence can be placed in the historicity of this document since it belongs to a class that consists of schoolboy copies of older documents into whose texts contemporary data have sometimes been introduced. Thus the document does not necessarily reflect an actual historical situation. Both Papyrus Anastasi II, 5, 6 ff. and Papyrus Anastasi IV, 5, 6 ff. preserve the same text—the one with the name of Merenptah, the other with that of Sety II.[24] Similarly, Papyrus Anastasi VI, 58, gives a Year 8 of what is theoretically the reign of Sety II,[25] but in fact the year must refer to the reign of Merenptah, inasmuch as Sety II did not reign beyond his sixth year (see below). Further on in the same papyrus, in lines 80–81, there are mentioned officials who are known to have served under Ramesses II and Merenptah,[26] yet the context assumes them to be alive and functioning in the reign of Sety II.

The jubilee of Osorkon II, dated to his Year 22,[27] seems clearly to be a case of anticipatory celebration taking place during a period when one would assume that the traditional pattern was still in force. From a chronological point of view, however, there is no document that would restrict the length of Osorkon II's reign to less than the requisite thirty years; and the accuracy of the copying of the date as Year 22 is itself open to question.[28] Thus the date of the jubilee of Osorkon II is not sufficiently well established to vitiate the thirty-year principle.

The jubilee attributed to Psamtik II, who reigned only six years (594–589 B.C.), is open to doubt. The view that it occurred is based upon the restoration of a damaged inscription on the obelisk of this king now at Monte Citorio in Rome. One of the columns of text ends with the phrase "first occasion" followed

[21] See Ricardo A. Caminos, *Late-Egyptian Miscellanies* (London, 1954) pp. 33–34.

[22] Page 1, ll. 3–9, and p. 4, ll. 1–10.

[23] Caminos, *Late-Egyptian Miscellanies*, p. 5.

[24] *Ibid.*, p. 50.

[25] *Ibid.*, p. 295.

[26] *Ibid.*, pp. 297–300.

[27] Edouard Naville, *The Festival-Hall of Osorkon II in the Great Temple of Bubastis* (*1887–1889*) (London, 1892) Pl. VI.

[28] See Wente, *JNES* 35 (1976) 275–78.

by a break.[29] An early and surprisingly accurate drawing done by James Stuart in 1750 shows what seems to be a tall *s* below the *zp*-sign,[30] and while the restoration *ḥb-sd* is plausible, it is by no means certain. There is therefore no way of being sure that this is an instance of an anticipatory celebration of a jubilee.

It seems clear that starting in the Middle Kingdom, the practice of celebrating a jubilee at set intervals beginning with Year 30 was established, and this practice continued until the Ptolemaic period with no exceptions that can be firmly established or that cannot be explained in some other way. Thus it seems reasonable to assume that wherever strong evidence exists that a king celebrated a jubilee or made preparations to do so, his reign must have approached his thirtieth year. The recording of a jubilee by a king thus becomes a significant *contemporary* statement as to the duration of his reign.

In establishing a chronology of the New Kingdom one must first consider the so-called "fixed" dates: the accessions of Amenhotep I, of Thutmose III, of Ramesses II, and of Shoshenq I. In a recent article it has been argued that perfect solutions of the two unemended lunar dates recorded during the reign of Thutmose III support his accession in 1504 B.C. rather than the generally accepted 1490 B.C.[31] Also in the same article a Memphite sighting of Sothis in the ninth year of the reign of Amenhotep I was deemed probable, supporting a higher chronology that would put the accession of Amenhotep I in the broad range of 1553–1545 B.C., with a possible refinement of the date to 1551 B.C. on the basis of the lunar calendar in Papyrus Ebers.

A lunar date in Year 52 of Ramesses II provides us with three possible dates for his accession: 1304, 1290, or 1279 B.C.[32] None of the solutions of this lunar date is perfect since they all assume an observational error in the early morning when the ancient Egyptians determined New Moon day. One type of observational error could easily be caused by unfavorable atmospheric conditions, when cloudiness, haze, or smoke from village fires might obscure the visibility of a final lunar crescent with the result that New Moon day would be declared one day in advance of actual conjunction. Both the 1304 and 1279 accession dates are based on solutions of the lunar date involving just such an observational error. The 1290 date, on the other hand, reflects a solution according to which the observer(s) thought that there was a final crescent when, in fact, there

[29] Orazio Marucchi, *Gli Obelischi egiziani di Roma* (Rome, 1898) p. 108.

[30] Erik Iversen, *Obelisks in Exile I. The Obelisks of Rome* (Copenhagen, 1968) Fig. 127.

[31] See Edward F. Wente, "Thutmose III's Accession and the Beginning of the New Kingdom," *JNES* 34 (1975) 265–72.

[32] See Richard A. Parker, "The Lunar Dates of Thutmose III and Ramesses II," *JNES* 16 (1957) 42–43.

actually was none, thus declaring New Moon day one day past actual conjunction. While atmospheric conditions might easily lead to failure to observe a final crescent, they would be less likely to give, to the trained eye of a professional observer, the impression that a final crescent existed when there actually was none. For this reason it would seem that either 1304 or 1279 B.C. is somewhat preferable to 1290 B.C. as the date of Ramesses II's accession, if only the astronomical evidence is taken into consideration.

The accession of Shoshenq I has been placed at 945 B.C. on the assumption that his Palestinian campaign, which occurred in the fifth year of Rehoboam, took place toward the end of his reign and was followed immediately by building projects in the fore part of the temple of Amon at Karnak.[33] The weaknesses in this argument have been discussed in a review of Kitchen's monumental work on the Third Intermediate Period.[34] At best the Palestinian synchronism tells us that Shoshenq I could have come to the throne no earlier than 948 B.C. but possibly as late as 929 B.C. In this review of Kitchen's work it was suggested that a better fixed date in the Twenty-second Dynasty is the accession of Takelot II in 860 B.C., as determined on astronomical grounds by Klaus Baer.[35] If one considers the jubilee evidence for certain predecessors of Takelot II, 946 B.C. can be determined by simple addition to be the probable date for Shoshenq I's accession, though this date could be raised or lowered in view of uncertainties surrounding the length of Takelot I's reign and the possibility of coregencies as yet undocumented. In spite of the fact that Kitchen's date for the beginning of the Twenty-second Dynasty differs from ours by only one year, it should be stressed that these two dates have been ascertained by entirely different means.

To determine the end of the Twentieth Dynasty, one simply adds the length of the Twenty-first Dynasty to the accession of Shoshenq I. Although Kitchen and Wente have proposed different genealogical reconstructions of the Twenty-first Dynasty, the chronological conclusions are similar.[36] In fact, Kitchen has succeeded in reducing the length of the dynasty by noting a very probable coregency between Psusennes I and his successor Amenemope. The only king about whose length of reign one might have some reservations is Psusennes II, for here we are dependent almost entirely upon Manetho. One excerptor, Africanus, assigns fourteen years to Psusennes II, while Eusebius gives him

[33] See Kitchen, *Third Intermediate Period*, pp. 72–76.

[34] See Wente, *JNES* 35 (1976) 275–78.

[35] "The Libyan and Nubian Kings of Egypt: Notes on the Chronology of Dynasties XXII to XXVI," *JNES* 32 (1973) 8–11.

[36] See Kitchen, *Third Intermediate Period*, Pt. I, and Wente, "On the Chronology of the Twenty-first Dynasty," *JNES* 26 (1967) 155–76.

thirty-five years. We agree with Kitchen that unless contemporary documentation should suggest the higher figure, it is safer to accept the lower one. Theban sources do give some king after Siamon a Year 13, which may belong to Psusennes II.[37] By adding the 124 years that comprise the Twenty-first Dynasty to the date of Shoshenq I's accession, one obtains the date of the beginning of the Twenty-first Dynasty, or the end of the New Kingdom, at 1070 B.C., one year earlier than Kitchen's 1069 B.C.

To ascertain the date of the beginning of the New Kingdom—that is, the accession of Ahmose I—it has been customary to add Manetho's figure of twenty-five years for the reign of Ahmose I to the date of Amenhotep I's accession as determined by considering the Sothic rising recorded in Amenhotep's Year 9. Some reservations have been expressed recently concerning this procedure.[38] There is some evidence to indicate that Ahmose I and Amenhotep I were coregents for perhaps as many as six years.[39] Consideration of the jubilee evidence pertaining to Amenhotep I suggests that the reign of twenty-one years usually accorded Amenhotep I on the basis of the biography of the astronomer Amenemhet and Manetho should be considered as the length of his sole reign after a period of coregency with his father Ahmose I. Thus a date ca. 1570 B.C. is proposed for the beginning of the New Kingdom.

Because the probable date of Amenhotep I's death coincided with the accession of Thutmose I, we know that they were not coregents.[40] The highest certain date for Thutmose I is a Year 4,[41] though some have adduced a Year 9 for him.[42] This Year 9 and a Year 8 appear in a very enigmatic cartouche in conjunction with what seem to be the leaves of an *ished*-tree carved on a block found in Thutmose III's portion of the sanctuary of Amon at Karnak.[43] We are thus far from certain that this block was contemporary with Thutmose I, and in view of the leaves of the *ished*-tree, one might suppose that the years are not even historical, for the leaves of this tree were supposed to be inscribed by the gods

[37] See Kitchen, *Third Intermediate Period*, p. 13.

[38] Wente, *JNES* 34 (1975) 270.

[39] See also Günther Vittmann, "Was There a Coregency of Aḥmose and Amenophis I?" *JEA* 60 (1974) 250–51.

[40] See Wolfgang Helck, "Zur Chronologie Amenophis' I.," in Helck, ed., *Festschrift für Siegfried Schott zu seinem 70. Geburtstag am 20. August 1967* (Wiesbaden, 1968) pp. 71–72, and Donald B. Redford, *History and Chronology of the Eighteenth Dynasty of Egypt: Seven Studies* (Toronto, 1967) pp. 51–53.

[41] "Urk" IV 91.

[42] E.g., Hornung (*Untersuchungen zur Chronologie*, p. 32) and Redford (*JNES* 25 [1966] 116).

[43] Kurt Sethe, *Das Hatschepsut-Problem noch einmal untersucht* ("[Königlich] Preussische Akademie der Wissenschaften, Abhandlungen der Philosophisch-historische Klasse," No. 4 [Berlin, 1932]) p. 85.

at the beginning of a king's reign.[44] We share William F. Edgerton's skepticism about the usefulness of this block.[45] Edgerton, who was very familiar with the Theban monuments of the Thutmosid rulers, concluded that if circumstances were to posit a short reign for Thutmose I, it could easily have been merely four or five years, a span of time quite sufficient for all the building projects carried out in his name.[46] If the Year 9 date is genuine, it could be accommodated in our chronology by elevating the accession of Amenhotep I to 1553 B.C., the highest possible date permitted by the Sothic rising in his Year 9.

By contrast, many scholars have granted Thutmose II only a very brief reign, rejecting a Year 18 ascribed to him on a monument copied by Georges Daressy, but since lost.[47] If Hatshepsut's jubilee, celebrated in her Year 16, conformed to the thirty-year principle, it is quite possible that she reckoned it from the death of her father Thutmose I, subsuming the reign of Thutmose II, her former husband, in her calculations. Hatshepsut, once she assumed the kingship, possibly as late as Year 7 of Thutmose III,[48] highly honored her father Thutmose I while she ignored entirely the reign of her dead husband. In fact, during her kingship she tried to make it appear that she was the direct successor of Thutmose I.[49] On the basis of her celebration of a Sed-festival in Year 16, it may be concluded that Thutmose II reigned thirteen full years, and one might therefore suggest that Daressy's Year 18 may have been a miscopy of a Year 14, whose tall unit-signs might easily have been damaged in midsection. Although Daressy was not noted for epigraphic accuracy, one cannot summarily dismiss his monument from consideration.

Some support in favor of a longer reign for Thutmose II is found in the biography of Aneni.[50] At the death of Thutmose I, the new king Thutmose II is described by Aneni as "a falcon who is in the nest," possibly a reference to his youth. Further on Aneni states that he reached old age under Thutmose II, a statement that implies a reign of some duration for Thutmose II during which there was sufficient time for Aneni to become old. By the end of his reign Thutmose II had two children: Neferure by Hatshepsut and Thutmose III by Isis; at the commencement of his reign in Year 1, however, it is significant that he did

[44] See Wolfgang Helck, "Ramessidische Inschriften aus Karnak I. Eine Inschrift Ramses' IV.," *ZÄS* 82 (1957) 117–40.

[45] "On the Chronology of the Early Eighteenth Dynasty (Amenhotep I to Thutmose III)," *AJSL* 53 (1937) 189, n. 4.

[46] William F. Edgerton, *The Thutmosid Succession* ("SAOC," No. 8 [1933]) p. 33.

[47] "La Chapelle d'Uazmès," *ASAE* 1 (1900) 99.

[48] See Roland Tefnin, "L'An 7 de Touthmosis III et d'Hatshepsout," *CdE* 48 (1973) 232–42.

[49] See Alan H. Gardiner, *Egypt of the Pharaohs* (Oxford, 1961) p. 186.

[50] "Urk" IV 58–59.

not personally participate in the Nubian war.[51] If his failure to appear in battle was because he was too young, his reign must have been of sufficient length to permit him to mature so as to beget two children. For what it is worth, Manetho, *apud* Helck, assigns to Thutmose II a reign of thirteen years.[52]

By-passing Thutmose III, the exact length of whose reign is well established at fifty-three years, ten months, twenty-six days, and who was coregent with his son Amenhotep II for two and one-third years,[53] we come to the reigns of Amenhotep II and Thutmose IV. For both of these kings there are jubilee inscriptions on monuments that read, "First Occasion and Repetition of the Jubilee."[54] The second phrase, *wḥm ḥb-sd*, is the technical term for the second jubilee, as we know from hieratic dockets from the Malkata palace of Amenhotep III[55] and from references to the second jubilee of Ramesses II.[56] What such texts on monuments tell us is that the king had already celebrated one jubilee and was on the verge of celebrating a second one in his Years 33–34, since the monument and the text would generally have been executed prior to the event of the second Sed-festival.

Some indirect supportive evidence for the length of Amenhotep II's reign is the inscription of Thutmose IV on the Lateran obelisk of Thutmose III.[57] It had probably been the intention to erect this obelisk for a jubilee of Thutmose III,[58] but the king died in Year 54 and the obelisk lay in the Karnak workshops until it was erected thirty-five years later by Thutmose IV. It is known that during his first year a king would undertake significant building projects,[59] and one might indeed suppose that the erection of the Lateran obelisk was carried out at the beginning of Thutmose IV's reign. If so, we then have a figure of approximately thirty-four years from near the end of Thutmose III's reign to

[51] "Urk" IV 137–41.

[52] Wolfgang Helck, *Geschichte des Alten Ägypten*, I. Abteilung, 1. Band, 3. Abschnitt of *Handbuch der Orientalistik*, ed. Bertold Spuler (Leiden and Cologne, 1968) pp. 142 and 151, n. 4.

[53] See Richard A. Parker, "Once Again the Coregency of Thutmose III and Amenhotep II," in *Studies in Honor of John A. Wilson* ("SAOC," No. 35 [1969]) pp. 75–82, and Wente, *JNES* 34 (1975) 267–68.

[54] For references see Hornung and Staehelin, *Studien zum Sedfest*, pp. 32–33.

[55] See William C. Hayes, "Inscriptions from the Palace of Amenhotep III," *JNES* 10 (1951) 84–85.

[56] See Hornung and Staehelin, *Studien zum Sedfest*, p. 38. It might be mentioned that in one of the Gardiner papyri *zp-sn*, "twice," is written with the *wḥm*-hieroglyph; see *ECT* III 115, n. 1.

[57] "Urk" IV 1550, ll. 2–8.

[58] See James Henry Breasted, "The Obelisks of Thutmose III and His Building Season in Egypt," *ZÄS* 39 (1901) 59.

[59] See Erik Hornung, "Politische Planung und Realität im alten Ägypten," *Saeculum* 22 (1971) 54–56.

the accession of Thutmose IV. In stating that the obelisk lay abandoned for thirty-five years, the Egyptians may simply have used the figure of Amenhotep II's highest regnal year to indicate the span of time. Thus the independent reign of Amenhotep II would have been thirty-four years less the period of coregency —two years, four months—that is, approximately thirty-one years, eight months in all. It might be mentioned that S. R. K. Glanville read a probable Year 30 on a document that he assigned to the reign of Thutmose III,[60] but Redford, in correctly reassigning the document to Amenhotep II's reign, rejected the reading of Year 30.[61] Although the date is broken, it may be that Glanville's earlier reading is correct, since he worked directly from the papyrus. In that case we would have a higher regnal year for Amenhotep II than the generally accepted Year 26 on a wine-jar docket from his mortuary temple.[62]

In connection with this Year 26 Redford has reasoned that it must lie at the very end of Amenhotep II's reign because wine would not have been stored a long time in porous jars before the inception of the king's mortuary cult that Redford believes commenced at the death of a king.[63] Helck, however, has provided some evidence for the long-term storage of wine in ancient Egypt,[64] and besides, it is quite well established that royal funerary temples of the New Kingdom functioned prior to the death of the king in whose honor the temple was erected.[65]

Acceptance of Year 26 as the final year of Amenhotep II's reign has received support through Helck's attributing the reign of Manetho's Mephramouthosis to Amenhotep II.[66] William C. Hayes, in stating, "Amenophis II, according to an inscribed jar from his funerary temple, was still on the throne in his own twenty-sixth year, but probably did not attain the thirty-one years assigned to him by Manetho," obviously did not follow Helck's interpretation of Manetho.[67]

[60] "Records of a Royal Dockyard of the Time of Tuthmosis III: Papyrus British Museum 10056," *ZÄS* 66 (1931) 120, with n. 3; cf. Jaroslav Černý, "The Contribution of the Study of Unofficial and Private Documents to the History of Pharaonic Egypt," in Sergio Donadoni, ed., *Le Fonti indirette della storia egiziana* (Rome, 1963) pp. 37–38.

[61] "The Coregency of Tuthmosis III and Amenophis II," *JEA* 51 (1965) 110.

[62] "Urk" IV 1365 (404).

[63] *JNES* 25 (1966) 119.

[64] "Die Sinai-Inschrift des Amenmose," *MIO* 2 (1954) 196 f.

[65] See Harold H. Nelson, "The Identity of Amon-Re of United-with-Eternity," *JNES* 1 (1942) 145–46; note wine deliveries to the mortuary temple of Siptah in his Year 4 (Jaroslav Černý, "A Note on the Chancellor Bay," *ZÄS* 93 [1966] 36–39).

[66] *Untersuchungen zu Manetho*, p. 66.

[67] In William C. Hayes, M. B. Rowton, and Frank H. Stubbings, "Chronology: Egypt, Western Asia, Aegean Bronze Age," in *Cambridge Ancient History* I (rev. ed.; Cambridge, 1962) chap. 6, p. 18.

This figure of thirty-one years, assigned to an Amenophis by Manetho, may reflect the length of Amenhotep II's sole rule, excluding the period when he was coregent with his father Thutmose III.

The possibility remains that Amenhotep II was also coregent with his son and successor, Thutmose IV. This suggestion was made by Cyril Aldred to help explain a seeming inconsistency within the reign of Thutmose IV, in that that king appears to have celebrated only a second, but no first jubilee during his supposedly short reign. Aldred considered that Thutmose IV was merely a cocelebrant with Amenhotep II in Amenhotep's second jubilee.[68] The discovery of blocks belonging to a large jubilee monument at Karnak built by Thutmose IV for his first jubilee vitiates this argument.[69]

More to the point are the unusual circumstances surrounding Thutmose IV's accession to the throne. His granite stele at the Great Sphinx records that the throne was granted to him through the agency of the god Harmakhis, and it implies that Thutmose IV was not originally destined to receive the throne.[70] The papyrus document that we have previously suggested dates to Year 30 of Amenhotep II mentions a prince Amenhotep, and this prince or some other prince may have been heir presumptive toward the end of Amenhotep II's reign. Some years ago there were discovered near the Great Sphinx a number of steles that depict a prince offering to a statue of Amenhotep II and the Great Sphinx.[71] The name of the prince, or of several different princes, has been erased on each stele, and such erasures, together with the implications that may be drawn from the granite stele of Thutmose IV, prompted Selim Hassan to suggest that a dynastic struggle had taken place preceding this king's elevation to the throne.[72] The fact that Tiaa, Thutmose IV's mother, was the Great King's Wife of Amenhotep II is not conclusive in establishing the legitimacy of his succession. Most, if not all, of the monuments of Tiaa were made only after Thutmose IV had succeeded to the throne, possibly to justify his right to the throne. These unusual circumstances, coupled with the complete absence of any evidence suggesting a coregency, should allay the suspicion that Amenhotep II and Thutmose IV were ever coregents.

[68] "The Second Jubilee of Amenophis II," *ZÄS* 94 (1967) 1–6.

[69] For a pillar mentioning the first jubilee of Thutmose IV, see Henri Chevrier, "Rapport sur les travaux de Karnak 1952–1953," *ASAE* 53 (1955), Pl. XX, right. The monument of Thutmose IV is to be published by Bernadette Letellier; for a progress report see Serge Sauneron, "Travaux de l'IFAO en 1972–73," *BIFAO* 73 (1973) 222–23, 241.

[70] William C. Hayes, "Egypt: Internal Affairs from Thutmosis I to the Death of Amenophis III," in *Cambridge Ancient History* II (rev. ed.; Cambridge, 1966) chap. 9, p. 11.

[71] Selim Hassan, *The Great Sphinx and Its Secrets* ("Excavations at Giza" VIII [Cairo, 1953]) Figs. 67–69.

[72] *Ibid.*, pp. 90–91.

Besides the jubilee evidence in favor of a long reign for Thutmose IV there are some additional bits of information that would indicate that his reign was not a short one. There are statues of Thutmose IV seated, not with his queen as is normal, but with his mother Tiaa.[73] At the time when he acceded to the throne, Thutmose IV was called a *ỉnpw*, a term applied to young princes and kings who had not yet reached puberty.[74] Yet by the time he died, this pharaoh had produced a rather large family, comprising at least seven sons and twelve daughters.[75] During his years as king, Thutmose IV had three queens, each of whom bore the title Great King's Wife.[76] The Eighteenth Dynasty evidence seems to indicate that a king had only one Great King's Wife at a time,[77] so that these three women must have held the title of principal queen consecutively. Another indication that Thutmose IV's reign was a long one is the large number of Theban tomb chapels that are assigned to his period.[78] No fewer than nineteen tombs can be specifically dated to his reign; for purposes of comparison, twenty tombs belong specifically to the reign of Amenhotep II and twenty to the reign of Amenhotep III.

Following a recent suggestion of J. R. Harris,[79] we have allowed for a maximum two-year coregency between Amenhotep III, who reigned just over thirty-seven full years, and Amenhotep IV (Akhenaton), whose highest regnal year was Year 17. Although certain scholars have given an independent reign to Akhenaton's successor Smenkhkare, the arguments are not entirely convinc-

[73] See Helck, *Geschichte des Alten Ägypten*, p. 164, n. 3.

[74] See Hellmut Brunner, *Die Geburt des Gottkönigs* ("Ägyptologische Abhandlungen" X [Wiesbaden, 1964]) pp. 27–29. When Amenhotep II was a youth (*ḥwn*) eighteen years of age, he was no longer a *ỉnpw*; see "Urk" IV 1279–81.

[75] See Henri Gauthier, *Le Livre des rois d'Egypte* II ("MIFAO" XVIII [1912]) pp. 302–5, and J. Vandier, *Manuel d'archéologie égyptienne* IV (Paris, 1964) 541–42.

[76] See John R. Harris, "Contributions to the History of the Eighteenth Dynasty," *SAK* 2 (1975) 95–98, for the three Great King's Wives of Thutmose IV, though his understanding of Nofretari as Ahmose I's Queen Ahmose-Nofretari is prejudiced by his assumption that Thutmose IV reigned less than ten years. The document in question comes from Giza, not Abydos or Thebes, where posthumous veneration of Ahmose-Nofretari might be expected.

[77] The title "Great King's Wife" is once accorded Satamon, the daughter of Tiye and Amenhotep III, while Tiye was still alive as the principal queen. This unique instance occurs on a kohl-tube (Alexandre Varille, "Toutankhamon est-il fils d'Aménophis III et de Satamon?" *ASAE* 40 [1941] 655, and Hayes, *The Scepter of Egypt* II [Cambridge, 1959] 257, Fig. 155) and may be simply an error on the part of the craftsman resulting from a confused conflation of the titles "Great King's Daughter" and "King's Wife."

[78] See Bertha Porter and Rosalind L. B. Moss, *Topographical Bibliography of Ancient Egyptian Hieroglyphic Texts, Reliefs and Paintings* I/1 (2d ed.; Oxford, 1960) 476.

[79] *SAK* 2 (1975) 98–101.

ing.[80] A recently published private stele suggests strongly that there had been a coregency,[81] and we have assumed that Smenkhkare's regnal years were reckoned from the time he was associated with Akhenaton as the junior ruler, in accordance with Middle Kingdom and Eighteenth Dynasty practice. For the reigns of Tutankhamon and Aye we have used the highest attested regnal years, though in our alternative chronology the reign of Aye has been lengthened slightly—by two years.

One of the more debatable points in this chronology is the length of Haremhab's reign.[82] While some might point to the unfinished state of his royal tomb and to the limited number of officials attested in Upper Egypt during his reign as indicative of a reign shorter than the twenty-eight years we have allotted him, we must reckon with the Year 59 of Haremhab in the inscription of Mes from the time of Ramesses II. In accordance with Ramesside prejudice against the heretic pharaohs—as exhibited, for example, in the statues of ancestral kings in the Ramesseum version of the Feast of Min, where Haremhab directly precedes Amenhotep III[83]—the Year 59 of Haremhab is to be explained as being the result of the addition of the reigns of the heretic pharaohs to the personal reign of Haremhab.[84] This total may possibly reflect the addition of highest regnal years of each of these predecessors without regard to any coregencies. At any rate a figure approaching fifty-eight years should separate the accession of Amenhotep IV from the death of Haremhab.

From the mortuary temple of Haremhab at Medinet Habu there is a graffito inscribed on a fragment of a statue of the king that gives a Year 27 and mentions, "Haremhab, l.p.h., beloved of Amon, he who hates his enemies and loves. . . ."[85] It seems that this text had been inscribed on the shoulder of the

[80] See Wolfgang Helck, "Amarna-Probleme," *CdE* 44 (1969) 203–8, and J. R. Harris, "Nefertiti Rediviva," *Acta Orientalia* 35 (1973) 5–9, on this coregency.

[81] See Julia Samson, *Amarna, City of Akhenaten and Nefertiti* (London, 1972) pp. 103–6, and review thereof by Geoffrey T. Martin in *JEA* 60 (1974) 268.

[82] See Erik Hornung, *Das Grab des Haremhab im Tal der Könige* (Bern, 1971) pp. 19–21, and Donald B. Redford, "New Light on the Asiatic Campaigning of Ḥoremheb," *BASOR* 211 (1973) 37–38, on the length of Haremhab's reign, though the bowl with a Year 16 date of Haremhab that is discussed by Redford is of quite doubtful authenticity. The short reign argued for by J. R. Harris ("How Long Was the Reign of Ḥoremḥeb?" *JEA* 54 [1968] 95–99) is based on evidence interpreted otherwise by Redford and by Hornung ("Neue Materialien zur ägyptischen Chronologie," *ZDMG* 117 [1967] 12–13).

[83] See The Epigraphic Survey, *Medinet Habu* IV ("OIP" LI [1940]) Pl. 213.

[84] See Alan H. Gardiner, *The Inscription of Mes* ("UGAÄ" IV [Leipzig, 1905]) p. 22, n. 72.

[85] See Uvo Hölscher, *Excavations at Ancient Thebes 1930/31* ("OIC," No. 15 [1932]) pp. 51–53 and Fig. 35, and Rudolf Anthes in Hölscher, *The Excavations of Medinet Habu* II: *The Temples of the Eighteenth Dynasty* ("OIP" XLI [1939]) pp. 106–8, Fig. 90, and Pl. 51*c*.

statue before it was fragmented.[86] Some have argued that the text was recorded during the reign of Ramesses II, to whom they would assign the date; but to understand the text as referring to Haremhab's mortuary temple appears to be forcing the interpretation of the king's name and epithets, which Redford has shown are appropriate for a living monarch.[87] Others, such as Hornung, have referred this date to the reign of Haremhab but have maintained that it contains a reference to his funeral.[88] This is highly unlikely since a king's funeral, occurring after an embalming period of seventy days, would have been dated in terms of his successor's regnal years, as we know from the Ramesside period.[89] Furthermore, British Museum ostracon 5624,[90] which Hornung adduces in support of his interpretation of the graffito, certainly does not refer to a funeral either.[91] It seems most probable that the graffito contains a reference to a visit made by the living Haremhab to his temple in his Year 27. Both this piece and the inscription of Mes support a long reign for Haremhab. Those who have attempted to shorten his reign have had to attribute the Mes date to scribal error, misinformation, or the like. For what it is worth, Manetho ascribes to a king who preceded Ramesses II a reign of fifty-nine years.[92]

It should be mentioned that Ramesses I, whose reign was less than two full years, may at the beginning of his rule have been a coregent of Haremhab,[93] and at the end of his reign he may have appointed his son Sety I as a coregent.[94] Although Year 11 is the highest attested regnal year of Sety I,[95] we have assigned him twelve years of rule. On the basis of the biographical inscription

[86] See Redford, *BASOR* 211 (1973) 37.

[87] *Ibid.*, p. 37, n. 5.

[88] Hornung, *Das Grab des Haremhab*, p. 20.

[89] See Jaroslav Černý, "Datum des Todes Ramses' III. und der Thronbesteigung Ramses' IV.," *ZÄS* 72 (1936) 113, and the oblique reference to the number of days for mummification in a variant of Papyrus Anastasi I, 3, 2–3, in Deir el Medineh ostracon 1077, ll. 3–4, published in Georges Posener, *Catalogue des ostraca hiératiques littéraires de Deir el Médineh* I ("DFIFAO" I [1938]) Pl. 43, "until you have completed your required time which is one twentieth of fourteen hundred at the hands of Anubis."

[90] "Urk" IV 2162 (844).

[91] It refers to the induction of a crew member into the Deir el Medineh workers' community at the time of its reconstitution in Year 7 of Haremhab; cf. Jaroslav Černý, *A Community of Workmen at Thebes in the Ramesside Period* ("BdE" L [1973]) pp. 25, 290–91.

[92] See Hornung, *Untersuchungen zur Chronologie*, p. 40, n. 83.

[93] See Cyril Aldred, "Two Monuments of the Reign of Ḥoremḥeb," *JEA* 54 (1968) 100–103.

[94] See Alain-Pierre Zivie, "Un Monument associant les noms de Ramsès I et de Séthi I," *BIFAO* 72 (1972) 99–114.

[95] See Redford, *History and Chronology*, p. 209.

of the High Priest Bakenkhons, Morris L. Bierbrier has recently argued that a reign of no fewer than fifteen years should be accorded Sety I.[96] There are, however, some uncertainties in his treatment of this inscription. In the first place, his restoration of the praenomen of Sety I is not the only possible one, for the praenomen of Ramesses I would also contain the *mn*-sign that is partially preserved. Secondly, in adding together the years spent in each post held by Bakenkhons, Bierbrier has proceeded in Western fashion, failing to take into account the ancient Egyptian's proclivity to express a span of time in terms of its extremes.[97] It is quite likely that Bakenkhons reckoned a year during which he changed office both as a full year assignable to the prior office and also as a full year assignable to the subsequent post.

Our alternative chronology has given Sety I a shorter reign of ten years, as Redford has proposed.[98] Since the death of Tutankhamon can hardly be placed later than 1325 B.C., as we shall discuss later, the reduction in the span of time between Ramesses I and the accession of Ramesses II means a shifting downward of the reign of Haremhab by lengthening the reign of Aye a corresponding amount. This alternative chronology is perfectly feasible and may, in fact, accord a bit better with the datum of the Mes inscription.

Some have wished to construct an argument on the basis of *apo Menophreos* ("from Menophris") and the beginning of a Sothic cycle in 1318 B.C. If Menophris is a rendition of either Menpehtyre (the praenomen of Ramesses I) or Merenptah Sety I, then neither the 1290 nor the 1279 B.C. accession date for Ramesses II fits very well with *apo Menophreos*. Rowton's original supposition that nominative Menophris derived from *Mn-nfr*, "Memphis,"[99] has since received additional support;[100] one might compare Onnophris from *Wnn-nfr*, a designation of Osiris. If one takes the era of Menophris as referring to a renewal at Memphis under Haremhab, then there is a fairly close correspondence between his accession in ca. 1321 B.C. and the beginning of a Sothic cycle in 1318 B.C. It is to be noted that the expression "Beginning of Eternity and the Inception of Everlastingness," used by Sety I and taken by some as connecting

[96] "The Length of the Reign of Sethos I," *JEA* 58 (1972) 303.

[97] See J. Capart, A. H. Gardiner, and B. van de Walle, "New Light on the Ramesside Tomb-Robberies," *JEA* 22 (1936) 177, and Edward F. Wente, "The Suppression of the High Priest Amenhotep," *JNES* 25 (1966) 82.

[98] *History and Chronology*, pp. 208–15.

[99] Michael B. Rowton, "Mesopotamian Chronology and the 'Era of Menophres,'" *Iraq* 8 (1946) 107–10.

[100] Gerhard Fecht, *Wortakzent und Silbenstruktur: Untersuchungen zur Geschichte der ägyptischen Sprache* ("Ägyptologische Forschungen," Vol. 21 [Glückstadt, 1960]) pp. 44–45, and Redford, *History and Chronology*, p. 214.

his reign with the era of Menophris and the Sothic cycle, is also attested for Haremhab.[101]

Having arrived at 1279 B.C. as the probable date for the accession of Ramesses II by adding the lengths of reigns from the accession of Thutmose III in 1504 B.C., let us now approach Ramesses II's accession from the opposite direction. Kitchen, who put Shoshenq I's accession in 945 B.C. and the beginning of the Twenty-first Dynasty in 1069 B.C., also calculated backwards and noted the possibility that Ramesses II could have come to the throne in 1279 B.C.[102] He rejected this date, however, and not on purely Egyptological grounds but because the date appeared incompatible with contemporary Near Eastern dates, "even those of Brinkman, *BiOr* 27 (1970), 301–14." Since Kitchen was committed—we believe correctly—to a ten-year reign for Merenptah, he proposed that in order to place Ramesses II's accession in 1290 B.C., some ten or more years must be dispersed "in much smaller amounts over the shorter reigns of the 19th Dynasty after Merenptah and in the 20th Dynasty." The question is whether such a procedure is warranted.

The lengths of certain of the reigns after Sety I down to the end of the Twentieth Dynasty are fixed. On the basis of evidence presented in several ostraca discussed by John A. Larson,[103] it appears that Ramesses II acceded to the throne between I *ꜣḫt* 16 and III *ꜣḫt* 5, or perhaps more specifically between III *ꜣḫt* 5 and 11 (September). Although Ramesses II had been a coregent with his father Sety I, consideration of the new range for his accession in connection with Ramesses II's activities in his Year 1, III *ꜣḫt*, as described in his Great Abydos Inscription, would tend to vitiate some of the conclusions of William Murnane.[104] The Abydos evidence would also support Keith C. Seele's previous view that Ramesses II began his regnal year count upon the death of his father,[105] which possibly occurred while Ramesses II was officiating in the Feast of Opet at Luxor. Ramesses II's appointment of the High Priest Nebwenenef following the Feast of Opet may reflect the new king's independently taking a firm hand in matters of appointment, rather than the absence of an incumbent High Priest of Amon during the Feast of Opet that we would otherwise have to assume. It is conceivable that Ramesses II relieved from his duties a high priest previously appointed by his father.

[101] See Hornung, *Untersuchungen zur Chronologie*, p. 62, n. 42.

[102] "Late-Egyptian Chronology and the Hebrew Monarchy," *JANES* 5 (1973) 232, with n. 28; see now also M. L. Bierbrier, *The Late New Kingdom in Egypt* (*c. 1300–664 B.C.*) (Warminster, 1975).

[103] "The Date of the Regnal Year Change in the Reign of Ramesses II," *Serapis* 3 (1975–76).

[104] "The Earlier Reign of Ramesses II and His Coregency with Sety I," *JNES* 34 (1975) 183–90.

[105] *The Coregency of Ramses II with Seti I and the Date of the Great Hypostyle Hall at Karnak* ("SAOC," No. 19 [1940]) chap. 4.

Ramesses II died in his Year 67, between I *ꜣḫt* 19 and II *ꜣḫt* 13; probably I *ꜣḫt* 19 was the actual date.[106] Thus he died in the month of July after a reign of sixty-six years, ten months.

We are certain of the length of the reign of Sety II, who came to the throne between the end of I *prt* and the beginning of III *prt* (December).[107] Since the transition from Sety II to Siptah occurred on IV *ꜣḫt* 28 in Year 6 (October),[108] the length of Sety II's reign was no more than five years, eleven months.

The length of Ramesses III's reign is well known. He acceded to the throne on I *šmw* 26 (March), and he died in Year 32, III *šmw* 15 (April) after a reign of thirty-one years, one month, nineteen days.[109]

Ramesses IX came to the throne in I *ꜣḫt* 18–23 (June)[110] and died in Year 19, I *prt* 17–27 (October)[111] after reigning eighteen years, four months.

The figure of nine years, six months that we have given to the reign of Ramesses X can confidently be said to be maximal. It is based on the consideration of a lunar feast mentioned in his third year that must be separated by thirty-one years from the same feast mentioned in Year 25 of Ramesses XI[112] and the consideration of the accession date of Ramesses XI, which is fixed at III *šmw* 20.[113] A date as high as Year 8 for Ramesses X now seems to be fairly certain,[114] providing some support for Parker's argument.

As for the remaining Ramesside pharaohs, the situation is as follows:

The highest attested regnal year for Merenptah is Year 10, IV *ꜣḫt* 7[115]—nine years, two months, eighteen days after his accession in I *ꜣḫt* 19. On the basis of the accession date of his successor Amenmesse, determined by Helck to be III

[106] See Wolfgang Helck, "Bemerkungen zu den Thronbesteigungsdaten im Neuen Reich," in *Studia Biblica et Orientalia* III: *Oriens antiqueus* (Rome, 1959) pp. 120–21.

[107] See *ibid.*, p. 123.

[108] See *ibid.*, pp. 123–24.

[109] See Hornung, *Untersuchungen zur Chronologie*, p. 97.

[110] See Helck, *Studia Biblica et Orientalia* III 128.

[111] See Giuseppe Botti, "Who Succeeded Ramesses IX-Neferkerēʿ?" *JEA* 14 (1928) 48, n. 3; cf. Černý, *Community of Workmen*, pp. 234–35. The Year 18 of W. Pleyte and F. Rossi, *Papyrus de Turin* (2 vols.; Leiden, 1869–76) Pl. V, l. 11, must belong to Ramesses IX, judging from the mention of the chief workman Userkhopeshef in the continuation of this inverted line on Pl. IV; cf. Černý, *Community of Workmen*, pp. 309–10.

[112] According to Parker, in "The Length of Reign of Ramses X," *RdE* 11 (1957) 163–64.

[113] See Alan H. Gardiner, "Adoption Extraordinary," *JEA* 26 (1940) 23 and 25; cf. *idem*, *Ramesside Administrative Documents* (Oxford, 1948) p. 67, ll. 14–16.

[114] See Bierbrier, *Late New Kingdom*, p. 126, n. 119.

[115] In Papyrus Sallier I, 3, 4; cf. Caminos, *Late-Egyptian Miscellanies*, p. 303.

šmw 18,[116] Merenptah's reign could have been as short as nine years, ten months. Elsewhere Helck has sought to demonstrate that Merenptah held the throne for the nineteen years attributed to his reign by Manetho,[117] but in doing so he is basing his argument on hieratic dockets from the Ramesseum that could equally well belong to the reign of either Ramesses II or Ramesses III, since no king's name is connected with the dates on these dockets. More recently Bierbrier has vigorously protested against a long reign for Merenptah on the basis of the genealogies of families living during the Ramesside period.[118]

For Amenmesse we have no regnal year higher than Year 4, III *šmw* 29.[119] If Year 4 was his highest, his reign lasted three years, eight months, for Sety II came to the throne between the end of I *prt* and the beginning of III *prt*. In spite of the implications of Černý's remarks that Cairo ostracon 25516 cannot mark the transition from the reign of Sety II to that of Siptah,[120] we must agree with Helck that this ostracon should indeed reflect this particular change of kings.[121] One need only compare the absence of dates for the consumption of lamps after I *prt* 18 and before I *prt* 23 (Cairo ostracon 25516, recto, lines 3–4) with the fact that the Deir el Medineh crew did no work during exactly the same span of time upon the announcement of Sety II's death on I *prt* 19 (Cairo ostracon 25515, verso, cols. ii–iii). Besides, in Cairo ostracon 25516 it is quite apparent that Hay and Paneb must be the two chief workmen on the left and right sides, respectively. Such a situation could not have obtained at the time of the transition from Amenmesse to Sety II.[122]

The regnal years of Siptah, who probably acceded to the throne on IV *ꜣḫt* 28 (October),[123] were all appropriated by Tausert, whose highest attested date is Year 8, III *prt* 5.[124] On the basis of the recently discovered stele of Setnakht from Elephantine,[125] there are once again grounds for assuming a short interregnum, for which we have allowed one year. Kitchen, on the other

[116] See Wolfgang Helck, "Zur Geschichte der 19. und 20. Dynastie," *ZDMG* 105 (1955) 43; *idem*, *Studia Biblica et Orientalia* III 121–23.

[117] *Materialien zur Wirtschaftsgeschichte des Neuen Reiches*, Pt. IV (Wiesbaden, 1963) pp. 733–34; cf. Hornung, *Untersuchungen zur Chronologie*, pp. 95–96.

[118] *Late New Kingdom*, chaps. 1–2.

[119] Cf. Hornung, *Untersuchungen zur Chronologie*, p. 96.

[120] *The Valley of the Kings* ("BdE" LXI [1973]) p. 47, with n. 5.

[121] See Helck, *ZDMG* 105 (1955) 41, n. 1; *idem*, *Studia Biblica et Orientalia* III 123.

[122] See Černý, *Community of Workmen*, pp. 125 and 302.

[123] See Helck, *Studia Biblica et Orientalia* III 123–24.

[124] See Hornung, *Untersuchungen zur Chronologie*, p. 97, n. 17.

[125] See Bidoli in Werner Kaiser *et al.*, "Stadt und Tempel von Elephantine," *MDAIK* 28 (1972) 193–200 and Pl. IL.

hand, allots eight years for the combined reigns of Siptah and Tausert without an interregnum between Tausert and Setnakht.[126] So far as computations are concerned, we are in agreement with Kitchen with regard to the interval of time between the accession of Siptah and the accession of Ramesses III, which follows upon Setnakht's reign of a minimum duration of one year, eleven months, sixteen days. This minimum reflects consideration of the Year 2, II *šmw* 10 date on Setnakht's Elephantine stele (the date being regarded as a theoretical accession date) and the accession of Ramesses III in I *šmw* 26.

Ramesses IV came to the throne in III *šmw* 15 (April) on the death of Ramesses III. It has been asserted that Year 6, III *šmw* 6 on Cairo ostracon 25291 is Ramesses IV's highest attested date and since this date lies only nine days before the beginning of his regnal Year 7, that he probably ruled at least six full years.[127] The photograph of this ostracon, however, clearly shows III *šmw* 16,[128] so that it must date to the very beginning rather than to the end of his sixth regnal year. Consequently the Year 6, I *prt* 19 of Cairo ostracon 25287 becomes the highest certain attested date in Ramesses IV's Year 6.[129] Nonetheless, as Hornung indicates,[130] the evidence of the Turin Indictment Papyrus does not entirely exclude the possibility that Ramesses IV ruled into his Year 7. Thus documents dated to Year 7 ought to be considered as possibly belonging to the reign of Ramesses IV. One such document is Ostracon Petrie 18, bearing a date Year 7 (or 17 or 27), IV *šmw* 11.[131] Since the two workmen Amenpahapy and Amenwa named on the ostracon are, to our knowledge, otherwise unattested in documentation from Ramesses III's reign, Year 7 is probably the correct reading of the year. While the prosopographical evidence of this document is of little value in determining to which of Ramesses III's successors the Year 7 date belongs, the writing of the prepositions *ḥr* and *r* in some of the pseudoverbal constructions might perhaps weigh in favor of the reign of Ramesses IV. Even more convincing is Bierbrier's argument that Deir el Medineh ostracon 207, bearing the date Year 7, III *ꜣḫt* 23, should be assigned to the reign of Ramesses IV.[132]

Regarding the accession date of Ramesses V, which would also be the death

[126] *JANES* 5 (1973) 232, n. 26.

[127] Hornung (*Untersuchungen zur Chronologie*, p. 98, n. 26), referring to Serge Sauneron, "Trois personnages du scandale d'Eléphantine," *RdE* 7 (1950) 56.

[128] See G. Daressy, *Ostraca* ("CCG" I [1901]), Pl. LVII, Cairo ostracon 25291, which is transcribed as C 25290 on p. 37. The date is III *šmw* 16, not 6.

[129] See Sauneron, *RdE* 7 (1950) 56, for the Year 6 documents.

[130] *Untersuchungen zur Chronologie*, p. 98.

[131] Jaroslav Černý and Alan H. Gardiner, *Hieratic Ostraca* I (Oxford, 1957) Pl. LXX, 1.

[132] *Late New Kingdom*, pp. 33 and 125, n. 111.

date of Ramesses IV, we have very little evidence. The sequence of dates in Papyrus Wilbour, columns 21, 44, and 75, from Ramesses V's Year 4, II *ꜣḫt* 15 to III *ꜣḫt* 1, rules out this span of time for his accession,[133] while the dates on Document 1 of the Will of Naunakhte possibly exclude the span III *ꜣḫt* 17 to IV *ꜣḫt* 5.[134] It may be suggested that the death of Ramesses IV probably occurred in Year 7, after IV *ꜣḫt* 5, that is, after September.

Although Černý in several places has adduced the evidence of Cairo ostracon 25598 in support of limiting Ramesses V's highest regnal year to Year 4,[135] he has in his posthumously published volume on the Deir el Medineh community proposed that both a Year 6 and a Year 9 must be attributed to Ramesses V.[136] In suggesting this, he has reasoned on the basis of the number of captains attached to the Deir el Medineh crew of workmen during the course of the Twentieth Dynasty, and also on the basis of the Egyptian spellings of the word for captains.[137] With regard to the evidence for Ramesses V's Year 6 in Papyrus Turin (unpublished continuation of 33, 10), the published text that precedes this continuation[138] is definitely assignable to the reign of Ramesses VI, not Ramesses IV.[139] The enigmatically written cartouche of Plate XXXII, line 3, gives the praenomen *Nb-mꜣʿt-Rʿ mr-ꜣImn* of Ramesses VI, for the hieroglyph of the seated king is to be read *nb*, not *ḥḳꜣ*.[140] This interpretation of the praenomen is confirmed by the signs preserved at the beginning of line 4: [*ꜣIm*]*n-ḫpš.f nṯr-ḥḳꜣ-ꜣIwnw*, which is unmistakably the conclusion of Ramesses VI's nomen. If a Year 6 actually appears in the unpublished continuation of Plate XXXIII,[141] and if this continuation was written after the text naming

[133] Alan H. Gardiner, *The Wilbour Papyrus* I (Oxford, 1941) Pls. 9, 20, and 36.

[134] Jaroslav Černý, "The Will of Naunakhte and the Related Documents," *JEA* 31 (1945) Pls. VIII–IX and p. 51, but cf. *idem*, *Community of Workmen*, pp. 343 and 353, for some reservations about the Year 4 date.

[135] See Černý, *JEA* 31 (1945) 42, n. 2; *idem*, "Egypt from the Death of Ramesses III to the End of the Twenty-first Dynasty," in *Cambridge Ancient History* II (rev. ed.; Cambridge, 1965) chap. 35, p. 8; cf. Jacobus J. Janssen, *Two Ancient Egyptian Ship's Logs* (Leiden, 1961) p. 56, n. 6, and Edward F. Wente, "A Prince's Tomb in the Valley of the Kings," *JNES* 32 (1973) 232.

[136] *Community of Workmen*, p. 217, n. 10, p. 233, n. 4, p. 235, n. 7.

[137] *Ibid.*, pp. 233–35.

[138] Pleyte and Rossi, *Papyrus de Turin*, Pls. XXXII–XXXIII.

[139] See *ibid.*, pp. 46–47, assigning the text to Ramesses IV; also apparently Černý, *Community of Workmen*, pp. 66–67, in speaking of "a statue of Ramesses IV."

[140] See Etienne Drioton, "Essai sur la cryptographie privée de la fin de la XVIIIe dynastie," *RdE* 1 (1933) 37; *idem* in Alexandre Piankoff, *Le Livre du jour et de la nuit* ("BdE" XIII [1942]), p. 106; The Epigraphic Survey, *The Temple of Khonsu* I (Chicago, forthcoming) Pl. 51, l. 5.

[141] In his *Community of Workmen* (p. 216, n. 9, p. 217, n. 10, p. 219, n. 3, p. 233, n. 4) Černý dates the unpublished continuation of Pl. XXXIII to a Year 6; but in one instance (p. 308, n. 1) he

Ramesses VI, we would then have mention of "the three captains" at a point in time when Černý would say that there should have been four captains, since between some time in the latter part of Year 1 and early in Year 3 of Ramesses VI the number of captains of the crew, according to Černý, was increased from three to four. On the same basis one might question Černý's assigning the Year 6 of Papyrus Turin Catalogue 2013, I, 6, to Ramesses V, because it speaks of "captains . . . , three men."[142]

Some uncertainty regarding the use of the number of captains for dating documents is raised by Deir el Medineh ostracon 381, whose recto and verso are each dated to a Year 4, obviously of the same reign.[143] On the recto one reads, "four captains," followed by their appropriate rations, whereas on the verso one reads, "three captains" and their corresponding rations. This evidence raises a doubt as to whether Černý was entirely correct in assigning all documents that mention only three captains to reigns prior to Ramesses VI's.

If one may draw any chronological conclusions from the number of captains mentioned and the spelling of the Egyptian word for captains, the situation might be stated in the following manner. All documents that display the spelling *ḥntyw*, with intrusive *n*, should date to Ramesses V or later, although the spelling *ḥ(w)tyw*, without *n*, also continued to be used sporadically even late in the Twentieth Dynasty.[144] While there is no evidence for the existence of four captains prior to Year 3 of Ramesses VI, in whose Year 1 three captains are still attested,[145] the mention of only three captains in a document does not necessarily preclude it from belonging to a period when there were actually four captains, as is nicely illustrated by Deir el Medineh ostracon 381.

On the basis of the mention of three captains,[146] Černý has assigned Papyrus Turin Catalogue 1900, containing a Year 9, to Ramesses V's reign, although elsewhere in his work he has suggested that the Year 9 of this papyrus pertains to the reign of Ramesses IX.[147] According to Černý, the word *smdt*, "serfs,"

---

lists this continuation among the *undated* documents referring to Nekhemmut and Anherkhau. This last reference makes one wonder whether the unpublished continuation of Pl. XXXIII actually does contain a Year 6, or whether Černý may not have been using the Year 6 of the recto of the papyrus, the so-called "Map of the Gold Mines"; see *ibid.*, p. 61. As Georges Goyon ("Le Papyrus de Turin dit 'Des Mines d'Or' et le Wadi Hammamat," *ASAE* 49 [1949] 343) points out, it is uncertain to which Ramesses this Year 6 belongs.

142 Černý, *Community of Workmen*, p. 234, with n. 4.

143 Published in Černý, *Catalogue des ostraca hiératiques non littéraires de Deir el Médineh* V ("DFIFAO" VII [1951]), Pl. 11.

144 See Černý, *Community of Workmen*, pp. 232–33.

145 *Ibid.*, pp. 234–35.

146 *Ibid.*, p. 235, with n. 7.

147 *Ibid.*, p. 157, p. 216, n. 10, p. 246, n. 4.

in this document is determined by the seated man with hand to mouth, a writing that he tells us is characteristic of the second half of the Twentieth Dynasty.[148] All parallel instances of such a spelling of *smdt* that Černý cites derive from documents from the reign of Ramesses X or later. Perhaps an even more compelling argument against assigning Papyrus Turin Catalogue 1900 to the reign of Ramesses V is the mention of a total number of four superiors (*ḥryw*) in the text.[149] Prior to the reign of Ramesses VI, the number of superiors was limited to three, their number being basically equivalent to the number of captains. In view of the spelling of *smdt* and the mention of four superiors in this papyrus, it would seem wiser to date it to Year 9 of Ramesses IX, in whose Year 17 we find the last attestation of the Scribe of the Tomb Hori named in the document.[150]

In view of the uncertainty regarding the existence of any regnal year higher than Year 4 for Ramesses V, and taking into account the evidence of Cairo ostracon 25598, one can deduce a probable length for his reign. Coming to the throne on the death of Ramesses IV, probably after IV *ꜣḫt* 5 (after September), Ramesses V witnessed the following dates in Year 4: (possibly) IV *ꜣḫt* 30,[151] I *prt* 24,[152] II *prt* 17,[153] and (possibly) III *ꜣḫt* 17.[154] Although the sequence of these dates in Year 4 is uncertain, it may be that since Ramesses VI came to the throne between the middle of I *prt* and the beginning of II *prt* (October),[155] the death of Ramesses V could well have occurred in his Year 5, possibly a month after the anniversary of his accession.

The highest attested regnal year of Ramesses VI seems to be Year 7.[156] More specifically, the date Year 7, II *šmw* 4 (not 5) that occurs in the first column of text in Pleyte and Rossi, *Papyrus de Turin*, Plate LXXII has been adduced by

[148] *Ibid.*, p. 184, n. 3.

[149] *Ibid.*, p. 246.

[150] *Ibid.*, p. 216.

[151] BM ostracon 5625, published by Aylward M. Blackman, "Oracles in Ancient Egypt," *JEA* 12 (1926) Pls. XXXV–XXXVI and XLI.

[152] Turin ostracon 2162, l. 4, published by G. Maspero, "Notes sur quelques points de grammaire et d'histoire," *RT* 2 (1880) 117; cf. Černý, *Community of Workmen*, p. 342.

[153] Černý and Gardiner, *Hieratic Ostraca* I, Pl. LV, 2.

[154] Černý, *JEA* 31 (1945) Pl. IX.

[155] See Helck, *Studia Biblica et Orientalia* III 125, referring to Černý and Gardiner, *Hieratic Ostraca* I, Pl. LXVIII, 1.

[156] See Hornung, *Untersuchungen zur Chronologie*, pp. 98–99, and Jacobus J. Janssen, "A Twentieth-Dynasty Account Papyrus," *JEA* 52 (1966) 91–92. The Karnak stele probably reads Year 6 rather than Year 7 of Ramesses VI; cf. Janssen, *JEA* 52 (1966) 92, n. 1, and Sauneron, *RdE* 7 (1950) 56.

von Beckerath as Ramesses VI's highest attested date.[157] Černý, however, has suggested that Years 7 and 8 may be attested for Ramesses VI in Pleyte and Rossi, *Papyrus de Turin*, Plates CVIII–CXI.[158] One reason that he gives for assigning the text of Plate CIX to either Ramesses V or VI is the mention of the vizier Neferronpe and of the overseer of the treasury Mentemtowe. These two officials, however, are not named at all in the verso of this papyrus (Pls. CVIII–CXI), but only on the recto, dated to a Year 1.[159] The recto and verso appear to comprise two unrelated texts, so that the criteria for dating the recto cannot be applied to the verso.

The suggestion that the text of the verso might indeed be assigned to Ramesses VI may find support rather in the mention (in the first line of the verso text, Pl. CVIII) that the chief of the Medjay Khensemhab arrived in Year 7, I *ꜣḫt* 4, for according to Černý this Khensemhab had already begun his career as a chief of the Medjay at the time of the announcement of the accession of Siptah;[160] the same text continues with Year 8 dates. If this verso text were to be assigned to the reign of Ramesses IX, as Černý has suggested elsewhere,[161] then Khensemhab would have served over seventy years as a chief of police, about fourteen years longer than if the Year 7 is attributed to Ramesses VI. Upon first consideration this would appear to be a rather compelling argument for dating the verso, Plates CVIII–CXI, to the reign of Ramesses VI. This attestation of a chief of the Medjay Khensemhab in a Year 7 cannot be divorced, however, from considering his mention in the same capacity in a Year 7 on the recto of another papyrus, one that also has Year 8 dates, namely Papyrus Turin Catalogue 1881.[162] Although there are some serious problems with the dating of various texts inscribed on this papyrus,[163] a subsequent page on the recto, Pleyte and Rossi, *Papyrus de Turin*, Plate VIII, line 4, mentions a Year 8 date under a king whose praenomen cannot possibly be that of Ramesses VI but probably is that

[157] "Ein Denkmal zur Genealogie der XX. Dynastie," *ZÄS* 97 (1971) 12.

[158] *Community of Workmen*, p. 235, n. 2, p. 268, n. 7.

[159] The recto is reproduced in Pleyte and Rossi, *Papyrus de Turin*, Pls. CII–CVII; cf. Schafik Allam, *Hieratische Ostraka und Papyri: Transkriptionen aus dem Nachlass von J. Černý*, Plate volume (Tübingen, 1973) pp. 132–33, for Černý's transcription of the relevant portion of the recto.

[160] *Community of Workmen*, p. 268.

[161] *Ibid.*, p. 141, n. 6, p. 216, n. 10, p. 219, nn. 2 and 4, p. 353, n. 8.

[162] Facsimiles in Pleyte and Rossi, *Papyrus de Turin*, Pls. II–X; cf. Allam, *Hieratische Ostraka*, Plate volume, pp. 108–10, for a portion of this papyrus and a diagram of the recto and verso. The chief of the Medjay Khensemhab is mentioned in Pleyte and Rossi, *Papyrus de Turin*, Pl. VII, l. 7; cf. Černý, *Community of Workmen*, p. 268, n. 7.

[163] See T. Eric Peet, "The Egyptian Words for 'Money', 'Buy', and 'Sell,' " in *Studies Presented to F. Ll. Griffith* (London, 1932) p. 125, and Gardiner, *Late-Egyptian Miscellanies* ("Bibliotheca Aegyptiaca" VII [Brussels, 1937]) p. xx (Turin B).

of Ramesses IX.[164] Ramesses IX's praenomen apparently also appeared in one of the original texts on the verso.[165] Perhaps an even more cogent reason for assigning Pleyte and Rossi, *Papyrus de Turin*, Plate VII to the reign of Ramesses IX is the mention of the chief workman Hormose in line 2, just five lines prior to the mention of the chief of the Medjay Khensemhab. Hormose as chief workman is characteristic of the reign of Ramesses IX,[166] and it is improbable that he served in this capacity as early as the reign of Ramesses VI.[167]

Thus we may infer that Khensemhab was indeed still active as a chief of police in Year 7 of Ramesses IX. Although Černý supposed that he had already been a chief of the Medjay at the commencement of Siptah's reign,[168] he was not actually accorded this title directly before his name until Year 20 of Ramesses III.[169] Thus Khensemhab may not have spent the entire seventy years from Siptah to Ramesses IX's Year 7 as a chief of the Medjay. In fact, the two chiefs of the Medjay during the last year of Sety II seem to have been Montmose and Nakhtmin,[170] and since Montmose continued in this post at least into the reign of Ramesses IV, the Khensemhab mentioned with the chief of the Medjay Nakhtmin in Cairo ostracon 25515 must not yet have become a chief of the Medjay, if there were only two such officers at any one time, as Černý has maintained.[171] If we are dealing with only one Khensemhab, he must have been in his mid or late eighties in Year 7 of Ramesses IX—by no means an impossibility. On the other hand, it is conceivable that the Khensemhab of the time of Siptah was a different person from the Khensemhab of the Twentieth Dynasty.

The evidence indicating that Khensemhab was still active as a chief of the Medjay in Ramesses IX's Year 7 does not necessarily mean, of course, that the Year 7 mention of him in Pleyte and Rossi, *Papyrus de Turin*, Plate CVIII, does not pertain to the reign of Ramesses VI. Probability, however, would seem to be against this, since according to the same papyrus (Pl. CXI, line 19) in Year 8,

[164] See Černý, *Community of Workmen*, p. 235, n. 2.

[165] See Gardiner, *Late-Egyptian Miscellanies*, p. 128*a*.

[166] See Černý, *Community of Workmen*, pp. 125, 308–9.

[167] See Bierbrier, *Late New Kingdom*, p. 38.

[168] *Community of Workmen*, p. 268, n. 5, referring to Cairo ostracon 25515, verso, col. iv, ll. 2 and 4.

[169] *Community of Workmen*, p. 268, n. 6, the document being published in Černý and Gardiner, *Hieratic Ostraca* I, Pl. XLIX, 3.

[170] See Černý, *Community of Workmen*, pp. 266–67.

[171] *Ibid.*, p. 263.

I *prt* 15 the deputy of the crew was Khons, who is known to have functioned in that capacity during the first half of the reign of Ramesses IX.[172]

There has been considerable discussion concerning the ordering of Ramesses VI's successors. Von Beckerath has been the staunchest supporter of interposing the brief reign of Ramesses-Sethhikhopeshef (Ramesses VIII) between Ramesses VI and Ramesses-Itamon (Ramesses VII);[173] Janssen, on the other hand, who initially accepted this sequence, has since expressed some reservations.[174] Most recently Kitchen has vigorously defended the traditional order of Ramesses VI, VII, and VIII, his major piece of evidence being a doorjamb dedicated by Ramesses-Itamon "for his father" Ramesses VI.[175] Kitchen is inclined to take "father" here in its literal sense and supposes that a normal father-son succession occurred. He adopts the view, still much disputed, that the Medinet Habu princes are the sons of Ramesses III, even though their names were not inscribed until after Ramesses III's death. Consequently Ramesses-Sethhikhopeshef, who, according to Kitchen, appears among these princes as a son of Ramesses III, would not have intruded himself into the direct father-son sequence of Ramesses VI and Ramesses-Itamon. However, just such an intrusion by an uncle between a father and a son seems to have occurred in the Nineteenth Dynasty, when Amenmesse, probably a son of Ramesses II and Queen Takhat, succeeded his half brother Merenptah, thus postponing the accession of Merenptah's son Sety II. Theoretically something of this sort may also have occurred in the Twentieth Dynasty.

If we adopt von Beckerath's ordering of Ramesses VI's successors, we can make some observations concerning the dating of documents and the transition of reigns. According to von Beckerath, the Year 7, II *šmw* 4 (not 5) date in column i of Pleyte and Rossi, *Papyrus de Turin*, Plate LXXII, is the highest attested in the reign of Ramesses VI, coming about four months after the beginning of his regnal year, between the middle of I *prt* and the beginning of II *prt*. Since Ramesses-Itamon came to the throne on IV *prt*,[176] his accession, if Year 7 was Ramesses VI's highest, occurred ten months after the II *šmw* 4 date in this Turin papyrus. Thus there is room between these two kings for the brief reign of Ramesses-Sethhikhopeshef—a maximum of ten months, according to von Beckerath's scheme.

[172] See Bierbrier, *Late New Kingdom*, pp. 33–34.

[173] Jürgen von Beckerath, *Tanis und Theben* ("Ägyptologische Forschungen," Vol. 16 [Glückstadt, 1951]) p. 87; *idem*, *ZÄS* 97 (1971) 7–12; cf. also Charles F. Nims, review of *Ägyptologische Studien*, ed. O. Firchow, in *BiOr* 14 (1957) 138.

[174] *JEA* 52 (1966) 92, n. 5.

[175] "Ramesses VII and the Twentieth Dynasty," *JEA* 58 (1972) 182–94.

[176] See Janssen, *JEA* 52 (1966) 92, and von Beckerath, *ZÄS* 97 (1971) 11–12.

There are some other documents with dates of Year 7 that should be considered. If, as von Beckerath maintains, Ramesses-Itamon directly preceded Ramesses IX, and if Year 7 was his final regnal year, Ramesses-Itamon's Year 7 began in IV *prt* and lasted about five months—until I *ꜣḫt* 18–23, when Ramesses IX came to the throne.[177] Thus, if Year 7 was the highest regnal year of Ramesses-Itamon, none of the following documents with Year 7 dates that fall outside this five-month range could belong to his reign: Papyrus Turin Catalogue 2008 + 2016;[178] Papyrus Turin Catalogue 2070, verso;[179] Ostracon Gardiner 181;[180] and Deir el Medineh ostracon 630.[181] Conceivably they could belong to Year 7 of Ramesses VI, as could also Ostracon Gardiner 36,[182] possibly providing us with higher dates in Ramesses VI's Year 7 than the II *šmw* 4 date. For example, the Year 7, IV *ꜣḫt* 30 date on Deir el Medineh ostracon 630, if it belongs to Ramesses VI's reign, would limit the reign of Ramesses-Sethhikhopeshef to three to four months, if Year 1 was his highest. Some may feel that this is a bit too brief a reign for this king in whose first year the Theban tomb chapel No. 113 was decorated, even if only in part.[183]

If, as Janssen has argued, Papyrus Turin Catalogue 2008 + 2016 is to be assigned to the reign of Ramesses-Itamon,[184] and if we accept von Beckerath's sequence of kings, then the Year 7, II *prt* 3 date in this papyrus,[185] rather than the Year 7, I *ꜣḫt* 10 of Papyrus Turin Catalogue 1907 + 1908,[186] becomes the highest date attested for Ramesses-Itamon. Ramesses-Itamon came to the throne in IV *prt*; and if we accept von Beckerath's view that this king was directly succeeded by Ramesses IX, who acceded to the throne in I *ꜣḫt* 18–23, then Ramesses-Itamon died in I *ꜣḫt* 18–23. Therefore the date Year 7, II *prt* 3 of Papyrus Turin Catalogue 2008 + 2016, if it is to be assigned to Ramesses-Itamon, would force us to conclude that he survived about five months into his Year 8, which is otherwise unattested in the documentation. Although Ramesses-Sethhikhopeshef's reign probably lasted less than one year, it is also

[177] See Helck, *Studia Biblica et Orientalia* III 128.

[178] Published in Janssen, *Two Ancient Egyptian Ship's Logs*, chap. 2.

[179] Published in transcription in Allam, *Hieratische Ostraka und Papyri*, Plate volume, Pl. 121.

[180] Published *ibid.*, Pl. 47.

[181] Published in Jaroslav Černý, *Catalogue des ostraca hiératiques non littéraires de Deir el-Médineh* VIII ("DFIFAO" XIV [1970]) Pl. 4.

[182] Černý and Gardiner, *Hieratic Ostraca* I, Pl. XXXVI, 1.

[183] See Porter and Moss, *Bibliography* I/1 230–31.

[184] *Two Ancient Egyptian Ship's Logs*, pp. 55–57; also von Beckerath, *ZÄS* 97 (1971) 11–12.

[185] Janssen, *Two Ancient Egyptian Ship's Logs*, p. 61.

[186] Janssen, *JEA* 52 (1966) Pl. XIX*A*.

conceivable that he reigned four or five months into his Year 2, as yet unattested in documents.

Now let us assume that Kitchen's traditional ordering of Ramesses VI's successors is correct. If we are in error in assigning the Year 7, II *šmw* 4 date of column i of Pleyte and Rossi, *Papyrus de Turin*, Plate LXXII to Ramesses VI, then his Year 7 may have been restricted to about three months, since he came to the throne between the middle of I *prt* and the beginning of II *prt*, and since his direct successor, this time Ramesses-Itamon, acceded to the throne in IV *prt*. If Pleyte and Rossi, *Papyrus de Turin*, Plate LXXII, column i, or any one of the Year 7 documents cited in the last paragraph but one should belong to the reign of Ramesses VI—and we believe that there is a strong probability that such is the case—then Ramesses VI must have reigned about three months into his Year 8, so far unattested in the documentation.

Since Ramesses-Itamon came to the throne in IV *prt*, his highest attested date can easily be that of Year 7, II *prt* 3 in Papyrus Turin Catalogue 2008 + 2016, which Janssen assigns to his reign. We are ignorant of the date of Ramesses-Sethhikhopeshef's accession, but he must have died in I *ꜣḫt* 18–23, when Ramesses IX came to the throne. Between II *prt* 3 and Ramesses IX's accession there are seven months, fifteen to twenty days, during which a brief reign of Ramesses-Sethhikhopeshef can be accommodated. If he ruled past his Year 1, his unattested Year 2 would have comprised seven months or less.

Perhaps Kitchen's solution of the problem of the succession of kings is a bit simpler than von Beckerath's, demanding less manipulation in the dating of the documents. Since the two texts in Pleyte and Rossi, *Papyrus de Turin*, Plate LXXII are unrelated in content and in script, we can infer very little about the sequence of the kings from this document. Von Beckerath's interpretation allows for a fifteen-month interval between the dates of the two texts, but the same separation applies also if Ramesses VI was followed directly by Ramesses-Itamon.

The highest attested regnal year of Ramesses XI, who acceded to the throne on III *šmw* 20, is Year 27, IV *šmw* 8.[187] Consideration of a series of letters written in Year 10 of the Renaissance, however, indicates that Ramesses XI was still alive at that time, so that Year 10 of the Renaissance would be equivalent to Year 28 of Ramesses XI.[188] In these letters there occurs a Year 10 (of the Renaissance, which was Year 28 of Ramesses XI), I *šmw* 25,[189] while a subsequent letter gives us a date I *šmw* 29, without any indication of the year.[190]

[187] Auguste Mariette, *Abydos* II (Paris, 1880) Pl. LXII (left) and p. 55; cf. Wente, *Late Ramesside Letters* ("SAOC," No. 33 [1967]) p. 12.

[188] See Kitchen, *Third Intermediate Period*, pp. 17–23, 252–54.

[189] Černý, *Late Ramesside Letters* ("Bibliotheca Aegyptiaca," IX [Brussels, 1939]), p. 17, l. 11.

[190] *Ibid.*, p. 48, l. 4.

Since at the time these letters were written, the General Paiankh was in Nubia, a graffito dated III *šmw* 23 (without any indication of the year), recording the return of the general from Nubia, should probably be placed just three days after the beginning of Ramesses XI's Year 29.[191] As is the case with Haremhab, we have no indication that Ramesses XI celebrated a jubilee, so that his Year 29 was probably his highest.

Admittedly both of the chronologies for the Ramesside period that we have presented are very tight, and the objection might be raised that any chronology of this period should be viable enough to accommodate the unforeseen. What contingencies might arise to affect the chronology? In view of the excellent spread of year-by-year documentation—including both contemporary and retrospective dates extending from Year 32 of Ramesses II to Year 3 of Ramesses X, a period of roughly 140 years—it is improbable that any one reign will be increased by more than one year. For the following years within the span of the chronology we have failed to find any documentary evidence: Ramesses II's Years 41 and 43, Sety II's Year 4, Setnakht's Year 1, Ramesses III's Year 1, Ramesses V's Year 5, Ramesses VII's Year 3, and Ramesses IX's Years 3 and 12. Thus within a span of 140 years, to our knowledge there are only nine years totally unaccounted for in the documentation. In addition, there is some uncertainty regarding the documentation attesting to Sety II's Year 3,[192] Ramesses III's Year 7,[193] and Ramesses VI's Year 8, which, if Kitchen's sequence of kings is correct, lasted only three months.[194] What we would stress is that even with the uncertain years included, totaling a maximum of twelve years, there is no definite instance of the absence of documentation for any two years in succession. The Year 3 of Sety II could conceivably belong to a later reign, but need not necessarily do so.

Such spread of documentation speaks strongly against adding a block of as many as ten years to the reign of Merenptah, whose highest attested regnal year is Year 10. But it also seems a bit difficult to follow the suggestion once made by Kitchen—that is, to distribute ten or eleven years in small quantities over the remaining reigns of the Nineteenth and Twentieth Dynasties. Within this 140-year period, the Ramesside pharaohs whose reigns might possibly be increased by one year each are Merenptah, Amenmesse, Tausert, Setnakht, and Ramesses-Sethhikhopeshef; and outside this 140-year span, Ramesses XI. If we adopt Kitchen's sequence of kings, we might also increase the reign of Ramesses-Itamon by a full year; in the alternative chronology, reflecting von Beckerath's

[191] Kitchen, *Third Intermediate Period*, p. 417.

[192] See Gauthier, *Livre des rois* III ("MIFAO" XIX [1914]) 131, IV.

[193] Possibly attested in Papyrus Greg, see Černý, *Valley of the Kings*, p. 51, n. 7.

[194] See above.

sequence, this additional year for the reign of Ramesses-Itamon has already been introduced in the computations. Thus there are seven kings whose reigns might each be increased by one year.

That any of these reigns should be increased by more than one year seems unlikely, but in order to elevate the accession of Ramesses II from 1279 to 1290 B.C., the reigns of four of these kings would have to be increased by two years each.

It may be objected that this revision of New Kingdom chronology does not make allowance for an eventual increase in the lengths of reigns more recent than that of Ramesses II. What would happen to this chronology if one or more of the Ramesside pharaohs were found to have reigned longer than indicated in our chronology? We would note the following possibilities for dealing with any such eventuality, which we regard as most unlikely in any case:

a) Our date for the accession of Shoshenq I at 946 B.C. is not as fixed as Kitchen's 945 B.C., for it is computed on entirely different grounds. Our date could be either elevated as high as 948 B.C. or lowered.

b) There is the possibility of a one-year reduction in the period from Siptah's accession to Ramesses III's accession.

c) The length of the reign of Ramesses X as determined by Parker is not entirely unassailable. Parker's argument does not carry quite the weight that a calculated solution of a specific New Moon date does. Should Parker's argument be discounted, the reign of Ramesses X could be reduced by two years. Any discrediting of Parker's argument would itself present an even more serious challenge to the proponents of Ramesses II's accession in 1290 B.C.

What we would emphasize regarding our lowering of the date of Ramesses II's accession to 1279 B.C. is that this date is suggested by a consideration of the earlier chronology of the Eighteenth Dynasty. So far as the Ramesside chronology alone is concerned, we have attempted to demonstrate merely that our current knowledge of the chronology of the second half of the New Kingdom comfortably permits such a lowering of the date of Ramesses II's accession.

We may now at last consider how this revised chronology of the New Kingdom meshes with the chronologies of Western Asia. From the Amarna letters it is known that Amenhotep III was contemporary with four Babylonian kings: Kara-indaš, Kurigalzu I, Kadašman-Enlil I, and Burna-Buriaš II, the last of whom was also contemporary with Amenhotep IV (Akhenaton) and Tutankhamon.[195] Thus Burna-Buriaš II should have been a late contemporary of

[195] See Hornung, *Untersuchungen zur Chronologie*, chap. 9; and specifically on the synchronism of Amenhotep III and Burna-Buriaš II, see Cord Kühne, *Die Chronologie der internationalen Korrespondenz von El-Amarna* (Neukirchen-Vluyn, 1973) p. 129, with n. 642. EA 9 is certainly

Amenhotep III. In EA 3, line 18, from Kadašman-Enlil I to Amenhotep III, there is a reference to a feast of Amenhotep III, which, in view of the number of Babylonian kings with whom Amenhotep III was contemporary, should refer to either the first or second jubilee of Amenhotep III, celebrated in his Years 29–30 and Years 33–34, respectively. The third jubilee, in Years 37–38, seems improbable, since by that date Amenhotep III should have been contemporary with Burna-Buriaš II. Since according to John A. Brinkman's most recent revision of Babylonian chronology,[196] Kadašman-Enlil I died in 1360 (±5) B.C., Amenhotep III's regnal Years 29–36 should be no later than 1360 (±5) B.C. In other words, Amenhotep III came to the throne either in 1396–1388 B.C. (without the factor of plus or minus five years) or, in the broadest range, 1401–1383 B.C. (taking into account the factor of plus or minus five years).

Even if we do not interpret the EA 3 letter as containing a reference to one of Amenhotep III's jubilees, the accession of Amenhotep III cannot be elevated higher in view of the synchronism with Burna-Buriaš II indicated in EA 11. Equating Year 38 of Amenhotep III with Burna-Buriaš II's first regnal year in 1359 (±5) B.C. gives the highest possible accession date for Amenhotep III. Without the factor of plus or minus five years Amenhotep III's accession would be in 1396 B.C., and with the factor of plus or minus five years it would be in 1401 B.C. at the earliest. In the light of Brinkman's revised Babylonian chronology, it is in no way possible for Amenhotep III to have come to the throne before 1401 B.C.

This fact has implications for the lengths of the reigns of Amenhotep II and Thutmose IV, which intervene between Thutmose III and Amenhotep III. A period of thirty-four years has normally been allotted to the span of time separating the death of Thutmose III from the accession of Amenhotep III. However, with Thutmose III's death now established in 1450 B.C. and Amenhotep III's accession, deduced on the basis of the Babylonian synchronisms, having occurred no earlier than 1401 B.C., this span of time must be at least forty-nine years at the very minimum. In other words, the commonly accepted lengths of the reigns of Amenhotep II and Thutmose IV cannot possibly be correct. In particular, a nine-year, eight-month reign suggested on the basis of Manetho (Josephus) for Thutmose IV is clearly too short and must be rejected, inasmuch as the Lateran obelisk inscription of Thutmose IV gives us a maximum

addressed by Burna-Buriaš II to Tutankhamon, in spite of Hornung's arguments to the contrary; see John A. Brinkman, "The Monarchy in the Time of the Kassite Dynasty," in *XIXe Rencontre assyriologique internationale, Paris, 29 juin–2 juillet 1971, Le Palais et la royauté* (Paris, 1973) p. 400, with n. 35.

[196] *A Catalogue of Cuneiform Sources Pertaining to Specific Monarchs of the Kassite Dynasty* ("Materials and Studies for Kassite History" I [Chicago, in press]).

of thirty-five years between the death of Thutmose III and the accession of Thutmose IV, leaving a minimum of fourteen years for Thutmose IV.

Our earlier consideration of the jubilee evidence for Amenhotep II and Thutmose IV has lengthened their reigns and placed the accession of Amenhotep III at 1386 B.C., a date that fits within the broad limits of 1401–1383 B.C. for his accession as determined in the light of Brinkman's Babylonian chronology. It does not, however, fall within the narrow limits of 1396–1388 B.C., determined without using the factor of plus or minus five years. It should be stressed that Brinkman's current Babylonian chronology is based upon accepting a thirteen-year reign for Ninurta-apil-Ekur, as given in the Nassouhi kinglist. There are more recent versions of the Assyrian kinglist that assign to this king a reign of only three years. Thus Brinkman's chronology is subject to an overall reduction by ten years; Brinkman himself has written: "There is not a single shred of positive evidence in favor of either alternative."[197] We would propose that Egyptian chronology strongly suggests a lowering of the Babylonian chronology by these ten years. If this is done, then the accession of Amenhotep III would fall within the narrow limits, now 1386–1378 B.C.

There may be one other fixed date in second millennium Near Eastern history. A Hittite text suggests that in the tenth year of the reign of Muršili II there occurred what may have been a solar eclipse.[198] Those who have favored understanding this text as referring to a solar eclipse have held that it was the eclipse of March, 1335 B.C., putting the accession of Muršili II at 1344 B.C.[199] On the basis of a letter written to the Hittite king Šuppiluliuma I by the widowed queen of Tutankhamon requesting a Hittite prince for a husband,[200] we know that the accession of Muršili II could have occurred no earlier than two years after the death of Tutankhamon. Tutankhamon would then have died in 1346 B.C. at the latest. Since he reigned at least nine full years, his accession would have been in 1355 B.C. at the latest. By adding the relevant figures we would then arrive at a date no earlier than 1371 B.C. for Amenhotep IV's (Akhenaton's)

[197] John A. Brinkman, "Comments on the Nassouhi Kinglist and the Assyrian Kinglist Tradition," *Or* n.s. 42 (1973) 313.

[198] See A. Götze, *Historische Texte* ("Keilschrifturkunden aus Boghazköi" XIV [Berlin, 1926]) p. 4.

[199] Emil Forrer, *Forschungen*, Vol. 2/1 (Berlin, 1926) pp. 1–9; Rowton in Hayes, Rowton, and Stubbings, "Chronology," in *Cambridge Ancient History* I (rev. ed.; Cambridge, 1962) chap. 6, p. 36 and p. 46, n. 2; Friedrich Cornelius, "Die Chronologie der Vorderen Orients im 2. Jahrtausend v. Chr.," *Archiv für Orientforschung* 17 (1954–56) 306–7.

[200] Hans Gustav Güterbock, "The Deeds of Suppiluliuma as Told by His Son, Mursili II," *JCS* 10 (1956) 94–95, Text A, col. iii, ll. 1–27; cf. Elmar Edel, "Neue keilschriftliche Umschreibungen ägyptischer Namen aus den Boğazköytexten," *JNES* 7 (1948) 14–15.

accession to the throne. This result is manifestly incompatible with our revised chronology.

In considering the possible dates for the above-mentioned eclipse of the sun, Forrer seems to have searched no later than 1330 B.C. It so happens that an even fuller eclipse of the sun took place in June, 1312 B.C.[201] Reasoning from this date as we have done from the date of the earlier eclipse, we find that the accession of Tutankhamon would have occurred in 1332 B.C. at the latest, and the accession of Amenhotep IV (Akhenaton) no later than 1348 B.C. The corresponding figures in our chronology are 1334 and 1350 B.C., and these fit well with understanding the phenomenon in Muršili II's tenth year to be the solar eclipse of 1312 B.C.

Less certain are the synchronisms with Near Eastern chronology at the time of Ramesses II. Much here revolves around the interpretation of a letter (KBo I 10) written by Hattušili III to the Babylonian king Kadašman-Enlil II seeking a treaty to counteract troubles the Hittites had been, or claimed to have been, having with Egypt. Was this letter written before Hattušili III's treaty with Egypt in Year 21 of Ramesses II, or was it written after this treaty in order to induce Babylonia to enter into a similar pact? The first alternative, favored by Edel and others, has supported 1290 B.C. as the date of Ramesses II's accession,[202] whereas the second interpretation has fitted in well with Rowton's position that Ramesses II came to the throne in 1304 B.C.[203] In terms of our revised Egyptian chronology, which lowers Ramesses II's accession to 1279 B.C., the Hittite treaty in his Year 21 would have been made in 1259 B.C. Brinkman puts the reign of Kadašman-Enlil II at 1263–1255 B.C., [204] but if his chronology is reduced by ten years overall, Kadašman-Enlil II's accession would have been in 1253 B.C., six years after our date for the treaty, and thus the letter would have been written after the treaty. In spite of the fact that our date for Ramesses II's accession is twenty-five years later than Rowton's, a comparable lowering of the chronologies of western Asia would seem to allow one still to accept Rowton's carefully worked-out interpretation of international diplomacy at the time of Ramesses II.

[201] See Manfred Kudlek and Erich H. Mickler, *Solar and Lunar Eclipses of the Ancient Near East from 3000 B.C. to 0 with Maps* ("Alter Orient und Altes Testament," Sonderreihe, Vol. 1 [Neukirchen-Vluyn, 1971]) p. 49.

[202] Elmar Edel, "Die Abfassungszeit des Briefes KBo I 10 (Hattušil–Kadašman-Enlil) und seine Bedeutung für die Chronologie Ramses' II.," *JCS* 12 (1958) 133.

[203] "The Material from Western Asia and the Chronology of the Nineteenth Dynasty," *JNES* 25 (1966) 240–58.

[204] *A Catalogue of Cuneiform Sources.*

TABLE 2

The Attestations of Dated Documents from Year 32 of Ramesses II to Year 3 of Ramesses X

The following symbols have been used in this table:

***	year without known attestations
—	no attestation
?	one or more questionable attestations
X	one certain attestation
X?	one certain plus one or more questionable attestations
X+	more than one certain attestation

		By type of document			
	Attestation(s)	Ostraca/Dockets	Papyri	Graffiti	Monuments
Ramesses II					
year 32	X	—	—	X	—
year 33	X+	X	X	—	X+
year 34	X+	X	—	X	X+
year 35	X+	X+	—	X	X+
year 36	X+	X	X	X	X
year 37	X+	X+	—	X	X+
year 38	X+	X+	—	—	X
year 39	X	X	—	—	—
year 40	X+	X	—	X	X+
year 41	***	—	—	—	—
year 42	X+	X	—	—	X+
year 43	***	—	—	—	—
year 44	X+	X	—	—	X
year 45	X	—	—	X	—
year 46	X+	X+	X	—	—
year 47	X+	X+	—	X	—
year 48	X+	X+	—	X	—
year 49	X	X	—	—	—
year 50	X	—	—	X	—
year 51	X	—	—	—	X
year 52	X+	X	X	—	—
year 53	X	X	—	—	—
year 54	X+	X	X	—	X
year 55	X+	—	X	X	X
year 56	X+	X	X	X	—
year 57	X+	X	—	—	X
year 58	X+	X	—	—	X

TABLE 2

THE ATTESTATIONS OF DATED DOCUMENTS FROM YEAR 32 OF RAMESSES II TO YEAR 3 OF RAMESSES X (*cont.*)

	By type of document				
	Attestation(s)	Ostraca/Dockets	Papyri	Graffiti	Monuments
Ramesses II (*cont.*)					
year 59	X	X	—	—	—
year 60	X	—	—	—	X
year 61	X?	—	X	—	?
year 62	X	—	—	—	X
year 63	X+	X	—	—	X+
year 64	X	X	—	—	—
year 65	X	—	—	—	X
year 66	X+	X	—	—	X?
year 67	X	—	X	—	—
Merenptah					
year 1	X+	—	X	X	X+
year 2	X+	X?	—	X	X+
year 3	X+	X+	X+	—	X
year 4	X+	?	—	X	X
year 5	X+	—	—	—	X+
year 6	X	—	—	—	X
year 7	X+	X	—	X	—
year 8	X+	X	X?	—	—
year 9	X	X	—	—	—
year 10	X	—	X	—	—
Amenmesse					
year 1	X	X	—	—	—
year 2	X?	X?	—	—	—
year 3	X+	X+	—	—	—
year 4	X	X	—	—	—
Sety II					
year 1	X+	X+	X	—	—
year 2	X+	—	X	—	X
year 3	?	?	—	—	—
year 4	***	—	—	—	—
year 5	X+	X+	—	—	X+
year 6	X+	X+	—	—	—

TABLE 2

THE ATTESTATIONS OF DATED DOCUMENTS FROM YEAR 32 OF RAMESSES II TO YEAR 3 OF RAMESSES X (*cont.*)

		By type of document			
	Attestation(s)	Ostraca/Dockets	Papyri	Graffiti	Monuments
Siptah					
year 1	X+	X+	—	—	X+
year 2	X	X	—	—	—
year 3	X+	—	—	X+	X
year 4	X+	X+	—	—	—
year 5	X	X	—	—	—
year 6	X	—	—	X	—
Tausert					
year 7	X+	?	—	X+	—
year 8	X+	X+	—	—	—
Setnakht					
year 1	***	—	—	—	—
year 2	X+	X	—	—	X+
Ramesses III					
year 1	***	—	—	—	—
year 2	X+	X+	—	—	X+
year 3	X+	X	—	—	X
year 4	X+	X+	—	—	X
year 5	X+	—	?	X+	X+
year 6	X+	?	X+	—	X+
year 7	?	—	?	—	—
year 8	X+	X	X	—	X
year 9	X	X	—	—	—
year 10	X?	X?	—	—	—
year 11	X+	X+	—	—	X+
year 12	X+	X	—	—	X+
year 13	X+	X+	—	—	—
year 14	X+	X+	—	—	—
year 15	X+	X+	—	—	X
year 16	X+	X+	X+	X+	X+
year 17	X+	X+	—	—	—
year 18	X+	X+	—	X+	X
year 19	X+	X+	—	—	—
year 20	X+	X+	—	X	X

TABLE 2

THE ATTESTATIONS OF DATED DOCUMENTS FROM YEAR 32 OF RAMESSES II TO YEAR 3 OF RAMESSES X (*cont.*)

	By type of document				
	Attestation(s)	Ostraca/Dockets	Papyri	Graffiti	Monuments
Ramesses III (*cont.*)					
year 21	X+	X+	X	X+	—
year 22	X+	X+	X	—	—
year 23	X+	X+	—	—	X
year 24	X+	X+	X	—	—
year 25	X+	X+	—	—	—
year 26	X+	X+	—	—	—
year 27	X+	X+	—	—	X
year 28	X+	X+	X	X	—
year 29	X+	X+	X	—	X+
year 30	X+	X+	X	X+	—
year 31	X+	X+	X	—	—
year 32	X+	X+	X	—	—
Ramesses IV					
year 1	X+	X+	X+	X+	X
year 2	X+	X+	X+	X+	X
year 3	X+	X+	X+	X	X+
year 4	X+	X+	X	X	X
year 5	X+	—	X	—	X+
year 6	X+	X+	X	X?	—
year 7	X?	X?	—	—	—
Ramesses V					
year 1	X	—	X	—	—
year 2	X+	X+	X+	X	—
year 3	X+	—	X+	—	—
year 4	X+	X+	X+	—	—
year 5	***	—	—	—	—
Ramesses VI					
year 1	X+	X+	X	X+	—
year 2	X+	X+	X	—	—
year 3	X	—	X	—	—
year 4	X	X	—	—	—
year 5	X	—	X	—	—
year 6	X	—	—	—	X
year 7	X	—	X	—	—
year 8	?	—	?	—	—

TABLE 2

THE ATTESTATIONS OF DATED DOCUMENTS FROM YEAR 32 OF RAMESSES II TO YEAR 3 OF RAMESSES X (*cont.*)

	By type of document				
	Attestation(s)	Ostraca/Dockets	Papyri	Graffiti	Monuments
Ramesses VII					
year 1	X+	—	X+	—	—
year 2	X	—	X	—	—
year 3	***	—	—	—	—
year 4	X?	?	X	—	—
year 5	X	—	X	—	—
year 6	X	—	X	—	—
year 7	X+	X	X	—	—
Ramesses VIII					
year 1	X	—	—	—	X
Ramesses IX					
year 1	X	—	X	—	—
year 2	X+	X	X+	—	—
year 3	***	—	—	—	—
year 4	X+	—	X	—	X
year 5	X	—	X	—	—
year 6	X+	—	X+	—	X
year 7	X+	?	X	X	—
year 8	X+	?	X+	—	—
year 9	X+	—	X+	X	—
year 10	X+	X	X+	—	X
year 11	X	—	X	—	—
year 12	***	—	—	—	—
year 13	X+	—	X+	—	—
year 14	X+	X+	X+	—	—
year 15	X+	—	X+	—	—
year 16	X+	—	X+	—	—
year 17	X+	X	X+	—	—
year 18	X	—	X	—	—
year 19	X+	—	X+	—	—
Ramesses X					
year 1	X	—	X	—	—
year 2	X	—	X	—	—
year 3	X	—	X	—	—

Register of Citations

Items in parentheses are questionable attestations

Ramesses II

For a listing of dated documents from his reign see John D. Schmidt, *Ramesses II: A Chronological Structure for His Reign* (Baltimore, 1973) chap. 2, to which add the following:

Year 32: Marek Marciniak, *Deir el-Bahari* I: *Les Inscriptions hiératiques du Temple de Thoutmosis III* (Warsaw, 1974) No. 17.

Years 35 and 37: O Chicago 17007 (unpublished).

Year 47: Schafik Allam, *Hieratische Ostraka und Papyri: Transkriptionen aus dem Nachlass von J. Černý*, Plate volume (Tübingen, 1973) p. 64.

Years 55 and 58: K. A. Kitchen, "Nakht-Thuty—Servitor of Sacred Barques and Golden Portals," *JEA* 60 (1974) 173.

Merenptah

Year 1: Alan H. Gardiner, *Ramesside Administrative Documents* (Oxford, 1948) p. 30 (hereinafter referred to as *RAD*); Wilhelm Spiegelberg, *Ägyptische und andere Graffiti (Inschriften und Zeichnungen) aus der thebanischen Nekropolis* (Heidelberg, 1921) No. 850*a*; Henri Gauthier, *Le Livre des rois d'Egypte* III ("MIFAO" XIX [1914]) 113–14.

Year 2: O DM 621 verso; (O Cairo 25581, see Jaroslav Černý, *The Valley of the Kings* ["BdE" LXI (1973)] p. 26); Gauthier, *Livre des rois* III 114–15.

Year 3: O Cairo 25540, 25552; P Anastasi III, 7, 11; P Bologna 1086, 10; Gauthier, *Livre des rois* III 115.

Year 4: (Bertha Porter and Rosalind L. B. Moss, *Topographical Bibliography of Ancient Egyptian Hieroglyphic Texts, Reliefs and Paintings* VII [Oxford, 1951] 371); Centre de Documentation et d'Etudes sur l'Ancienne Egypte, *Graffiti de la Montagne Thébaine* (Cairo, 1969– –) No. 3012 (hereinafter referred to as Centre, *Graffiti*); K. A. Kitchen, *Ramesside Inscriptions* IV (Oxford, 1968) 1.

Year 5: Gauthier, *Livre des rois* III 116–17.

Year 6: Porter and Moss, *Bibliography* VII 159 (6).

Year 7: O Cairo 25504 recto; Gauthier, *Livre des rois* III 117.

Year 8: O Cairo 25504 verso; P Bologna 1094 verso 2; (P Anastasi VI, 58).

Year 9: O Gardiner 197, see Jaroslav Černý, *A Community of Workmen at Thebes in the Ramesside Period* ("BdE" L [1973]) p. 331.

Year 10: P Sallier I, 3, 4.

Amenmesse

Year 1: O Cairo 25779.

Year 2: O DM 209; (O Varille 26, see Jacobus J. Janssen and P. W. Pestman, "Burial and Inheritance in the Community of the Necropolis Workmen of Thebes," *JESHO* XI [1968] 142, n. 2).

Year 3: O Cairo 25780, 25782, 25783.

Year 4: O Cairo 25784.

Sety II

Year 1: O Cairo 25509, 25560; Jaroslav Černý and Alan H. Gardiner, *Hieratic Ostraca* I (Oxford, 1957) Pl. LXIV, 1; P Anastasi IV 1*a*, 1.

Year 2: Gardiner, *RAD*, p. 15; Gauthier, *Livre des rois* III 131.

Year 3: (Gauthier, *Livre des rois* III 131, IV).

Year 4

Year 5: O Cairo 25542, 25556; Georges Goyon, *Nouvelles inscriptions rupestres du Wadi Hammamat* (Paris, 1957) No. 95; Wolfgang Helck, "Zwei thebanische Urkunden aus der Zeit Sethos' II," *ZÄS* 81 (1956) 86–87.

Year 6: O Cairo 25515, 25517; Černý and Gardiner, *Hieratic Ostraca*, Pl. XLVI, 2.

Siptah

Year 1: O Cairo 25515–25519, 25521; Gauthier, *Livre des rois* III 140.

Year 2: O Cairo 25521.

Year 3: Gauthier, *Livre des rois* III 141.

Year 4: Jaroslav Černý, "A Note on the Chancellor Bay," *ZÄS* 93 (1966) 36.

Year 5: Černý and Gardiner, *Hieratic Ostraca*, Pl. XVII, 4.

Year 6: Gauthier, *Livre des rois* III 142.

Tausert

Year 7: (O Cairo 25610); Sir Alan Gardiner, "The Tomb of Queen Twosre," *JEA* 40 (1954) 43; Marciniak, *Deir el-Bahari* I, No. 3.

Year 8: O DM 594; O Cairo 25293, see Gardiner, *JEA* 40 (1954) 43, n. 3.

Setnakht

Year 1

Year 2: Kitchen, *Inscriptions* V (Oxford, 1970) 1–2; Werner Kaiser, Dino Bidoli, *et al.*, "Stadt und Tempel von Elephantine, dritter Grabungsbericht," *MDAIK* 28 (1972) 193 ff., Pl. IL.

Ramesses III

Year 1

Year 2: Černý and Gardiner, *Hieratic Ostraca*, Pl. XXVI, 4; Porter and Moss, *Bibliography* I/2 (2d ed.; 1964) 845; Bernard Bruyère, *Mert Seger à Deir el Médineh* ("MIFAO" LVIII [1930]) p. 14; Siegfried Schott, *Wall Scenes from the Mortuary Chapel of the Mayor Paser at Medinet Habu* ("SAOC," No. 30 [1957]) Pl. 1.

Year 3: Černý and Gardiner, *Hieratic Ostraca*, Pl. LXXVII, 5; Schott, *Paser*, Pl. 1.

Year 4: O Cairo 25589 recto; Černý and Gardiner, *Hieratic Ostraca*, Pl. LXXVII, 9; Gauthier, *Livre des rois* III 157.

Year 5: (P Greg, see Černý, *Valley of the Kings*, p. 37); Gauthier, *Livre des rois* III 157–58; Porter and Moss, *Bibliography* VII 162.

Year 6: P Chester Beatty XI verso; (P Greg); Gauthier, *Livre des rois* III 158–59; Porter and Moss, *Bibliography* II (2d ed.; 1972) 409; G. A. Gaballa, "Three Documents from the Reign of Ramesses III," *JEA* 59 (1973) 111.

Ramesses III (*cont.*)

Year 7: (P Greg, see Černý, *Valley of the Kings*, p. 51, n. 7).

Year 8: O DM 672; P Bulaq 10 verso; Gauthier, *Livre des rois* III 159.

Year 9: O Cairo 25589 recto.

Year 10: O Cairo 25589 verso; O Michaelides 1, but probably emend to Year 16, see Černý, *Community of Workmen*, p. 306, n. 7.

Year 11: O Cairo 25589 verso; Allam, *Hieratische Ostraka*, Plate volume, p. 55; Gauthier, *Livre des rois* III 159; Porter and Moss, *Bibliography* VII 162.

Year 12: O Cairo 25553; Gauthier, *Livre des rois* III 160.

Year 13: O Cairo 25555; O DM 432; O Turin 6629, see Černý, *Community of Workmen*, p. 271, n. 5.

Year 14: O Cairo 25555, 25703; Černý and Gardiner, *Hieratic Ostraca*, Pl. LVII, 2.

Year 15: O DM 92, 406; Černý and Gardiner, *Hieratic Ostraca*, Pl. XXXIX, 2; Gauthier, *Livre des rois* III 160.

Year 16: O Wien 18; O Michaelides 2; Allam, *Hieratische Ostraka*, Plate volume, p. 94; P Turin 99, 2–3, see Černý, *Community of Workmen*, p. 344; *idem*, *Graffiti hiéroglyphiques et hiératiques de la Nécropole thébaine* ("DFIFAO" IX [1956]) Nos. 1111, 1143; Gauthier, *Livre des rois* III 161.

Year 17: Černý and Gardiner, *Hieratic Ostraca*, Pl. LXXVII; O DM 176 verso; O Cairo 25584.

Year 18: O DM 422 verso; O Cairo 25584; Černý, *Graffiti*, Nos. 1149 and 1296; Spiegelberg, *Graffiti*, No. 508; Schott, *Paser*, Pl. 1.

Year 19: O Cairo 25584; O DM 424; O Berlin 11254.

Year 20: Černý and Gardiner, *Hieratic Ostraca*, Pls. XLIX, 3, LIII, 2; O DM 73; Centre, *Graffiti*, No. 1928; Porter and Moss, *Bibliography* II 131.

Year 21: O Florence 2621; O DM 364; Ernesto Schiaparelli, *Relazione sui lavori della Missione archeologica italiana in Egitto* (*anni 1903–1920*) I (Turin, 1924) Figs. 126–27; Allam, *Hieratische Ostraka*, Plate volume, p. 81; Spiegelberg, *Graffiti*, Nos. 99, 245, 253.

Year 22: Černý and Gardiner, *Hieratic Ostraca*, Pl. XLIX, 1; O DM 222; Schiaparelli, *Relazione* I, Fig. 128; P Harris I, 17*a*, l. 4.

Year 23: Černý and Gardiner, *Hieratic Ostraca*, Pls. LXIV, 2, LXXII, 3; O DM 625; Sinai Inscription No. 273.

Year 24: O DM 137, 164, 451; Allam, *Hieratische Ostraka*, Plate volume, p. 83.

Year 25: O DM 32, 56; Černý and Gardiner, *Hieratic Ostraca*, Pl. XXXIV, 1.

Year 26: O DM 142, 410; O Michaelides 5.

Year 27: Černý and Gardiner, *Hieratic Ostraca*, Pls. XVI, 4, LXI, 1; O DM 33, 151 verso; M. L. Bierbrier, *The Late New Kingdom in Egypt* (*c. 1300–664 B.C.*) (Warminster, 1975) pp. 7–8.

Year 28: Černý and Gardiner, *Hieratic Ostraca*, Pls. XLV, 1, LXIII, 2; O DM 62, 138, 168; Gardiner, *RAD*, p. 79; Spiegelberg, *Graffiti*, No. 609.

Year 29: O DM 64, 152; O Cairo 25530; Gardiner, *RAD*, p. 46; Gauthier, *Livre des rois* III 162–63.

Year 30: O DM 74, 98, 145; Černý and Gardiner, *Hieratic Ostraca*, Pl. LXXI, 1 verso; Gardiner, *RAD*, p. 58; Černý, *Graffiti*, No. 1165; Spiegelberg, *Graffiti*, No. 1012.

Year 31: Černý and Gardiner, *Hieratic Ostraca*, Pl. LXXI, 1 verso; O DM 36, 37, 55; P Mallet I, 3.

Year 32: O DM 38, 39; P Harris I, 1, 1.

Ramesses IV

Year 1: O DM 41–44, 47, 70; Gardiner, *RAD*, p. 81; P Turin 1949 + 1946, see Jaroslav Černý, "Datum des Todes Ramses' III und der Thronbesteigung Ramses' IV," *ZÄS* 72 (1936) 111; P Turin 2044, see Černý, *Community of Workmen*, pp. 277–78; Spiegelberg, *Graffiti*, Nos. 298 and 839; Kitchen, *Inscriptions* VI (Oxford, 1969) 1–2.

Year 2: O DM 44, 45, 401; Černý and Gardiner, *Hieratic Ostraca*, Pl. LXXIII, 1; P Turin 49; Gardiner, *RAD*, p. 80; Černý, *Graffiti*, Nos. 1288, 1405; Kitchen, *Inscriptions* VI 9.

Year 3: Černý and Gardiner, *Hieratic Ostraca*, Pls. XLVIII, 2, LXXVII, 5; Gardiner, *RAD*, p. 80; P Mallet I; Kitchen, *Inscriptions* VI 12–16.

Year 4: Černý and Gardiner, *Hieratic Ostraca*, Pl. LXXVII, 9; O Chicago 12073, see Černý, *Community of Workmen*, p. 136, n. 8; Gardiner, *RAD*, p. 80; Centre, *Graffiti*, No. 2609; Kitchen, *Inscriptions* VI 17.

Year 5: Gardiner, *RAD*, p. 80; Kitchen, *Inscriptions* VI 26–27.

Year 6: Černý and Gardiner, *Hieratic Ostraca*, Pl. XVI, 2; O Cairo 25273, 25274; Gardiner, *RAD*, p. 80; Spiegelberg, *Graffiti*, No. 790; (Centre, *Graffiti*, No. 2577).

Year 7: O DM 207; (Černý and Gardiner, *Hieratic Ostraca*, Pl. LXX, 1).

Ramesses V

Year 1: Gardiner, *RAD*, p. 80.

Year 2: Černý and Gardiner, *Hieratic Ostraca*, Pls. XXVIII, 2, LXIX, 2; Gardiner, *RAD*, p. 80; P Chester Beatty I, Pl. 19; Černý, *Graffiti*, No. 1252.

Year 3: Gardiner, *RAD*, p. 80; Will of Naunakhte, Doc. 1 in Jaroslav Černý, "The Will of Naunakhte and the Related Documents," *JEA* 31 (1945) Pl. 8.

Year 4: Černý and Gardiner, *Hieratic Ostraca*, Pl. LV, 2; O Cairo 25598; O Turin 2162, see Černý, *Community of Workmen*, p. 342; Gardiner, *RAD*, p. 81; Wilbour Papyrus.

Year 5

Ramesses VI

Year 1: Černý and Gardiner, *Hieratic Ostraca*, Pl. LXVIII, 1; O Cairo 25598; P Bibl. Nat. No. 237, see Jaroslav Černý, "Egypt: From the Death of Ramesses III to the End of the Twenty-first Dynasty," in *Cambridge Ancient History* II (rev. ed.; Cambridge, 1965) chap. 35, p. 11; Černý, *Graffiti*, No. 1269; Centre, *Graffiti*, No. 2876.

Ramesses VI (*cont.*)

Year 2: O Cairo 25254; Allam, *Hieratische Ostraka*, Plate volume, p. 13; P Turin 1923 verso, see Černý, *Valley of the Kings*, p. 21, n. 1, p. 25.

Year 3: P Bibl. Nat. No. 237, see Černý, *Community of Workmen*, p. 356, n. 8.

Year 4: O Cairo 25566 recto.

Year 5: P Turin 1907/8 recto 3, 13, see Jacobus J. Janssen, "A Twentieth-Dynasty Account Papyrus," *JEA* 52 (1966) 84.

Year 6: Karnak stele, see Janssen, *JEA* 52 (1966) 92, n. 1.

Year 7: P Turin 72, col. i.

Year 8: See discussion above concerning the reign of Ramesses VI.

Ramesses VII

Year 1: Gardiner, *RAD*, p. 9; P Turin 72, col. ii.

Year 2: Gardiner, *RAD*, p. 10.

Year 3

Year 4: (O DM 133, see Bierbrier, *Late New Kingdom*, p. 38, p. 128, n. 167); P Turin 1907/8 recto 2.

Year 5: P Turin 1907/8 recto 2.

Year 6: P Turin 1907/8 recto 3, 7.

Year 7: O Strasbourg H 84, see Janssen, *JEA* 52 (1966) 91, n. 1; P Turin 1907/8.

Ramesses VIII

Year 1: Theban Tomb No. 113.

Ramesses IX

Year 1: P Turin 2084 + 2091, see Bierbrier, *Late New Kingdom*, pp. 33–35, p. 126, n. 121, p. 127, n. 139.

Year 2: O Gardiner 143, see Černý, *Community of Workmen*, p. 267, n. 2, p. 275, n. 3; Wolfgang Helck, "Eine Briefsammlung aus der Verwaltung des Amuntempels," *JARCE* 6 (1967) 147; P Turin 2084 + 2091.

Year 3

Year 4: P Turin 1900, III, see Černý, *Community of Workmen*, p. 157, n. 4; Gauthier, *Livre des rois* III 207.

Year 5: P Turin 1881, see Allam, *Hieratische Ostraka*, Plate volume, p. 109.

Year 6: P Turin 1881; P Turin 1930, I, see Černý, *Community of Workmen*, p. 308, n. 6; Porter and Moss, *Bibliography* VII 159.

Year 7: (O IFAO 1274, see Černý, *Community of Workmen*, p. 308, n. 3); P Turin 1881; Uvo Hölscher, *The Excavation of Medinet Habu* IV: *The Mortuary Temple of Ramses III*, Pt. II ("OIP" LV [1951]) p. 12, Fig. 11.

Year 8: (O DM 672); P Turin 1881; P Turin 29.

Year 9: P Turin 1900 verso I–II, see Černý, *Community of Workmen*, p. 157, n. 5, p. 216, n. 10; P Turin 2072, see Allam, *Hieratische Ostraka*, Plate volume, p. 130; graffito in tomb of Ramesses VI, see Bierbrier, *Late New Kingdom*, p. 14.

Year 10: Gauthier, *Livre des rois* III 208, V; P Turin 2071/224, see Černý, *Community of Workmen*, p. 203, n. 7; P Turin 2072; Gauthier, *Livre des rois* III 217.

Year 11: P Turin 50, see Černý, *Community of Workmen*, p. 127, n. 7, p. 157, n. 8.

Year 12

Year 13: Giuseppe Botti and T. Eric Peet, *Il Giornale della necropoli di Tebe* (Turin, 1928) Pls. 1 ff.; P Turin 2087/29, see Černý, *Community of Workmen*, p. 356, n. 1; P Leopold II-Amherst 1, 15; P BM 10054 verso 1, 6.

Year 14: O Leningrad 2973, see Černý, *Community of Workmen*, p. 197, n. 8; O Cairo 25362, see Černý, *Community of Workmen*, p. 197, n. 8; O Cairo 25299, see Černý, *Valley of the Kings*, p. 40, n. 6; P Abbott 4, 15–16; P Turin 2071/224 + 1960, see Allam, *Hieratische Ostraka*, Plate volume, p. 123.

Year 15: P Turin 2071/224 + 1960; Botti and Peet, *Giornale*, Pls. 28–29.

Year 16: P Abbott; P Leopold II-Amherst; P BM 10054 verso 1; P Turin 2057–2058, see Černý, *Community of Workmen*, p. 220, n. 4.

Year 17: O IFAO 1258, see Černý, *Community of Workmen*, p. 127, n. 4; P BM 10053 recto; Botti and Peet, *Giornale*, Pl. 16.

Year 18: P Turin 5, l. 11.

Year 19: P Turin 1932 + 1939, see Černý, *Community of Workmen*, p. 234; P Turin 2075, see Černý, *Community of Workmen*, p. 193, n. 5, p. 200, n. 10.

Ramesses X

Year 1: P Turin 1932 + 1939.

Year 2: P Turin 1932 + 1939.

Year 3: Botti and Peet, *Giornale*, Pls. 58 ff.; Gauthier, *Livre des rois* III 217.

SOME FRAGMENTARY DEMOTIC WISDOM TEXTS

Ronald J. Williams

The genre of "teachings," which first made its appearance in the Old Kingdom, remained an important and popular feature of Egyptian literature right down to the Greco-Roman period. In the Demotic script two lengthy treatises are known. The first is contained in the Leyden Pap. Insinger[1] and turns up in different editions in four other manuscripts now in Copenhagen (with fragments in Florence).[2] Somewhat earlier in origin are the "Instructions of ʿOnchsheshonqy" in the British Museum.[3] A much briefer work has survived on a papyrus now in the Louvre, Pap. Louvre 2414.[4] Unfortunately, none of these works has reached us intact.

The great vogue of this type of literature in the late period is attested by a number of tantalizingly small fragments. Part of one column of an anthology of maxims in a private collection in Cairo has been published.[5] Long before this, a tiny scrap of papyrus that may have formed part of yet another such work was made available.[6] In the rich collection of Demotic papyri in the Austrian National Library at Vienna there are scores of fragments of what must have been a long work of the same kind that still awaits publication.

Many years ago I read Pap. Insinger with the distinguished scholar in whose honor the present volume of essays has been prepared. As a modest tribute to his friendship and scholarly assistance at that time and during the years that have followed, three more examples of Demotic didactic texts are here discussed

[1] François Lexa, *Papyrus Insinger* (Paris, 1926).

[2] Aksel Volten, *Kopenhagener Texte zum demotischen Weisheitsbuch* ("Analecta Aegyptiaca" I [Copenhagen, 1940]).

[3] S. R. K. Glanville, *The Instructions of ʿOnchsheshonqy* ("Catalogue of Demotic Papyri in the British Museum" II [London, 1955]).

[4] Aksel Volten, "Die moralischen Lehren des demotischen Pap. Louvre 2414," in *Studi in memoria di I. Rosellini* II (Pisa, 1955) 271–80.

[5] Edda Bresciani, *Testi demotici nella Collezione Michaelidis* ("Orientis Antiqua Collectio" II [Rome, 1963]) 1–4 and Pl. I.

[6] Wilhelm Spiegelberg, *Die demotischen Papyrus* II ("CCG" [Strassburg, 1908]) 103.

All of these have been available to scholars for a long time but have been understandably neglected because of their fragmentary condition.

The first two are papyri that have been in the possession of the Louvre for nearly a century and a half. They were found in the Memphite area together with Pap. Louvre 2414, to which we have already alluded. Wilcken has shown that the drafts of Greek documents inscribed on all three papyri were written by the same hand within a period of four years and are to be dated from 163 B.C. to 159 B.C.[7] The excellent photographs of the papyri were obtained through the kindness of Professor J. Vandier, the late lamented curator of the Egyptian Department of the Louvre.

I. PAP. LOUVRE 2377 VERSO

The fragment Pap. Louvre 2377 verso (Fig. 50) is a palimpsest that contains one column of thirteen lines of text. The end of a long line from the preceding column has been preserved to the right of it. It was published in a careful facsimile by J. A. Letronne in 1865,[8] and the indefatigable Revillout made a pioneer attempt to interpret it in his classes.[9] The Greek texts were thoroughly dealt with by Wilcken.[10] In view of the date of the latter, the Demotic text must be assigned to the middle of the second century B.C.

TRANSLITERATION

1. *mn*[a] *pꜣ mr pꜣ ḫy ḥꜣṯ m-dr pꜣ tꜣ*
2. *sdm ḫrw* ⌈*s*⌉[b] *nb gm=k pꜣ nty nꜣ-nfr=f r ḏd=s*
3. *mn*[a] *pꜣ* ⌈*tn*⌉[c] *m-dr pꜣ sp n pꜣ nty ỉw bw-ỉr=w rḫ sʿḥʿ=f*
4. *mn*[a] *pꜣ ỉy m-dr md.t-nfr.t n pꜣ nty ỉw=s ẖn ḥꜣṯ=f r ḏd* ⌈*tꜣ*⌉ *ḫ*[. . .]
5. *bn ỉw lḫ r pꜣ ỉ-ỉr dỉ ꜣḳ pꜣy=f ʿš-sḥn ḏd bn ỉw=y dỉ . . .*[d]
6. *m-ỉr ḥwrʿ bw-ỉr=f*[e]
7. *m-ỉr ṯy ẖrỉ ḫr ḫb pꜣ* ⌈*ʿḥʿ*⌉[f] *n pꜣ nty ỉr=s*
8. *pꜣ nty ỉw=f ḏd bn ỉw=y rḫ šsp mr*[g] *my wšd=f pꜣ Rʿ*
9. *pꜣ nty ỉw=f ḏd bn ỉw=y rḫ ỉr tꜣ wp.t my wšd=f pꜣ Rʿ*
10. *pꜣ nty ỉw=f mḥ*[h] *rꜣ=f bw-ỉr=f rḫ ʿm=f my ỉn wʿ . . .* ⌈*bnr*⌉ *. . .*[i]

[7] Ulrich Wilcken, *Urkunden der Ptolemäerzeit* (*ältere Funde*) I (Berlin and Leipzig, 1927) 133 ff.

[8] *Papyrus grecs du Louvre et de la Bibliothèque Impériale: Planches* ("Notices et extraits des manuscrits de la Bibliothèque Impériale et autres bibliothèques" XVIII, seconde partie [Paris, 1865]) Pl. XXXV, No. 54 verso.

[9] Eugène Revillout, *Quelques textes traduits à mes cours*, Première série (Paris, 1893) pp. lxxiii–lxxvii.

[10] *Urkunden* I 386–92, No. 84.

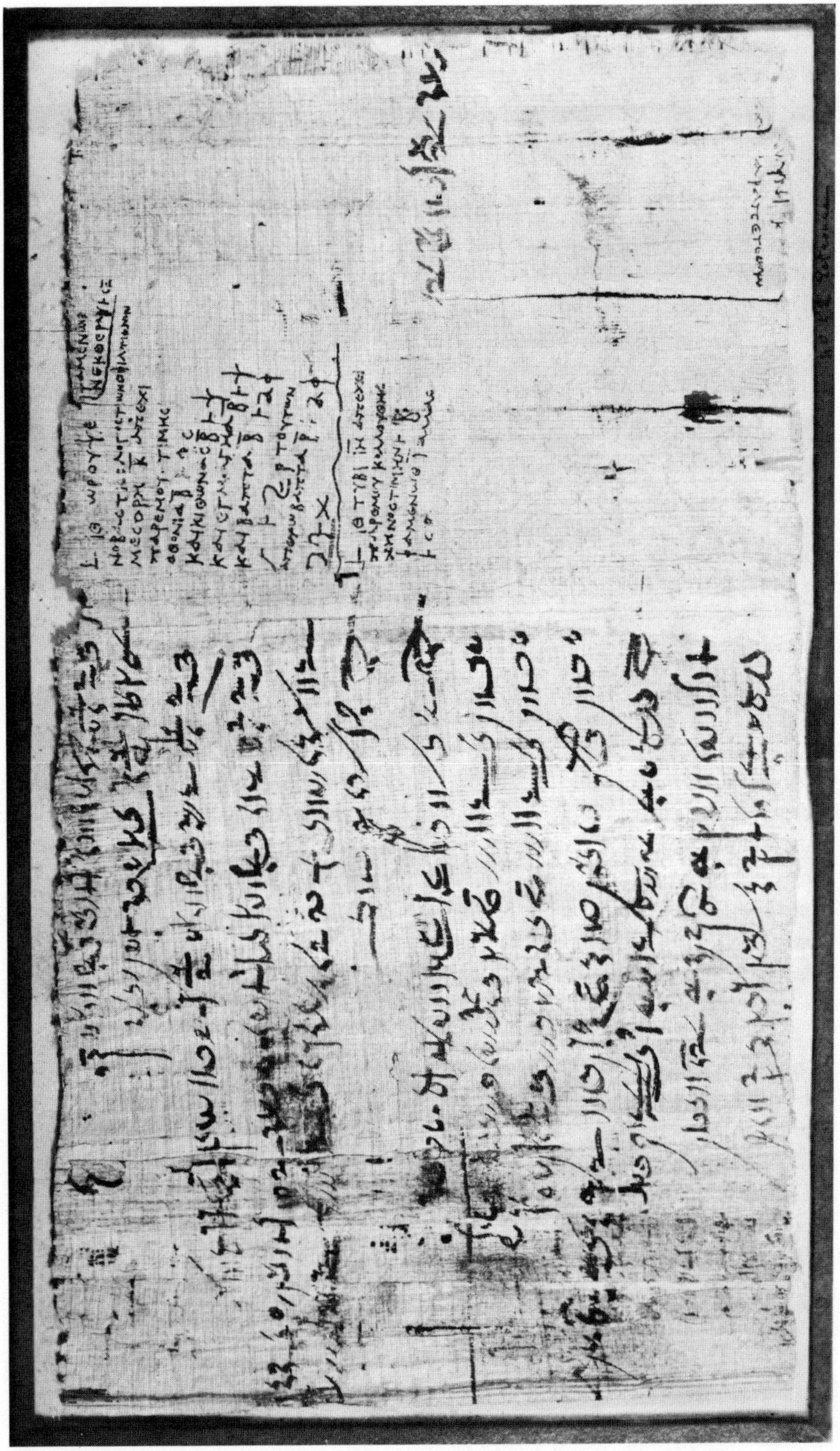

FIG. 50.—Papyrus Louvre 2377, verso

11. *m-ỉr ḫꜣ*ʿ *pꜣy=k gy*[j] *(n)* ʿ*.wy pꜣy=k sꜣ ḏd dỉ=k n=f nk*
12. *ḏwy*[k] *ỉrm rmt ḫm nk=f tꜣy=k ḥm.t ỉ-ỉr-ḥr=f*
13. *ḫꜣ*ʿ *pꜣ btw*[l] *n w*ʿ *ḫrš (n) sm ỉr=f w*ʿ *ỉḥ*

TRANSLATION

1. There is no[a] loving of the haughty by the land.
2. Listen to the voice of every ⌈man⌉,[b] that you may discover what is good to say.
3. No deed brings ⌈honor⌉[c] to him whom they cannot reprove.
4. No favor comes to him who has it in mind to say the . . .
5. There is no one more foolish than him who has ruined his commission, saying, "I will not let . . ."[d]
6. Do not defraud, ⌈that he may not⌉[e] . . .
7. Do not seize food; the ⌈lifetime⌉[f] of the one who does it is shortened.
8. He who says, "I will not be able to endure suffering,"[g] let him pray to Phrēʿ.
9. He who says, "I will not be able to do the task," let him pray to Phrēʿ.
10. He who would fill[h] his mouth cannot swallow it; let one . . . forth . . .[i]
11. Do not leave your ⌈intention⌉[j] in the hands of your son, because you have given him your property.
12. A thief[k] and a common man, he violated your wife before him.
13. Leave the ⌈wrongdoer⌉[l] to a bundle of hay, that he may be an ox!

NOTES

[a]This writing of *mn* occurs also in lines 3 and 4 as well as in Pap. Louvre 2380, 2/10. Although *mn* is normally followed by an indefinite noun, there is an instance of an infinitive with the definite article in Dem. Chron. 3/19.

[b]There is no exact parallel for this unusual writing of a word that is ordinarily found in a different context.

[c]In the light of the parallels in lines 1 and 4, an infinitive seems to be required.

[d]The word after *dỉ* looks like *wp.t*, "task," as in line 9, but no satisfactory reading of the traces at the end of the line suggests itself.

[e]If the reading is correct, the rest of the line has disappeared or has been omitted. Perhaps one should read *pꜣ ỉ-ỉr=f*, "what he has done."

[f]The reading is uncertain but makes good sense.

[g]For the word *mr* meaning "suffering" see Mythus 18/10, Sat. Poem 2/2, ʿOnchsh. 1/17, 6/21, 24, 12/2, 15/12, 16/4, 13, and *nꜣ-mr* in 26/9.

[h]The sign resembling an *f* after *mḥ* is perhaps part of the word itself.

[i]The end of the line is baffling. The remains of the previous text, which has been erased, add to the confusion.

[j]This meaning of *gy* occurs in the phrase *ḫr pꜣ gy* in II Kh. 6/21, 7/3, Pap. Krall 11/30f., 23/13.

[k]The word *ḏwy* in Pap. Ins. 15/9 means "robbery"; its use here seems unique. The sense of the whole line is obscure.

[l]Although *btw* means "crime," "wrongdoing," it must here have the unusual connotation of "wrongdoer," unless it is a most peculiar spelling of *bn* (*bỉn*), "bad," "evil."

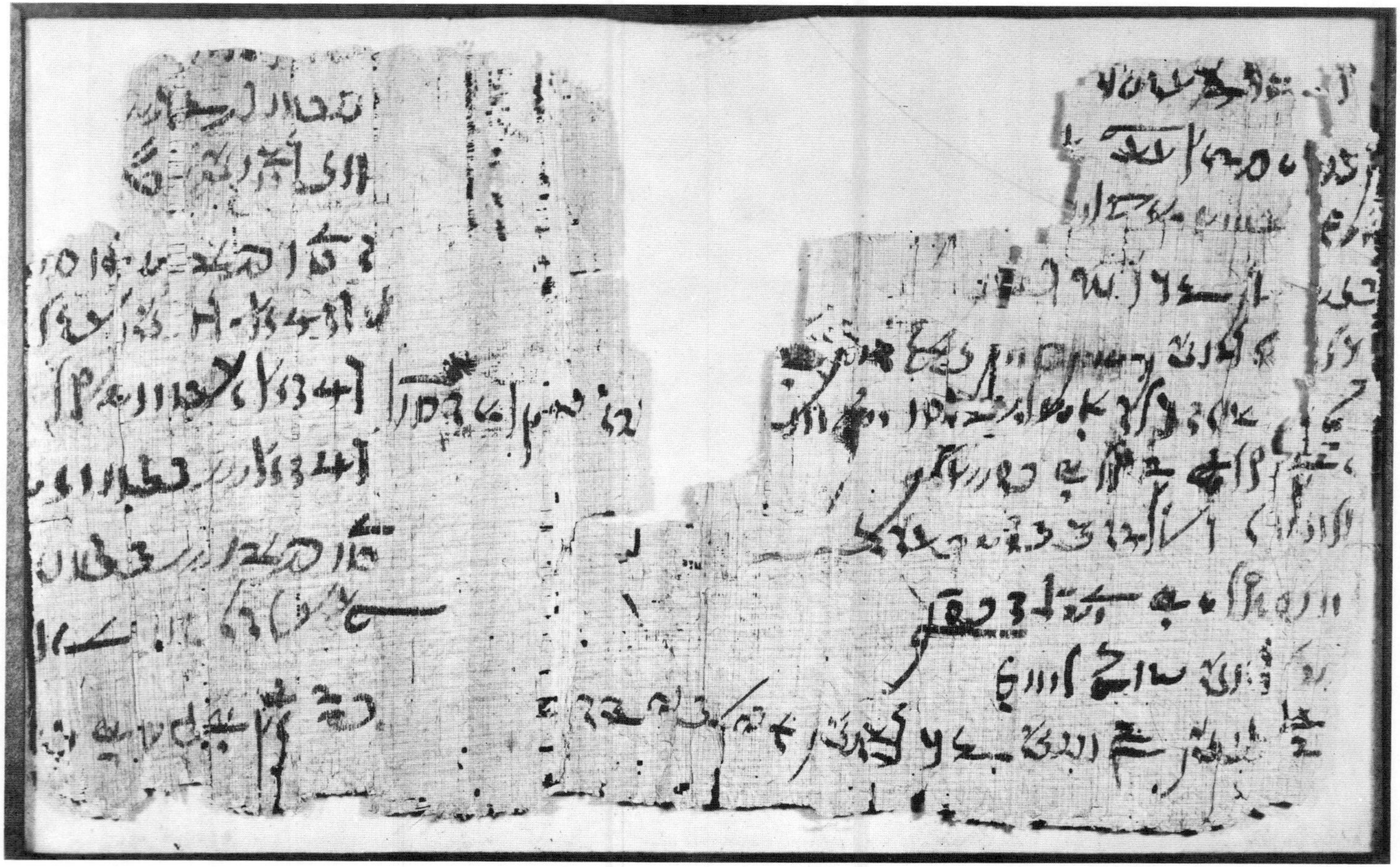

FIG. 51.—Papyrus Louvre 2380, verso

II. PAP. LOUVRE 2380 VERSO

The damaged Pap. Louvre 2380 verso (Fig. 51) contains the end of one column and the beginning of a second. The top has been torn off, but the bottom margin is preserved. The Demotic text was also reproduced by Letronne,[11] and the Greek documents on the recto were published by Wilcken.[12] Like the preceding text, it dates from the middle of the second century B.C.

TRANSLITERATION

Column i

1. [. . .] . . . [a]⌜*=tn*⌝ *ỉw=s* ⌜*ꜥꜣ*⌝ [. . .]
2. [. . .]*=f ḫrw pꜣ hp ky šrỉ* [. . .][b]
3. [. . .] . . . ⌜*m-sꜣ*⌝ *pꜣy=w mr* ⌜*wp*[*.t*]⌝[c] . . .[b]
4. [. . .] *mtr=f bn-pw=w ms.ṯ=f*
5. [. . .] *sw*[*g*][d] *ḥꜣṯ=f n pꜣy=f ḥry ỉw=f ỉr bꜣk tꜣy=f* ⌜*ḥm.t*⌝ [. . .]
6. [. . .] *ꜥn*[e] [. . .] . . . *tꜣ swḥ*[f] *šsp*[g] ⌜*pꜣy=f*⌝ . . . *fy* [. . .] . . . *rmt.w nꜣ.w nꜣ pr.w*
7. [. . .] *wꜥ ntr ꜥꜣ wꜥ ntr ḫm* ⌜*m-sꜣ*⌝*=f*
8. [. . .] . . . ⌜*srw*⌝ *šm*[h] *pꜣ nty ỉw=s ḫpr*
9. [. . .] *ỉrm pꜣ ntr pꜣy=k dmy nꜣ nty nḥm=k*
10. [. . .] . . . *sp-sn*[i] *bw-ỉr=k wy*
11. [. . .] *sp . . . =f pk*[j] *bn-pw ḥꜣṯ=f dỉ* ⌜*ꜣrmꜣ*⌝[k]*=s*

Column ii

1. [. . .] . . . [. . .]
2. *hmy r bn-pw=y* [. . .]
3. *ỉ-ỉr ḥꜣṯ* [*rmt*][l]*-rḫ* [. . .]
4. *nꜣ-tkn*[m] *pꜣ* ⌜*bn*⌝[n] [. . .]
5. ⌜*tꜣ*⌝ *sbꜣ n ḥꜣṯ lḫ* [. . .]
6. *sbꜣ nb my pꜣ ntr* [. . .]
7. *sbꜣ=y m-ḳdy* [. . .]
8. *tkn=y m-ḳdy* [. . .]
9. *ỉw=k lwḥ*[o] . . . *dỉ* [. . .]
10. *mn rmt ḫm* ⌜*ỉn*⌝[p] *pꜣ ḫm* [. . .]

TRANSLATION

Column i

1. [. . .] . . .[a] it being great [. . .]
2. [. . .] his [. . .] voice ⌜of⌝ the law ⌜of⌝ another child [. . .][b]

[11] *Papyrus grecs*, Pl. XXXVI, No. 53 verso.

[12] *Urkunden* I 392–96, No. 85.

3. [. . .] after their love of wo[rk[c] . . .][b]
4. [. . .] to instruct him; he has not been born.
5. [. . .] foolish[d] ⌜of⌝ his heart for his master, he will serve his ⌜wife⌝.
6. [. . .] again[e] [. . .] . . .[f] men, those of the households.
7. [. . .] a great god or a little god ⌜except/after⌝ him.
8. [. . .] . . . . . .[h] that which will happen.
9. [. . .] with the god of your town are those who save you.
10. [. . .] . . . . . .[i] that you may not be distant.
11. [. . .] time . . .[j] his heart did not . . .[k] it.

Column ii

1. (Only traces remain)
2. If only I had not [. . .]
3. The mind of a wise [man[l] . . .]
4. The wicked[n] is ⌜swift⌝[m] [. . .]
5. ⌜The⌝ teaching of a foolish mind [. . .]
6. As for every teaching, let the god [. . .]
7. I have taught like [. . .]
8. I have ⌜hastened⌝ like [. . .]
9. When you are ⌜at⌝[o] fault . . . give [. . .]
10. There is no[p] common man [. . .]

NOTES

[a] The traces of the word preceding *ỉw=s* are too damaged to be read, but the final group is probably the pronominal suffix.

[b] If one compares the copy of Letronne with the photograph, it is apparent that a small piece of papyrus has been dislodged at the end of lines 2 and 3, resulting in the loss of some signs. In its present condition the line defies a sensible translation.

[c] The traces suggest either *wp.t*, "task," "work," or *šms*, "to serve."

[d] The determinative makes it likely that the missing sign is either *g* or *k*.

[e] Perhaps this is the beginning of a damaged *fy*, "to carry," "to lift."

[f] If this word is to be read *swḥ* or *swꜣ*, it lacks any determinative and is so far unknown. The meaning of this part of the line is unintelligible.

[g] This might also be read as *dr=w*, "all of them."

[h] Neither *srw* nor *šm* are known, unless the latter be the verb meaning "to diminish," "grow smaller," Coptic ϢⲘⲀ. The preceding traces are enigmatic.

[i] The sign read *sp-sn* may just as likely be the flesh determinative.

[j] After *sp* there is a group with the flesh determinative and the third masculine suffix. The traces hardly fit *rꜣ=f*, "his mouth." The following *pk* may be the verb meaning "to be weak" (Coptic ⲠⲀⲔⲈ), as in Pap. Ins. 22/22, Pap. Krall 12/20, or the ancestor of Coptic ⲠⲰϬⲈ, "to break," "to burst." The following flesh determinative, however, suggests otherwise.

[k] The word *ꜣrmꜣ* is a hapax legomenon.

[l] A vertical strip of papyrus has been torn off; *rmt* may have occupied the space originally.

[m]If rightly understood, this is the only instance of *tkn* used as an adjective-verb.

[n]Only the beginning of the word remains. The signs might also be read as *ḏn* or even *ḏh*[. . .].

[o]Some preposition might have been expected before this word.

[p]If this is the negative particle *ỉn*, it is unexpected after *mn*. The writing of the latter word resembles that in Pap. Louvre 2377, lines 1, 3, and 4.

III. OSTRACON FROM DEIR EL-BAḤRI

The third text is a broken ostracon (Fig. 52) said to come from Deir el-Baḥri. A hand copy was included by Hess in his monograph on the Rosetta Stone as evidence for the meaning of the word *lwḥ*, "fault."[13] The present whereabouts of this ostracon is unknown to the writer, so that no photograph could be obtained. The hand is late Ptolemaic or early Roman.

TRANSLITERATION

1. *twy=s ẖ.t wꜥ.t sbꜥ.t r.dỉ n=w ⸢sẖ pr-ꜥnẖ⸣*
2. (*n*) *ky*[a] *šrỉ ỉw=f sbḳ n ms m-šs sp-sn*
3. *m-ỉr nḳ s-ḥm.t ỉw bn tꜣy=k ꜥn*[b] *tꜣy*
4. *bw-ỉr=w gm n=k lwḥ r-dbꜣ.ṯ=s*
5. *⸢k.t ꜥn tꜣy⸣*[c] *ỉw*[d] *bn ⸢nꜣ⸣ nty nꜣ- . . .*[e] *ḥm.t.w n pꜣ ẖyr dỉ*
6. *ḫpr tꜣy=k ḫnšṯ(.t) ⸢n⸣* [. . .]
7. *k.t ꜥn tꜣy m-ỉr ⸢sdm⸣* [. . .]

TRANSLATION

1. Here is a copy of a teaching that a ⸢scribe of the House of Life⸣ gave them
2. (for) a little[a] child who is very, very young.
3. Do not sleep with a wife who is not[b] yours,
4. that no fault may be found with you because of it.
5. Here is another one:[c] Those who are . . .[e] are not[d] women in the street (to)
6. create your bad odor ⸢in⸣ [. . .]
7. Here is another one: Do not listen [. . .]

NOTES

[a]This is a well-attested spelling of the adjective that appears in Coptic as ⲔⲞⲨⲒ. Or, of course, it may be the very common word meaning "another."

[b]The word *ꜥn* here is the negative particle.

[c]The expression *k.t ꜥn tꜣy* occurs elsewhere in Mythus 5/13, 19/34, Pap. Krall 6/3, 7/17, 11/29, 23/11 f. Meaning literally "it is another also," it is used to introduce an additional item and may be rendered as "Here is another thing," or "furthermore." In line 7 it is

[13] J. J. Hess, *Der demotische Teil der dreisprachigen Inschrift von Rosette* (Freiburg, 1902) p. 56.

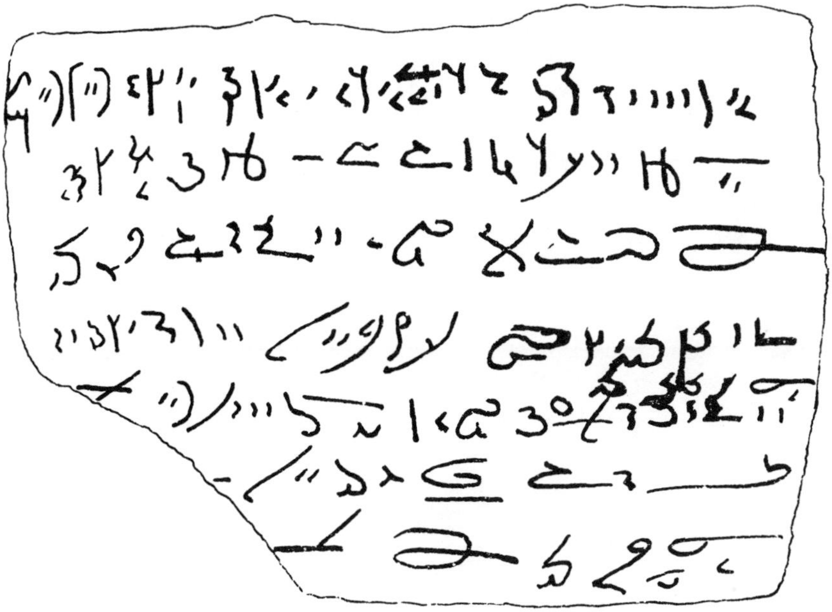

FIG. 52.—Inscription on ostracon from Deir el-Baḥri

clearly used to present a further maxim. In line 5 it appears to have been omitted and later inserted above the line. If so, the signs *ʿn tȝy* seem to have been repeated, perhaps because their crowded condition made them difficult to distinguish the first time.

[d]The *ỉw*, if such it be, is difficult. Possibly the scribe intended to write *bn ỉw*, a familiar form of introduction for a negative equational sentence.

[e]No satisfactory reading of this group occurs to the writer.

The significance of these texts is their further witness to the popularity of collections of aphorisms as late as the Demotic period. It is very likely that some, if not all, were schoolboy copies. The two Louvre texts are perhaps portions of larger treatises like those mentioned at the beginning of this article. Or they may have been random collections of maxims drawn from various sources. This is certainly the case with the ostracon from Deir el-Baḥri.

Because of the damaged condition of these documents and the frequent difficulty of the scribal hands, much remains obscure. Admittedly, even when the reading of the text is certain, many passages in Demotic wisdom texts still raise problems of interpretation. This seems to be inherent in the nature of the material. If these notes will stimulate some to contribute to the clarification of these texts, the purpose of the present writer will have been achieved.

MRS. ANDREWS AND "THE TOMB OF QUEEN TIYI"

John A. Wilson†

In January, 1907, Theodore M. Davis found a tomb in the Valley of the Kings. Davis persistently urged that he had found the burial of Queen Tiyi, the wife of Amen-hotep III, and his published report emphasized that belief. Arthur Weigall, the Chief Inspector of the Antiquities Service for Upper Egypt, sought every evidence that the burial was that of the heretic pharaoh Akh-en-Aton. There was argument from the very day on which the tomb was penetrated.[1] The varied attribution of the materials placed in the tomb, the scattered confusion of objects, the equivocal nature of altered inscriptions, and the absence of any methodical recording of the discovery made certainty about the burial impossible and opened the way to elaborate theories. Later analysis by other authorities disagreed on the history of the burial and of the funerary furniture but came to some consensus that the skeletal remains were those of Smenkh-ka-Re, the elder son-in-law of Akh-en-Aton.[2] Into the argument have entered the names of Tiyi, Akh-en-Aton, Smenkh-ka-Re, Merit-Aton, and Tut-ankh-Amon. The Amarna period of Egyptian history always seems to foster controversy. It

[1] The primary reports are those of Theodore M. Davis, Gaston Maspero, G. Elliot Smith, Edward Ayrton, and George Daressy, *The Tomb of Queen Tîyi* (London, 1910); E. R. Ayrton, "The Tomb of Thyi," *PSBA* 29 (1907) 277–81; G. Elliot Smith, *The Royal Mummies* ("CCG" [1912]) pp. 51–56; Georges Daressy, "Le Cercueil de Khu-n-Aten," *BIFAO* 12 (1916) 145–59; Arthur E. P. Weigall, *The Life and Times of Akhnaton, Pharaoh of Egypt* (Edinburgh and London, 1911) pp. 276–84; *idem*, "The Mummy of Akhenaton," *JEA* 8 (1922) 193–99; and Joseph Lindon Smith, *Tombs, Temples and Ancient Art* (Norman, 1956) pp. 54–75.

[2] R. Engelbach, "The So-called Coffin of Akhenaten," *ASAE* 31 (1931) 98–114; *idem*, "Material for a Revision of the History of the Heresy Period of the XVIIIth Dynasty," *ASAE* 40 (1940) 148–52; D. E. Derry, "Note on the Skeleton Hitherto Believed To Be That of Akhenaten," *ASAE* 31 (1931) 115–19; and R. G. Harrison, "An Anatomical Examination of the Pharaonic Remains Purported To Be Akhenaten," *JEA* 52 (1966) 95–119. Three important articles in *JEA* are the following: Sir Alan Gardiner, "The So-called Tomb of Queen Tiye," *JEA* 43 (1957) 10–25, with his addition, a review of *Tombs, Temples and Ancient Art*, by Joseph Lindon Smith, in *JEA* 45 (1959) 107–8; H. W. Fairman, "Once Again the So-called Coffin of Akhenaton," *JEA* 47 (1961) 25–40; and Cyril Aldred, "The Tomb of Akhenaton at Thebes," *JEA* 47 (1961) 41–65. Not listed here are theories and conclusions by about a dozen other scholars.

may be of some use to add the record of those days in 1907, as it appeared in the journal of Davis's sister, who kept house for him on his boat at Luxor.

Mrs. Emma B. Andrews accompanied her brother Theo from 1889 to 1911 and kept a journal of her doings on the *Bedawin* and of her brother's observations at the end of each digging day. This diary was deposited with the Metropolitan Museum of Art in 1919. In 1944 a copy was given to the Library of the American Philosophical Society.[3] I am grateful to Dr. Whitfield J. Bell, Jr., the librarian of the society, who called it to my attention in 1969. In a 1919 Foreword to the journal Albert M. Lythgoe wrote: "the charming description which she gives of their river-life on the 'Bedawin' . . . is certainly worthy of a wider public and more permanent form in print—though she could not be prevailed upon to consider this." A copy of some pages of the diary was sent by William C. Hayes of the Metropolitan Museum to Warren R. Dawson in England, and the entry for January 19, 1907, appeared as a postscript to Sir Alan Gardiner's article, "The So-called Tomb of Queen Tiye" (*JEA* 43 [1957] 25). I therefore understand that pertinent excerpts from the journal may be released.

Davis records elsewhere that that season's work in the Valley of the Kings began on January 1, 1907. At that time the dahabiyeh *Bedawin* was moored on the west bank, across from Luxor. E. R. Ayrton was the archeologist directing the actual digging for Davis in the Valley. Weigall, Egyptian government representative for antiquities, had a house in Luxor. Davis and Mrs. Andrews were busy with a round of social engagements; Davis usually visited the excavation when summoned by Ayrton. The published record shows that recording of the process of work and of the finds was minimal. It was not until a sensational tomb was discovered that a photographer and two artists were enlisted to detail the finds. The accounts published later by Davis, Weigall, and Joseph Lindon Smith, the American artist, are based on self-justifying recollections and differ decidedly in details. Mrs. Andrews's diary has the virtue of recording what she saw or what she was told, with no desire to advance a theory. Naturally it does echo her brother's hope that he had found "the Queen." But it serves as a control and corrective on some of the impassioned writing about the tomb and its contents.

Copied here are the days from January 4 through January 29. I make no attempt to correct a few misspellings of names or to identify persons immaterial to the account.

Friday, Jan. 4th.

Mr. Ayrton wrote a note this morning to Theo saying he had found a tomb. Theo had intended going over today, so when he returned he reported that it promised something—but was still uncertain. Jean and I went over to the hotel to pay some visits.

[3] Accessioned February 16, 1944, 84653–54.

Saturday, Jan. 5.

Another note from Mr. Ayrton saying the tomb was not a tomb! Nettie was so disappointed. Dr. Wiedemann and his wife dined with us tonight. They are delightful people, and we had a charming evening.

Sunday, Jan. 6.

A quiet delightful morning—Mr. Dalison came to lunch—some of Jean's friends to tea.

Monday, Jan. 7.

Theodore went over to the Valley this morning—found it very hot—and when he got back quite late, told us that Ayrton had this time found a real tomb. We are all going over tomorrow, and so are Mr. and Mrs. Weigall. Joe Smith is staying at the Valley tonight with Ayrton. Jean went to the hotel to lunch with Mrs. Peckett—Nettie and I had a beautiful lunch on deck, and at 3 o'clock went over to the hotel for her—Mrs. Peckett, the Misses Collins, and Carter were there—we brought Carter home with us, calling on our way back on their dahabya "Stella" on the Smiths. Mr. and Mrs. Weigall came to tea.

Tuesday, Jan. 8th.

All of us went over to the Valley this morning—found Mr. Ayrton had cleared enough to show a small chamber which he thought was the whole tomb. But after lunch it was found that a doorway which had been sealed up as that in the tomb of Touyou and Iuia led to a corridor. In removing some of the blocks of stone which hindered progress, a fine broken alabaster vase, and some bits of gold foil were found; so the work for the day was stopped, as it was too late to open it, the guards and police were sent for, and we rode home—speculating as to who the tomb had belonged. Mr. Weigall and his wife were already camping in the Valley—and wanted Nettie and Jean to stay with them the night—which they did—delighted at the opportunity. Joe Smith and his wife also stayed. A very nice man, an Englishman, whom Theo had met the day before, lunched in the tomb with us, Mr. David Erskin M.P. Theo and I had a quiet evening alone—a most unusual thing.

Jan. 9. Wednesday.

We made rather an early start this morning—Theo and I, with Amelie and Jones, and Hassein. When we arrived at the tomb, every one was waiting for us as the doorway and steps had been cleared, and everything ready for an entrance. Ayrton, Weigall and Theo scrambled along the corridor over the stones, and made a very difficult entrance. Mr. Erskine, by invitation had joined us, we women, with Mr. E., Mrs. Weigall, and Joe and his wife, sat about on the rocks above, and waited straining our ears to catch the broken exclamations that reached us from below—"Aton! The rays of the Sun" Tut-ankh-amen" etc. and at last Mr. Davis's voice rang out, "By Jove, Queen Tyi, and no mistake" and so it proved. On the rough stones of the corridor rested a wooden door, 12 × 14 ft. long—6 ft. wide, and a smaller one about 2 × 4—with bronze doors and hinges—both doors covered with gold foil—the smaller one in quite good condition, and on it the cartouche of Tyi, and that of her husband Amenhotep III. The burial chamber was not large, but in a state of great confusion. The Queen would seem to have been laid in a great, highly decorated, wood shrine—parts of which were on the floor, or leaning against the wall,—the coffin on the floor—all showing hasty burial, or robbery or desecration. I did not go down—but Nettie, Mrs. Weigall, and Jean went down—one by one—Theo was determined that Nettie should be the first one to see it, and she was the first woman to enter. All the men had been down. We had a big lunch with everyone, and a charming day. Very warm today.

Thursday, Jan. 10.

Theo and the girls went again to the Valley. I wouldn't face that long ride in the hot sun today—and so had a nice quiet day at home. They came back very tired, bringing word of the many treasures of the tomb. Tomorrow the tomb is to be given over into the hands of a skillful photographer sent for from Cairo—and Joe Smith is also painting there.

Jan. 11. Friday.

Theo came over in the Valley again—had Carter lunching with us.

Jan. 12. Saturday.[4]

Theo at home for a rest. The girls and I over at Luxor—visiting and shopping. Mr. Erskine dined with us. A nice, big, handsome Englishman.

Jan. 13. 1st Sunday after Epiphany.

M. and Mme. Naville dined with us.

Luxor, Jan. 14. Monday.

A quiet day at home. The Maspero's boat arrived this morning. Theo went over to see them—they are delighted with the finding of Tyi's tomb—weather cool and pleasant—the mountains were wonderful at dawn this morning—the first rosy touch of the sun on their highest peaks until the whole range burned with a rosy light—transfused as it were—as if its colour came from itself.

Tuesday, Jan. 15.

It has been a dull, dark day with north wind in squalls. A pleasant visit from M. and Mme. Maspero this afternoon and a nice cable from Mr. Robinson of congratulations to Theo. This evening we had a gale, and were battered about—and rain fell for a time.

Wednesday, Jan. 16.

We had a hard rain for 2 hours this A.M. and it was cold. The Masperos went to the Valley in spite of it. Mme. Maspero had my chair. Theo went over later, and they had lunch with him.

Thursday, Jan. 17.

Theo and Jean went over to the Valley this morning. Theo reports that they were clearing the corridor and bracing up stones which held part of wooden

[4] On January 12, 1907, George R. Hughes was born in Wymore, Nebraska.

shrine. It is all under Ayrton's charge. Nettie and I crossed to Luxor this morning. I went to the Luxor Hotel to see Mrs. Congdon, who is better, and then joined Nettie at the Temple, and we took a carriage and drove to the Girls Mission School but found Miss Buchanan was in Asyût attending the yearly conference. Stopped at Mohassibs for a little visit. The poor man looks old and ill. Mr. Carter and Rev. Mr. Samms came to tea.

Friday, Jan. 18.

We all went over to Karnac this afternoon—met Mme. Maspero and a friend there. Mr. Sayce arrived early in the day—I sent him a note asking him to come to tea.

Saturday, Jan. 19.[5]

At the Valley. Dr. Wiedermann and wife, and Mr. Sayce were over and lunched with us in the lunch tomb. I went down to the burial chamber and it is now almost easy of access—and saw the poor Queen as she lies now just a bit outside her magnificent coffin, with the vulture crown on her head—all the woodwork of the shrine, doors, etc. are heavily overlaid with gold foil—which under the influence of the outer air is now peeling off—and I seemed to be walking on gold—and even the Arab working inside had some of it sticking in his wooly hair. Here is the sketch of the tomb and situation of objects.

No. 1. mummy of Queen—partly overlaid by coffin No. 2—both on the floor. 3,3,3,3, doors or panels—very large, heavily overlaid with gold,—the one with the x, has a beautiful portrait of Queen. All of them beautifully incised on the gold leaf. *Aton* rays on all and Khuenatens cartouche followed by an inscription "I made this for the great Queen Tyi, royal mother." The 4 x-s against the wall are 4 large panels, all gold and inscriptions.

Second Sunday after Epiphany—Jan. 20.

Home all day—Theo and Nettie went to Karnac in the afternoon. Many visitors. Mrs. Smith, Sir Benjaman Stone, Mr. Briggs and Currelly; Mr. Sayce dined with us. Cool, all day—cold, now. My mountains were wonderful this A.M.

Monday, Jan. 21.

Theo at the Valley all day—he reports all the panels being treated to paraffin to hold the gold in place. Weidermans dined with us. Our new moon should have shown.

Tuesday, Jan. 22.

Prof. Tarbell, Chicago University, called with a letter from Mr. Lythgoe. Robert Trefusis and Harold Jones arrived from Abydos—on coming back after some visits this afternoon found them here. They came back to dine.

Wednesday, Jan. 23.

Robert and H. Jones to dine again—discussed how to treat the panels and

[5] The entry for this day was published by Gardiner, *JEA* 43 (1957) 25. The accompanying sketch plan reproduced there is omitted here.

doors of shrine. H.J. came here to paint or draw them, finds it very difficult—decided to take an impression of inscriptions by wax and plaster of paris—our little new moon showed for the first time tonight.

Thursday, Jan. 24.

Theo at home today. Ayrton and Mr. Dalison lunched with us. We all went over to the new hotel, the "Winter Palace" to have tea and called on Mrs. Harriman, who is lying opposite us in the new private steamer the Soudan. Robert and H. J. dined with us. Lovely day.

Friday, Jan. 25.

Theo was all day at the Tomb—entertained at luncheon, Prof. Tarbell and M. Lacau—Ayrton, Weigall, Robert and Harold Jones. They at last lifted the coffin off the mummy without much damage. Owing to the past presence of water in the tomb, the coffin, except for the cover which is made of gold inlaid with lapis and carnelian, had gone into ruins—and her poor mummy turned into dust. They took off the vulture crown and saw a necklace and bracelets—but did not disturb them as they want a doctor to examine the skeleton and pronounce on her sex, scientifically. They found the body wrapped in thick gold plates rather than foil. Theo brought the crown home with him—and it now lies in the closet at the head of my bed! It is of solid gold, and represents the royal vulture, with out-spread wings and meeting behind the head, beautifully done in a fine répoussé style—every feather perfect. Robert and H.J. dined here.

Saturday, Jan. 26.

We all went over to the Valley this morning and I made my last descent into the tomb. The morning was warm—my poor little donkeys were tired—for Luxor has been the prey of countless multitudes of tourists for weeks. It was our last opportunity to see the tomb and the Queen. She is nothing but a mass of black dust and bones. Everything is now to be taken out of the tomb, as soon as Harold Jones finishes the drawing of the big door—everything has been likewise photographed. Mr. David Erskine, M.P. a delightful Englishman, Theo fell in with awhile ago, lunched with us for the 2d time in the lunch tomb. We had a merry lunch. Mrs. Harriman and daughter, and Miss Bishop came to see the tomb.

Septuagesima Sunday, Jan. 27.

I had my quiet little church today—about 4 o'clock as we were waiting for tea, on deck, we saw coming across the distant sands the procession of the treasures of the tomb on its way to us—Weigall and Ayrton on horses led the way, and a long procession of Arabs following carrying the boxes—and the sun striking the rifles of the accompanying sailors. It was really impressive. Our feluccas were sent for them, and a large native gyassa pressed into service—and they are now safely stowed on deck—the smaller things below. Dr. Weideman and his wife and Mr. Sayce dined with us.

Monday, Jan. 28.

A lovely warm day—Theo in the Valley. He says everything that is to be moved is out of the tomb. The ashes and bones of the Queen have been reverently gathered and put into a box—and left there—and the tomb is to be hermetically sealed. Mr. Erskine dined with us.

Tuesday, Jan. 29.

Theo took over Mrs. Harriman and party to Medinet Habu today. Mr. Sayce came to tea, and we looked over many of the interesting treasure we have on board. Jones had a carpenter here early this morning to construct a big box to hold everything that must stay on deck—and now this box 8-1/2 ft. long by 5 ft. high and broad is on our back upper deck and looks formidable and is safe against everything but a concerted raid.

In my *Signs and Wonders upon Pharaoh*[6] I drew upon the published accounts and thereby compacted the exciting events of discovery into a single day. Mrs. Andrews's diary shows that the affair moved over several days, that Weigall and Joseph Lindon Smith were present at the first penetration of the tomb, but that Maspero did not reach Luxor until five days later. There was no immediate examination of the bones of the mummy by a physician who just happened to be in the Valley that day. As seen through Mrs. Andrews's eyes there was no running argument between Davis and Weigall as to whether they had discovered the burial of Queen Tiyi or of Akh-en-Aton. She is aware of that problem, because she does mention the desire to have a doctor look at the skeleton to "pronounce on her sex, scientifically." She is wrong in understanding that the bones were left in a box inside a sealed tomb; Elliot Smith examined them in Cairo some months later. But her day-by-day record is a detached account of one of the extraordinary episodes in Egyptian archeology.

Not all of the diary is germane to the central problem of the history and contents of the tomb. But I trust that George and Maurine Hughes may find the account of Luxor at the height of the tourist season in 1907 evocative of pleasant memories of their long residence there.

[6] Chicago and London, 1964, pp. 117–20.

BIBLIOGRAPHY OF GEORGE R. HUGHES

Book reviews, newspaper articles, lectures, and the like have been omitted.

BOOKS

Saite Demotic Land Leases. ("SAOC," No. 28.) 1952.

Demotic Ostraca in the Brooklyn Museum. ("Wilbour Monographs.") Brooklyn, forthcoming.

JOINT PUBLICATIONS

Reliefs and Inscriptions at Karnak III: *The Bubastite Portal.* By the Epigraphic Survey. ("OIP" LXXIV.) 1954.

Medinet Habu V: *The Temple Proper.* Part I: *The Portico, the Treasury, and Chapels Adjoining the First Hypostyle Hall, with Marginal Material from the Forecourts.* By the Epigraphic Survey. ("OIP" LXXXIII.) 1957.

Medinet Habu VI: *The Temple Proper.* Part II: *The Re Chapel, the Royal Mortuary Complex, and Adjacent Rooms, with Miscellaneous Material from the Pylons, the Forecourts, and the First Hypostyle Hall.* By the Epigraphic Survey. ("OIP" LXXXIV.) 1963.

Medinet Habu VII: *The Temple Proper.* Part III: *The Third Hypostyle Hall and All Rooms Accessible from It, with Friezes of Scenes from the Roof Terraces and Exterior Walls of the Temple.* Includes concordance of Berlin *Zettel* numbers with all Medinet Habu epigraphic publications. By the Epigraphic Survey. ("OIP" XCIII.) 1964.

The Beit el-Wali Temple of Ramesses II ("Oriental Institute Nubian Expedition" I.) With Herbert Ricke and Edward F. Wente. Chicago, 1967.

Medinet Habu VIII: *The Eastern High Gate, with Translations of Texts.* By the Epigraphic Survey. ("OIP" XCIV.) 1970.

The Demotic Legal Code of Hermopolis West. By Girgis Mattha. Edited by George R. Hughes. ("BdE" XLV.) 1976.

The Temple of Khonsu I: *Scenes of King Herihor in the Court, with Translations of Texts.* By the Epigraphic Survey. ("OIP.") Forthcoming.

The Tomb of Kheruef. By the Epigraphic Survey. ("OIP.") Forthcoming.

ARTICLES

"Some Observations on the British Museum Demotic Theban Archive," *AJSL* 57 (1940) 244–61. With Charles F. Nims.

"A Demotic Astrological Text," *JNES* 10 (1951) 256–64.

"Recording Egypt's Ancient Documents," *Archaeology* 5 (1952) 201–4.

"Are There Two Demotic Writings of *šw*?" *MDAIK* 14 (1956) 80–88.

"A Demotic Letter to Thoth," *JNES* 17 (1958) 1–12.

"The Sixth Day of the Lunar Month and the Demotic Word for 'Cult Guild,'" *MDAIK* 16 (1958) 147–60.

"The Cosmetic Arts in Ancient Egypt," *Journal of the Society of Cosmetic Chemists* 10 (1959) 159–76.

"Work in the Field and at Home: The Epigraphic Survey and the Expedition to Nubia," Oriental Institute *Report for 1961/62*, pp. 6–9.

"Serra East: The University of Chicago Excavations, 1961–62. A Preliminary Report on the First Season's Work," *Kush* 11 (1963) 121–30.

"A Coptic Liturgical Book from Qasr el-Wizz in Nubia," Oriental Institute *Report for 1965/66*, pp. 10–13 and cover photograph.

"No Ramesses III Funerary Estate in Pap. Louvre E 7845A," *JEA* 52 (1966) 178–79.

"A Demotic Plea to Thoth in the Library of G. Michaelides," *JEA* 54 (1968) 176–82.

"The Cruel Father: A Demotic Papyrus in the Library of G. Michaelides," in *Studies in Honor of John A. Wilson.* ("SAOC," No. 35.) 1969. Pp. 43–54.

"Notes on Demotic Egyptian Leases of Property," *JNES* 32 (1973) 152–60.

"The Oriental Institute Archaeological Report on the Near East," *AJSL* 52 (1936) 123–42; 53 (1937) 256–62; 54 (1937) 71–75; 55 (1938) 97–100, 209–13, 319–23, 426–33; 56 (1939) 95–97, 162–64, 310–14, 423–28; 57 (1940) 102–5, 188–89, 321–23; 58 (1941) 104–5, 405–8.

"The Oriental Institute Archeological Newsletter," March 30, 1951, from Luxor, Egypt; November 13, 1951, from Luxor, Egypt; February 25, 1952, from Luxor, Egypt; April 10, 1953, from Luxor, Egypt; April 13, 1954, from Luxor, Egypt; January 4, 1955, from Luxor, Egypt; October 18, 1955, from Luxor, Egypt; November 23, 1956, from Luxor, Egypt; December 7, 1957, from Luxor, Egypt; May 19, 1958, from Luxor, Egypt; November 23, 1959, from Luxor, Egypt; December 23, 1961, from Serra East, Sudan; March 22, 1962, from Serra East, Sudan; December 30, 1963, from Luxor, Egypt.

"To the Members and Friends of the Oriental Institute," Oriental Institute *Report* for 1968/69, 1969/70, 1970/71, 1971/72.